Telling the Story of Mormon History

William G. Hartley

Editor

Proceedings of the 2002 Symposium
of the Joseph Fielding Smith Institute for Latter-day Saint History
at Brigham Young University

Symposium Proceedings in Latter-day Saint History

Produced by the Joseph Fielding Smith Institute for Latter-day Saint History

Volumes in the series:

Times of Transition, 1890–1920

Lives of the Saints: Writing Mormon Biography and Autobiography

Cover images:

Background text is a note written by William Clayton, on behalf of Joseph Smith, to Dan Jones, captain of the *Maid of Iowa,* Courtesy James B. Allen
Andrew Jensen, Courtesy Church Archives
Leonard J. Arrington, Courtesy Joseph Fielding Smith Institute
B. H. Roberts, Courtesy Church Archives
A detail of Emmeline B. Wells, *The Relief Society Magazine* 3 no 2 (February 1916): 62–63

Cover design by Kimberly Chen Pace

© 2004 Joseph Fielding Smith Institute for Latter-day Saint History. All rights reserved.

No part of this book may be reproduced in any form or by any means without permission in writing from the publisher. To contact the Joseph Fielding Smith Institute for Latter-day Saint History, write to: 121 KMB, Brigham Young University, Provo, Utah 84602. To contact BYU Studies, write to 403 CB, Brigham Young University, PO Box 24098, Provo, Utah 84602.

ISBN 0-8425-2558-0

Printed in the United States of America
10 9 8 7 6 5 4 3 2 1

Contents

INTRODUCTION	v
HISTORIANS AND INTERPRETING THE STORY	
The Story of *A Disciples Life:* Preparing the Biography of Elder Neal A. Maxwell Bruce C. Hafen	1
George Q. Cannon and the Faithful Narrative of Mormon History Davis Bitton	9
Telling the Untold Story: Emmeline B. Wells as Historian Carol Cornwall Madsen	17
Humor on the Trail of Mormon History Melvin L. Bashore	23
Writing Ward Histories: Mormon Wards as Communities Jessie L. Embry	27
Improving the Telling of Native American and Mormon Contacts in Frontier Utah Robert H. Briggs	31
Handling Sensitivities in LDS History: A Panel Discussion John W. Welch (moderator), Richard C. Bennett, Doris R. Dant, and Steven Sorensen	41
HISTORIANS' THEORIES AND METHODS	
The Mormon *Positivismußtreit:* Modern vs. Postmodern Approaches to Telling the Story of Mormonism Alan Goff	49
Many Mansions: The Postmodern Critique and a New Faithful History Stephen C. Taysom	65
Telling the Story of Mormon History: The James Moyle Oral History Program Matthew K. Heiss	75
Education in Pioneer Utah: A Quantitative Approach Tally S. Payne	81

SEEKING THE STORY OF THE INTERNATIONAL CHURCH
    African Converts without Baptism: 97
        A Unique and Inspiring Chapter in Church History
        E. Dale LeBaron

    The Historiography of Latter-day Saints in the Pacific   101
        Grant Underwood

    Selected Bibliography: Historiography of the Church in Eastern Europe   119
        Kahlile B. Mehr

HISTORIC SITES AND PERIOD LIFE STYLES
    Historic Sites as Institutional Memory   121
        Steven L. Olsen

    Nineteenth-Century Latter-day Saint Immigration: 125
        Lessons from Sea Trek 2001 for Telling the Story Better
        William G. Hartley

HISTORY IN THE CLASSROOM
    An Extraordinary Influence: Church History in the Classroom Setting   135
        Susan Easton Black

    T. Edgar Lyon: Teaching LDS History by Faith and by Fact   141
        Thomas E. Lyon Jr.

AUTHOR BIOGRAPHIES   149

Introduction

William G. Hartley

History serves many purposes. Professors publish it for other scholars. Teachers present it to infuse students with their heritage. Fiction writers draw from it for historical novels, as do playwrights for dramas. TV program producers shape powerful documentaries from it. Religious leaders and teachers instill values and life lessons from it. Families form identities from it. Museums display it. Historic sites present it through restoration and replication of artifacts. The history of The Church of Jesus Christ of Latter-day Saints serves all of these purposes and more.

On March 16, 2002, the Joseph Fielding Smith Institute for Latter-day Saint History hosted a history conference designed to explore the ways in which Mormon history is presented and the range of purposes it serves. Approximately 350 people attended one or more of the sessions that addressed the theme of the conference, "Telling the Story of Mormon History." Sessions involved formal papers and panel discussions and in some cases audio-visual presentations. Most presenters were from Utah, including a number of BYU faculty; others came from Canada, Indiana, Washington, New York, California, and elsewhere.

Elder Bruce C. Hafen opened the conference with a keynote address explaining some of the challenges he faced when writing his biography of Elder Neal Maxwell, *The Story of a Disciple's Life*.

During concurrent sessions, speakers covered a range of topics: postmodernist influences on history writing; George Q. Cannon and Emmeline B. Wells as historians; historians' treatment of the history of Nauvoo, the matter of Mormon-Indian relations, and Church history beyond North America; new angles for viewing Mormon Trail history and for telling the history of a ward; and the types of records historians rely on (Joseph Smith's record keeping, the Church's oral history program, and Church periodicals, for example). Nonprint modes for telling history received attention, too, in sessions that dealt with classroom teaching, interactive CDs and DVDs, film documentaries, quantification, oral history, and historic sites and artifacts.

Non-Mormon historian Klaus Hansen, from Queens College in Ontario, shared ideas about how Mormon history can be written for the non-Mormon audience. During a noon panel, Richard Bushman of Columbia University identified challenges he has faced in writing a biography of Joseph Smith, and former Assistant Church Historian James B. Allen shared his experiences writing *The Story of the Latter-day Saints* (co-authored with Glen Leonard).

To conclude the conference, a panel explored the thorny issue of how to handle sensitivities in LDS history.

This volume contains some, but not all, of the presentations. Of the thirty-four presenters, twenty submitted their materials for this publication. Some authors presented their materials orally or as visual presentations that did not lend themselves to publication, and others chose not to include their contributions in the proceedings. Readers should note that although we have published the papers here without formal editing or source checking, we have reformatted and lightly copyedited them for the collection.

As general editor, I extend thanks to the program committee—Mel Bashore, Mary Jane Woodger, Reid Neilson, and Marilyn Parks—who helped frame the conference and solicit presentations; to the individual presenters; and to Heather Seferovich, Anastasia Sutherland, and Shannon Thurlow for their work in preparing these papers for publication.

Elders Neal A. Maxwell, *left*, and Bruce C. Hafen, 2003.

The Story of *A Disciple's Life*: Preparing the Biography of Elder Neal A. Maxwell

Bruce C. Hafen

The story behind my work on the biography of Elder Neal A. Maxwell actually began in 1976, when he invited me to take leave from Brigham Young University and work for two years under his daily direction in the new Correlation Department at Church headquarters. In later years, when I was an administrator and a teacher at Ricks College and then at BYU, I saw him often in Church Educational System meetings, where he was a key figure on the Church Board of Education.

In 1996, I was called to the Seventy and assigned to an Area Presidency in Australia, where I would remain until returning to Utah in August 2000. Like so many other Church members, my wife, Marie, and I were stunned by the news of Elder Maxwell's leukemia in late 1996, and we worried and prayed about his health. During October conference 1999, he invited me to come by his office. As we talked, he was quite uncertain about his condition. He was receiving an experimental treatment, but "one of these days," he said, he fully expected the leukemia to return. That was the main reason why he had finally yielded to prodding from others that he allow the writing of his biography. I thought a book on his life story would be wonderful—until he asked if I would write it.

As honored as I felt, I honestly thought my doing this was not a good idea. I believed that he, his family, and the Church deserved thorough research and writing, and the work needed to be done at once to maximize the possibility of being published during his lifetime; he shared those hopes. But given the frightening uncertainty of his health; given that acceptable biographies can take years to document and write; given that he hadn't kept a personal journal, which would necessitate additional months of original research; and especially given that I was half a world away on a full-time Church assignment, I thought we needed to find someone else who could give this project immediate and full-time attention.

Nonetheless, after more visits with Elder Maxwell and others, within a few days I had accepted the project and agreed to begin working on it as quickly as possible. In the weeks that followed, I still worried about having committed myself to something as unreachable as this task seemed. As I would awaken to hear the colorful birds that rule those fresh Australian mornings, I would sometimes wonder if—indeed, I would hope that—I had agreed to write Elder Maxwell's biography only in a dream. Then the reality would hit me again. At times I would remember Nephi's words about the Lord preparing a way for people who have a work to do.

As time went on and as I found able people who were eager to help, my anxiety gradually subsided. I learned about peaceful intensity. Marie and I increasingly sensed that we had been given a rare privilege and that whatever came of this experience would bless us. As we worked, we also prayed often that the Lord would lengthen Elder Maxwell's life. After such prayers, I would sometimes recall a scriptural phrase I first heard him quote from the book of Daniel: "*But if not . . .*" (Dan. 3:17–18)—meaning, we must do everything we can to make each assignment work, and then if it doesn't, as Abinadi said, "it matters not" (Mos. 13:9).

Looking back now, I feel that I—and all of us in the Church—have witnessed firsthand a genuine miracle. Elder Maxwell's oncologist, a Church member named Clyde Ford, told me that Elder Maxwell had beaten the statistical odds when his leukemia went into its first remission, which lasted fifteen months. When the illness returned in 1998, the odds were much worse. Dr. Ford knew that even if the standard medical treatment brought about a second remission, it would inevitably be shorter than the first remission. So he prayerfully studied the research journals until he discovered some reported success with leukemia patients in Sweden whose doctors were using a new treatment pattern. The sample size wasn't large enough to justify predictable results, but the Maxwells and Dr. Ford decided to try it.

In April 2003, Elder Maxwell is still taking this same treatment as he goes about his normal duties each day. The preservation of his life was not, and could not have been, anticipated by medical science. Along with its far more substantial blessings, this miracle made it possible to have a biography that draws on lengthy interviews with him and reflects his having reviewed the entire text. Like you, I pray that the miracle will continue.

∽

My work on this project has caused me to ask myself, Why do we read, let alone write, biographies? Since ancient days, we have been taught the gospel by stories. The accounts of the war in heaven, the Garden of Eden, and Cain and Abel are the first stories showing what happens when people try to live or don't live God's teachings. The New Testament is itself a story about Jesus—who he was, what he taught, and what he did. Christ's life is the story of *giving* the Atonement. The story of Adam and Eve is the story of *receiving* the Atonement. As we experience mortality the way our first parents did, struggling with the oppositions between good and evil, we can look at Eve or at Adam and say, "That is the story of *my* life." When we tell our own stories to others, we realize that the cosmic quest to overcome evil and find God is our very personal quest.

Our own testimonies are simply true stories that can capture in vivid detail how the Lord blesses us, protects us, changes us, and helps us to overcome. Nothing brings the Spirit into a conversation or a classroom more than hearing people bear honest testimony by telling the story of their personal experience. The Church membership is itself the aggregation of thousands of personal stories, or testimonies, from people all over the world. Every one of those stories is unique, richly textured, full of meaning, and full of lessons about life. Each story is daily developing its own fresh narrative, against the many oppositions in mortality.

The scriptures, too, are primarily a collection of stories, given to us because God directed prophets to recount their experiences to his people. In his desire to give us guidance about life, God could have given us a large rulebook or a series of grand philosophical essays. But he didn't. He gave us stories—stories about people like ourselves. Again and again, the Book of Mormon writers tell us about some person's experience and then say, "And thus we see . . ."

What *do* we *see* from these stories? We can see, for example, that "by small means the Lord can bring about great things" (1 Ne. 16:29) and that if people keep God's commandments "he doth nourish them, and strengthen them, and provide means" for them to keep going (1 Ne. 17:3). These stories teach us that "the devil will not support his children at the last day" (Alma 30:60), that "the children of men [are quick to] forget the Lord. . . . And we also see the great wickedness one very wicked man can cause" (Alma 46:8–9).

J. R. R. Tolkien's understanding of the power of stories played an important part in the conversion of his friend C. S. Lewis to Christianity. Tolkien helped Lewis see that the *story* of Christ's life conveys a fuller meaning to our minds than abstract statements of doctrine and reason can convey. He explained that the abstract "ideas" of Christianity "are too large and too all-embracing for the finite mind to absorb them. That is why the divine providence revealed himself in a story." This insight helped Lewis realize why he had *felt* that certain classical stories were "profound and suggestive of meaning beyond [his] grasp even tho' [he] could not say in cold prose 'what it meant.'"[1]

Elder Maxwell's biography is the story of one man's discoveries from applying the story of Jesus to his own life. The *story* of Elder Maxwell does offer more understanding than at least my "cold prose" could offer in an essay about Christian discipleship and "what it means."

His life story is valuable at two levels: one as a chapter in the history of the Church and the other as an illustration of the process of trying to become a follower of Christ. One of my hopes in telling this story, then, was not only to record the life of a Church leader but also to offer his experience as one model to any individual for whom discipleship is a personal quest. The Latter-day Saint Bible dictionary defines "disciple" as "a pupil or learner; a name used to denote (1) [capital *D:*] the twelve, also called apostles, [and] (2) [lower case *d*:] all followers of Jesus Christ." I have wanted to speak to both meanings, as suggested by the biography's opening sentence: "All Apostles are Disciples of Jesus, but not all of Jesus' disciples are Apostles."

In fall 2001, Jeff Keith, a BYU geology professor, spoke at a campus devotional. At one point he quoted the last verse in the Gospel of John: "And there are also many other things which Jesus did, the which, if they should be written every one, I suppose that even the world itself could not contain the books that should be written" (John 21:25). Then Brother Keith explained why he believes Christ's biography is so large that the world itself cannot contain it: because "the most complete biographies of each of our lives . . . are really contained in His biography."[2] In other words, because of the Atonement, his life story includes the life story of every one of his disciples, both with a capital *D* and with a small *d*. For the same reason, our life stories can each include his life story. No wonder that in some personal histories and biographies, we find real evidence of the Savior's influence and tangibly feel his love.

Church history work at Church headquarters is concerned primarily with the history of the institutional Church, which includes the experiences of its leaders. However, the "personal history" accounts of all disciples' lives—quite apart from any role they may have played in Church institutional affairs—are also a crucial element in the history of the Lord's people. We Church members typically view these "personal histories" as a part of *family history* more than of *Church history*. Perhaps an examination of that assumption will help us see new value in the recent merger of the departments of Family History and Church History at Church headquarters. Both parts of the new department, each in its own way, are engaged in "telling the story" of the Lord's dealings with both his Church collectively and his followers individually.

∽

Regarding the research and writing process, I am now grateful I was forced to conduct the research as I did, because other people did much better work than I ever could have done had I been in Utah trying to do it myself. The day after I agreed to proceed, I had a heaven-sent conversation with my friend Elder Marlin K. Jensen, who had once worked as an adviser to the Church Historical Department. After hearing my worries about doing the needed research from Australia, Elder Jensen suggested I contact Gordon Irving, one of the Church's primary oral historians.

I called Gordon on the phone but didn't actually meet him until we had worked together via email for six months. As it turned out, Gordon became my principal collaborator. Using an agenda of research questions that we developed together in our frequent emails, he conducted eighteen interviews with Elder Maxwell, which when transcribed filled 560 pages. In addition to interviews I later did, Gordon also recorded, had transcribed, then edited interviews about Elder Maxwell with each member of the First Presidency, a number of other General Authorities, and several other people. Gordon would email the edited transcripts to me for my research base. His well-schooled and faithful touch made the biography a much better book.

My other indispensable email companion was Elder Maxwell's son, Cory, who combed, inventoried, copied, and shipped, as weekly care packages across the Pacific, portions of large annual scrapbooks that Elder Maxwell's secretaries have been compiling since the late 1960s.

As helpful as these materials were, I soon realized why a biography cannot be better than its primary source material. The parts of Elder Maxwell's story that draw on such contemporaneous documents as letters, journals, and his personal writings are richer than other parts of the story. Always a "clean desk man," he has not kept a great deal of correspondence and other personal papers. His written personal history is very brief, dealing with only a portion of his ministry. It was written mostly as an annual summary of key events in the 1970s and early '80s without much commentary. I asked him if he had written letters to his family during his service in World War II and on his mission. He said, "Oh, there might be a few things around, but there is nothing profound in those old letters." When I finally received copies of those letters and began reading them, that was a turning point in my feeling for the entire process. Suddenly, I could sense for myself why Churchill's biographer, Martin Gilbert, called such letters "history's gold."[3] The issue here is the depth of real evidence. Memories recalled years after an event are helpful, but they are not the same as uninterpreted, contemporaneous evidence that allows readers to draw their own conclusions.

Here is one small example. Neal Maxwell's experience as an eighteen-year-old infantryman on Okinawa was a defining moment for his entire life. He was in a mortar crew during a ferocious battle. One night in May 1945, the shrieking noise of artillery fire caught Neal's attention with a frightening realization. Three shells in a row had exploded in a sequence that sent a dreadful message—the enemy had completely triangulated his position, and the next series of shots would hit home.

Suddenly a shell exploded no more than five feet away from him. Terribly shaken, Neal jumped from his muddy foxhole and moved down a little knoll seeking protection, and then, uncertain what to do, he crawled back to the foxhole. There he knelt, trembling, and spoke the deepest prayer he had ever uttered, pleading for protection and dedicating the rest of his life to the Lord's service. In his pocket, he was carrying a smudged copy of his patriarchal blessing, which gave him a special promise of protection. No more shells exploded near him after that moment. He came to know God that night in a way that changed him and directed his life's course. When the leukemia came, he would often compare that experience with Okinawa, both in its terror and in its deep spiritual impact on him.

I knew this was a significant event, but I knew almost nothing about Okinawa, so I began reading some historical sources about World War II. In addition to learning why the Japanese defense of Okinawa was so fierce, I came across some detailed accounts of the miserable battlefield conditions there. During the time of Neal's key battle, the place was a mess. The intensity of the fighting combined with the deplorable conditions made some people who survived this trauma unable to talk about it for decades. Heavy rains turned the battlefield into such a mud puddle that even "tanks disappeared into the ooze." Disease and dysentery plagued the soldiers. They were so exhausted that what little sleep they got was often while standing up in the mud. Supply trucks couldn't provide consistent food and ammunition, so the troops were always hungry and, especially, thirsty. One account recorded that the soldiers lived with "almost constant thirst," and even when they had water, it was too foul and oily to drink.

According to this account, the only thing that saved them from the unrelenting thirst was coffee, which, having been boiled, was at least edible.[4]

Not long after reading these military histories, I came across this brief paragraph in the letters Neal hastily scrawled to his family during the battle for Okinawa:

> Had a dream the other night. You folks were holding Carol [his sister] up to a window and I was saying Boo to her, and she laughed just as she does. Boy, if that didn't make me blue. . . . It's rough here. . . . It will be wonderful to bathe again. Still not smoking, drinking tea or coffee, nothing great, but the coffee is tempting some times.[5]

When I showed Elder Maxwell this letter, I asked him, "Do you remember why the coffee tempted you?" He couldn't remember. I asked if he remembered how thirsty he was and how hard it was to get water. He did remember that he had to collect rain water in his helmet to provide water for the sacrament he blessed for himself each Sunday. But he didn't remember the thirst, and he didn't remember the connection between the thirst and his comment in the family letter about the coffee.

Well, he never would drink the coffee. The combination of knowing the messy battlefield context and seeing his innocent reference to being tempted but not giving in was for me a moving discovery about the way that battle shaped his character. I believe his determination to avoid the coffee was a very practical, youthful expression of the commitment he made there to serve the Lord. I only dared hint about this in writing the Okinawa chapter, because I wanted to let the reader draw his or her own conclusion. I offer more about my conclusion here because of what this experience showed me about the place of specific details and contemporaneous sources in "telling the story."

∼

Another area that offers rich contemporaneous evidence about Elder Maxwell's personal development is his prolific writing and speaking. Neal Maxwell has a very interesting personality, and his verbal style is so distinctive it can only be called, well . . . Maxwellian. As President Hinckley said, "[Neal] speaks differently from any of the other General Authorities. He just has a unique style all his own. We all admire it."[6]

I'll offer only a brief comment about Elder Maxwell's form and will later illustrate the development of his content. One distinctive aspect of his style is that his handwriting is nearly illegible. When his son, Cory, was in his teens, Elder Maxwell left him a handwritten note before going on a trip. Cory couldn't read the note, so he took it to his mother for help. She told him he was looking at it upside down. But even when they turned it around, they still couldn't read it. President Hinckley said at a recent dinner tribute for Elder Maxwell at the University of Utah, "Surely a man who has so many virtues must have a vice or two. Have you ever seen Neal's handwriting? . . . I don't know how in the world Colleen ever derived any comfort from the letters Neal sent."[7]

The tales about Elder Maxwell's use of language are legendary. A returned missionary who was translating general conference live into Mandarin Chinese a few years ago told me that the translation staff said they had categorized the conference talks according to "four . . . , well, five levels of difficulty for translators. Levels one through four are for everybody else, and level five is for Elder Maxwell."[8] The translators' challenge is not that he uses big academic words but that his language is so compressed and full of carefully chosen imagery, metaphors, and allusions. "One of his talks is like a bouillon cube," said his daughter-in-law, Karen B. Maxwell, using a pretty good metaphor of her own. Metaphors "are a great way to say a lot in a few words," but the listener must bring something to it before "it can expand for you."[9] Consider, for example, his general conference comment about religious risk takers who engage in "intellectual bungee jumping." Try translating that into Chinese!

∼

At first I thought the main theme of Elder Maxwell's life might be his memorable contributions to the Church as a role model for educated Latter-day Saints. The evidence from my research, however, revealed a different focus: *discipleship* is without question the central message of his life and of his teachings. His background and contributions as an educator still matter—indeed, they matter even more in light of his life's more fundamental theme of personal discipleship. Consider some autobiographical reflections of my own about those two issues in his life.

In his generally sympathetic 1957 book *The Mormons,* a Catholic sociologist named Thomas O'Dea summarized the major "sources of strain and conflict" he believed the Church would face in the near future. Heading his list was the conflict he saw coming between the Church's emphasis on education and its authoritarian theology. He wrote, "Perhaps Mormonism's greatest and most significant problem is its encounter with modern secular thought." He noted that the Church had long emphasized education, but he observed correctly that higher education tends to reflect the secular culture of our age. O'Dea predicted that Latter-day Saint youth, who he said "usually [come] from a background of rural and quite literal Mormonism," would encounter in their university studies much "doubt and confusion," bringing "religious crisis to [them] and profound danger" to the Church. O'Dea believed this conflict was so significant that "upon its outcome will depend in a deeper sense the future of Mormonism."[10]

I encountered this conflict for myself as a university student. When I enrolled at BYU in 1963 after my mission, I seemed to bump against it everywhere I turned. A friend who was a seminary teacher told me to avoid classes in subjects like history, literature, and philosophy because they would lead me into intellectual apostasy. Yet some of my professors in liberal arts classes told me to beware of anti-intellectual religion teachers who, as one person put it, "expect the Holy Ghost to do their thinking for them." That year I took a superb religion course from West Belnap called Your Religious Problems. Here each student presented to the class the issue that concerned him or her most. I called my topic "Liberalism vs. Conservatism in the Church." I was looking for a general framework in approaching many specific issues, from evolution and politics to women's rights and constitutional law.

To one degree or another, I suspect my experience was not unusual. And the potential for the problem O'Dea identified was growing in the Church because the American boom in higher education in the last half of the twentieth century drew an ever higher percentage of young Latter-day Saints to college campuses. The apparent conflict between submissiveness to religious authority and the independence fostered by a liberal education creates a paradox that can seem difficult to resolve, both in general and in the specific issues in one's field of interest. I suspect many of you have sat through sessions like those I have known where people talk and write at length in efforts to resolve such issues analytically. Those discussions can help, but I have found that the best resolution of this paradox lies not in abstract analysis, but in the lives of real people, whose actual experience demonstrates how a faithful spiritual life and a rigorous education can work together to yield *both* greater spiritual depth and a more abundant intellectual life.

The best way for Latter-day Saint students to grow their way through the natural paradox of freedom versus authority, then, is to have a good teacher—a mentor, whose modeling they can watch and follow. Usually such mentoring occurs in a personal, student-teacher relationship. That is a core part of the educational vision that guides everything that BYU aims to do. During the 1970s, I was blessed to enjoy such mentoring when I was invited into daily working relationships with Dallin Oaks and then with Neal Maxwell—both of them so competent academically and yet so faithful. Because of what these relationships meant to my own resolution of the O'Dea paradox, I was not surprised to discover in my research for the biography this statement from former BYU social sciences dean Martin Hickman regarding Elder Maxwell's influence as commissioner of education. He said Neal Maxwell had become "a legend in the Church for the depth of his thought, his knowledge of the scriptures, the elegance of his language, . . . and for his compassion for those in and out of the Church who need comfort." Martin said that what a good mentoring teacher does for his college students "Neal Maxwell now provides for a generation of young Latter-day Saints, who come not only from the valleys of the Wasatch front but from the continents and isles of the sea" all over the Church.[11]

When I am on BYU campus, I can still hear the sound of Commissioner Maxwell's voice from the 1970s echoing off Y Mountain in these quotes and paraphrases: "We cannot let the world condemn our value system by calling attention to our professional mediocrity."[12] A disciple's excellent scholarship is a form of consecration.[13] In a morally deteriorating culture, we must lean "into the fray" like Joseph of Egypt, rather than just being another hungry mouth to feed.[14] Keep your citizenship in Jerusalem, but use your passport to Athens.[15]

In this role, Commissioner Maxwell became a principal mentor for three future members of the Twelve whom he helped bring into leadership positions in the Church Educational System in the 1970s: Dallin H. Oaks, Jeffrey R. Holland, and Henry B. Eyring. Neal Maxwell learned the need for and the art of such significant mentoring from his two principal mentors during his own younger years: G. Homer Durham, who was Neal's college professor at the University of Utah, and Harold B. Lee, whom he came to know through an assignment on the Church leadership committee in the 1960s.

When I learned who Elder Maxwell's mentors were, I reflected on what I had learned from my earlier reading in the biographies of other Church leaders. I saw a short but potent "chain of title" for Neal's own tutoring process in a complete vision of Church education. Karl G. Maeser had originally tutored Brigham Young's children. Then Brigham Young sent him to Provo to start the Brigham Young Academy in 1876. There Karl Maeser let the best of his German intellectual discipline serve the broader aims of his unqualified commitment to Brigham Young's primary request—not to teach even the alphabet or the multiplication tables without the Spirit of God.

As the first general superintendent of Church schools from 1888 to 1901, Karl Maeser passed the torch of this vision to an entire generation of Latter-day Saint teachers, including young James E. Talmage, who mentored young J. Reuben Clark, who mentored young Harold B. Lee, who mentored young Neal A. Maxwell. And as if that weren't enough, another young teacher mentored by Karl Maeser was Joseph Tanner, who later mentored young John A. Widtsoe, who later mentored young G. Homer Durham, who later mentored young Neal A. Maxwell.

My work on the biography reminded me, then taught me again with the depth that only experience and detail can provide, about the blessing of being mentored by teachers and leaders for whom Thomas O'Dea's paradox is ultimately not a conflict but a source of great strength.

Neal Maxwell came from "a background of rural and quite literal Mormonism." His parents had desired, but never enjoyed, higher education. He then encountered with zest the confusion and doubts of the modern secular world at sophisticated levels, emerging with a spiritual maturity that was enriched rather than undermined by his educational and professional experiences. Then, as a role model, Neal Maxwell taught what he had learned to other educated Latter-day Saints, nurturing and encouraging teachers and leaders whose encounters with O'Dea's concerns had been as valuable and positive as was his own. I thank the Lord for raising up such teachers, not only in my own life, but in today's generation of Latter-day Saints.

~

My final comment is about the doctrinal insight that comes from viewing through Elder Maxwell's eyes the unfolding meaning of discipleship. His talks and his prolific writing over the years are a veritable library of his "letters to the Saints." These messages also reveal a great deal about him. As much as any other biographical evidence, the evolving "wordprint" of Neal's writing faithfully tracks and illustrates both his personality and his spiritual growth. He has written autobiographically, even if he has never said so—or thought so—about his life's journey. The eventual but central theme of his writing has become discipleship, becoming a true follower of Jesus. Discipleship has also been the central preoccupation of his own life, how he has tried to live and what has made him tick. So most of his writing consists of little notes he has left tacked on the trees for those who come afterward on his path of discipleship. "Having found the only passage," he once wrote, "we should . . . willingly serve as guides for other wanderers."[16]

Consider just a brief summary of the way his understanding of the term *disciple* moved gradually from bud to blossom, as reflected in his writing (his writing also reflected his life experience). In the 1960s when he was a teacher and leader at the University of Utah, Neal Maxwell used the word *disciple* essentially as a synonym for *Church member*. In the early 1970s, when he was commissioner of education for the Church, he saw further that a disciple was a Church member who disengaged from the unclean things of the secular world. A few years later, just after his call as a General Authority, his experience with two young fathers who had terminal cancer expanded his understanding, as he began seeing connections between discipleship and adversity. In a book he dedicated to these young men, he used a phrase that hauntingly anticipated the leukemia that would strike him nearly two decades later: "The very act of choosing to be a disciple . . . can bring to us a certain special suffering. . . . [A]ll who will can come to know [what Paul called] 'the fellowship of his suffering.'"[17]

About three years after writing these words, Elder Maxwell was called to the Twelve. That call soon focused him intently on discipleship as a personal relationship with Jesus—a master-apprentice tutorial in which the disciple has the duty to become more like the master. Now he began to see discipleship as a personal growth process designed to develop Christlike attributes. This understanding let him see that suffering, when it is part of a divine tutorial, can be sanctifying in the sense of developing the very virtues a particular disciple needs to learn.

During the late 1980s and into the 1990s, Elder Maxwell built on this foundation to focus both his personal discipline and his writing on such qualities as meekness and submissiveness—not only submitting to the commandments, but accepting whatever the Master may inflict on the apprentice to teach him how he, personally, may become more like the Master. Elder Maxwell then sensed that, in his words, "if we are serious about our discipleship, Jesus will eventually request each of us to do those very things which are most difficult for us to do."[18]

This was what he came to call the "wintry doctrine." At the funeral of a young father in 1996 he put it this way:

> There are in the gospel warm and cuddly doctrines, and then there are some that are just outright wintry doctrines. . . . One of them, frankly, is that we cannot approach [real] consecration without passing through appropriate clinical experiences, [because we don't achieve consecration] in the abstract.
>
> . . . Sometimes [therefore,] the best people . . . have the worst experiences . . . because they are the most ready to learn.[19]

Just a few months later, the dark shadows of leukemia entered Neal Maxwell's life. He immediately saw that his readiness to learn had qualified him for his own clinical experience in what he called the graduate curriculum in the school of discipleship. In his recent season of the wintry doctrine, Elder Maxwell says he has learned much about empathy. Now he is more able to know and feel what others are going through in their own wintry trials. He discovered experientially what he had already sensed and taught about Christ's empathy for us: Christ understands and succors us in our sicknesses and afflictions because he has tasted such sorrow himself. Elder Maxwell calls this "earned empathy."[20]

As I stretched to understand all of this enough to describe it, I realized that I can never really grasp it until I have been down a few more wintry roads myself. But I did see a fresh doctrinal link. The increased empathy Elder Maxwell had found looked more and more to me like what the scriptures call charity. He was coming to taste more fully the pure love that Christ has for other people. Then came what was for me the most significant doctrinal link—the connection between charity and affliction.

Perhaps those who seek apprenticeship with the Master of mankind must emulate his sacrificial experience to the fullest extent of their personal capacity. Only then can they taste his empathy and his charity. For only then are they like him enough to feel his love for others *the way he feels it*—to love "*as I have loved you*" (John 13:34). That is a deeper, different love from "love thy neighbour as thyself" (Matt. 19:19). Perhaps it isn't possible to have Christ's charity without submitting to some form of his affliction—not only through physical pain but in many other ways—because they are two sides of the same, single reality.

Christ's love for all mankind is fully bound up in his exquisite pain—"How sore you know not . . . how hard to bear you know not" (D&C 19:15). Perhaps we cannot know his love without knowing his pain. If so, the personal suffering we confront in the sanctification process, "the fellowship of his suffering," could move the pure love of Christ from a concept in one's head to a spirit in one's heart. And once in the heart, charity will circulate all through the body, because it is being moved by "a new heart" (Ezek. 36:26).

I pray that I, and each of us, may learn from the lives of people such as Neal A. Maxwell how better to prepare ourselves to sacrifice and submit ourselves in whatever will help us to know the Savior and become more like him. May we not be surprised and may we not shrink when we discover, paradoxically, how dear a price we may need to pay to receive what is, finally, a gift from him—charity, the pure love of Christ.

Notes

1. A. N. Wilson, *C. S. Lewis: A Biography* (New York: W. W. Norton, 1990), 126, quoted in Bruce C. Hafen, *A Disciple's Life: The Biography of Neal A. Maxwell* (Salt Lake City: Deseret Book, 2002), xiv.

2. Jeffrey D. Keith, "Feeling the Atonement," *Brigham Young University 2001–2002 Speeches* (Provo, Utah: Brigham Young University, 2002), 114.

3. Martin Gilbert, *In Search of Churchill: A Historian's Journey* (New York: John Wiley and Sons, 1994), 20, quoted in Hafen, *Disciple's Life,* xv.

4. Hafen, *Disciple's Life,* 107–8, quoting George Feifer, *Tennozan: The Battle of Okinawa and the Atomic Bomb* (New York: Ticknor and Fields, 1992), 299–307.

5. Hafen, *Disciple's Life,* 108, quoting Neal A. Maxwell to family, May 13, 1945.

6. Hafen, *Disciple's Life,* 520, quoting Gordon B. Hinckley, oral history, 1.

7. Hafen, *Disciple's Life,* 530, quoting Gordon B. Hinckley, remarks at inauguration of Neal A. Maxwell Presidential Endowed Chair, video recording.

8. Hafen, *Disciple's Life,* 521, quoting David K. Hafen, conversation with author, about 1993.

9. Hafen, *Disciple's Life,* 521, quoting Karen B. Maxwell, oral history, 30–31.

10. Hafen, *Disciple's Life,* 333, quoting Thomas O'Dea, *The Mormons* (Chicago: University of Chicago Press, 1957), 222, 225–27, 235–36, 240.

11. Hafen, *Disciple's Life,* 397, quoting Martin B. Hickman, introduction of Neal A. Maxwell, G. Homer Durham Lecture Series, in 1987 scrapbook.

12. Hafen, *Disciple's Life,* 380.

13. Hafen, *Disciple's Life,* 379–80, quoting Neal A. Maxwell, "The Disciple-Scholar," in *On Becoming a Disciple-Scholar,* ed. Henry B. Eyring (Salt Lake City: Bookcraft, 1995), 7–22.

14. Hafen, *Disciple's Life,* 380, quoting Neal A. Maxwell, *The Mormon Milieu,* Brigham Young University Speeches of the Year, Provo, Utah, February 23, 1971, 5.

15. Hafen, *Disciple's Life,* 379.

16. Hafen, *Disciple's Life,* 520, quoting Neal A. Maxwell, *A Time to Choose* (Salt Lake City: Deseret Book, 1972), 19.

17. Hafen, *Disciple's Life,* 544, quoting Neal A. Maxwell, *All These Things Shall Give Thee Experience* (Salt Lake City: Deseret Book, 1979), 30, 32.

18. Hafen, *Disciple's Life,* 547, quoting Maxwell, *Time to Choose,* 46.

19. Hafen, *Disciple's Life,* 20, quoting Neal A. Maxwell, remarks at Joseph S. Clark funeral, February 23, 1996, in Douglas Parker, oral history, 55–57.

20. See Neal A. Maxwell, "From Whom All Blessings Flow," *Ensign* 27 (May 1997): 12.

George Q. Cannon and the
Faithful Narrative of Mormon History

Davis Bitton

I have no desire to argue that George Q. Cannon (1827–1901) was a great historian. It is stretching the point even to say he was a historian at all. And I do not pretend that his view of history was any different from that of John Taylor or Wilford Woodruff or other Church leaders of his generation. Even B. H. Roberts (1857–1933) shared many of the same presuppositions, although I think that Roberts moved the writing of "inside" Mormon history to a new level.[1] What I will attempt to demonstrate is that Cannon exerted an extraordinary influence on the self-conception that became standard among faithful Latter-day Saints. Let us briefly notice the areas in which George Q. Cannon promoted a way of thinking about the past.

1. He talked about history in his sermons. I have read every surviving Cannon sermon. It would be going too far to say that when he stood at the pulpit he always talked about history. Instead, like his brethren among the general authorities, he typically talked about current situations and offered counsel. I can say that one of his frequent topics was a quick review of the history of the restoration, showing how, in the face of seeming insuperable odds, the work had continued to progress.[2]

2. He participated in the dedications of monuments and in celebrations commemorating the achievements of the past. I have attempted to put this kind of memorialization into a larger framework in an article I did on "The Ritualization of Mormon History."[3]

3. He showed an interest in the preservation of primary sources and, at the end of his life, began the large multi-volume work we know as *History of the Church of Jesus Christ of Latter-day Saints* by Joseph Smith. The project was taken over and carried to a successful completion by B. H. Roberts.[4]

When we remember that George Q. Cannon was a general authority from 1860 to his death in 1901, first as an apostle; then as a counselor to President Brigham Young; and from 1880 as the first counselor to Presidents John Taylor, Wilford Woodruff, and Lorenzo Snow; and that his publishing house, George Q. Cannon and Sons, published the great majority of titles intended for the Mormon audience, it should not be surprising that his way of thinking, talking, and writing about history had a powerful shaping influence on the collective memory of the Saints.

From the beginning of the *Juvenile Instructor* in 1866, he was its editor and publisher, and in its pages appeared many short, first-person narratives. Then in 1879 Cannon and Sons published the first volume of the Faith-Promoting Series. Thirteen more volumes, for the most part first-person narratives, followed over the next nine years.[5] Cannon's *My First Mission*, a distillation of his experience, led the way as volume 1. Volume 3 was the remarkable *Leaves from My Journal* by Wilford Woodruff, and volume 7 was the *Journal of Heber C. Kimball*. Other first-hand accounts included C.V. Spencer's mission to Great Britain in the 1850s; William Budge's 1878–80 mission to England and Switzerland; Thomas Shreeve's mission to Australia and New Zealand in 1878–80; Llewelyn Harris's 1878 experience with the Zunis; Amasa Potter's mission to Australia in 1856–58; David P. Kimball's experience on the Salt River in 1881; and life sketches of Robert Aveson, William Anderson, John Tanner, Briant Stevens, and Daniel Tyler.

No documentation supports these narratives. Historians using this material must assess its authenticity by comparing it to diaries, letters, or other documents close to the events. Judging by George Q. Cannon's account of his sojourn in Hawaii, the changes could be as innocent as casting an experience into a retrospective mode rather than recounting it day by day. Some omissions and highlighting were of course inevitable.

Surviving handwritten documents by some of these authors force us to conclude that the manuscripts received revision—correction of spelling, recasting of sentences, insertion of paragraph divisions—as they were prepared for publication.

Describing travel, persecution, healings, dreams, and visions, the Faith-Promoting Series books cumulatively comprise a *Foxe's Book of Martyrs* for Latter-day Saints. Suffering and frustration were not omitted; for example, the series included descriptions of Wilford Woodruff's accidents and also the misfortunes of many others. Daniel Tyler even admitted to lack of proselytizing success, but he did it in such a way as to encourage rather than dissuade other young Latter-day Saints. "I baptized none personally while on that mission of about three and a half years," he wrote, "and yet, although I suffered much affliction and persecution, I look back upon it as one of the happiest times of my life."[6] A Mormon convention was being established.

The inclusion of many specifics, including the names of witnesses who could confirm or deny stories, lends credibility to these accounts. But they are selective. Tales of disillusionment or apostasy were disqualified. And accounts had to have a moral.

Most of the volumes of the Faith-Promoting Series were published during the 1880s, a time of intense pressure for Cannon. In 1887, the year of the Edmunds-Tucker Act, *Eventful Narratives*, the thirteenth volume in the series, appeared. The preface clearly states the purpose of the series: "The principal object in issuing them has been and is to increase faith in the hearts of those who peruse them, by showing how miraculously God has overruled everything for the benefit of those who try to serve Him." The Faith-Promoting Series was Cannon's way of conveying this lesson to the broad reading audience of Mormons.

Cannon's magnum opus was *The Life of Joseph Smith, the Prophet* (1888; 2nd ed. 1907; in Tahitian, 1925). This work was reprinted in 1986 as part of the Classics in Mormon Literature series. In a preface, historian Donald Q. Cannon notes that it has been "a very popular book for a long time"; that it is eulogistic, "designed to build faith"; that it "tells the story of the Prophet, but . . . does not attempt to analyze him or to probe deep beneath the surface events of his life in a critical way"; and that it "always presents Joseph Smith and the Church in the most favorable light."[7] All of this is true enough, but more needs to be said.

George Q. Cannon's original preface, penned in late 1888, brings the reader into the intense religious atmosphere of the prison cell—he was serving a term in the territorial prison for unlawful cohabitation.[8] Cannon does not hide his own fervent conviction about Joseph Smith as a prophet. Rather than allowing it to emerge as a conclusion reached after telling Smith's life story, the author's testimony is trumpeted in the opening lines: "Joseph and Hyrum are now dead; but like the first martyr they yet speak. Their united voice is one of testimony, admonition and warning to the world." Cannon's motive in writing the book is stated forthrightly: "It is in the hope that the Saints may find joy in reading of their beloved Prophet and Patriarch, and that the world may judge more fairly of these benefactors of mankind, that this book is written."

Although working on the project "in the midst of a somewhat busy and laborious life"—an understatement—Cannon considered the labor a "loving duty" that had brought him comfort. The closing chapters, he says, "were finished in prison for adherence to the principles which they [Joseph and Hyrum Smith] taught, and for this, the life is invested with a dearer regard." He even hated to send the completed manuscript off for publication: "To send the work away now is like being torn from a beloved companion, when most the solace of his friendly presence is needed."

Cannon had help on this project. "To many friends the author is indebted for information here embodied," he wrote; "and he takes this occasion to thank them, hoping to live yet to meet them and express his gratitude in the flesh." We wish he had been more specific about these "many friends." It would seem natural for a member of the First Presidency such as Cannon to enlist the help of the Church Historian's Office in preparing his work. Whether he spent time in that office or had material delivered to his own office is not known. His three oldest sons all worked on the project. As early as fall 1882, Frank J. Cannon was "preparing the History of Joseph Smith."[9] Abraham H. Cannon also had a hand in it. "We revised what Frank had written of the Prophet's history," Abraham wrote on August 20, 1886.[10] A year later John Q. Cannon went over the whole thing and revised it.[11] Therefore, a draft manuscript by George Q. and his three oldest sons was in existence even before 1888.

George Q. Cannon was writing and revising through much of the summer of 1888, and in the fall spent many hours in proofreading and preparing the manuscript for the press.[12] He thoroughly reworked and approved the finished product. He would not have allowed this work to appear under his name if it did not represent his views on the life of Joseph Smith. "Every spare moment of my time," he wrote on June 15, "I have worked on my History of Joseph."[13] He regarded it as his work.

After an introductory section about the primitive Christian church, the Apostasy, the Reformation, the French Revolution, and the rise of modern sectarianism, Cannon offered what is no less than a hymn of praise to his subject. Joseph Smith's "lofty soul," he said, "comprehended the grandeur of his mission upon earth." In his physical appearance "he seemed to combine all attractions and excellencies." Joseph Smith, he said, had been "a retiring youth," but the Spirit made him bold; had been a humble farmer, but "divine authority sat so becomingly upon him that men looked at him with reverent awe"; had been unlearned, but "he walked with God until human knowledge was to his eye an open book, the celestial light beamed through his mind."

Just as Jesus was ridiculed during his life and only later could be seen "illuminated by the eternal sunshine of heaven," standing "outlined against the blue vastness of the past in sublime simplicity," so Joseph Smith should now be seen "as he towered in the full radiance of his labors. . . the reconciler of divergent sects and doctrines, the oracle of the Almighty to all nations, kindreds, tongues and peoples." Joseph Smith's "life was exalted and unselfish," his death "a sealing martyrdom, following after that which was completed upon Calvary for the redemption of a world."[14]

Whether the casual, unbelieving reader would be drawn in or turned off by these opening pages, there was no false advertising. This book would not be history or biography in the dispassionate mode.

After such an opening, it is no surprise to find in the following sixty-five chapters a Joseph Smith without fault, a persecuted people, knavish enemies, and the eventual martyrdom that concludes the book. Good and evil are as clearly contrasted as in any medieval morality play or modern western novel.

Cannon's *Life of Joseph Smith the Prophet* was not merely grandiloquent. Holding it together is a string of factual statements that no one would contest—although, as suggested, some might well take exception to the spin he put on them. Cannon's comments are interlarded with many documents. Available to Cannon were early newspapers and published works by George A. Smith, Thomas Ford, and Josiah Quincy. Documents such as the Wentworth letter of 1842, including the Articles of Faith, are printed in their entirety.

A short chapter that deserves careful attention is chapter 56, "Eternal Marriage." Did George Q. Cannon give a clear account of the origins of plural marriage? Did he, in prison, defend it? The answer to the first question is no, but he comes close. "Eternity and plurality of marriage" are not distinguished but melded together and explained as the product of revelation. Joseph Smith "did not write it [the revelation] for a time," Cannon says, "although he obeyed its commands and taught it to Hyrum and other faithful men, who, in prayer and humility before God, accepted and fulfilled its requirements." It was on July 12, 1843, Cannon explains, that the revelation was dictated to William Clayton, on July 13 that a copy was made by Joseph C. Kingsbury, and on August 12 that it was presented to the stake presidency and high council of the Nauvoo Stake. He acknowledges Emma Smith's ambivalence. At first she did not accept it, "but later she became convinced of its truth and gave good women to her husband to wife as Sarah of old administered to Abraham."[15]

Then Cannon inserts this editorial comment: "There is not one word in the revelation, nor was there one word in the Prophet's teaching other than purity and self sacrifice." It was a system that would make possible the satisfaction of every woman's right to "virtuous wifehood and maternity"; it was "a code of moral law by which the modern world, under the light of Christian truth, may achieve social redemption and be forever purified." An experienced soldier in the defense of polygamy for nearly forty years, Cannon could have said much more. But he said something about the subject, and it was not an apology or retraction.

In chapter 48, "Manliness of Joseph," we are treated to several complimentary quotations from contemporaries. Cannon does not choose to quote those who derided Joseph Smith, for his point is that even some who were not Church members were able to recognize some of the greatness of the man. He did not claim more than he should:

> The foregoing opinions quoted from the Prophet's contemporaries and observers—his opponents, candid though they were—are as favorable as could be looked for in a skeptical, materialistic age. They prove all that can be asserted of the Prophet by his believers, except the essential feature of his inspiration. This could not be testified to by any except a believer. His reviewers, whom we have quoted, judge entirely from external evidence. They saw the phenomenon presented by his life and work, and recorded it, excluding entirely from their consideration of his character and deeds all thought of the superhuman. . . . It cannot be expected that any non-believer will testify to the prophetic power of Joseph Smith. To admit it is to believe.[16]

It is a thoughtful analysis. "No words of a believer can of themselves convince an unbeliever," he wrote. "There is but one power of demonstration, and that is to seek by humble prayer for the voice of the Holy Spirit. So surely as man prays in faith and meekness, so surely will the answer come."[17]

The book concludes with a vivid, rapid-fire description of the martyrdom of Joseph and Hyrum Smith. There is no epilogue or concluding chapter describing the trial of the assassins, the continued persecutions, or the expulsion of the Saints from Nauvoo. With Joseph Smith dead and buried, author Cannon had finished his work—except for this final paragraph:

> The enemies of truth were sure that they had now destroyed the work. And yet it lives, greater and stronger after the lapse of years! It is indestructible for it is the work of God. And knowing that it is the eternal work of God, we know that Joseph Smith, who established it, was a Prophet holy and pure.[18]

Such, even in prison, was the powerful conviction of George Q. Cannon.

Cannon was not trying to satisfy a doctoral committee or to please reviewers in secular journals. Readers would not have expected from him the flat exposition of an encyclopedia article. What they got—and arguably what was and is valuable—was not merely a life of Joseph Smith but what George Q. Cannon thought and felt about the life of Joseph Smith.

Cannon's work served a purpose. For Latter-day Saints, it was a reassuring and satisfying reaffirmation. For outsiders, the book, even with its heavy moralizing, told the Prophet's life in its essentials. The discerning reader would have little difficulty in recognizing that it told as much about Latter-day Saint self-perception as about Joseph Smith.

Already simple, the work was not, in Cannon's estimation, simple enough for children. In 1898, George Q. enlisted the help of his twenty-one-year-old son Joseph J. "My son Joseph submitted to me some manuscript of a 'Child's History of Joseph' which he is compiling under my directions," George Q. wrote.[19] "Under my directions"—that is the key. Knowing how to use assistance, George Q. Cannon would again review the work, make whatever changes he thought necessary, and take responsibility for it. When published in 1900, *The Latter-day Prophet: History of Joseph Smith Written for Young People* must have filled a niche, for it came out again with a different subtitle—*Young People's History of Joseph Smith*—in 1912, 1914, and 1918. Always interested in children, Cannon was anxious to provide the new generation with a life of the Prophet that would stick in their minds.

To call *The Latter-day Prophet* a Mormon version of Parson Weems's mythologized life of George Washington may be too strong. But Cannon was not afraid of indoctrination. Some kind of societal indoctrination would take place under any circumstances, as he well knew, and he wanted the rising generation of Latter-day Saints to understand and feel something of what he understood and felt about Joseph Smith.

The closest thing to a general history that Cannon produced, *The History of the Mormons: Their Persecutions and Travels* appeared in 1890, just two years after his Joseph Smith biography.[20] He of course knew this short, quick survey of article length was not a "full" history. When that full history was written, whether the author was friendly or hostile, every reader would recognize two "remarkable facts":

One is that in all the course of their interesting and troublous [sic] career, though marked at every stage by honesty, thrift and good order, the people were constantly maligned by their neighbors and accused of views and practices inimical to the peace and welfare of the country. The other is that no sooner was one subterfuge of their opponents pierced by the light of truth and utterly disproved, than a second was brought forward and urged successively throughout the confines of township, county, state and nation.

He added a third obvious fact: "After each onslaught, no matter how great the increase in virulence, the people have gained in strength, in numbers, in prosperity and in the ability to withstand every kind of attack."

Cannon was writing in 1889 or early 1890. The federal onslaught was indeed increasing in virulence. It was about to force a momentous capitulation. Not knowing what was just around the corner, he considered the time ripe to review the sixty years of Mormon history.

Essentially, this little work is a lawyer's opening speech on behalf of a defendant. From the beginning, he writes, the Saints had been persecuted. Starting with the Missouri persecutions and the driving of Mormon refugees from the state, the pattern had continued in Illinois, forcing the massive flight to the Rocky Mountains. What were the motives? What caused these other Americans to hate the Latter-day Saints? For Cannon, the truth of the matter was made clear in Missouri:

> It is true the mobocrats laid numerous offenses at their [the Saints'] doors. Cunning villains have always been ready with stories calculated to inflame the ignorant mind and appeal to popular clamor. It was at first charged against the Mormons that their religion was an imposture—they believed in revelation from on high. Another offense was that in their domestic affairs they were "peculiar"—they were reserved in their deportment and dealing; they did not mix with the wild elements of mankind which surrounded them; in short, they minded their own business. These were atrocious crimes indeed! For these were they outraged, plundered and butchered! Many of them came from New England, where the antislavery movement was beginning. They were recognized as "Yankees," were accused of secreting and "stealing" negroes, and were hated as abolitionists with all the bitterness that the men who lived on the border of the slave states at that time felt for adherents of that doctrine. This was held up as a most grievous offense, and they were driven out at the point of the bayonet.

This catalogue of charges is not quite complete, for it omits the apprehensions of the Missourians that the Saints would somehow stir up the Indians. But here is Cannon's fundamental point:

> No charges of immorality then! No talk of *imperium in imperio*! No holy abhorrence of polygamy! No loyal anxiety to repress violations of law, for there were charges neither of misdemeanor nor of felony! No high-voiced hypocrisy about disloyalty or treason; for they [the Saints] were law-abiding, obedient to judicial summons and patriotic.

A prosecuting attorney might point out that in the late stages of the Missouri conflict some Saints were indeed charged with crimes. But Cannon would stick to his allegation: the original case against the Saints did not include charges of polygamy or grandiose aspirations of political independence.

In Illinois, Cannon said, the old charges of fanaticism were raised, but in this Northern state allegations of abolitionism carried less terror. A new objection must be found. It was found in the Mormons' bloc voting. The members believed that in union there is strength. They carried the theory into practice—not only in religion, but in commerce and politics. It was a great stumbling block to their neighbors. The independence which made them free to select the best candidates, and the good sense which caused them to cast a united vote for them, gave their enemies a weapon which has ever been readily used against them.

Only now, according to Cannon, did various other charges begin to be hurled against the Mormons:

> Having started out to give the Mormons a bad name, it was easy to charge them with the prevailing crimes of horse-stealing, counterfeiting, harboring vile characters, and of living, as a community, by a system of plunder. Lawless persons from up and down the river found it to their advantage to shield their own practices and divert suspicion from themselves by attaching it to the unpopular citizens.

Cannon recognized that the charges were made, dismissed them as essentially groundless, and tried to explain them. More recent research showing some basis for the charges of counterfeiting and theft might throw doubt on his claims of complete Mormon innocence, but his understanding of the general group psychology remains plausible. If any individual Saints were guilty of crimes, he insisted, they could have been tried and punished; after all, they lived as a minority in a country of law. Such charges were really a smoke screen. "The people were objectionable—

that was all. That was the head and front of their offending."

He traces the forced departure from Illinois, the hardship on the plains, the service in the Mormon Battalion, and the raising of the American flag in the Salt Lake Valley when it was still Mexican territory. For a brief period the Saints enjoyed peace in their valley home. Then came false and corrupt officials, who perjured themselves in making baseless charges. The result was the Utah expedition of 1857, a "senseless and unjustifiable expedition" that was not only "a farce, but a costly crime."

Then came the anti-Mormon legislation. Now Cannon is speaking as if cornered. Many times he had been told that if the Saints would only stop polygamy, all would be well. "How hollow and mocking these phrases. . . sounded to a people who had passed through every form of tribulation before polygamy was known! We saw the old spirit of mobocracy which had driven us out from civilization in a new garb, to fit the changed circumstances of the case."

The closing pages are Cannon's address to the world, as it were. Standing his ground, with the shells of the Edmunds-Tucker Act and confiscations and imprisonment and denial of the franchise exploding around him, he proclaimed: "We mourn for our unhappy country and those who will have to reap the whirlwind after such abundant sowing of the wind." For Cannon, it was the Latter-day Saints who were the defenders of liberty—meaning of course freedom of religion as they understood it: "When we shall have emerged from under the clouds and the sorrows, the love of freedom will have left an impress so indelible upon us that we will hold it as priceless to ourselves but too precious to be denied to others."

Looking back over the tortuous path his people had followed, he saw clearly "the fate of those who have pitted themselves against the work and have sought to destroy the people":

> We have had presidents, governors, judges and other prominent and noted men, who have undertaken the task of "solving the Mormon problem" by violence and by the framing of various devices and schemes having in view the overthrow of the people. But who of them has prospered? Who has achieved fame or credit? It is true that some have attained some notoriety for the time being. this was not because of any superior merit which they possessed, but because their names have been [?] with that of the Mormons.

> This notoriety has, of course, been only temporary. Everyone has sunk into dishonor and oblivion.

Governor Thomas Ford's published apprehension that his name would be remembered only for his role in the Mormon conflict had, as far as Cannon was concerned, been fulfilled, and the same was true of the other leading men in the hostilities.

Cannon concluded by lauding the Saints for their "high conception of the rights of man," frugality, temperance, industry, perseverance, honesty, virtue, and "our hatred to vice in every form, and to litigation and violence."

> We have been the pioneers in western civilization. About forty-five years ago we were compelled to leave the cities and pleasant places of our race and launch forth into an unknown wilderness. From that day until the present we have been the pioneers of the regions where we settled. We carried with us the printing press. Among the first buildings erected by us have been school-rooms. The first American paper published in California was issued from a Mormon press. The first farming operations performed by American labor there were carried on by the Mormons. The first gold discovered in California, which has created such a revolution, was dug by Mormons. We are the first Anglo-Saxons who have practiced irrigation. We came to Utah as religious exiles. We came here with a determination to make it our home, because we desired to be where we could worship God according to the dictates of our own consciences, undisturbed by mobs and religious bigotry.

He contrasted these achievements with the desolation of places in Illinois and Missouri once occupied by Saints and now showing signs of blight.

He was proud of the high credit rating of his people: "In the commercial world our credit is of the highest. We can be trusted in financial circles because we always fulfill our obligations. Merchants, bankers, business men of all parts of the country, yield us freely this praise." He was speaking from experience, but this was before the extreme financial difficulties that would follow the Panic of 1893.

The short "history" concluded with the manifesto of December 12, 1889. Just a year later, a new printing of Cannon's short history also included the Woodruff Manifesto of 1890.[21]

The History of the Mormons was not so much a history as it was an oration. The main value of such "history" is to serve as a reminder of the framework within which people like Cannon saw themselves and their past. They were not aloof bystanders but actors in the drama. To step back and see things neutrally was impossible for a committed participant. Concessions on details could be made, perhaps, but the essential pattern—a wronged people driven from place to place while sustained by their God—was not negotiable.

While encouraging a remembrance of things past, Cannon wished that remembrance to serve a present purpose. It should explain, create empathy with those who had gone before, and evoke admiration and appreciation. Above all, for Latter-day Saints, it should reinforce faith in the restored gospel. To subordinate the priceless jewel of religious faith to the paltry prattle of secular historians, incurably handicapped in their blindness and deafness to the spiritual dimension, would be a pitiful thing indeed. For Cannon, it was unthinkable.

Throughout Cannon's life, Latter-day Saints were the object of outrageous vilification. I am referring not to mild ridicule or a tendency to see them as curiosities—strange people to be ogled at and whispered about. Eskimos and Zulus and headhunters in New Guinea received similar bemused appreciation. I am referring rather to the hate-filled denunciations that effectively defined the Saints as less than human, especially those calling for their extermination. With anti-Mormon newspapers, magazines, and travel books being published every year, Cannon could easily conclude that it was not his responsibility to represent the critics but to describe events as they appeared to the Saints, even if this was "apologetic" in the sense of being a one-sided defense. The prosecution was already being heard and in many venues it was the only voice being heard.

It probably helps, also, to remember the importance of *testifying* to George Q. Cannon and his colleagues among the general authorities of the Church. He had observed much of Mormon history and was an important participant in certain parts of it. Why should he write as if he were a disinterested observer? He would testify of what he was convinced of, of what he "knew." We don't read the words "I testify to the truth of these things in the name of Jesus Christ," but his tone is often one of proclaiming or bearing witness. This, needless to say, is not the history of a textbook or a learned treatise but the fervent witness of a believer.

If George Q. Cannon had models, historical works that were widely read and admired, they would include Thomas Babington Macaulay's popular *History of England*, perhaps J. L. Motley's *History of the United Netherlands*, and George Bancroft's *History of the United States*. While based on extensive research, these works all had a strong point of view and did not mind letting the reader know who wore the white hats and who wore the black hats. If we think Cannon was too severe in his condemnation of Governor Lilburn W. Boggs, we might find it illuminating to read Motley's description of Philip II of Spain: "If Philip possessed a single virtue it has eluded the conscientious research of the writer of these pages. If there are vices—as possibly there are—from which he was exempt, it is because it is not permitted by human nature to attain perfection even in evil."[22]

With the introduction of the seminar system and training of graduate students in history, followed by the organization of historical associations and the publication of professional historical journals, readers of history became familiar with norms that included careful documentation, reliance on primary sources, and avoidance of rank partisanship.[23] At least these were the stated goals. Whether they were realized is another question.[24]

What academic historians have a hard time realizing is that most people who enjoy reading history are not interested in footnotes. They may not even care about "objectivity," if that frequently misused term is in their vocabulary. They do like to think that what they are reading is true in the sense of being faithful to the reality of the past, but they seldom wish to go through the tedious exercise of looking at events from different points of view or weighing the evidence and assigning degrees of probability. What they want is a *story* compellingly told. They like strong, colorful characters and dramatic confrontations. Admittedly, there may be a certain audience for detailed, analytical works, but the biographies and histories most widely read for pleasure by the general public will continue to be those that, like novels, tell a story and let us know who are the good guys and who are the bad guys. For his generation—and apparently for many believing Latter-day Saints right down to the present—George Q. Cannon satisfied that desire.

The fact remains that for every chapter George Q. Cannon wrote, if not for almost every page, significant scholarship has been produced during the past century. A perusal of the substantial bibliography in my *Images of the Prophet Joseph Smith* (1994) or the massive bibliography in *Studies in Mormon History, 1830–1997* demonstrates how far we have come since Cannon wrote. Even with all of the available information, there is still value in the shorter histories. The student or casual reader may not think it necessary to delve into the intricacies of economic life at Nauvoo, for example, and may be quite satisfied with a simplified survey. I think that any intelligent reader should exercise sufficient critical faculty to recognize the point of view of the book in question and its limitations.

The historian cannot avoid thinking about audience. For whom does he or she write? The tone and terminology appropriate to the in-house audience might not be easily understood by others, and the audience might also be turned off by a testimony-bearing tendency or a partisanship so extreme as to lack credibility. The chasm between faith-promoting history and critical history is impossible to ignore, at least in its extreme manifestations on both sides. To some extent I blame readers who, professing interest in the subject, refuse to read works from the other side—believers so easily offended that they are unwilling to learn from outside historians and "outsiders" who turn up their noses at all in-house history. But writers of history bear responsibility as well. One longs for the kind of history that can be read with profit by everyone. It is a goal seldom achieved perhaps, but well worth pursuing.

Notes

A modified version of this article was published in *FARMS Review of Books* 14.1–2 (2002), 275–93.

1. Davis Bitton, "B. H. Roberts as Historian," *Dialogue* 3 (winter 1968): 25–44; revised as a chapter in Bitton and Leonard J. Arrington, *Mormons and Their Historians* (Salt Lake City: University of Utah Press, 1988).

2. For example, George Q. Cannon, in *Journal of Discourses,* 26 vols. (Liverpool: F. D. Richards, 1855–86), 10:340–48, October 28, 1864; 23:114–23, April 3, 1881.

3. Davis Bitton, "The Ritualization of Mormon History," *Utah Historical Quarterly* 43 (winter 1975): 67–85; revised as a chapter in Davis Bitton, *The Ritualization of Mormon History and Other Essays* (Urbana: University of Illinois Press, 1994).

4. Davis Bitton, *George Q. Cannon: A Biography* (Salt Lake City: Deseret Book, 1999), 446. For Roberts' evaluation of this whole project, which is quite critical of Cannon, see B. H. Roberts, *The Autobiography of B. H. Roberts,* ed. Gary James Bergera (Salt Lake City: Signature Books, 1990), 222–23.

5. Cannon's *The Life of Nephi* (Salt Lake City: Juvenile Instructor, 1883), vol. 9 of Faith-Promoting Series; and George Reynolds, *The Myth of the "Manuscript Found"* (Salt Lake City: Juvenile Instructor, 1883), vol. 11 of Faith-Promoting Series, a refutation of the Spaulding theory of the origin of the Book of Mormon, were not first-person narratives and in this respect were different from the others.

6. Daniel Tyler, "Incidents of Experience," in *Scraps of Biography* (Salt Lake City: Juvenile Instructor, 1883), 46.

7. George Q. Cannon, *Life of Joseph Smith, the Prophet* (Salt Lake City: Juvenile Instructor, 1888). My references are to the pagination of the reprint edition (Salt Lake City: Deseret Book, 1986), which inserts dates of death in the genealogical data of note 1 and references to the published Joseph Smith Jr., *History of The Church of Jesus Christ of Latter-day Saints,* ed. B. H. Roberts, 2d. ed., rev., 7 vols. (Salt Lake City: Deseret Book, 1971) in parentheses after some quotations.

8. For the details, see Davis Bitton, *George Q. Cannon,* 292–96.

9. Abraham H. Cannon, Journal, October 24, 1882, holograph, 19 vols., L. Tom Perry Special Collections, Harold B. Lee Library, Brigham Young University, Provo, Utah. Photocopies of the original are in Church Archives, The Church of Jesus Christ of Latter-day Saints, Salt Lake City, and Special collections, J. Willard Marriott Library, the University of Utah, Salt Lake City.

10. Abraham H. Cannon, Journal, August 20, 1886.

11. Abraham H. Cannon, Journal, November 7, 1887.

12. George Q. Cannon, Journal, March 31, May 26, May 31, June 2, June 5, June 7–9, June 15–16, June 23, August 6, August 15, August 25, August 30–31, September 4–8, 1888. I was given access to this journal during the preparation of my biography of Cannon, cited in note 4.

13. George Q. Cannon, Journal, June 15, 1888.

14. George Q. Cannon, *Life of Joseph Smith,* 19–21.

15. Among scholarly analyses of the origins of plural marriage are Danel W. Bachman, "A Study of the Mormon Practice of Plural Marriage Before the Death of Joseph Smith" (master's thesis, Purdue University, 1975); James B. Allen, *Trials of Discipleship: The Story of William Clayton, a Mormon* (Urbana: University of Illinois Press, 1987), reprint as *No Toil Nor Labor Fear;* and Todd Compton, *In Sacred Loneliness: The Plural Wives of Joseph Smith* (Salt Lake City: Signature Books, 2001).

16. Cannon, *Life of Joseph Smith,* 357–58.

17. Cannon, *Life of Joseph Smith,* 360.

18. Cannon, *Life of Joseph Smith,* 527.

19. George Q. Cannon, Journal, August 23, 1898.

20. Salt Lake City: Juvenile Instructor, 1890.

21. James R. Clark, comp., *Messages of the First Presidency of The Church of Jesus Christ of Latter-day Saints, 1833–1964,* 6 vols. (Salt Lake City: Bookcraft, 1965–75), 3:183–87, 193–95. The 1890 manifesto is now printed as Official Declaration 1 in the Doctrine and Covenants.

22. J. L. Motley, *History of the United Netherlands* (ed. 1867), 3:534–43, as quoted and cited in Dom David Knowles, *The Historian and Character* (Cambridge: Cambridge University Press, 1963), 3.

23. See summary of this development, with references, in Davis Bitton and Leonard J. Arrington, *Mormons and Their Historians* (Salt Lake City: University of Utah Press, 1988), 126–29.

24. The most stimulating analysis and critique is Peter Novick, *That Noble Dream: The "Objectivity Question" and the American Historical Profession* (Cambridge: Cambridge University Press, 1988).

Telling the Untold Story: Emmeline B. Wells as Historian

Carol Cornwall Madsen

A talented writer, a compulsive record-keeper, a woman of great ambition, and a thoughtful participant in the events of her time and place—these were the attributes that found expression as Emmeline Wells fashioned her life on an insight she learned when she was growing up in her native New England: "There is no excellence without labor," she discovered; "you must work, toil, not sit idly indulging in fruitless day-dreams, but active work must be done if you would attain to any degree of honor, or be useful to yourself and others."[1] Idleness and daydreaming were luxuries that never found their way into Emmeline Wells' peripatetic life.

Born in a small mill-town of central Massachusetts in 1828, Emmeline Woodward showed an early penchant for writing. She first thought about writing when, as a young child, she discovered a packet of her grandmother's letters and other papers tucked away in a corner of the garret of her grandparent's home. "A light had dawned upon me in that out of the way place," she wrote in 1888, looking back on that fateful day. "I had found that women sometimes put their thoughts upon paper, and I conceived the idea of making rhymes, or jingles."[2] But it would not be rhymes and jingles that would flow from her ambitious pen. Though poetry remained her favored mode of expression and the hoped-for avenue to public recognition, destiny had other plans for her. Conversion to Mormonism in 1842 and removal to far-off Utah Territory diverted her path to a more significant destination and wider renown than she could have imagined in that New England garret so many years earlier.

The *Woman's Exponent* was the vehicle that would take her along this alternate path and become her historical magnum opus. Established in 1872 by Edward Sloan, editor of the *Salt Lake Herald*, the *Woman's Exponent* promised in its first issue that it would "endeavor, at all times, to speak freely on every topic of current interest, and on every subject as it arises in which the women of Utah, and the great sisterhood the world over, are specially interested."[3] Thus, it reported on both national and international topics relating to women while also responding to the controversial questions raised by the woman's movement of the time. It served also as a public forum for Latter-day Saint women to represent themselves to a censorious nation during a violent anti-Mormon period. It covered half a century of the Church's most volatile history with its editor's astute observations, detailed descriptions of people and events, and well-reasoned commentary. These accounts, preserved by a historically minded Emmeline Wells, who became editor of the *Woman's Exponent* in 1877, constitute an untold history of the Latter-day Saints. Untold, because the paper and its angle of vision have not been included as a historical resource for the official record nor its commentary utilized as a viable source of historical understanding.

The same is true of another lengthy chronicle of Mormon life preserved by Wells—her forty-seven diaries, which offer thoughtful insights into the lives and actions of numerous individuals and firsthand information about public and, more particularly, private exchanges and decisions that underlay many of the significant events of the time. Letters, articles, newspaper stories, and talks augment the large paper trail this inveterate writer left behind. Hers is an authentic and uniquely female perspective so long missing from recorded history.

Wells was fully immersed in the historic events of the age in which she lived, especially those relating to women. That the nineteenth century was "woman's era" and that the history of women in that century was unfolding in unimagined and dramatic ways were obvious and inevitable truths to Wells. But she was aware that women had long been a missing element in the written record. "History tells us very little about women," she wrote in 1881. "Judging from its pages, one would suppose their lives were insignificant and their opinions worthless." At that time, she had much evidence to support this observation. Thus, she added, "Volumes of unwritten history, yet remain, the sequel to the written lives of brave and heroic men." Lamenting this historical oversight, she promised that "although the historians of the past have been neglectful of woman, and it is the exception if she be mentioned at all; yet the future will deal more generously with womandkind." As a warning she concluded, "the historian of the present age will find it very embarrassing to ignore woman in the records of the nineteenth century."[4] This was an astute and visionary statement from a woman so long sequestered in a remote territory who did not make contact until midlife with the center of women's agitation for public participation and recognition. She set out to help rectify this omission.

Emmeline Wells was not a historian in a professional sense, nor might her abundant writings be considered more than historical documents. But her sense of history pervades them all, and they have made her a major contributor to Mormon historiography.[5] She wrote, even in much of her diary, as if to educate and inform a later audience, explaining motives, detailing events, preserving names, locations, and dates, and offering her own insights and interpretations, as historians do. She was therefore more than just a chronicler of her times. She left a record of nineteenth-century Mormon life in its broad social context as filtered through the mind and experience of a woman who transcended the narrow provincialism that characterized many of her Mormon contemporaries. Mormonism was not the end of the journey for Emmeline Wells but the beginning. It served as the center point of a social cosmology that encompassed a broad universe of ideas, people, experiences, and commitments. These informed both the personal and public records she so laboriously created.

She might well be classified as a social historian, recording history from the bottom up, not from the perspective of those making the national political, economic, and judicial decisions, but from those most affected by them. Moreover, she functioned at the center of many of those historic events that engrossed American society in the nineteenth century and made Mormonism front-page news. She was also a vital part of the history of the organized movement to attain equal rights for women, a local player who acted on a national stage in a drama she helped to write and faithfully record. The multivolumed *History of Woman Suffrage,* hailed as the definitive record of the struggle for the vote for women, is no better a history of the national movement than the multivolumed *Woman's Exponent* is of the local movement in which Utah women were so critically involved.

Of the many areas of Mormon women's lives and interests covered by the *Exponent,* three are representative. Though the paper was never officially connected to the Church, it nonetheless published editorials and articles that reveal the religious thought and activities of Mormon women along with the sermons and reviews of Church and Relief Society conferences and newsworthy items about Church leaders. Juxtaposing Wells's diary entries with her public words often reveals some disjuncture between the public and private. Though she published a long editorial eulogy in the *Exponent* at the death of Brigham Young in 1877, her diary indicates that "he is not so much mourned as one would imagine." She added that the presidency of John Taylor would cause "some dissatisfaction."[6] In October 1901, on the occasion of a specially called "solemn assembly" to sustain Joseph F. Smith as President of the Church, she also added some anecdotal, but important, information. In a small notation in her Relief Society minute book, she observed that the sustaining of a new Relief Society general presidency in that same solemn assembly was unprecedented. "It was a very grand and impressive spectacle to witness," she wrote, "to see the uplifted hands of all the several Quorums of the Holy Priesthood raised to sustain them [the women]." It was the "first of its kind on record when women were the officers to be elected [sustained]."[7]

Her sense of history prompted her to publish minutes of the semiannual women's conferences as well as those of quarterly stake Relief Society conferences and to request that ward and stake units of the women's auxiliaries along with the

Retrenchment Society submit minutes of their meetings, thus providing an easily accessible record of their officers, members, projects, financial status, discussions, and the counsel of their leaders. At a conference of the newly organized Salt Lake Stake Relief Society in 1877, she was invited to speak as the newly appointed editor of the *Woman's Exponent*. She chose that occasion to instruct the ward secretaries, admonishing them to record not only financial statistics but also names of members and officers, types and numbers of meetings held, numbers in attendance, the work accomplished, and especially the spiritual development of each ward Relief Society, such instructions reflecting her innate penchant for thorough record keeping. "We are the pioneer workers in these institutions," she said, convinced of the great value to later generations of a written record of their pioneering efforts.[8]

These reports provide insight into the character and mission of Eliza R. Snow and the Relief Society during its formative years in Utah, as well as those of later Relief Society leaders. Their sermons, instructions, and visits to the wards and branches were carefully recorded by conscientious secretaries and permanently preserved on the pages of the *Woman's Exponent*. There we learn, for instance, how impressive a leader Eliza R. Snow was in encouraging the faithful sisters of the Relief Society to do their share of kingdom building even as they struggled to establish homes in new settlements throughout the territory. Her words inspired and motivated the women who flocked to hear her speak when she visited their communities. Her talk to one group of Relief Society sisters, so ably recorded and submitted to the *Woman's Exponent*, showed the power of her own example as she exhorted them to be "prayerful and [to] humble themselves" so that God might not have to do it for them. "I want my feelings absorbed in Zion," she declared. "I don't call in question am I able? I ask the Lord to give me strength to do what is required of me, but I do not wait for the strength to come before I make the effort." If that is what Eliza R. Snow chose to do, it was surely a model for them all. "We must start," she encouraged, "then [God] will help us. We want a determination as strong as the everlasting hills, to do the will of God."[9] Few other public sources reveal as completely as the *Woman's Exponent* the understanding that women had of their role in the Church, their place in God's plan, and the eminence in which they held their Relief Society leaders. The sisters of the Kanab Relief Society expressed their regard for this extraordinary woman in their report to the *Exponent*. "We welcome sisters Eliza and Zina [D. H. Young] as our Elect Lady and her counselor, and as presidents of all the feminine portion of the human race, though comparatively few recognize their right to this authority," the Relief Society secretary recorded in 1881. "Yet, we know," she continued, "they have been set apart as leading Priestesses of this dispensation. As such we honor them."[10] Together, these reports and the accounts of the general and local women's conferences constitute an impressive history of women's work in the Church.

Even more than information on Church affairs was the attention Wells gave to the woman's movement of her time. Many historians of woman's past begin their analysis with the viewpoint of woman's enduring subjugation and fashion a women's history as a long, hard-fought struggle to overcome the social elements restricting women's autonomy. Others focus on the wide and varied experiences of women, noting racial, regional, religious, and class differences as well as the commonalties women have shared over time. The history that emerges from Emmeline Wells's pen details the efforts to alter the laws and traditions that limited women's experience while also documenting the rich and satisfying camaraderie and unique culture that women developed in their various settings. Her own involvement in that long crusade for women's rights turned the *Woman's Exponent* into a major historical resource as she documented and reflected upon each development, the national and international conventions of women's organizations, and the guiding spirits of this controversial campaign.

Several issues of the *Exponent* (and many pages of her diary) recount the proceedings of the 1879 woman suffrage convention in Washington, D.C., the first Emmeline Wells attended and her maiden foray into the national suffrage movement. She wrote of its origins, its founders, its historical context, and made it a compelling topic, when she entered the campaign herself. She wrote a number of articles describing the procedures at each session, the different attributes and effectiveness of the leading women of the movement, particularly Elizabeth Stanton and Susan B. Anthony, their interactions with one another, their varied styles of public speaking, and, her general impression of each convention.

She did not fail to also include some of the human interest stories that appealed to her readers. For example, immediately following the 1879 convention an exchange occurred between two major suffrage leaders, Lucy Stone, founder of the American Woman Suffrage Association, and Elizabeth Stanton, founder of the rival National Woman Suffrage Association, whose convention Wells attended. An article in Stone's suffrage paper, the Boston *Woman's Journal*, expressed outrage that the National Association would accept the membership of Mormon women, then the object of almost universal derision and threats of disfranchisement for practicing polygamy. Stanton immediately responded by chiding Lucy Stone for not refuting the article. "If George Q. Cannon [Utah's delegate to Congress and a polygamist] can sit in the Congress of the United States without compromising that body on the question of polygamy, I should think Mormon women might sit on our platform without making us responsible for their religious faith." She then added, "When the women of a whole Territory are threatened with disfranchisement where should they go to make their complaint but to the platform of the National Suffrage Association?"[11]

Between the formal record of the proceedings of these annual conventions in the *Woman's Exponent* and the anecdotal addendums in both the *Exponent* and her diary, Emmeline Wells provided an eyewitness account of how suffrage leaders managed their long, difficult campaign and gave an insider's view of the subtle intrigues over power and philosophy, as well as a front-row perspective of how problematic the involvement of Mormon women was to the unity and success of the suffrage movement. She also showed just how deeply involved Church leaders were in many aspects of the woman's movement beyond suffrage. The value of her diary as a historical account becomes evident in Wells's frank appraisals of the men and women she met, details of the meetings she attended, and her disclosures of unofficial interviews and conversations.

It is especially useful in delineating the close working partnership of Mormon women representatives to these national organizations and the First Presidency of the Church.

The nomination of B. H. Roberts for Congress in 1898, occasioned one of these interviews. His nomination had outraged many Utah women, since Roberts had almost derailed woman suffrage at Utah's constitutional convention in 1895 and now expected Mormon women to vote for him. Taking the matter to newly sustained Church President Lorenzo Snow and his counselor George Q. Cannon, Wells explained the dilemma women faced in feeling obliged to vote for Roberts as the Mormon candidate. Her diary indicates both President Snow's and Cannon's own opposition to his candidacy and their consent for the women to work against him either "privately or publicly," including the possibility of holding a mass meeting, which the women chose not to do.[12]

Her diary also mentions a private meeting in 1902 with Reed Smoot, a soon-to-be candidate for the U.S. Senate, and Anthon Lund of the First Presidency of the Church concerning the funding for Susa Young Gate's travel to an executive meeting of the International Council of Women in Copenhagen and the problem of funding Latter-day Saint women to attend any of these women's conventions. Her diary reveals Smoot's strong support of continued association with the necessary assistance of Church and auxiliary funds. That he would be the object of an intensive, nationwide effort to unseat him after his election to the Senate by these same women's organizations did not dissuade him from continuing to believe such association was in the best interest of Mormon women as well as the Church.[13]

The *Woman's Exponent* also provides information not found in other Church histories, such as Elder Franklin D. Richards' 1888 sermon to the Weber Stake Relief Society explaining to his attentive audience the relationship of women and the priesthood, and Elder Joseph F. Smith's startling and encouraging talk in support of woman's rights in 1895, as woman suffrage was being debated in Utah's constitutional convention. Both of these talks give insight into the personal views of these Church leaders on subjects that few biographies have explored.[14] As an inside player,

Wells was in a position to provide an interpretation of events and individuals that has often eluded modern historians.

Not only did Emmeline Wells devote much of her journalistic energy to the women's movement, to which she was personally connected, but through her experience with anti-polygamy women, clergy, journalists, and congressmen, she was able to grasp the full implications, particularly for women, of every step of the long crusade to eradicate plural marriage. Few could better define the elements of confrontation, measure the strength of public opinion, or more ably trace the subtle transition of her own people from an impassioned defense, to resignation, and eventually to conciliation.

Not content to deal only with national issues that affected Latter-day Saint women, Wells also documented their local interests including the clubs they organized, the socials they planned, the legislation they fostered, the political parties they joined, and the homes and families they managed.

A third major historical contribution that became increasingly more urgent to her was "collecting and publishing" the lives of the women of the Church. In 1908 she wrote that she felt strongly impressed that this was to be her lifework from that point on. "I really feel," she confided to her diary, "that I can keep their memory before the women of today, and in doing so leave a record of them for the coming generation."[15] With advancing age and most of her commitments successfully behind her, her focus turned from national concerns to local, and she was finally able to concentrate on a charge given to her by Brigham Young when she became editor of the *Woman's Exponent* thirty-one years earlier. "I give you a mission to write brief sketches of the lives of the leading women of Zion, and publish them," he instructed her. Expressing his confidence in the historical value of the paper, he admonished Wells to "tell the sisters to take the *Exponent* and keep it, for it will contain the record of their work and a portion of church history."[16]

Enlisting the help of her contributors, she urged her readers to submit life sketches about others as well as about themselves. "The columns of this paper are ever open to publish such sketches and incidents," she informed the sisters, and encouraged them to submit accounts "of their experiences and testimonies for the benefit of others and to leave them upon record."[17] Included in many of the life stories are personal reminiscences of historical events that occurred during the organizational period of the Church, the western migration, and settlement in Utah. In addition to these individual sketches, Wells wrote and published numerous collective biographies of women in journalism, medicine, literature, politics, education, philanthropy, and other vocational and volunteer fields that women were beginning to enter. She also included brief obituaries submitted by friends and families of the deceased. As a result of this commission, the *Woman's Exponent* contains nearly eight hundred obituaries and close to two hundred multicolumned biographical sketches of Wells's contemporaries. The paper is an impressive biographical dictionary of nineteenth-century women.[18]

In 1911, three years before Emmeline Wells lay down her editorial pen and yielded to changing times and needs of women, she looked over the forty years the *Woman's Exponent* had been keeping a record of women's work and expressed her hope that future historians would "remember the women of Zion when compiling the history of this Western land."[19] She was confident that "no work had been commenced by women that had not been considered and helped" by her paper. She may well have added her diary, a historically valuable companion to the *Exponent,* for she wrote it also with a historian's eye. These two documents divulge a great swath of untapped history unprecedented in Mormon women's historiography. Lamentably, when Emmeline Wells finally lay down her editorial pen in 1914 at the age of eighty-six, the *Woman's Exponent,* after a forty-two year run, slipped quietly into an archival grave, forgotten for more than half a century.

Ever protective of the place she had hoped her paper had filled for the women of her time and the value it would be to future generations, she confidently asserted at the end that the paper had "performed a mission in the midst of Zion for the women of Zion, holding as it does within its leaves the history of their work."[20] Because of her reputed memory for details in Mormon history, for the origins and growth of the Relief Society and other women's activities, and for other information long forgotten by her peers, Wells was frequently considered a historian by her contemporaries and her paper a repository of valuable historical information. In 1918, when Wells was ninety years old and still serving as general president of the Relief Society, a friend interviewed her for a talk she was to give before the Daughters of Utah Pioneers. She had chosen to write about Wells as a historian, a decision that was very satisfying to Wells.[21]

As a preserver of the record, Emmeline Wells was deeply sensitive to the historic changes of the times in which she lived and responded to an inner compulsion to be a conduit through which the past could join the future. While she did not have the passing of time, as most historians do, to fully reflect on the world she so keenly observed, she nonetheless served as an incisive, if not wholly unbiased, interpreter of her generation for ours. Her records help to guide the reader through the ambiguities of a shadowed past toward a clearer view of a complex, intriguing, and challenging time in Mormon history.

Notes

1. "Midnight Soliloquy," *Woman's Exponent* 8 (May 1, 1880), 175–76.
2. "The Old Garrett," *Woman's Exponent* 17 (October 1, 1888), 67.
3. "Our Position," *Woman's Exponent* 1 (June 1, 1872), 4.
4. "Self-Made Women," *Woman's Exponent* 9 (March 2, 1881), 148.
5. The multivolume series edited and compiled by Kate B. Carter through the Daughters of Utah Pioneers is another and later valuable collection by a woman of Utah and Mormon history.
6. Emmeline B. Wells, Diary, August 29, 1877, L. Tom Perry Special Collections, Harold B. Lee Library, Brigham Young University, Provo, Utah. The dissatisfaction to which Wells referred may have related to the fact that both Orson Hyde and Orson Pratt, who were ordained apostles before John Taylor, had each been out of fellowship with the Church for a period, during which time John Taylor and Wilford Woodruff were appointed to the Quorum of Twelve. When Elders Hyde and Pratt were reinstated, Brigham Young ranked them in seniority according to their second ordinations to the Quorum, rather than their first, putting them behind both Elders Taylor and Woodruff. Some Church members may not have been comfortable with this procedure.
7. Relief Society Record (n.d.), November 1901. She mentions at another time, however, that in April 1878, women were voted on for the first time at the annual conference of the Church. "I am glad our labors are coming in to notice," she remarked. See Salt Lake Stake Relief Society Conference Record Book, 1868–1903, December 22, 1877.
8. Salt Lake Stake Relief Society Conference Record Book, 1868–1903, June 22, 1878, Church Archives, The Church of Jesus Christ of Latter-day Saints, Salt Lake City.
9. "R.S. Reports," *Woman's Exponent* 4 (October 1, 1875), 67.
10. "A Welcome," *Woman's Exponent* (April 1, 1881), 165.
11. *National Citizen and Ballot Box,* May 1879. See also *Woman's Exponent* 7 (May 15, 1879), 240.
12. Emmeline B. Wells, Diary, September 20, 1898. It was generally considered by Church as well as the state's political leaders that it would be more beneficial to Utah to elect non-Mormons or at least monogamous Mormons to national office until time had extinguished the still burning anti-Mormon and anti-polygamous feelings both locally and nationwide. Their fears proved to be well founded. See Truman G. Madsen, *Defender of the Faith: The B. H. Roberts Story* (Salt Lake City: Bookcraft, 1980), 242–72.
13. Emmeline B. Wells, Diary, June 10, 1902.
14. For Apostle Smith's talk, see "Relief Society Conference," *Woman's Exponent* 24 (August 15, 1895), 45–46.
15. Emmeline B. Wells, Diary, May 23, 24, 1908.
16. "The Jubilee Celebration, The Need of Press Representation," *Woman's Exponent* 20 (March 15, 1892), 132.
17. "Editorial Thoughts," *Woman's Exponent* 18 (November 15, 1889), 92.
18. A compilation of all of the obituaries and "In Memoriam" notices as well as the biographical sketches which ran from one column to several pages reveals how persistent Emmeline Wells was in fulfilling this charge and particularly after her own determination to devote more time to it. This compilation is in my possession.
19. "Volume Forty," *Woman's Exponent* 40 (July 1911), 4.
20. "Heartfelt Farewell," *Woman's Exponent* 41 (February 1914), 100.
21. Emmeline B. Wells, Diary, April 23, 1918.

Humor on the Trail of Mormon History

Melvin L. Bashore

If you were to pick some words to describe major themes of Mormon history in the nineteenth century, no doubt those words might include persecution, mobs, extermination, exodus, martyrdom, war, or imprisonment. These words evoke our perception of serious happenings in Mormon history.

The traditional way that the Mormon story is recounted leaves little room for laughter or lightheartedness. For a historian to try to make light of these traditional stories would show a lack of good sense or sensitivity. People are used to hearing and reading the story in a serious way. The traditional recounting of the Mormon story is stylized, expected, almost formulaic—with no room for surprises or levity. It would take courage or foolishness to tell the story otherwise. Well, fools walk in where angels fear to tread.

For fifteen years, I've been reading Mormon Trail journals. I have found much in them that was funny. But when we hear the pioneer story recounted every July, what do we hear about? We generally only hear about any one of three companies who came to Utah: 1847 Brigham Young pioneer company or the 1856 Willie and Martin handcart companies. We also hear about death and suffering. Why? The Latter-day Saint migration movement is widely regarded as the most successful organized migration during the nineteenth century. When other historians emphasize the success of the Church migration, why do Latter-day Saints want to dwell on the deaths? Death casualties evidence a lack of success. My wife theorizes that it may have something to do with Latter-day Saint teachings about the purpose of earth life. We are put on earth to be tested. If we meet our challenges successfully, we can gain exaltation. The challenges of the Mormon Trail prove that our pioneer ancestors suffered and deserve exaltation. Latter-day Saints tell the story of the Mormon Trail to emphasize death and suffering in order to demonstrate that their pioneers are worthy of eternal glory for what they went through. In doing so, they skew the story of the Mormon Trail to make it appear more challenging and fraught with dangers than it really was.[1]

I don't have any Mormon pioneer ancestry. This dwelling on death and suffering is foreign to what little I had learned about the Latter-day Saints in public schools. They emphasized the positive—the success of the Church in colonizing the West.

During the past three years, I have given a very popular, award-winning lecture sponsored by the Utah Humanities Council Speakers Bureau. For two years, I was their most requested speaker, traveling throughout the state. My lecture was entitled "A Funny Thing Happened on the Way to Utah: Laughable Incidences on the Mormon Trail." I gave my program to Sons of Utah Pioneer and Daughters of Utah Pioneer groups, book clubs, various nonprofit organizations, and even whole communities. After this experience, I'm convinced that people are tired of the old, shopworn traditional telling of the pioneer trail story. When you tell something so often and in the same way, pretty soon people stop listening. They want to hear something fresh and new. The way that Latter-day Saints usually tell the Mormon Trail story is designed to elicit tears and impress others with the sacrifice and hardships faced by the pioneers. Oftentimes traditional recountings of the Mormon Trail story seem to hover close to a desire on the part of the speaker or writer to manipulate emotions.

In my lecture on the Mormon Trail, I presumed that there would be people in my audiences who would be open to a new way of looking at the trail. I also assumed there would be some who would be puzzled by my lecture title. They would be wary of and prepared to defend their traditional view of the Mormon pioneer. Knowing this, I started my program this way: Generally when the title of my program is given to an audience, "A Funny Thing Happened on the Way to Utah"—I get these angry looks and furrowed brows that convey the message, "I dare you to tell me that anything funny happened on the trail!" While saying that, I would display the "angry looks and furrowed brows" and bang my fist on the podium for dramatic emphasis. That was usually enough to defuse the puzzled, warning looks that I would get prior to beginning my lecture. I guess the underlying psychology of this approach is that if you can get the audience to laugh at you at the beginning, they'll probably laugh with you thereafter.

Some of the funny things that happened on the trail may not have been funny at the time, but with the passing of years they were probably funny to the pioneers—and they are funny now. They also tell us about trail life without causing us to cry a bucket of tears. If I had my choice, I'd rather laugh than cry. Those lucky pioneers—they got to take a hike every day. Get up. Take a hike. Go to bed. Get up and take another hike. What a fortunate life. Just like in my hikes, certain things happened to the pioneers to spoil things. Running into snakes, mosquitoes, or skunks put a damper on their daily hike.

One very old Danish man, who had completely lost his sense of smell, wanted to be helpful in procuring game and food to share with his company. He had seen the other men in his company going out and bringing back buffalo and antelope for dinner. He wanted to do his part. He saw a little furry black and white animal scurrying along the ground. I guess they don't have those animals in Scandinavia. Remember, I told you he'd lost his sense of smell? He took his cane and clubbed it to death, grabbed it's tail and threw it over his shoulder, and headed back to camp. He intended to make skunk soup. I would suspect that the company knew he was coming several hundred yards before he got to camp and that for several weeks, he probably walked several hundred yards behind and downwind from the company.

There are also lots of funny snake stories. One time, Willard Richards pulled out his gun when he found a snake blocking his path. "He fired at it 3 times with his pistol, but the Snake dodged each time."² On the fourth shot, he cut him in two. If a Mormon pioneer was bitten by a rattlesnake (and at least seven were), they either put a poultice on the place where bitten or gave the person the usual all-around medicine they used for anything that ailed you—whiskey. They didn't just pour it on the wound—they believed the more you got down the throat, the better the rattlesnake victim's chances for survival. One day a small company of Latter-day Saints were traveling in southern Iowa heading for the outfitting place on the Missouri River. They stopped to corral their wagons at a place aptly-named Whiskey Point. As they were circling their wagons "a man came on the run across the prairie with his hat off. [He] wanted some whiskey very bad. His child had just been bitten by a rattle snake." The diarist wrote

> I gave him some and he was soon out of sight again. Shortly after we camped for [the] night some 6 or 8 men came to our camp for whiskey. Some more snakes had inserted their poisonous fangs into them, or their wives. But I was quite well aware of the trick by this time and would not let any more go.³

On another occasion a mule was bitten on his belly by a rattlesnake. The pioneers poured a quart of whiskey down its throat, and this saved its life.⁴

There are dozens of funny stories about teenage night guards. Their job was to stay awake all night watching out for the safety of the camp and livestock. Many of them were converts from the cities and towns of Europe. They sometimes brought their city customs with them in the performance of their camp duties. One British teenager, while making his rounds, overheard Hiram Gates arguing late at night with his wife. He called out for all the camp to hear: "Eleven o'clock and all is well and Gates is quarreling with his wife like hell."⁵

Mosquitoes were the pest of the plains. In July 1997, we drove up to Wyoming to see the new Latter-day Saint handcart interpretive center at the Sun Ranch by Devil's Gate. One of my married sons was with us. He had never seen that part of Wyoming and was ecstatic about the beauty of the land. As we neared the center, he asked, "Why didn't the Saints just stop here?" We found out why as soon as we got out of the car.

Don't go in July and, if you do, don't forget your mosquito repellent like we did. My wife proposed a theory—that mosquitoes were the real reason and motivation for the Saints coming all the way to Utah. They kept being bitten until Brigham Young exited Emigration Canyon and found that a mosquito abatement program was in effect in Salt Lake Valley and he said, "This is the right place." Isn't that the story they tell at This Is the Place State Park? Upon later reflection I realized that we were bitten by descendants of the original mosquitoes who bit the pioneers.

I recognize that in a Latter-day Saint audience, it almost borders on sacrilege to poke fun at Brigham Young's entry into the Salt Lake Valley. Every year we celebrate it with a state holiday. But every time I tell that story with my own little perverse and twisted slant—people laugh. You can find a humorous or comic side to even those historical stories that we consider almost sacred. The Willie and Martin handcart story is venerated for its tragic and telling sacrifice. The zeal with which those poor Mormon pioneers pushed ahead under conditions that took lives at every turn of the trail commands nothing but admiration and respect. Who would dare find something funny in that story? I did. Two Latter-day Saint wagon companies followed those handcart companies, one of them reaching the Salt Lake Valley a couple of weeks behind the last handcart company. As their story was little known and they froze and suffered in the same miserable weather as the Willie and Martin companies, I decided to tell their forgotten story. It was published in *Annals of Wyoming*. John Bond, twelve years old, was in one of those wagon companies. His family's story is doubly tragic. Latter-day Saint converts from England, his family had sufficient means to travel without Church financial assistance. They were among the very first to arrive on the Iowa City campground to outfit for the plains. Through bureaucratic oversight on the part of Church leaders, his family ended up being among the last to leave the outfitting place. To lighten their wagon load and preserve the strength of their ox team, they cast out food staples and supplies. One day, when the company was called to gather for prayer meeting, young John was too much tempted to linger behind by the smell of some baking bread on someone else's campfire. Bond wrote:

I saw sister Scott cooking a nice pot of dumplings just before the bugle sounded. She hid the dumplings under the wagon, being a zealous woman, and went to prayer meeting, but I did not go this time. I stood back and looked for the dumplings, found them and being so hungry I could not resist the temptations, sat down and ate them all. I admit that those dumplings did me more good than all the prayers that could have been offered.[6]

Does humor have a place in Mormon history? In a historiographical essay in a western history journal, Charles S. Peterson wrote that humor played no "part of Utah/Mormon history's repertoire."[7] In a later issue of that same journal, Leonard Arrington disagreed with Peterson and countered with dozens of funny stories that he had culled from Latter-day Saint diaries, sermons, and minute books.[8] In my more focused study of Church emigration, like Arrington, I have found much to laugh at. In my public speaking about the Mormon Trail, I have found that humor has a way of breaking the ice—be it a Mormon or non-Mormon audience, scholarly setting or general public. Latter-day Saint historians have been criticized for being too narrow, for not reaching out to a wider audience.[9] Humor can bridge that gap between town and gown, between Mormons and non-Mormons, between Mormon history (narrowly defined) and Western, American, and international history. Humor may even be an antidote (not a cure-all) for those who are of the opinion that Mormon history is boring and tiresome.[10]

Humor is a great leveler. It is one of the joys of being human. Out of our recent experience in the Winter Olympics, observers noted with surprise that Mormons are "normal" and not at all "weird."[11] The world learned that Latter-day Saints are nice, friendly, and hospitable. They also learned that Latter-day Saints like to have fun. Most of us didn't want the party to end. We need to communicate those characteristics in telling the story of our past. We are not staid and preponderantly serious. We have a lighter side. The Mormon past has a lighter side. Mormon history often deals with serious matters, but there is no reason why humor can't coexist with the serious. In fact, when our history is most grim is when we most need to laugh. Stanley L. Witkin, a social worker, attested to the benefits of humor during bleak and morbid times. He wrote, "In these situations humor can provide a perspective that enables us to distinguish the annoying from the intolerable, the unfortunate from the disastrous, and the unpleasant from the awful."[12] There is no call for history to be humorless. We need to mine our documents and records for evidence of the humor in our history. It is there waiting to be discovered—and we need to inject it into our history.

Maybe if enough of these funny stories get written and recounted, our perception of Mormon history will become more faithful and true to what life was really like. At the very least, our telling of the story will become less serious, more fresh and engaging. Is it too much to hope that in ten or twenty years—if enough of these funny stories get told—that our images of what happened in the Mormon past might be very different than is generally the case today? In the future, if one were to mention that river and stream crossings presented challenges on the Mormon Trail, people wouldn't immediately think of the three young men who carried the handcart pioneers across the freezing Sweetwater River to the detriment of their own health. They might instead recall and picture the young man who tried to carry a hefty, Mormon pioneer lady across a stream, but lost his footing midstream and landed on his backside with the lady sprawled on top of him. It really happened, and by telling this story, it helps give balance to the story of what really happened in the Mormon past. And besides—it's entertaining.

Notes

1. Heretofore most comments and discussions about death on the Mormon Trail have been generalized because there has been no accurate accounting of either who or how many people died on the trail. The author has been studying Mormon Trail mortality for several years, compiling a list of people who died, and an article on his research findings is in preparation.

2. Thomas Bullock, *The Pioneer Camp of the Saints: The 1846 and 1847 Mormon Trail Journals of Thomas Bullock,* ed. Will Bagley (Spokane, Wash.: Arthur H. Clark, 1997), 168.

3. David Moore, Writings, typescript, 44, Church Archives.

4. "Biographical Sketch of John Hindley," 143, in Histories of Utah Pioneers of Adams Camp, Daughters of Utah Pioneers, American Fork, vol. 2, L. Tom Perry Special Collections, Harold B. Lee Library, Brigham Young University, Provo, Utah.

5. Oliver B. Huntington, Diary, July 9, 1848, in Digital Archive Collections, Overland Trails, Utah and Inter-mountain West, Harold B. Lee Library, Brigham Young University, Provo, Utah (catalog.lib.byu.edu/Archimages/1181722.PDF).

6. Melvin L. Bashore, "On the Heels of the Handcart Tragedy: Mormondom's Forgotten 1856 Wagon Companies," *Annals of Wyoming* 68, no. 3 (summer 1996): 45.

7. Charles S. Peterson, "The Look of the Elephant: On Seeing Western History," *Montana: The Magazine of Western History* 39, no. 2 (spring 1989): 73.

8. Leonard J. Arrington, "The Looseness of Zion: The Lighter Side of Mormon History," *Montana: The Magazine of Western History* 40, no. 2 (spring 1990): 73–78.

9. Among those who have criticized Mormon historians for writing to a narrow audience is Charles S. Peterson. He faulted Mormon historians for writing "to themselves and to themselves alone" (Peterson, "The Look of the Elephant," 71).

10. For an essay critical of the sameness of Mormon history, see Isleta L. Pement, "The Boring of Mormonism," *John Whitmer Historical Association Journal* 15 (1995): 3–8. Roger Launius, a past president of Mormon History Association, has observed that Mormon history has lost the excitement present during the 1970s and early 1980s; see "The 'New Social History' and the 'New Mormon History': Reflections on Recent Trends," *Dialogue: A Journal of Mormon Thought* 27, no. 1 (spring 1994): 109–27. He appealed for Mormon historians to "shake up" and reinvigorate the field.

11. For comments on Mormons not being weird, see excerpt in "Media React to Church," *Deseret News Church News,* March 2, 2002, 2, from Tim Dahlberg, AP article published in *Los Angeles Times.* For comments on Mormons being normal, see R. Scott Lloyd, "Communicating with the World," *Deseret News Church News,* March 2, 2002, 13.

12. Stanley L. Witkin, "Taking Humor Seriously," *Social Work* 44, no. 2 (March 1999): 104.

Writing Ward Histories: Mormon Wards as Community

Jessie L. Embry

The Lord revealed to Joseph Smith Jr. the necessity of keeping records and histories. "It is the duty of the Lord's clerk whom he has appointed to keep a history . . . of all things that transpire in Zion" (D&C 85:1). Ward clerks followed that advice and chronicled events. Ward members frequently use this information along with all data to write ward histories. Many examples are at the Brigham Young University Library; countless others remain only in their local areas. These histories list names and refresh memories. They are invaluable for those who know the people and the events. But they usually isolate the ward experience, limiting their usefulness. They are an interesting read for those from the area; they lack significance for those who know nothing about the ward or the people.

Ward histories are not unique though. Most local histories focus on only the area. They lack the historical panorama that give added meaning. They ignore theories that help understand why things happen. These weaknesses limit the usefulness of the study. But with some additional research, the local history and the ward history can be more valuable for those who directly relate to it and others who know nothing about the area.

For example, in the 1960s the Daughters of Utah Pioneers in Wasatch County compiled historical information and asked newspaper administrator William Mortimer to edit *How Beautiful Upon the Mountains*.[1] As a Utah State Historical Society preservation intern during the 1970s researching buildings in Wasatch County, I found the book to be very helpful. It had the names of all county, city, and Latter-day Saint Church leaders. It included a short biography of many of the county's pioneers. But I had to add the required historical significance to my National Register nomination forms. I longed for a history of the area that would put the county into a historical setting.

In the 1990s, I had the opportunity. After some arm twisting, the Utah State Historical Society and the county commissioners hired me to write a history as part of Utah State centennial series. I used the information from *How Beautiful Upon the Mountains* and other sources to explore how Wasatch County was similar and different from other parts of Utah and the United States. I included United States and Utah history to show how they impacted Wasatch County. My goal was to produce a history that county residents and others would enjoy and learn from.[2]

An example illustrates the difference in the histories. *How Beautiful Upon the Mountains* tells about the remodeling of the Midway Second Ward chapel in 1952. The history detailed the new building that surrounded the old. Other chapters talked about new construction in the towns of Heber City, Wallsburg, and Center during the 1950s. There was no attempt to show how all this new construction related to each other and to United States history.

But there is a direct connection. Following World War II, Americans wanted to return to normalcy. The war required them to "make do or do without." Once rationing ended, they wanted to buy new cars, homes, and household appliances. They wanted new public buildings—schools, post offices, and churches. Across the United States, Americans constructed new or remodeled buildings. The Midway Second Ward followed this pattern. What started as a simple fix-up project expanded until a church was built that looked completely different but used the same foundation. Just as throughout the United States, new was essential in Midway.[3]

This example illustrates the value of American history in understanding local history. The same applies to ward histories. By studying other histories, we can better understand how our wards reacted to the world around them. In the same way, using social science theories can help appreciate how our wards are similar and different from other organizations. By adding background historical information and social science theories, we can take our ward listings and expand them into new histories just like the Midway Second Ward transformed their meeting house.

To illustrate this point, I will examine community research. During the 1990s community became a catchword in American popular and academic circles. The Unabomber published a letter blaming "the social and psychological problems of modern society" on a system that "compelled people to live under conditions radically different from under which the human race evolved." Technology left people isolated and took them out of small, caring communities.[4] Hillary Rodham Clinton, the U.S. president's wife, used an African proverb "It takes a village to raise a child" to call for more interaction.[5]

The concept was not new. As early as 1887 German sociologist Ferdinand Toennies described a shift from *gemeinschaft*—usually translated as community—to *gesellschaft*—society in an industrial society. His theories went in and out of fashion over the years but by the 1980s community studies returned to importance.[6] Sociologist Robert Wuthnow's *Sharing the Journey: Support Groups and America's News Quest for Community* explained, "Ours is a highly fluid society. Many of us live anonymous lives" and cry for support groups. Wuthnow argues that twelve-step programs are "clearly rooted in the breakdown of these traditional support structures and the continuing desire for community."[7] More recently organizational behaviorist Robert Putnam called for Americans to return to participation in all aspects of civic involvement in his study *Bowling Alone: The Collapse and Revival of American Community*.[8]

Religious scholars have asked similar questions. James P. Wind and James W. Lewis published a two-volume history that looked at religious congregations as communities. Volume one examined specific churches, including a chapter on The Church of Jesus Christ of Latter-day Saints and a case study of the Salt Lake City Sugar House Ward.[9] Other religious scholars have also examined the interrelationship between congregations and communities, including E. Brooks Holifield's "Towards a History of American Congregations."[10]

Scholars studying The Church of Jesus Christ of Latter-day Saints have also been concerned about community. Sociologist Lowry Nelson praised the Latter-day Saints' adaption of the farm village and their "intense religious motivation" in his 1952 study.[11] Scholars continued to examine Mormon communities and congregations. In 1979 historians Leonard J. Arrington and Davis Bitton wrote, "In pioneer Utah, the ward [was] more than the basic ecclesiastical unit—it was the most important political unit, and except for the family, the most important social unit as well."[12]

Do wards still play that role? In his 1978 Mormon History Association presidential address, historian Douglas D. Alder asked if Latter-day Saint wards were communities where people shared experiences or congregations where people simply worshipped together.[13] Historians Jan Shipps, Dean May, and Cheryll May saw the pattern continuing, "For more than a century the church has kept wards at village size by altering ward boundaries."[14] General Relief Society President Mary Ellen W. Smoot expressed the same hope at Brigham Young University in 2000, "We have been told that the Church will never be larger than our ward boundaries. Each of us has an opportunity to be an instrument in the Lord's hands in making our ward so strong and filled with so much love, devotion, and acceptance that everyone feels a part of our ward."[15]

This information about community can provide a framework for a ward history. In *Mormon Wards as Community* I asked a question very similar to Douglas Alder's, "Do wards provide a community for Latter-day Saints?"[16] I discovered that a number of factors determined the answer to that question and that each individual's experience was unique. Jan Shipps and the Mays feared that the consolidated meeting schedule adopted in the 1980s would remove the sense of community.[17] I found that while it had an effect, there were other important factors such as location, a person's stage of life, the ward membership, and the person's attitude. I use personal examples to prove my points. The theories, though, provided structure and ideas that others who knew about the wards I discussed understood.

Besides using the community theories, I also used my training as a historian to explain what happened in the wards. United States, Utah, and Church history all added to my narrative. For example, I examined ward divisions. As Shipps and the Mays suggested, wards have been divided to keep the membership about the size of a village. For the most part, Latter-day Saints accept these changes, only "whining" when the new boundaries force them to make a new community. Still, there was some pain. Some members "lament[ed] the day the ward was divided." According to Dean May, a ward division "was a rite of passage for Alpine [Utah]."[18]

The Provo Sixth Ward, which celebrated its one-hundredth anniversary in 2002, provided a classic example of how I used history and social science theory to understand ward division. Brigham Young initially formed four wards in Provo in the 1850s. Even though the city grew rapidly, the wards were not divided until 1902 when President Joseph F. Smith decided the congregations should be smaller. In April that year, Apostle Reed Smoot, a Provo native, organized the Provo Fifth and Sixth Wards.

Provo continued to grow. The Provo Sixth Ward went from 935 members in 1914 to 1,100 in 1950. Following World War II, Church leaders again desired to make wards smaller and more personal. The Provo Sixth Ward was split, and church leaders created the Provo Fourteenth Ward. But location changed those boundaries. The Sixth Ward was near the city center and the Fourteenth Ward was on the edge of town. As the city grew, the central business district spilled over into the residential area. Homes in the Provo Sixth Ward were torn down and replaced by stores. The ward became very small. At the same time, farmers in the Provo Fourteenth Ward sold their property and new subdivisions brought more residents. Eventually all of the original Fourteenth Ward was returned to the Sixth Ward.

The growth of Brigham Young University also changed the Provo Sixth Ward. Following World War II, returning servicemen used the G.I. bill to attend colleges and universities. BYU's enrollment soared and students moved into neighborhoods around the city. This added to the transient nature of the Provo Sixth Ward, but it also provided fresh faces to fulfill church callings.

Those who moved in often found a community because they were immediately put to work.

My home town of North Logan, Utah, experienced similar changes. It started as a small farming community, not settled until 1884 because there was no water. While the farmers lived on scattered homesteads, they developed a community through the ward and school. After World War II, increased enrollment at Utah State University brought more students and faculty to town. New faculty who grew up in small towns liked the rural atmosphere just north of the university campus and bought property in town. New construction boomed. I felt that I grew up in a unique town where farmers and academics mixed very well, but some complained that sometimes professors wanted to be known as "Doctor" in the classroom and at church. For these people, profession was a dividing line. For me the problem came when the ward was actually divided in 1962. True, the ward was too large, but it split the community down the middle. Members were so involved in their new ward that they rarely saw the people on the other side of the street.

While wards in Utah provide communities for members, those outside the state where Mormons are a minority have stronger bonds. My family lived in Iran from 1960–1962. My father, Bertis L. Embry, was a professor at Utah State University and part of a contract that the university had with the U.S. government to provide agricultural education. Brigham Young University had a contract at the same time to provide teacher education. The contracts had started during the 1950s, and the federal programs were part of the foreign aid given to combat the Russian influence in the area. (Iran shared a long northern border with the USSR.) The little branch that we attended provided a home for the American Mormons who were very different from the Muslims and from the other American service personnel and business representatives. My knowledge of history and the community theories helped me understand why the Latter-day Saints in Iran depended on each other so much.

I had a less dramatic experience when I lived in Columbia, Missouri in 1966. The small branch there was our home. Everyone attended MIA dances; they became ward socials. While I rarely saw the girls in Mutual class at school, they were my safety net outside of class. I tried to develop other friends with my 4-H club, but there was not the same connection. In the ward our beliefs tied us together; in the 4-H club our interest in rural life was not as great as my religious convictions. The 1960s were a time of civil rights change, and I felt it hard to understand why the African Americans in my homeroom had to sit on the back row. But everything was too new for me, and I wanted the safety of the Church.

Mormons relate to these examples because they have experienced wards dividing and lived in places where they were the minority. They have lived in wards where they felt at home or where they felt they were different. Yet they do not always know the impact of national and state events on their wards. Nor do they understand why changes take place. Social science theories can help answer those questions.

But how can a ward historian find this information? The history is easiest to find. General U.S. and state history books outline events that impacted local areas. Latter-day Saint history books such as James B. Allen and Glen Leonard's *Story of the Latter-day Saints* does the same for the Church.[19] There are many social science theories, so selecting one might not be as easy. My focus was community, so I searched card catalogues and basic sociology textbooks. I found more information than I could write about. Other theories that impact wards are economic divisions, ethnic mixes, and involvement levels. While it make take some searching, it will be worthwhile to answer why.

By putting our ward histories in historical and theoretical frameworks rather than listing the names of bishops and Relief Society presidents and the dates of the Gold and Green Balls, our ward histories can have greater meaning.

Notes

1. William James Mortimer, ed., *How Beautiful Upon the Mountains* (Wasatch County: Daughters of Utah Pioneers, 1963).

2. Jessie L. Embry, *A History of Wasatch County: Utah Centennial County History Series* (Salt Lake City: Utah State Historical Society and Wasatch County Commission, 1996).

3. Embry, *A History of Wasatch County,* 220, 249.

4. Robert Wright, "The Evolution of Despair," *Time* 28 (August 1995), 50–57.

5. Hillary Rodham Clinton, *It Takes a Village and Other Lessons Children Teach Us* (New York: Simon and Schuster, 1996).

6. Larry Lyon, *The Community in Urban Society* (Philadelphia: Temple University Press, 1987), xii.

7. Robert Wuthnow, *Sharing the Journey: Support Groups and America's News Quest for Community* (New York: The Free Press, 1994), 5.

8. Robert D. Putnam, *Bowling Alone: The Collapse and Revival of American Community* (New York: Simon and Schuster).

9. Jan Shipps, Cheryll May, and Dean May, "Sugar House Ward: A Latter-day Saint Congregation," *American Congregations: Volume One,* James P. Wind and James W. Lewis, eds. (Chicago: University of Chicago, 1994), 293–348.

10. E. Brooks Holifield, "Towards a History of American Congregations," *American Congregations: Volume Two,* James P. Ward and James W. Lewis, eds. (Chicago: University of Chicago, 1994).

11. Lowry Nelson, *The Mormon Village* (Chicago: University of Chicago Press, 1952), xiii.

12. Leonard J. Arrington and Davis Bitton, *Mormon Experience: A History of the Latter-day Saints* (New York: Alfred A. Knopf, 1979), 208.

13. Douglas D. Alder, "The Mormon Ward: Congregation or Community," *Journal of Mormon History* (1979), 23–26, 70.

14. Shipps, May, and May, "Sugar House Ward," 325.

15. Mary Ellen W. Smoot, "Seeking Solutions," *Ensign* 32 (February 2002): 47.

16. For more information and the sources for the Provo Sixth, North Logan, and Iran congregations, see Jessie L. Embry, *Mormon Wards as Community* (Binghamton, N.Y.: Global Publications, 2001).

17. Shipps, May, and May, "Sugar House Ward," 293–348.

18. Shipps, May, and May, "Sugar House Ward," 325; Dean May, "The LDS Ward as Congregation," Sunstone Symposium, 1995 Salt Lake City, Cassette Tape, Learning Resource Center, Harold B. Lee Library, Provo, Utah.

19. James B. Allen and Glen Leonard, *Story of the Latter-day Saints* (Salt Lake City: Deseret Book, 1992).

Improving the Telling of Native American and Mormon Contacts in Frontier Utah

Robert H. Briggs

The Broader Context:
Indian Studies in the United States

By the middle of the twentieth century, nearly thirty thousand books had been published on the American Indians. Some were positive in their portrayal, but the large majority were negative.[1] Writers and scholars alike wrote in a descriptive vein, usually about "bloody Indian wars or courageous native patriots fighting to save their people." Not surprisingly, the vast majority were also written by non-Indians. Thus, American Indian history was dominated by "non-Indian historians who used non-Indian sources to create non-Indian interpretations about American Indians and their past." Angela Cavender Wilson argues that this has been the case even up to the present and that such histories should be called "non-Indian perceptions of American Indian history."[2]

Most of the earlier generation of Mormon writers followed these trends. Most dealt with conflict or war with Indians. While the "wars" in Utah occurred during relatively brief and discrete periods (the so-called Walker War of 1853–54 and the Black Hawk War of 1865–68), these accounts imparted to the rising generation the risks involved in contacts with Indians. There were, however, several exceptions to this, one of which was the biography of Jacob Hamblin, the Latter-day Saint "Apostle to the Lamanites."[3] While it had its share of adventures and breathtaking escapes, generally it conveyed Hamblin's view of the Indian tribes as having distinct cultures as well as the positive features Hamblin observed in these cultures. More important, Hamblin portrayed his identification with and empathy for the Indians he came to know, conveying their essential "humanness" and fundamental similarities to whites.

Meanwhile, in academia in the United States and Europe, the discipline of anthropology (and its allied fields) was developing. Beginning with E. B. Tylor and continuing with the theoretical work of Boas, Benedict, Kroeber, Steward, White, Durkheim, Radcliffe-Brown, Evans-Pritchard, and Malinowski, the new science developed from the 1860s to the 1950s.[4] For all of its grand promise,[5] however, anthropology settled into the comfortable academic niche of explaining the myriad manifestations of "culture" and, particularly, documenting "primitive" and, in many cases, vanishing peoples.[6] It became the primary discipline for studying Native Americans.

A further step occurred in the 1950s, when anthropologists and historians interested in Indian studies first began looking enviously over the academic fences separating their disciplines. They began borrowing data and then methods from each other. From this academic cross-fertilization, ethnohistory was born.[7] Since then, ethnohistory has developed as the primary vehicle for studying Native Americans and, despite some criticisms,[8] has supplied the main interdisciplinary methods for Indian studies.

In the late 1980s, a new movement labeled the New Western History emerged.[9] Some also perceived the emergence of a New Indian History. But for ethnohistorians, the New Indian History had its roots in the ethnohistory that had flourished since the 1950s. To the traditional category of narrative history, the methodologies of New Indian History have added oral history, environmental history, biographical history, women's history, quantitative history, agricultural history, and demographic history, to name only a few.[10]

There are signs that these larger trends in western and Indian studies are having a positive impact on Mormon studies, particularly on the subject of Native American-Mormon contacts in frontier Utah. Using methods from ethnohistory and the New Indian History, some important new studies have emerged in various genres such as studies of war, tribal histories, frontier contacts, and biographies. Recently, titles such as these have been published: John A. Peterson's *Utah's Black Hawk War;* a collection of introductory essays on the six major Utah Indian tribes edited by Forrest S. Cuch and entitled *A History of Utah's American Indians;* Robert S. McPherson's study entitled *The Northern Navajo Frontier, 1860–1900: Expansion through Adversity;* and two biographies, *The Journey of Navajo Oshley: An Autobiography and Life History* edited by Robert S. McPherson; and *Sagwitch: Shoshone Chieftain, Mormon Elder, 1822–1887* by Scott R. Christensen.[11]

Despite these positive steps, Forrest Cuch has recently contended that persistent myths in Utah history must be dispelled. Among these myths, Cuch argues, is first that "'no one' (or no people of importance) lived in [Utah] prior to Mormon settlement," second, that "Utah's American Indians were treated better than 'other Indians' outside [Utah]," and third, the "common perception . . . that all Indians are the same, when, in fact, Indians are a very diverse group." On the two latter issues, Cuch argues for a more nuanced approach. Further, he challenges the marginalization of Native American accounts. "[T]he histories of Utah's American Indian tribes have not been considered a viable and integral part of the history of the state." Citing Will Numkena, Cuch notes that "a one-sided perspective without presentation of the Indian experience" has been offered. As has happened elsewhere, "Indian history has been written by the conqueror, with little or no regard for those conquered."[12]

Suggestions for Improving the Telling of Native American-Mormon Contacts in Frontier Utah

Having provided this brief historical overview, we turn to the central question of this brief study: How can we improve our histories of the contact between Native Americans and Euro-Americans, especially Latter-day Saints, in Utah and the larger regions of the Great Basin and Colorado Plateau?[13] I offer the following suggestions, most of which are drawn from the experience of the practitioners in ethnohistory and the New Indian History.

1. The consensus among ethnohistorians is that *the first step in improving our understanding of American Indians is to look closely at Indian cultures and their communities.*[14] Practically speaking, this means making judicious use of Native American materials gathered from anthropology, ethnology, and ethnohistory. It means studying Indian languages, oral histories, and tribal histories. *Rethinking American Indian History,* edited by Donald L. Fixico, discusses some of the new and promising methodologies in detail.[15] We should also admit how challenging this enterprise is. Its interdisciplinary approach is a strong call for collaboration, discussed below at item nine.

2. Viewing five hundred years of contact between Euro-Americans and Native Americans has led some observers to discern repeating patterns and issues. *Among these frequently occurring issues are: disruption, disease and die off, dispossession, disintegration (of culture), and detribalization.* What has been the Indian experience with these issues in Utah?

Disruption. In the context of the Great Basin and Colorado Plateau, the influx of Euro-Americans into the region was rapid, steady, and unabating. The ten-year census records convey part of the story. From no presence in 1840 to slightly more than 11,000 in 1850, the white inhabitants grew to 40,000 in 1860, nearly 87,000 in 1870, nearly 144,000 in 1880, and a whopping 211,000 by 1890.[16] For the Native Americans who had lived sedately on the banks of perennial streams for hundreds of years, the invasion of Mormons, miners, and military men was a calamitous flood, sweeping everything indigenous before its path. The engulfing tide of newcomers increased the already stiff competition for scarce resources in the Great Basin. Within a brief span of years, the Indians of the Great Basin were pushed to the margins of the useful land. Furthermore, the Mormons also hunted game animals in direct competition with Native Americans. Thus, within a few years, game near the most inhabited areas had noticeably declined. As for the livestock that the Mormons introduced into the environment, they grazed on the native browse that also contained the seeds and plant foods that Indians collected. Thus, staples of the Native American diet, seeds and plant foods, likewise declined in areas frequented by the Mormons' livestock. Whether from loss of game animals, seeds, plant foods, or choice riparian bottom lands for Indian horticulture or agriculture, the traditional subsistence patterns of the Ute,[17] Goshute,[18] and Paiute[19] were disrupted.

Disease and Die Off. The Northwestern Shoshone experienced a devastating die off, although less from disease than from a single calamitous event, the Bear River Massacre. On January 29, 1863, Col. Patrick Edward Connor lead a column of California Volunteers in a massacre of an estimated 250 Shoshone men, women, and children near the Bear River in southern Idaho. Here was a significant "die off" from which the Shoshone has never recovered. It is a central event in their tribal history of the last two centuries and perhaps the largest slaughter of Native Americans in a single-day engagement in American history.[20]

In contrast, the Ute, Goshute, and Paiute suffered the more gradual effects of disease leading to declining populations. In the 1850s to 1860s, both the Latter-day Saints and the Paiute in southern Utah suffered from epidemics of cholera, scarlet fever, whooping cough, measles, mumps, tuberculosis, and malaria. But having less acquired immunity than the Latter-day Saints, the Paiute suffered greater losses. In some bands, the mortality ran as high as 90 percent.[21] The Ute population declined as well. Disease was a factor, such as the smallpox epidemic in winter 1864–65.[22] But for the Ute, losses in battle from two wars (the Walker War and Black Hawk War) plus numerous sanguinary skirmishes spanning more than two decades also took their toll. Brigham Young himself noted the declining Indian population.[23]

The Navajo fared better. They were exposed to the same Euro-American diseases but during the nineteenth century their population declines were far less severe than among their Indian neighbors to the north. In fact, while most Indian populations in Utah had declined, the Navajo population remained robust. Only a small portion of their reservation lies within Utah, yet the Navajo constitute the majority of the American Indians living in Utah. Why have they flourished so? Evidently, their prior contact with the New Mexicans to the east of their traditional lands gave them a greater degree of resistance to the European diseases that the Latter-day Saints and others inevitably brought with them. This, however, needs further study.

Finally, the recent experience of the Paiute during and after the Termination Period of 1953–70 (discussed below) is an indication that this issue has not been limited to the period of first contact in the nineteenth century. After termination in the 1950s, support for the Paiute under the federal trusteeship vanished. This led to a precipitous decline in the Paiute standard of living. By the early 1980s, the dispirited Paiute suffered a skyrocketing death rate due to alcoholism, the average life expectancy for Paiute males dropped to forty-two years and, with only one birth for every three deaths, the Utah Paiute population sagged. More recently, however, better medical care and other services have improved both their life expectancy rates and their lot in general.

Dispossession. The effects of dispossession have varied widely among the tribes of Utah. As we have seen, the Shoshone decline is tied to the 1863 Bear River Massacre. Their traditional lands were enormous, covering portions of Utah, Nevada, Idaho, and Wyoming. But after being decimated in 1863, their land holdings have dwindled to the current level of 184 acres.[24]

In the 1850s, Latter-day Saints began settling in traditional Goshute lands in future Tooele County. By 1860 with the settlement of Ibapah (or Deep Creek), "the last of the favored regions in the Goshute homeland had been invaded."[25] The influx of Mormons, the U.S. Army, the Pony Express, the Overland Stage, as well as fluctuating federal Indian policy and unfulfilled promises bred frustration, mistrust, and suspicion. When whites made permanent use of previous Goshute resources, the Goshute retaliated. Raiding began as early as 1851 and continued sporadically through the 1860s. The 1860s were also years of wrangling over proposed reservation lands. In 1883, the Church of Jesus Christ of Latter-day Saints (hereafter Church of Jesus Christ) placed the Goshutes on a thousand acre farm which was later deeded to them. And finally, after years of federal neglect, two federal reservations were established early in the twentieth century.[26] These reservations at Skull Valley and Deep Creek currently contain some 17,000 and 108,000 acres, respectively.[27]

The cases of the Navajo, Ute, and Paiute are a study in contrasts. Each has a history of dispossession, although in sharply differing ways. In 1846 the Navajo encountered Americans who displaced the Mexicans in controlling the territory now comprising the state of New Mexico. The 1850s and 1860s were calamitous times as conflict grew between Americans and the Navajo. It culminated in the punishing forays of Indian fighter Christopher "Kit" Carson into the heartland of Navajo country—the Dinétah—with disastrous results. Carson destroyed much of the Navajo subsistence base and forced their capitulation. During the winter of 1863–64, under the direction of General James Carleton, the Navajo endured the Long Walk from their traditional lands to Fort Sumner at Bosque Redondo in central New Mexico. Within a year, eight thousand Navajo had been relocated to Fort Sumner. But the deaths of three thousand Navajo at Bosque Redondo, corruption among some federal officials, and the obvious failure of the relocation policy lead to its reversal. In 1868 the Navajo were allowed to return to the Dinétah, now greatly reduced in size. Yet over the next four decades, through impressive and astute resistance to encroaching miners, Mormons, and other white settlers, the Navajo successfully recaptured large portions of their traditional lands, winning eight boundary changes between 1868 and 1905, with additional expansions in 1933 and 1958. The modern Navajo reservation is the largest in the United States.[28]

In contrast, the Ute experience followed the pattern more typical of American Indians during the nineteenth century: steady white encroachment into their traditional lands followed by concentration under federal policy onto "reserved" lands. Today the Ute occupy only a tiny fraction of their former territories. The Southern Ute live on a reservation in the southwestern corner of Colorado near Ignacio. The Ute Mountain Utes descend from the Weminuche band who moved to the western end of the Southern Ute Reservation in 1897. Their reservation is located in the Four Corners area near Towaoc, Colorado, and includes small sections of Utah and New Mexico. The Northern Ute live on the Uintah-Ouray Reservation near Fort Duchesne in northeastern Utah.[29]

Finally, the Southern Paiute suffered dispossession but in its own unique way. In the latter nineteenth century they were pressed to the periphery of their traditional lands. During the Reservation Period of federal policy, several small and inadequate reservations were created in the southern portions of Utah and Nevada. Some gathered to these reservations, but others did not. However, in the Termination Period of the mid-twentieth century, the Paiute were terminated from their trusteeship with the Bureau of Indian Affairs (BIA). Being thus "set free," the Paiute "suffered the loss of land, federal expertise and legal protection, federal health and education funds to individuals, . . . training, housing, and business grants . . . and . . . the limited sovereignty they had enjoyed [previously]." After two decades under "termination," the Paiute's deplorable condition was recognized and efforts were undertaken to pass a restoration bill that would create a federally recognized tribal entity for the Paiute. Restoration was enacted in 1980 during the Carter administration. Yet the net loss of land is an indication of how the process of dispossession has continued: For the 29 million acres lost in termination they were paid a paltry 27 cents per acre. The restoration act of 1980 promised restoration of 15,000 acres. The Paiute were also given access to a $2.5 million trust fund for economic development and tribal services. To date, however, less than 5,000 acres have been restored.[30]

Cultural Disintegration. Not surprisingly, the above factors have also negatively impacted the cultures of Utah's Indians. Of special concern is the decline in those who speak their native language. This is particularly true among the Northwestern Shoshone, Goshute, and Southern Paiute. Other forms of cultural decline are in evidence and are addressed in *A History of Utah's American Indians.*

Detribalization. Detribalization—the widespread loss of identification with one's particular tribe—has occurred less frequently in the United States. It is widespread in Mexico and other areas of Latin America where most are biracial with indigenous roots, yet they have de-emphasized or lost their identification with a particular indigenous tribe. However, detribalization has had differential impact on Utah's tribes, with relatively less effect on the larger tribes such as the Navajo but marked effects on, for example, the Northwestern Shoshone who have never recovered from Colonel Connor's near genocidal attack of 1863.[31]

3. Another broad approach is *the study of changes in federal Indian policy* and its varying impacts on the tribes of Utah. The evolution of federal policy toward American Indians is divided into the following periods:

    Treaty Period, 1789–1871

    Reservation Period, 1871–1887

    Allotment Period, 1887–1934

    Reorganization Period, 1934–1953

    Termination Period, 1953–1970

    Self-Determination Period, 1970–1994

    Self-Government Period, 1994–present

As with the other general approaches described here, each period reflects new legislation and a shift in federal policy. Yet despite the supposed uniformity of federal policy in each period, the impacts among the various tribes were variable instead of uniform.[32]

4. There are other *commonalities* among the tribes of Utah. Cuch notes the "high value placed on family and spirituality, nuclear family and extended family and extended kinship structures; similar tribal spiritual philosophies; [and] a high regard for the elderly, who sometimes serve as the educators and second parents."[33]

5. Some commonalities notwithstanding, a point explicitly made in the New Indian History is *the great diversity among Indian tribes*. There are 540 federally recognized Indian tribes within the United States, while 340 Indian languages are still in use. Cuch notes differences in "customs, practices, clothing, housing, and foods."[34] Thus, we must be aware of the broad diversity of Native Americans, even among those of the same region. Centuries-old, Euro-American generalizations about "Indians" are now seen as problematic at best. The preferable course in most contexts is to limit our generalizations to a particular tribe, thus avoiding our past penchant for over-generalization.

6. The trends in the larger historical community can profitably be considered. Critiques of the older descriptive histories have produced new methods, new questions, and arguably a new movement: the New Indian History. Among the *fruitful areas of study within the New Indian History* are statistical studies of the impact of disease on Indians in the Western Hemisphere; period histories; regional Indian studies; tribal Indian studies; studies of colonial and nineteenth century Indian warfare; treatment of captives and adaptation of technology; missionary work among Indians; the role and contributions of Indian women particularly as preservers of traditional Indian society and resisters of cultural change and religious conversion; Indian use of natural resources (land and non-land); white acquisition of Indian lands (both governmental and individual); federal and individual state Indian policies; general histories following changes in federal Indian policies and the resulting impacts on Indians in general; contemporary Indian problems and issues; studies of modern urban Indians and modern reservation Indians; and biographies.[35] To these could be added mistreatment studies (studies of victimization, exploitation, and cultural dissolution) and its flip side, contribution studies (studies of decisive action and resistance to oppression, particularly by Indian women).[36]

7. Despite past neglect, in some quarters of the dominant culture there is *a growing interest and respect for Native American culture and history*. In Utah, the positive signs include six initiatives identified by the Utah Division of Indian Affairs. The first initiative has been achieved. In 2000, *A History of Utah's American Indians,* edited by Forrest S. Cuch, was published jointly by Utah's Division of Indian Affairs and Division of History. The second identified need is expanding basic research in Indian history. A third initiative is developing curricula on Utah Indian history for the public schools, train teachers in Indian history and integrate Indian studies into the core curriculum. Fourth is expanding programs of public and educational lectures. Fifth is expanding Indian oral history projects, and sixth is broadening Indian history projects using audiovisual and other media.[37]

Another positive sign in Utah is a sea change in the perception of the Indian role in the Mountain Meadows Massacre. Early accounts squarely laid blame for the massacre on Utah's Indians, particular the Southern Paiute and the Corn Creek Pahvant, a Ute tribe in southern Ute territory. This perception continued for more than a century. Recent studies, however, have diminished both the role and the blameworthiness of Indian participation. While controversy still surrounds some details of the massacre, a broad consensus supported by substantial evidence shows that the Southern Paiute were incited by Mormon militia leaders in southern Utah who encouraged and provided material incentives to them for cooperation with militiamen from the Iron Military District. Yet even today the Paiute remain reluctant to discuss the massacre for fear of inciting prejudice against them.[38]

Positive as these steps are, they need expanding. Those within the nascent Indian history movement in Utah should be encouraged to attend, offer papers, and participate on panels at annual conferences and symposia of the Utah State Historical Society, Mormon History Association, Western History Association, the Smith Institute of Latter-day Saint History, and similar venues of the various universities and colleges of Utah. In particular, the voice of Native Americans themselves should be sought. Their perspective is necessary, of great value and should be included in accounts of the Great Basin and Southwest in the nineteenth century.

8. As we have seen, *to be successful in this field, future work must involve collaboration across multiple disciplines.* To illustrate the benefits of a multidisciplinary and collaborative approach as well as some of the other contributions from the New Indian History, two of the most recent and best book-length treatments on Indians in Utah are illustrative.

By far the best study of the Black Hawk War of 1865–72 in Utah is John A. Peterson's *Utah's Black Hawk War,* published in 1998 by the University of Utah Press. In it, the interdisciplinary and collaborative nature of Peterson's work is revealed. How is it interdisciplinary? The book reflects the dual nature of Peterson's methodology. First, Peterson worked as a traditional documentary historian, pouring over documents in many repositories that hold the two major white sources on the Indians of Utah: government documents, especially those of the Department of Indian Affairs, and documents from the Church of Jesus Christ. Second, Peterson consulted with Ute tribal informants for tribal records plus oral histories and traditions among the Ute.

To be sure, the writing of history has always been collaborative. The acknowledgments in most histories reflect the collaboration of the author with many individuals and institutions in preparing the text. But for the documentary historian, this is a new form of collaboration. Again Peterson's case is instructive. By using Ute tribal informants, Peterson's work achieves a degree of balance not seen in earlier treatments of Utah's Black Hawk War. The sense of balance is due in large measure to Peterson's presentation of the Ute perspective on both the causes of the conflict and the details of many individual skirmishes, engagements, and battles throughout its course.

Another work noteworthy for collaboration and its interdisciplinary approach is Forrest S. Cuch's *A History of Utah's American Indians.* Written from the perspective of the Indians themselves, it presents the history of Utah's six tribes plus several major sub-tribes. Once again the methods of document historian and ethnohistorian are used. Editor Forrest S. Cuch is a Ute who provides an overall introduction. Robert McPherson, a non-Indian anthropologist, provides a historical introduction and conclusion. The chapter on the Northwestern Shoshones is written by Mae Parry. Ms. Parry is a member and leader of the Northwestern Shoshone and, clearly, one of its defacto historians. Dennis Defa prepared the chapter on the Goshutes. Defa, who holds a graduate degree in history, collaborated with Milton Hooper of the Goshute tribe. The Paiute history was coauthored by Gary Tom, a Paiute who is the education director for Utah's Paiute tribe. His coauthor was non-Indian anthropologist Ronald Holt. Clifford Duncan, a Northern Ute active in Northern Ute government and cultural affairs, prepared the chapter on Northern Ute tribal history. The history of the White Mesa Ute was the collaborative effort of Mary Jane Yazzie, of the Ute Mountain tribe, and non-Indian anthropologist Robert McPherson. The chapter on the Navajo was co-written by Nancy Maryboy and David Begay of the Navajo Nation. Each holds a Ph.D. and works with the Diné College and its eight satellite campuses in New Mexico and Arizona.

In the future this approach will yield the best results. The reason is that this field requires dual competencies: in history and anthropology; in tribal culture and the larger dominant culture; and in a tribal language and the English language. Also, there will be a special place for those biracial individuals who are also bilingual and bicultural. Such individuals would have much to offer and may make major contributions.

9. To do this collaborative, interdisciplinary work, the future researcher will need appropriate academic training from the colleges and universities of Utah and the Inter-Mountain West. Many of these schools now offer *programs in Indian (or Native American) studies*. To the extent they have languished, they should be appraised for their strengths and weaknesses and areas needing improvement. Improving recruitment of students and curriculum offerings in core and elective classes should be improving. And since these programs will inevitably languish if students in Indian Studies are unable to find adequate employment and compensation for their skills, job placement efforts should be reexamined and strengthened.[39]

The Final Point: Thinking like an Indian

Many have noted the differences and even polarity between western (that is, Hellenistic) and Native American worldviews. Calvin Martin argues that native peoples lived in a mythic world which is "eternal, cyclical, endlessly repetitive, powered by Nature, and cosmogonic." In contrast, the western historian has a sharply limited sense of time which is "linear, remorselessly historical, profane and anthropological." To understand a culture and worldview so different from our own, the historian must, at least temporarily, transcend his or her own worldview and enter the worldview of native peoples.[40]

Others have reminded us that western history has long used "imaginative double vision."

> We use deep research and empathy to see other people as they saw themselves, but we also use hindsight and objectifying scholarship to see them as they could not see themselves, as only we can. Thus we achieve historical vision, at once "loving and scrutinizing," for our own human purposes without needing to commit professional or cultural suicide.[41]

Thus, knowing only the material culture of a tribe, their surrounding environment, their subsistence patterns, etc., will not suffice. We must also understand their worldview, the mental constructs from which they built their conception of reality. Having said that, Euro-American Latter-day Saints may find that this effort at a deeper understanding and at least provisional acceptance of the worldview of the indigenous peoples of the Americas may contribute to the Latter-day Saint understanding of their unique scripture, the Book of Mormon. I will conclude by elaborating on several possibilities.

The worldview of Euro-American Latter-day Saints has a western orientation. In modes of perception and thinking, Euro-American Latter-day Saints owe as much to Athens as to Jerusalem. Latter-day Saints from the Euro-American tradition are (or think they are) logical, rational, and analytical. Although most of the Book of Mormon is couched in narrative—stories—frequently Euro-American Latter-day Saints place great stress on the analytical. Latter-day Saints from this tradition are also linear thinkers. For them, reality is like a great river, flowing in one direction and never returning.

For Native Americans, however, there is another aspect of the natural world that they find striking and from which they find an analogue for the nature of reality. For Native American peoples, the nature of reality is revealed by standing at any point in the world, looking to any point on the horizon and following the horizon. What do they see? Following the cardinal points, Native Americans' vision travels from north to east to south to west, then back to north. They have traced a circle. Similarly, tracing the nadir on earth through the zenith in the sky and back to the nadir, they also trace a circle. For Native Americans, then, the circle is their reality. It is beneath, above and around the people. The circle is reality. Within the circle is a dualism of contrasting forces: the cardinal directions, night and day, moon and sun, moist and dry, dark and light, life and death, etc.[42] These are not viewed as polar opposites but as existing in a state of balance and harmony.[43] Everything that exists is within the circle. Thus, the circle becomes one of their primary symbols.

Native Americans convey the meaning of life through narratives or stories. They are comfortable with stories and story cycles. In the Book of Mormon there are stories of peoples who lived in harmony, walked in right ways, and prospered. Then they grew in pride and lapsed into unbelief. Finally, they returned to harmony and the right path and again prospered. The cycle (or circle) then begins again. These are story cycles. For Indians, they have a familiar ring. Also sounding a familiar note to indigenous peoples is the Book of Mormon notion of chosen peoples and promised or sacred lands.[44]

In the Latter-day Saints' Book of Abraham, there is an unusual document known as a hydrocephalus.[45] It presents the elements of reality not linearly, but within a circle. I am not suggesting a direct linkage between an Egyptian hydrocephalus several millennia old and modern Native Americans. I am suggesting, however, that it reflects a view of the cosmos that is symbolized within a circle. The Latter-day Saints' founding prophet, Joseph Smith, was sufficiently impressed with it that he included it within the Latter-day Saint canon of scripture.

I conclude with a final example from the Book of Mormon about the circle. In Alma 7:20, we read:

> I perceive that it has been made known unto you, by the testimony of his word, that he [that is, God] cannot walk in crooked paths; neither doth he vary from that which he hath said; neither hath he a shadow of turning from the right to the left, or from that which is right to that which is wrong; therefore, his course is one eternal round.

The concluding phrase, "his [that is, God's] course is one eternal round," sounds foreign and catches our attention. It occurs twice more in the Book of Mormon.[46] This is a confusing phrase. The statement begins by informing us that the Lord "cannot walk in crooked paths." This seems sufficiently clear. The Lord walks in a straight path, that is, a direct, linear, unswerving path. It also seems clear that the Lord does not have "a shadow of turning" from the "right to the left" or "from that which is right to that which is wrong." Again, the Lord walks in a straight, direct, linear, unswerving path without a "shadow of turning" from that path.

However, the conclusion is confusing. The passage continues, "Therefore" (that is, as a consequence of the Lord walking in a straight, direct, linear, unswerving path, it follows that) "[God's] course is one eternal round." From his straight path, it follows that God's course is "one eternal round"? Latter-day Saints with thoroughly Hellenized, linear-thinking minds may have difficulty determining the meaning of the last expression. It is not a common expression in our modern western world. Nor does it appear to have been a common expression in Joseph Smith's world either.

But from a nonlinear mode of thinking, for instance, a mode of thinking that views reality as a circle, the phrase resonates. Reality is like a circle. When Native Americans represent the world, the natural, appropriate "frame" to contain its elements is a circle. What better way, then, to express a cosmic view of things than to say God's course is one eternal round?

I close not with neat conclusions but with questions. Would understanding the worldview of indigenous peoples in the Americas shed light on some aspects of Latter-day Saint religion? Most would concede that we don't yet know all there is to know about the gospel or our scriptures. Is it possible, then, that cultures with a non-western worldview, Native Americans being one of them, may contribute something of value to our understanding of the gospel and our scriptures? The source of the Book of Mormon was a non-Hellenistic source. Its provenance is, quite literally, a Native American source or, more properly, sources. In anthropological terms, its sources derive from some indigenous Native American groups several millennia ago.[47] I have no objection to using Hellenistic and rationalistic methods to probe its meaning. Yet, since it is a Native American document, would it not be useful to determine whether Native American modes of thought might assist to plumb its depths? At least in the case I have raised, would not Native American modes of thinking—viewing reality as a circle—give a fresh perspective to the otherwise mysterious phrase, "[God's] course is one eternal round"?

Can the indigenous worldview shed light on a text that describes chosen peoples living on sacred lands; cherishes narratives (i.e., stories); has repeating patterns or story cycles; and alludes to space, time, and reality as one eternal round? Might these non-western thinkers provide a perspective that would further unlock the nonlinear, non-western aspects of Latter-day Saint scriptures?[48] I think it is worth exploring.

Notes

1. Donald L. Fixico, ed., *Rethinking American Indian History* (Albuquerque: University of New Mexico Press, 1997), 3.

2. Angela Cavender Wilson, "Power of the Spoken Word: Native Oral Traditions in American Indian History," in *Rethinking American Indian History*, 101.

3. James A. Little, *Jacob Hamblin* (Salt Lake City: George Q. Cannon, 1881), reprinted in Preston Nibley, comp., *Three Mormon Classics: Leaves From My Journal, My First Mission and Jacob Hamblin* (Salt Lake City: Bookcraft, 1997, 1988).

4. Elvin Hatch, *Theories of Man and Culture* (New York: Columbia University Press, 1973).

5. For a grand vision of the potential of anthropology, see Ernest Becker, *The Lost Science of Man* (New York: George Braziller, 1971). In his essay, "Sketch for a Critical History of Anthropology," Becker presents a bold, passionate, protean, synthetic, yet maddening review of two hundred years of intellectual history from Rousseau to Erich Fromm. Becker traces the origin, development, and decline yet continuing relevance and promise of anthropology to further a great moral vision: to reduce "inequality" (126, 131, 133–34, 139), provide a "complete theory of human alienation in society and history" (143), and reduce the "constrictive national state" (152); thus expanding "human freedom" (120–21) or "freedom in community," that is, achieving "maximum free individuality and maximum community, at the same time" (141). Thus conceived, anthropology was a bold program indeed.

6. Carol R. Ember and Melvin Ember, *Cultural Anthropology*, 2d ed. (Englewood Cliffs, N.J.: Prentice-Hall, 1977); William A. Haviland, *Cultural Anthropology*, 4th ed. (New York: Holt, Rinehart and Winston, 1983); Elmer S. Miller and Charles A. Weitz, *Introduction to Anthropology* (Englewood Cliffs, N.J.: Prentice-Hall, 1979); L. L. Langness, *The Study of Culture*, rev. ed. (Novato, Cal.: Chandler & Sharp, 1987); Robert F. Murphy, *Cultural and Social Anthropology: An Overture*, 3d ed. (Englewood Cliffs, N.J.: Prentice-Hall, 1989).

7. William T. Hagan, "The New Indian History," in *Rethinking American Indian History*, 30.

8. James Axtell, "The Ethnohistory of Native America," in *Rethinking American Indian History*, 20–24. Axtell addresses five main criticisms of the ethnohistorical enterprise.

9. Hagan, "The New Indian History," 29–30.

10. Fixico, *Rethinking*, 118–19.

11. John A. Peterson, *Utah's Black Hawk War* (Salt Lake City: University of Utah Press, 1998); Forrest S. Cuch, ed., *A History of Utah's American Indians* (Salt Lake City: Utah State Division of Indian Affairs/Utah State Division of History, 2000); Robert S. McPherson, *The Northern Navajo Frontier, 1860–1900: Expansion through Adversity* (Logan: Utah State University Press, 2001); Robert S. McPherson, ed., *The Journey of Navajo Oshley: An Autobiography and Life History* (Logan: Utah State University Press, 2000); and Scott R. Christensen, *Sagwitch: Shoshone Chieftain, Mormon Elder, 1822–1887* (Logan: Utah State University Press, 1999).

12. Cuch, *Utah's American Indians*, xii–xiv.

13. Due to space limitations this discussion is generally confined to the modern state of Utah. However, it has some application to the broader area of the Great Basin and Colorado Plateau beyond Utah. For a helpful webpage on the geographic features of the Colorado Plateau and its native peoples, see "Canyon, Cultures and Environmental Change: An Introduction to the Land Use History of the Colorado Plateau" at the Colorado Plateau—Land Use History of North America (CP LUHNA) homepage, 1999, <www.cpluhna.nau.edu/index.htm>.

14. Fixico, *Rethinking*, 8. Among our tools will be those from anthropology. Perhaps, however, we should be sensitive in using the standard anthropological terms, "myth" and "mythology." Although variously defined, myth does not denote falsity. Rather, it denotes a "deeply held belief beyond truth or falsity" or "a verbal rationale for religion, differing from other kinds of verbal material in having the connotation of the sacred." Miller and Weitz, *Introduction to Anthropology*, 638. Myths are "the powerhouses of culture." Robert S. McPherson, "Setting the Stage: Native America Revisited" in *History of Utah's American Indians*, 6, quoting anthropologist Victor Turner. Yet such terminology is just as foreign to Native American spirituality as to Mormonism. What anthropologists call "myth" and in common parlance we might call "legend" or "folklore" are to Indians the "sacred stories" or simply "stories." For example, in discussing Native American spirituality, Peggy V. Beck, Anna Lee Walters, and Nia Francisco, *The Sacred: Ways of Knowledge, Sources of Life* (Tsaile, Ariz.: Navajo Community College Press, 1996), repeatedly use "story" while terms such as "legend" or "myth" (60, 63) are used much less frequently. This usage is preferred to "myths," "legends," "folklore," or "folktales."

15. I have found Donald L. Fixico, ed., *Rethinking American Indian History*, enormously helpful, have cited it frequently and recommend it highly.

16. McPherson, "Setting the Stage," 20.

17. As to the Northern Ute, see Clifford Duncan, "The Northern Utes of Utah," in *History of Utah's American Indians*, 187–91. As to the White Mesa Ute, see Robert S. McPherson and Mary Jane Yazzie, "The White Mesa Utes," in the same source, 242–43.

18. Dennis R. Defa, "The Goshute Indians of Utah," in *History of Utah's American Indians*, 75, 97–98.

19. Gary Tom and Ronald Holt, "The Paiute Tribe of Utah," in *History of Utah's American Indians*, 130–31, 139–41.

20. Brigham D. Madsen, *The Shoshoni Frontier and the Bear River Massacre* (Salt Lake City: University of Utah Press, 1985); David L. Bigler, *Forgotten Kingdom: The Mormon Theocracy in the American West, 1847–1896* (Spokane, Wash.: Arthur H. Clark, 1998), 228–32; Mae Parry, "The Northwestern Shoshone," in *History of Utah's American Indians*, 33–44. Brigham D. Madsen states that of the six major Indian massacres in the Far West, from Bear River in 1863 to Wounded Knee in 1890, the Bear River Massacre had the most Indian victims. Brigham D. Madsen, "Bear River Massacre," in *Utah History Encyclopedia*, ed. Allan Kent Powell (Salt Lake City: University of Utah Press, 1994), 35–36.

21. Tom and Holt, "Paiute Tribe," 131.

22. Duncan, "Northern Utes," 190.

23. Duncan, "Northern Utes," 186–94.

24. Parry, "Northwestern Shoshone," 67.

25. Defa, "Goshute Indians," 96.

26. Defa, "Goshute Indians," 92–113.

27. Defa, "Goshute Indians," 119–20.

28. An extended treatment of the Long Walk period is in Lynn R. Bailey, *Bosque Redondo: The Navajo Internment at Fort Sumner, New Mexico, 1863–68* (Tucson, Ariz.: Westernlore Press, 1998). For the post-Bosque Redondo period, see William Haas Moore, *Chiefs, Agents and Soldiers: Conflict on the Navajo Frontier, 1868–1882* (Albuquerque: University of New Mexico Press, 1994). See also Nancy C. Maryboy and David Begay, "The Navajos of Utah," in *History of Utah's American Indians*, 280–89 and Robert S. McPherson, "Navajo Indians," in *Utah History Encyclopedia*, 392.

29. Duncan, "Northern Utes," 185–94; McPherson and Yazzie, "White Mesa Utes," 239–50; David Rich Lewis,

"Ute Indians—Northern" in *Utah History Encyclopedia*, 608–9; and Robert S. McPherson, "Ute Indians—Southern" in *Utah History Encyclopedia*, 609–11; "Ute," Colorado Plateau—Land Use History of North America (CP LUHNA) staff, 1999, CP LUHNA homepage, <www.cpluhna.nau.edu/People/ute_indians.htm>.

30. Tom and Holt, "Paiute Tribe," 151–52. Ronald L. Holt, "Paiute Indians of Utah," in *Utah History Encyclopedia*, 409–10.

31. With the rise in awareness of "ethnic cleansing" in genocide studies, I suspect that at a minimum we should view the 1863 Bear River massacre as an example of Euro-American ethnic cleansing of a group of Shoshone Indians.

32. Cuch, *Utah's American Indians*, xv–xvi.

33. Cuch, *Utah's American Indians*, xii–xiii.

34. Cuch, *Utah's American Indians*, xii.

35. Hagan, "The New Indian History," 34–40.

36. Glenda Riley, "The Historiography of American Indian and Other Western Women," in *Rethinking American Indian History*, 51.

37. Alan Kent Powell in preface to *History of Utah's American Indians*, vi–vii.

38. For a Paiute account of the Mountain Meadows Massacre, see Tom and Holt, "Paiute Tribe," 131–39. See also my studies, "'They're Trying to Hang a Man and I Want What Was Said!': Mining the Militia Narratives of the Mountain Meadows Massacre for Confessions, Evasions and Moonshine," forthcoming; and "Tragedy at the Mountain Meadows Massacre: Toward a Consensus Account and Time Line" (St. George: Dixie State College of Utah, 2002), 16–20. Will Bagley, *Blood of the Prophets: Brigham Young and the Mountain Meadows Massacre* (Norman: University of Oklahoma Press, forthcoming in 2002), also discusses a limited Paiute role at the massacre. I am indebted to Logan Hebner, a student of anthropology and friend of the Cedar City Paiute for pointing out the continuing fear they feel about discussing the massacre. Email communication, Logan Hebner to Robert Briggs, March 20, 2002, in author's possession.

39. The Native American Studies minor at Brigham Young University is currently being revised under the direction of Jay H. Buckley, Ph.D. Personal communication, Jay Buckley to Robert Briggs, March 22, 2002, in author's possession. At College of Eastern Utah, San Juan Campus, which services a large Native American population, Robert S. McPherson, Ph.D., is creating a two year degree in Native American Studies. Knowledgeable about such programs in higher education in Utah, Dr. McPherson suggested that a good program would include a core of North American Indians, Contemporary Indian Affairs, Native American Literature and Philosophy, Native American History and Culture, and Introduction to Native American Studies. Electives may include American Indians and the Environment, American Indian Business Practices, American Indian Arts and Crafts, Native American Government, Cross Cultural Psychology, and American Indian Education. Email communication, Robert McPherson to Robert Briggs, March 19, 2002, in author's possession.

40. Axtell, "Ethnohistory of Native America," 22–23, quoting in part Calvin Martin.

41. Axtell, "Ethnohistory of Native America," 22–23, quoting in part Christopher Vecsey.

42. Beck, Walters, and Francisco, *The Sacred*, 15. See also 2 Nephi 2:11–12 in which Book of Mormon prophet-philosopher Lehi speaks of "an opposition in all things." To Euro-American Latter-day Saints, this is commonly understood to mean that in the nature of things some form of moral opposition is required against the righteous. However, I suggest that the opposition, or opposites, Lehi had in mind included actual, physical dualities such as light and darkness, hot and cold, etc. If these dualities did not exist, he says, "all things [would be] a compound in one" and thus "dead." Of course, Lehi wasn't thinking in terms of modern quantum mechanics, but it may help us to briefly do so. According to that model, before the first dualities, light and darkness, appeared, the physical cosmos was a mass of undifferentiated matter and was, in a sense, dead. In that early stage of our universe, our current physical reality was nonexistent. Had things remained in that condition, none of the conditions of our current state of reality would or could exist—life and death, corruption and incorruption, happiness and misery, sense (consciousness?) and insensibility (unconsciousness?). Instead our reality would have been "a thing of naught,"or nothingness, which condition would have "destroyed the wisdom[,] . . . power[,] . . . mercy, and . . . justice of God." Without the presence of these physical dualities, Lehi seems to say, the moral dualities—happiness and punishment, righteousness and wickedness, holiness and misery, good and bad—could not exist either. These dualities are in some sense balanced against one another. In line with what I argue here, a Native American perspective on Lehi's views of dualities should be explored.

43. Beck, Walters, and Francisco, *The Sacred*, 13, 15, 95–96 concept of balance; 102, 165–66, 309 balance and imbalance; and 168–74 rebalancing.

44. I am indebted to Jane Hafen for this insight. P. Jane Hafen, Professor of English at University of Nevada at Las Vegas, is a Taos Pueblo.

45. Book of Abraham, 36.

46. 1 Nephi 10:19 and Alma 37:12. It also occurs twice in the Doctrine and Covenants in D&C 3:2 and 35:1, where Joseph Smith's use of that phraseology may have been "borrowed" from the Book of Mormon.

47. The Latter-day Saint understanding of where the Book of Mormon occurred has changed considerably over the years. During the nineteenth century the American Indians were commonly assumed to be the descendants of Book of Mormon peoples and the book's setting was assumed to extend over a large portion of the western hemisphere. In recent years, however, a closer reading of the Book of Mormon text itself has lead many to favor a more limited setting. In 1985, John L. Sorenson argued that "the *Book of Mormon* story took place in a limited portion of the western hemisphere . . . [and that the] size of that territory was measured in hundreds, not thousands, of miles." John L. Sorenson, *An Ancient American Setting for the Book of Mormon* (Salt Lake City: Deseret Book, 1985), 22. He proposed Mesoamerica as the text's setting and FARMS scholars have followed his lead. Others, however, continue to pursue possible North American settings. Given the lack of consensus as well as the traditional nineteenth-century belief among Latter-day Saint leaders and lay members alike in a North American setting, there seems to be no reason at present for rejecting the possibility of connections between the Book of Mormon and the Indians of North America.

48. For a treatment of this issue in another cultural context, see Louis Midgley, "A Maori View of the Book of Mormon," *Journal of Book of Mormon Studies* 8, no. 1 (1999), 4–11. Midgley profitably examines how Maori culture both shapes their interpretation of and elucidates the meaning of the Book of Mormon.

Handling Sensitivities in LDS History: A Panel Discussion

John W. Welch (moderator), Richard C. Bennett,
Doris R. Dant, and Steven Sorensen

Opening Remarks

John W. Welch

Throughout this conference, numerous ideas, tools, suggestions, and most of all role models have been discussed and displayed in ways that should help any thoughtful historian to increase his or her skills in handling sensitive issues in writing Church or family history. This panel discussion seeks to infuse those who tell the story of the Latter-day Saints with a desire to write and publish first-rate scholarly materials that are fully appropriate. All Latter-day Saint historians know that many sensitivities are out there, but do we see all of them, and do we think carefully enough about how to handle them?

One scholar came up to me during the lunch break of this conference and told me that he would not be coming to this panel discussion. He said, "I'm not coming to that session. I'm tired of talking about sensitivities." I suppose in one sense the purpose of our panel had already been served in his case. Whether he liked it or not, unwittingly he had already been reminded of the need to think about sensitive issues.

But more than that, all professionals need to be reminded of professional responsibilities and to continuously rethink their ethical considerations. We strive to be professional historians. Professions are characterized by codes of professional responsibility and collective efforts within the guild to reinforce and on some occasions even enforce professional standards and duties. Lawyers certainly have their code of professional responsibility, and they take that code very seriously. Members of the bar are prosecuted and disbarred for violating their professional responsibilities. Each year, every practicing lawyer is required to receive continuing legal education regarding professional responsibilities. No matter how many years a person has been in practice, ethical sensitivities must be updated and revisited. Even lawyers who have been in practice for twenty or thirty years are affected, because each new case presents new potential ethical considerations.

So it is important for historians also to think about the ethical dimensions of their craft. I like the line that says, "We are closest to sin when we think we are farthest from it." I am pleased to have on this panel today four outstanding writers, scholars, and editors who deal with sensitive issues on a daily basis. Doris Dant is Executive Editor of *BYU Studies*. Richard Bennett teaches in the Department of Church History and Doctrine at Brigham Young University and is on the BYU Studies editorial board. Jill Durr serves on the Executive Committee of the Joseph Fielding Smith Institute for Latter-day Saint History. Steve Sorensen is the head of the Manuscripts Division at Church Archives and serves on the BYU Studies editorial board.

To start the discussion, perhaps the main advice I would offer, especially to young historians, is to collaborate with others in their field and to have a mentor. It is important for everyone to discuss perceived problems with reliable and trustworthy people. Listen to what they say. Lawyers are often required, especially in cases involving potential conflicts of interest, to seek a second opinion regarding their ethical decisions. In the ethical business, two heads are almost always better than one. I like to circulate drafts of things I have written among a wide variety of readers to get their reactions. Listening to them helps me become more sensitive to my audiences and to potential areas of misunderstanding or unintended offense.

Richard Bushman has informally suggested that, in a certain way, as a LDS historian he needs to be "double-minded," meaning that he tries to keep two audiences in mind: faithful readers and skeptical scholars. But there are also other audiences: a sensitive historian may need to be triple- or quadruple-minded. In an interesting sense, at least for a religious historian, God himself is inevitably one of our audiences.

Various other obliging values for a Christian scholar are suggested in the guidelines for authors that are used by *BYU Studies*. I am inclined to call these points a "code of academic responsibility." The following has been published in the thirty-year index and the forty-year commemorative issue of *BYU Studies,* and I try to keep these points in mind as I make decisions as a scholar, writer, editor, and publisher. This code consists of six points related to responsible scholarship.

Code of Academic Considerations

Scholarship is like any other tool; it can be used either for good or for evil. A hammer can be used to build up or tear down, to help or hinder. A tool can even injure the person using it, if the person does not know how to use it correctly and carefully. Knowledge confers a type of power that inevitably will be exercised either righteously or unrighteously, and indeed the natural tendency is to misuse any power that is given (D&C 121:39). Thus I would think that all who venture to speak and write in Church circles must morally confront certain responsibilities that may be said to comprise a sort of academic code of professional conduct. Some important components of such a code, in my opinion, would embrace at least the following precepts:

1. Unity. The Lord has clearly stated: "If ye are not one ye are not mine" (D&C 38:27). This principle stands as a beacon for all who strive "for the perfecting of the saints . . . till we all come in the unity of the faith, and of the knowledge of the Son of God" (Eph. 4:12–13). In a shifting world that necessarily and fortunately features diversity, individuality, heterodoxy, and change, the goal of unity with God and our fellow beings must be continually cultivated and nourished.[1] The goal of unity does not imply that all scholarly methods or personal approaches must be the same. As Paul explained, we are "many members, yet but one body" (1 Cor. 12:20). Indeed, even those members "which seem to be more feeble" turn out to be among the "necessary" (1 Cor. 12:22).

2. Harmony. A gospel-scholar needs to be committed to seeking truth "by study and also by faith" (D&C 88:118), on the premise that faith and reason, revelation and scholarly learning, obedience and creativity are ultimately compatible. One of the great strengths of Mormonism, in my opinion, is its ability to harmonize and transcend in a spiritual, intellectual, and practical unity, elements of this mortal existence that appear to most people to be incompatible contradictions. Traditional dichotomies such as mind and body, God and man, spirit and matter, time and eternity, are not viewed in the gospel of Jesus Christ as competing opposites but as companions on a spectrum of degrees of refinement or as opposites whose existence is unified in higher intents and purposes.[2] The objective is to embrace both: ancient and modern, word and deed, intellectual and spiritual, research and teaching, reason and revelation, the "ought" and the "is," community and individuality, diversity and unity, male and female, nature and custom, induction and deduction, analysis and synthesis, rights and duties, subjectivity and objectivity, theory and practice, even mortality and godhood. We can grow beyond issues over which is greater, the spirit or the intellect, the liahona or the iron rod. For Lehi, both symbols were concurrent. For purposes of the spirit, the spirit is greater; and for purposes of the mind, the mind is greater. For Latter-day Saint study and faith, the one is not without the other. As Elder Boyd K. Packer has stated, "Each of us must accommodate the mixture of reason and revelation in our lives. The gospel not only permits but *requires* it."[3] Kierkegaard offered the world an Either/Or; Joseph Smith, a Both/And.

3. Honesty. As a primary trait of character, "we believe in being honest" (A of F 13). Accuracy and reliability are of the essence in scholarship. All scholars worth their salt have wrestled long with the questions of what can and cannot, what should and should not, what must or must not be said. They acknowledge and evaluate data both for and against their ideas and theories. They eschew all forms of plagiarism and generously recognize their indebtedness to other scholars. They guard on all sides against the covert influences of unstated assumptions, bias, and esoteric terminology. They describe shades of grey where they exist. They identify clearly their personal opinions as such. Finally, they avoid material omissions, for often what is not said can be as misleading as what is said.

4. Thoroughness. "If there is anything virtuous, lovely, or of good report or praiseworthy, we seek after these things" (A of F 13). Latter-day Saint scholarship welcomes a wide range of subjects, addressing

> all things that pertain unto the kingdom of God, that are expedient for you to understand; of things both in heaven and in the earth, and under the earth; things which have been, things which are, things which must shortly come to pass; things which are at home, things which are abroad, . . . that ye may be prepared in all things when I shall send you again to magnify the calling whereunto I have called you. (D&C 88:78–80)

This is a fulfilling, but sobering mandate.

5. Humility. Pride has been identified as the pervading sin of our day. Scholars have more than their share of exposure to this problem. Arrogance, disdain, overconfidence, dogmatism, and many other manifestations of intellectual and spiritual pride may well be the main occupational hazards of academia. But the perspectives of scholarship and the gospel can also provide the antidote. First is the acknowledgment that all people are at different stages in the eternal journey toward the glory of God, which is intelligence. No person says or understands everything perfectly, and a variety of opinions on a shared scale of progression are expected. Hence, a person's direction is more important than his or her present stance. Second is the humble awareness that scholarship is not an end in itself. Research cannot create faith; it can only set the stage for greater light and knowledge. As B. H. Roberts once wrote, "The clearer and more complete the statement is, the better opportunity will the Holy Spirit have for testifying to the souls of men that the work is true."[4]

6. Charity. In order for communication to occur, there must be charity, for no statement exists (including this one) that cannot be misconstrued. If fellowship and good will does not exist, especially in an academic setting, we will not communicate with each other. Paul's confession comes to mind: "Though I have the gift of *prophecy,* and understand all mysteries, *and all knowledge* . . . and have not charity, I am nothing" (1 Cor. 13:2, emphasis added). Charity is essential to avoid disputation. Left untempered by love, scholarly debate and critical inquiry will be divisive and unhealthy.[5] Charity is also necessary to avoid offending even the weakest of the Saints. Jesus said: "It is impossible but that offences will come: but woe unto him, through whom they come! It were better for him that a millstone were hanged around his neck, and he cast into the sea, than that he should offend one of these little ones" (Luke 17:2).[6] Perhaps this is part of what Jesus meant when he told his disciples: "Be ye therefore wise as serpents, and harmless as doves" (Matt. 10:16).[7]

Questions for Handling Sensitivities

To apply these principles more concretely to the subject of this panel, I pose the following questions, to which the panelists may desire to respond:

- What factors make a topic or issue or item "sensitive"?
- What things should be kept private? and why?
- In writing about a person, how do you deal with things in his or her life that are embarrassing, disgracing, regrettable, or make that person look bad?
- What makes something unsettling to faith or values?
- Specifically which words or phrases might be offensive or problematic?
- How do you avoid being unintentionally offensive? What land mines are often stepped on unawares?
- Are we better off stating our assumptions, beliefs, and biases openly or leaving them unstated?
- Is a "balanced approach" always appropriate?
- How do you know your audience?
- How does the nature of the audience determine what may or may not be sensitive?
- How does the audience's likely uses of the material determine what may or may not be sensitive?
- How does an author or publisher build credibility and confidence in dealing with sensitive issues?
- Do you use any personal rules or rhetorical techniques for handling sensitive issues?
- Does context explain everything?
- Is writing religious history a special case, or is it just like writing any other history?
- Is there a duty to avoid giving offense?
- What final word of advice would you give to a person trying to deal with sensitive issues in telling the story of Mormon history?

The Myths and Mists of Darkness

Richard E. Bennett

> Oh say, what is truth! 'Tis the fairest gem
> That the riches of worlds can produce.
> And priceless the value of truth will be when
> The proud monarch's costliest diadem
> Is counted but dross and refuse.[8]

Some time ago, a colleague of mine approached me with a question. He had just been reading in one of my books a chapter on the succession of Brigham Young to the presidency of the Church in the Kanesville (Iowa) log tabernacle in December 1847. "Why didn't you tell about the earthquake?" he wondered. "What earthquake?" I asked. "The one some later said happened on that day in that place. Surely it was a sign of God's benediction." I could respond only that there may have been a retrospective account somewhere that spoke of such things, but from my research into scores of contemporary letters, diaries, and sermons, the Spirit of the Lord was in abundance without any earthquake occurring. "But it's such a faith-building story," he argued. "It had to have happened!"

I have reflected on our conversation many times since. Why is it, I wonder, that some Latter-day Saints go "beyond the mark" in wanting to believe in that which never happened, in seeking more than truth, in relying on myth when fact and faith are ever sufficient? Elder Bruce R. McConkie, when discussing the miracle of the 1978 revelation on the Priesthood, spoke of this tendency to rely on myth:

> Latter-day Saints have a complex; many of them desire to magnify and build upon what has occurred, and they think of miraculous things. And maybe some of them would like to believe that the Lord himself was there [at the temple], or that the Prophet Joseph Smith came to deliver the revelation, which was one of the possibilities. Well, these things did not happen. The stories that go around to the contrary are not factual or realistic or true, and you as teachers in the Church Educational System will be in a position to explain and to tell your students that this thing came by the power of the Holy Ghost, and that all the Brethren involved, the thirteen who were present, are indispensable personal witnesses of the truth and divinity of what occurred.[9]

None of us appreciate being purposely deceived. Bearing false witness is both a crime and a sin. There is only hurt, sorrow, and diminishment in lying and deception. Satan himself is sometimes called the "father of lies." Why is it, then, that we hate lies but often love myths and the persistent believing in that which is not so? I believe that in doing so we not only twist the truth but also destroy faith for the simple reason that faith is based on truth. As the Apostle Peter said, "Faith is the substance of things hoped for, the evidence of things not seen" (Heb. 11:1). Alma added, "Faith is not to have a perfect knowledge of things; therefore if ye have faith ye hope for things which are not seen, which are true" (Alma 32:21). Truth, not deception, is the bulwark of faith.

The dictionary defines *myth* as "a belief, opinion, or theory that is not based on fact or reality," an "invented story," or "made-up person or thing."[10] Mormon history, or rather Mormon memory, is strewn with such masquerades for truth and misconceptions of fact. Spurious accounts of Three Nephite appearances are everywhere, blotting out those that may be genuine. There are even published accounts of oversized Nephite warriors protecting temple doors during the anti-polygamy raids of the late nineteenth century. Some still persist in believing that lightning struck dead those who were poised to mutilate the body of the Prophet Joseph on that sad day in Carthage, despite the fact there is no historical evidence whatsoever to back up such a story. I remember reading, as a child, *The Fate of the Persecutors of the Prophet Joseph Smith*, which assigned the most cruel sufferings and ignominious deaths to those responsible for the martyrdom.[11] If they escaped justice from the courts of the land, surely they deserved divine punishment. Never mind that Dallin Oaks and Marvin S. Hill debunked these accounts in their excellent history, *Carthage Conspiracy*. The stories just have to be true.

This is not to say that myth and fiction are one and the same. The former masquerades as truth; the other makes no such attempt. Great literature seeks not to be factual, as myth pretends to be. As with Shakespeare's *Julius Caesar*, *Macbeth*, and *Romeo and Juliet* or the Greek legends in Homer's *Iliad* and *Odyssey*, literature often takes license with historical accuracy but still teaches the truths of human nature—our noble virtues as well as our tragic flaws—characteristics that define our very being. Literature reflects the lasting truths of our nature whatever they may be; the mythic is a shortcut to resolution, a simplistic, exaggerated stretch of the truth to arrive at some pretended, artificial end, and a feeble attempt to square what some think should have happened to what was. Myth is neither history nor literature but, rather, deliberate distortion. It is an unnecessary fabrication, a subterfuge that the Spirit of the Lord rejects in the end. And because it is at war with truth, myth is an enemy to the miraculous. Unfortunately, when finally dispelled and proven wrong, it often leaves an ugly scar imprinted upon one's page of faith. Unlike the innocent childhood belief in Santa Claus, myths in Latter-day Saint history are an adult phenomenon. They mislead and eventually contend with the truth. "Why didn't you tell me the truth sooner?" inquirers will inevitably ask. "How could such an untruth continue to circulate?" my students ask. "What really happened? Please tell me!"

I return to Kanesville. Careful students of Mormon history realize that Brigham Young's call to the presidency of the Church came only after years of training and preparation. If Joseph Smith gained his prophetic call in his visions in upstate New York and Ohio, Brigham found his in the mud and mountains of the Mormon exodus. The miracle of his call came in God's careful tutoring of a modern Moses. And by the time December 1847 rolled around, most everyone in camp knew who should be president. When the vote was taken, every one of the over one thousand people packed into that makeshift tabernacle raised their hand in perfect unison. The Spirit was real and powerful, and the faith of a mighty people was on the line and in full view. Why muddy it with myth? Why exaggerate the revelation on the Priesthood with that which did not happen? Why contaminate the faithful story of the martyrdom with that which did not occur?

One final, very related point. There is yet another enemy to credible, faithful history, what I call the "mists" of darkness. If the truth will eventually prevail, then let the truth be told. Having been both an archivist and historian for most of my professional life, I have learned that the truth will eventually come out. While it is true that the faithful historian need not tell all the truth all of the time, he or she is justified in seeking to know what happened and why. There is no room for obfuscation. Making archival sources open and more readily available to responsible scholars is in our lasting best interest. Some in the recent past, having been given access to sensitive Church documents, may have betrayed their trust and sought to embarrass the Church and its people. Such actions are despicable to us all. Nevertheless, if believing Latter-day Saint scholars are not trusted and encouraged to tell our story honestly and independently, inevitably others will sooner or later do it for us, often at great cost to faith. It is hard, if not impossible, to answer their claims without more reasonable access to the materials.

The future of Latter-day Saint history has never been more bright. There is so much yet to discover, so much in our history to celebrate. The finest histories have yet to be written, despite the excellence of those histories written in the past. New generations of Latter-day Saint historians reserve the right to reinterpret everything in our past for their times and purposes. They need neither our myths nor unnecessary barriers but deserve our trust and support as they go forward reexamining, redefining, and reinterpreting the Lord's work in these latter days.

> Yes, say what is truth? 'Tis the brightest prize
> To which mortals or God's can aspire;
> Go search in the depths where it glittering lies,
> Or ascend in pursuit to the loftiest skies:
> 'Tis an aim for the noblest desire.[12]

The Case for Humility When Writing Mormon Biography

Doris R. Dant

> And inasmuch as they were humble they might be made strong, and blessed from on high, and receive knowledge from time to time.
> —D&C 1:28

When the desirable traits for biographers are inventoried, humility is typically not mentioned. It is usually not even a minor consideration lurking on the horizon. Therefore, the topic may seem tangential in a discussion of Mormon biography. I justify inclusion with a bold claim: when written with humility, Mormon biography tends to be more representative, more balanced, more complete, more honest.

The case for humility in writing biography begins with the premise that only one person made a perfect journey through mortality and he was not a biographer. The conclusion, while obvious, is one that we sometimes lose sight of. We are imperfect—no exceptions. Conscious acknowledgement of this fact can have a dramatic impact on our attitude toward our work and our subjects.

For example, humility is an antidote for the inherent problems of the "Aha! I gotcha!" form of biography, a form that too often misrepresents the subject or the subject's associates. Rather than aiming to depict a person holistically, the I-gotcha biography prefers disclosing "dirt" regardless of that finding's overall significance. Sometimes these biographies verge on muckraking, on distorting the picture for the sake of sensationalism. Always they suffer from inadequate balance and charity.

Biographers of the I-gotcha genre seem to mentally downplay or justify their own failings, weaknesses, and errors while condemning those they write about—the beam-and-mote syndrome. Sometimes, in their view, the failings they detail are too despicable to be explicable. Other times, I have noticed, researchers obtain a high from the addicting thrill of "discovering" that an icon or otherwise admirable person is flawed. Yet what is so new? The person is mortal; therefore, the person is guaranteed to be imperfect. Only the specific nature of the failings will differ from person to person. Whatever the self-righteous feel, scorn, disgust, or glee—in the heat of that emotion, their judgment seems to desert them, resulting in descriptions that are lopsided or wholly one-sided. If the descriptions are of supporting players, those people may be presented as cardboard villains. Descriptions become diatribes.

Given adequate resources, a researcher will find negative elements in any person's life. The issue is how to treat the flaws. Recognizing their own failings and the existence of their own dirt, humble biographers first of all ponder whether to include a particular negative. If the item is necessary to understanding the person, the humble biographer seeks to place the negative in the contexts of the person's milieu, aspirations, and preceding and subsequent life experiences. This process can lead biographers into considerations they might not have explored otherwise. The biography becomes more complete and balanced.

Note I am not recommending that imperfections be automatically ignored. Unalloyed praise is also misguided, resulting, as reviewers remind us, in another form of distortion and subsequent loss of credibility. But even here humility plays a role, for with its premise of the fallen state of all humanity, it can rein in an impulse to gallop off into hagiography or panegyric—no matter how much a biographer may admire or identify with the person being researched.

A variation of this problem exists when a biographer so esteems the person depicted that all who opposed, mistreated, or disliked that person are treated as scoundrels. Sometimes the perceived wrongdoing is stated baldly in a negative context, a treatment that can make even innocent actions seem evil. In the same biography, the main subject's significant failings are contextualized as understandable or they are downplayed as foibles or lovable eccentricities. In other words, descriptive standards are inconsistently applied. Humble biographers recognize they can fall prey to this human response. They do enough research into the lives of the opponents to determine (or hypothesize) why those people acted as they did. Readers can then understand the opponents even though the audience and the biographer may still decry the opponents' actions.

Terminology also becomes an issue for the biographer, who typically can select from multiple terms meaning roughly the same thing. In the biographer's hands, a decision may be cautious or timid, an action aggressive or assertive. A committee may engage in a lively discussion or a heated debate. Readers' attitudes are shaped by whichever terms are selected. Hopefully, the chosen descriptor captures the flavor of the event, but wording can also be manipulated. Without the self-awareness that humility can bring, biographers can wield terms as inappropriately as research has shown psychologists and news writers have. Style guides and bias reference guides for these professionals warn about promoting personal agendas or biases through labels. Mormon biography can fall prey to any of the standard biases and agendas as well as some specific to the field (such as *hierarchy* versus *leadership*). But the biographer humble enough to be tutored in charity will guard against inadvertent labeling and will abstain from manipulative stereotypes.

In the twilight zone between the time a biography is written and the time it is printed, humility can again improve quality. As an editor, I have noticed that humble authors are aware that, in spite of their best efforts and those of their research assistants, mistakes and omissions are inevitable. Those problems may be relatively minor, or they may involve major reorganization, significant rewriting, material excision, or additional research. Regardless of whether an editor or the author makes these changes, there is a drain on the author's time and energy that is irritating at the least, especially if the biographer has hoped to turn his or her attention to another project. But the humble biographer painstakingly persists and thereby eliminates some of the concerns a reviewer or reader might raise.

The more arrogant writers resist suggestions; their work, after all, is already worthy of an award, and they see no need to be bothered by editors who are nitpicky and mistaken anyway. When these authors deign to address problems, their efforts tend to be half-hearted, hasty, and sloppy. And while their work may still be prize-winning material, their lack of humility during the editorial process reduces their potential degree of greatness.

Humility can dissolve the stereotyped dichotomies that produce contention over the quality of printed biographies. An example is the dichotomy of objective history and faithful history. The humble biographer is cognizant of the incompleteness of the human record, of a human's inability to access all the records that do exist (the existence or location of some being unknown to the biographer), and of the length limitations of all books and articles, which necessitates choosing what to include (to privilege) and, therefore, what to exclude in any written work. Without full access to God's records and his knowledge of an individual's heart, human biographers are constrained by their own incompleteness and fallibility, their subjectivity. Thus the human condition moots claims to objectivity.

On the other hand, all biography has the potential to be faithful—faithful to the biographers' own worldviews and their understanding of their subjects' worldviews. I admit my play on the word *faithful*. In the Mormon history debate, *faithful* has been restricted to history that was seen as skewed toward supporting the institutional church's views. My point is, however, that any sincere biography subscribes to—is faithful to—some set of beliefs. (Interestingly, the word *faithful* has now been appropriated by a group of historians to describe, approvingly, history granting the existence of divine influences.) A humble recognition of one's "faithfulness" and constraints resolves the dichotomy between objective and faithful history and provokes an honest appraisal of what biography can be.

By issuing this call for humility, I risk an attack of hubris. Therefore, I hereby acknowledge my fallibility as a writer, an editor, and a commentator on biography. As a writer, I confess I have made choices requiring repentance: I have desired to exclude items that did not neatly fit my schema. I have faltered when faced with negatives about which I had inadequate information. As an editor, I hope the humble biographer will engage me in a dialogue aimed at remedying our respective errors. As a commentator on biography, I have created this brief presentation with very broad strokes indeed. But this I know: excellence is more likely when quested with humility. With this paradox, I rest my case.

Church Archives

Steven Sorensen

As Director of Church Archives, Steve Sorenson read the archive's policy on confidentiality of records. For the most recent copy of this statement, researchers should visit the archives of The Church of Jesus Christ of Latter-day Saints in Salt Lake City.

Concluding Remarks

John W. Welch

In conclusion, to tie this together, it occurs to me that behind the comments of most of our panelists, stand the scriptures. For Doris Dant, humility is crucial: "Be thou humble and the

Lord thy God shall lead thee by the hand and give thee answers to thy prayers" (D&C 112:10). For Richard Bennett, a key scripture might be "be not afraid" (Mark 6:50), or from the hymns, "Do what is right, let the consequence follow." For Jill Derr, charity: "Though I have all knowledge and have not charity I am nothing and have become as sounding brass and tinkling symbols" (1 Cor. 13:1).

Thus, it occurs to me that for Mormon historians, the scriptures will be our best allies in dealing with sensitive issues. I hope you have your favorite scriptures that guide your thinking and writing. Dealing with sensitive issues in Church History is difficult, but it is no more difficult than dealing with sensitivities in any other part of our lives. Sensitive problems arise in dealing with our children, spouses, friends, students, ward members, or professional associates. Just as the scriptures guide our thoughts, words, and actions in other parts of our lives, the scriptures can guide us successfully in our professional work as well. As Jesus instructed his disciples, "Be ye as wise as serpents, and harmless as doves" (Matt. 10:16). This advice is just as valid today as it was then; it applies to the discipline of history as much as it applies to any other form of discipleship, and it will help us earn true empathy with our subjects.

Notes

1. For interesting discussions on these topics in the *Encyclopedia of Mormonism*, ed. Daniel H. Ludlow, 4 vols. (New York: Macmillan, 1992), see Howard M. Bahr, "Individuality," 2:680–82; M. Gerald Bradford, "Orthodoxy, Heterodoxy and Heresy," 3:1054–55; F. Neil Brady, "Unity," 4:1497–98.

2. David L. Paulsen, "Doctrine: Harmonization of Paradox," in *Encyclopedia of Mormonism*, 1:402–403.

3. Boyd K. Packer, "'I Say Unto You, Be One' (D&C 38:27)," BYU Devotional Address, February 12, 1991 (emphasis in original).

4. B. H. Roberts, *New Witnesses for God*, 3 vols. (Salt Lake City: Deseret Book, 1909), 2:vii.

5. Dallin H. Oaks, *The Lord's Way* (Salt Lake City: Deseret Book, 1991), 138–52.

6. Jesus gave this saying on several occasions. Matthew places it in the context of offending a little child (Matt. 18:6); Mark uses it to caution disciples against restraining anyone who does any good deed in the name of Christ (Mark 9:42); Luke makes it a general instruction.

7. Adapted from John W. Welch, "Moving On," *BYU Studies* 38, no. 1 (1999): 226–28; and John W. Welch, "*BYU Studies*: Into the 1990s," *BYU Studies* 31, no. 4 (1991): 24–26.

8. From John Jacques's hymn "Oh Say, What is Truth?" in *Hymns of The Church of Jesus Christ of Latter-day Saints* (Salt Lake City: The Church of Jesus Christ of Latter-day Saints, 1985), no. 272.

9. Bruce R. McConkie, "All Are Alike Unto God," Brigham Young University devotional address, August 1978.

10. *The World Book Dictionary* (Chicago: World Book, 2000), 2:1377.

11. N. B. Lundwall, comp., *The Fate of the Persecutors of the Prophet Joseph Smith* (Salt Lake City: Bookcraft, 1952).

12. "Oh Say What is Truth."

The Mormon *Positivismuẞtreit*: Modern vs. Postmodern Approaches to Telling the Story of Mormonism

Alan Goff

The meaning of a word is its use in the language.
—Ludwig Wittgenstein

The problem of representation is a primary battleground in the struggle between modernity and postmodernism. Modernity emerged in the fifteenth century; as it broke into several divisions, modernity struggled with medieval and classical systems of thought for a few centuries before gaining dominance. The most important subdivision of modernity turned out to be the Enlightenment.

Enlightenment thinkers (Locke, Voltaire, Kant, the philosophes, and the American founding fathers) adhered to a cluster of important ideas that we still debate today: (1) reason, rather than tradition or revelation, is the pathway to truth; (2) scientific and moral progress is inevitable; (3) humans are fundamentally rational creatures, so the way to change the world is to educate people, show them the direction universal reason would lead them; (4) progress in the natural sciences has shown us how to progress in social and moral endeavors (science is the pattern of all human knowledge with universal laws and experimentation as the model epistemological method); (5) humans must be seen historically in order to be understood; and (6) freedom of the individual is the primary goal of philosophy and public policy (governments, churches, families, or any institutions that dictate to individuals should be restricted from dominating people so they can make up their own minds freely about their own purposes and means).

After the Enlightenment further fragmented, one of the most important subdivisions was positivism. August Comte (1798–1857) founded positivism with the idea that humans still need religion (ritual, communion, and instruction) but the influence of the Catholic Church in particular was harmful. He founded his own church, called the Church of Humanity, blatantly stealing from Catholicism a similar liturgical calendar, rites, and organization. (Comte himself dressed in robes and became the Pope of this new church.) Instead of celebrating St. Francis or Mary, this new church celebrated Newton or Shakespeare. Popular in Paris and London, this church even had a few branches in New York City and Long Island. Comte saw historically and believed history inevitably developed in three progressive stages: (1) a theological phase in which humans attribute actions in the world to deities (a person would pray to be healed of smallpox, and when recovery occurred, the person would mistakenly attribute the result to God), (2) a metaphysical stage in which humans evolve to a higher level and believe in abstract ideas such as first causes, political contracts, and human rights, and (3) a positive stage (Comte's own beliefs here being the highest attainment of human thought) where humans finally see things the way they are by doing away with all theology and metaphysics to see that truth is revealed only through empirical observation. Positivism articulated a new version of Enlightenment epistemology with the following principles: (1) empirical observation is the only path to truth (any claim to truth must be verified by appeal to reality observed through the senses and subject to scientific methods), (2) the goal of knowledge is to reveal universal truths, and (3) the world outside our minds is straightforwardly accessible through observation without our projecting preconceptions on it if we have made it to that positivistic/scientific plateau.

Enlightenment epistemologies are based on the confidence that the human mind can understand the world free of distortion. The most common way this idea has been articulated in our day is for researchers to claim objectivity: others, those with whom I disagree, impose their desires and subjectivities on the past while I view the world without bias or preconception.

Modernity shares the notion, which philosophers call realism, that there is some kind of verisimilitude between the world outside and what goes on in my thoughts. Positivism shares this Enlightenment and modern view of realism, narrowing it to mean that the only valid way the mind understands the world around it is through sensory experience.

Since the 1960s a new philosophy has examined this realist view of the world adhered to by modernity generally, and positivism particularly, and undermined all of the latter's claims. Between the 1880s and the 1960s positivist epistemology dominated all inquiry in the natural sciences, social sciences, and humanities.

The post-WWII period brought a new version of positivism to dominate university life in Western culture. This movement was initially called Logical Positivism and was articulated by the Vienna School of Logical Positivism (Ernst Mach, Moritz Schlick, Rudolf Carnap, and A. J. Ayer are names associated with this school of thought). Logical positivists asserted that the only knowledge worthy of being called "knowledge" is derived from sensory experience or directly abstracted from sense data. As with most philosophical movements, positivism diffused throughout the disciplines of the university in a debased, commonsense form, its adherents hardly aware of the intellectual heritage of the ideas they advocated as the only way to truth.

After WWII, positivism came under fierce attack by members of the Frankfurt School of Critical Theory (Max Horkheimer, Theodor Adorno, Herbert Marcuse, Jurgen Habermas), most of whom had moved to the United States to escape Nazi persecution and murder. This debate became known as the German Positivismußtreit. The upshot of this strife was that positivism was thoroughly discredited and abandoned as an explicit way of justifying knowledge claims. However, Positivism's eighty-year domination of universities still has its effects. Theoretically- and philosophically-sophisticated practitioners of every discipline actively attack positivism, but this theory of knowledge still dominates economics, history, political science, and virtually every other field of inquiry. When postmodern thinkers emerged in the 1960s and 1970s, they further discredited positivism.

This paper will be concerned mainly with positivism among historians. Shortly before Thomas Alexander's "Historiography and the New Mormon History: A Historian's Perspective" appeared in Dialogue in 1986, Brigham Young University political scientists David Bohn and Louis Midgley had begun calling New Mormon Historians positivists. Alexander and a series of other professionally-trained and amateur historians entered the debate, all denying that any New Mormon Historians could be positivists. I call this the Mormon *Positivismußtreit*. The Latter-day Saint debate about positivism will end up the same way the German debate did—with the claims of the positivists being abandoned.

Exotic Definitions of Positivism among Mormon Historians

All versions of positivism are united by the attempt to solve the problem of representation. How does the mind (the thinking subject) bridge to the outside world to understand something outside itself (the object)? The past is the object in question for historiography. Questions of representation address the chasm between the present and the past or the bridge across that chasm. Positivists claim that truthful understanding must be realist in some way; the mind must accurately perceive the object without contaminating ideological biases or preconceptions.[1] Postmodern thinkers (whatever their wide variety of positions about other matters) agree that all human understanding is perspectival, always affected by the ideology of the group or the individual. If postmodern epistemologies are accepted, positivism faces an insurmountable obstacle.

Positivism denigrates knowledge unless it qualifies as understanding according to its own methods. Positivism has always rejected religious claims to truth because religions claim access to knowledge independent of sensory experience. The New Mormon History emerged since the 1950s under a positivist understanding of how the past ought to be interpreted. To have Mormon historians called positivists has unnerved New Mormon Historians. Thomas Alexander has responded to this problem by attempting to redefine positivism so it no longer poses a problem for Mormon historians: "It is my belief that most New Mormon Historians, although they differ considerably in their views, would perceive their work as a part of the human studies rather than as a part of the natural sciences under which positivism would fall."[2] This definitional strategy would work if positivism were somehow prohibited from the social sciences and the humanities, relegated only to the natural sciences. The body of theoretically-sophisticated historians and social scientists understands that not only is positivism possible in the social and human studies, it was the dominant understanding in the twentieth century. Note a claim made about the same time Alexander was making his assertion about positivism: "The positivist posture, while discredited by vanguard thinkers in every known discipline, continues to this day to guide the efforts of practitioners of inquiry, particularly in the social or human sciences."[3] The point is also true of history as a discipline; positivism has been the natural set of categories within which historians have described what they do:

> In sum, most historians have been unwilling—unwilling, rather than unable—to think about the historicity of knowledge (including their own knowledge). Thereby the historical profession has been, by and large, unable to liberate itself from the wholly outdated, and badly leaking, categories of materialism and of positivism and their implicit 'laws' of causality.[4]

Dominick LaCapra has noted that most historians are positivists unawares and they just assume everyone else in the profession will agree with them about epistemological issues.[5] Alexander's attempt to sequester the threat of positivism by exiling it to the natural sciences will not work because one of the main thrusts of positivist claims in the social sciences and humanities has been the unification of science presumption: the social studies must model themselves on the method used so successfully in the natural sciences, physics in particular.

These odd claims about what positivism means haven't been isolated to professional historians. An amateur historian has also denied that New Mormon Historians can be positivists. Edward Ashment, instead of relegating positivism to the natural sciences, seems to believe the concept is bordered chronologically: Ashment is incensed that some Mormon historians, including himself, have been called positivists:

> In their efforts to neutralize historiography, Mormon theologians, at least, anachronistically equate today's historiography with that of the "positivists" and "historicists" of the late 19th and early 20th Centuries. For example: Apologists have condemned the writings of Thomas Alexander, Fawn M. Brodie, Klaus J. Hansen, Marvin S. Hill, Lawrence Foster, Sterling McMurrin, Dale Morgan, Jan Shipps, and, most recently, this writer as "positivist."[6]

At the least, Alexander and Hill are apologists for positivism because they offer weird definitions of positivism with the ideological purpose of absolving New Mormon Historians of the charge of being positivists while they make patently positivistic claims. McMurrin is a positivist because not only has he defended a positivist epistemology but also because he has applied the label to himself.[7] Ashment has more recently modified that essay, asserting that "modern historiographical methodology is neither positivistic nor objectivistic. But because Latter-day Saint apologists rely so heavily on identifying historiography with positivism, it is important to consider how historiographic methodology evolved."[8] Ashment refers his reader to history to resolve the question. Historiographical developments over the past century would indeed be a good place to resolve this question about positivism. We shall see if historians themselves admit that historiography has been subjugated by positivism.

Yet a third New Mormon Historian has involved himself in the Mormon *Positivismußtreit*. Marvin Hill resorts to a standard, unabridged dictionary to give a definition: "By positivism, again in its simplest dictionary sense, I mean that history is taken to be potentially verifiable—that the mind can know the outside world as it is and was." I too feel Hill's discomfort with this definition, but not quite in the way Hill does. He apologizes for this definition:

> These definitions are drawn from the Webster's *New Twentieth-Century Unabridged Dictionary*. Although historians, social scientists, and philosophers have constructed complex and elaborate definitions of these two terms [subjectivism and positivism] and their relationship to each other, I am deliberately using simple meanings that are juxtaposed to each other to try and move the discussion from technical definitions to awareness of meanings and implications. Webster's definition indicates that the positivists refuse to consider ultimate origins, but this does not necessarily mean they are atheists, as some would hold. They may be agnostics or simply unwilling to impose their religious values upon their readers.[9]

These aren't simple meanings but simplistic and deceptive ones. All historians must believe that the past is verifiable in some way or there wouldn't be much reason to do history. I believe the past is, in variable and partial ways, verifiable, so according to this definition I would be a positivist. Positivism doesn't twist on this fulcrum of verifiability but upon an entirely different one—ideology.

This simplistic definition is merely an attempt to deny that New Mormon Historians are positivists and turn the charge against anti-positivists. All three of these odd definitions of positivism are ideological and presented at the same time the truly positivist historian claims to be beyond all ideology. Positivism has a complex and ramifying history. Any attempt to define it must take into account that complexity, or fall into another version of positivism:

> When I have lectured to audiences of literary critics, I have found two pervasive philosophical presuppositions in the discussions of literary theory, both oddly enough derived from logical positivism. First there is the assumption that unless a distinction can be made rigorous and precise it isn't really a distinction at all. Many literary theorists fail to see, for example, that it is not an objection to a theory of fiction that it does not sharply divide fiction from nonfiction, or an objection to a theory of metaphor that it does not sharply divide the metaphorical from the non-metaphorical. On the contrary, it is a condition of the adequacy of a precise theory of an indeterminate phenomenon that it should precisely characterize that phenomenon as indeterminate; and a distinction is no less a distinction for allowing for a family of related, marginal, diverging cases.[10]

Any adequate definition of positivism must be complex because the very object under study is indeterminate.

How Can We Recognize a Positivist?

Though positivism was a French export, it quickly took root in America, especially at the university once positivism was shorn of the outer shell of religion that Comte personally imposed on it. Perhaps only Brazil experienced a more profound penetration of positivist thought in intellectual institutions than the U.S. did: "nowhere did positivism become more deeply rooted than in the United States."[11] We now live in a time that makes positivism looks ridiculous and illusory, so Nancy Partner too assuredly claims that historians have overcome it: "All historians know that history is no longer the discipline busily fulfilling its positivistic promise to tell it all as it really happened."[12] Partner represents that thin layer of theoretically-informed historians, so we can pardon her too-easy confidence that positivism has been driven from the profession.

The one element that bridges various positivist claims is the concept of ideology. Positivists claim to have struck through the mask to uncover without bias, distortion, and particularity the way the world really is. The claims come in stereotypical bromides under the umbrella of objectivity; the positivist historian claims to be free of ideology while his or her opponent is in the grip of an ideology. It is useful to think of the following family of claims to cover the phenomena:

1. Sergeant Joe Friday Positivism, or Brute Fact Positivism
2. Empiricist Positivism, or I'll-Believe-It-If-I-See-It Positivism
3. Preconceptionless Positivism
4. Anti-Metaphysical Positivism, or I-Don't-Do-Metaphysics-Said-the-Historian-Metaphysically
5. Value-Free Positivism
6. Anti-Particularity Positivism

I'll offer a definition of each of these six versions of positivism, provide an example or two from New Mormon Historians, then show that the center of gravity within the historical profession has shifted to undermine these positivist claims. Other positivist claims are equally common among Mormon historians, but I can't explore all claims in this paper.

1. Sergeant Joe Friday Positivism, or Brute Fact Positivism

This form of positivism asserts that some facts exist entirely free of interpretation; the facts interpret themselves. The historian can and should find facts completely divested of the subjectivity of interpreters. This version of positivism attempts to still the claims that ideology has intervened in the construction of the past by asserting that some facts are free from all interpretation. Here is how the positivist claims appears:

> But there are facts in history that are separate from interpretation. Harvey points to police files and scientific notebooks that are full of facts "that we simply are unable to interpret in any meaningful way"

and "the unintelligible cuneiform tablet, the discovery of a third-century Roman coin in a first-century ruin, the discovery of a diary that contradicts a widely accepted version of an event. All these require interpretation. They are facts in search of meaning, so to speak."[13]

Ashment points to other brute facts, perceiving that if some explanations of the past are free of interpretation, his own stand some chance of also claiming to be free of ideology: "Harvey points to the death of Hitler as an example which demonstrates that facts exist separate from interpretation. The fact is that Hitler died."[14]

Similarly, when FARMS and Signature Books got in a dustup after Signature's threat to sue over negative reviews by a FARMS publication of books published by Signature, the exchange resulted in the following positivist assertion reported by Daniel Peterson:

> There is, of course, nothing morally wrong with having an agenda or a point of view. Certainly there is nothing illegal about it. Deseret Book represents an unmistakable worldview, and F.A.R.M.S. advocates several agendas, as well. The puzzling thing for many of us who have observed Signature Books over the years is the apparent reluctance on the part of at least some of its principal figures to admit what seems obvious to us, namely that Signature too has a none-too-obscure point of view. In the telephone call that, for me, began the episode under consideration here, my acquaintance at Signature Books informed me that, while F.A.R.M.S. has a point of view, Signature does not. At Signature, he said, people simply *allow the facts to speak for themselves* (italics added).[15]

Anyone who claims to let the facts speak for themselves is a positivist. One of the central positivist claims is empiricist: the researcher can access uninterpreted facts by depending solely on empirical evidence. This idea of objectivity

> is represented by the positivists, who commit the so-called Baconian or inductivist fallacy. They hold that historians should let the evidence or data speak for themselves. Not only should the historians' present commitments (religious, moral, political, or whatever) be systematically and rigorously excluded from the inquiry; but even their perceptions should be formally and mechanically ordered by a technique that will render impressions into knowledge without distortion of any sort.[16]

Facts, even the simplest facts, never come to us free of interpretation; it is a positivist delusion to think so.

This claim to have found some Archimedean point free of bias or interpretation is a delusion and has been widely criticized among historians. Facts are never "brute facts" but always correspond to problems and questions the historians pose of them. The historian also applies metaphors and other tropes not inherent in the facts:

> we should no longer naively expect that statements about a given epoch of complex of events in the past "correspond" to some pre-existent body of "raw facts." For we should recognize that *what constitutes the facts themselves* is the problem that the historian, like the artist, has tried to solve in the choice of the metaphor by which he orders his world, past, present, and future.[17]

The coin that the archaeologist finds and the fact of Hitler's death (both of them brute facts according to Ashment) belong to a certain chronological framework that the archaeologist or historian contributes to the process of understanding.[18] Certainly these objects are real and independent of the researcher's mind, but when the researcher explains them to colleagues and writes up an essay or even tries to make sense of them in his or her own mind, they always mix with certain layers of meaning that aren't brute matter:

> "Fact" is another word that has fallen on hard times. Just as there are many historians out there who need to be reminded that, for all their differences, the writing of history and the writing of fiction are kindred activities, so there are also historians who still need to learn that facts only take shape under the aegis of paradigms, presuppositions, theories, and the like. There are even historians who might benefit from writing on the blackboard twenty times, "facts are just low-level interpretive entities unlikely for the moment to be contested."[19]

Similarly, Hans Kellner asks if facts exist at some "zero degree" of interpretation. "George Washington was born" is one that Kellner cites, similar to Ashment's fact about Hitler:

> I grant that there are plenty of cultural and linguistic forces in the constitution of these statements, but they are safe enough for my purposes here. As Fish puts it: "A sentence that seems to need no interpretation is already the product of one." That is not my point. What I want to ask is, is this *historical* knowledge?[20]

These issues have been discussed extensively in the larger historiographical field. Ashment needs to take up these positivist claims with this community for

> only the most innocent kind of positivist could now suppose that "facts" add up to anything in and of themselves, or that the scholar can move inductively from particulars collected at random

to broad theories somehow generated by meaning or order inherent in the facts themselves.[21]

That Ashment can assert there are facts free of interpretation demonstrates how uncritically he accepts his own positivistic interpretive scheme.

2. Empiricist Positivism

Positivism has always had a strong empiricist bent. At times during the history of the movement, positivists have insisted on being called empiricists, and sometimes the empiricists insisted on being called positivists. This occurred before the word *positivist* became a pejorative. This version of positivism claims that the only valid form of knowledge is that based upon empirical observation. If an assertion can't be verified empirically, it has no valid claim to knowledge. The empiricist claim becomes positivistic when the researcher asserts empirical data are superior to other forms of evidence because they bypass any need for interpretation and the concerns of ideology involved in representation. Most notably articulated by Comte, this tradition achieved its apogee among the Vienna School of Logical Positivists in the 1950s. Critics have pointed out that even though a work of art can't be analyzed in any meaningful way numerically or by observing color pigmentations, we still can make knowledgeable assertions about aesthetics. We can't analyze right or wrong conduct quantitatively, but ethics provides reasoned knowledge nevertheless. One Latter-day Saint critic, commenting on the Book of Mormon, insists that the ecclesiastical understanding of Latter-day Saint scriptures is dubious because it is insufficiently empirical. For this positivist, empirical history would revise such understandings. This attempt to revise the understanding of the Book of Mormon from within the community of Latter-day Saints aims to expose the text "to the scrutiny of reason and empirical research."[22] One wonders how his reading the Book of Mormon is more empirical than mine is, but the insistence that only empirical approaches yield knowledge is the positivist claim.

Similarly, James Clayton asserts that religious knowledge is non-knowledge, non-sense, because it does not apply sufficiently sensory data.

> That is a theological statement, not a historical statement. Historians can say very little about the actual relationship between God and Christ, since there is virtually no historical *evidence* to deal with. All historians can do is to analyze what people say they think of that relationship. The same problem exists in the quotations from Herbert Butterfield. When Butterfield mentions the Incarnation, the Crucifixion, and the Resurrection, he is in the realm of metaphysics and well beyond the realm of history. One deals with these sorts of things on the basis of faith, not on the basis of empirical data. One asserts their ultimate truth, one does not calculate their probabilities.[23]

Another critic within the Latter-day Saint community has also asserted this empiricist/positivist claim about an attempt by Joseph Smith to provide witnesses of his work by supplying witnesses to the plates from which the Book of Mormon was translated:

> Because they experienced the plates in a religiously ecstatic context, the experience is best approached from within a visionary tradition. Such a testimonial vision from God is not designed to address the empirical world of its human participants and cannot lend itself to historical-critical assessment.[24]

Jan Shipps also claims the Book of Mormon can't really be regarded as an ancient text because it can't stand up to empirical verification: "Yet it has never lent itself to the same process of verification that historians use to verify ordinary accounts of what happened in the past." For Shipps, empirical verification is something the book could never live up to—the best that could be hoped for is plausibility. Demonstrations of ancient patterns in the text are suspect because "such demonstrations point, finally, only to plausibility. Proof is a different matter."[25]

This idea that religious claims must measure up to some standard of proof is astounding, for no historical account achieves the level of proof. Why such an impossibly high standard for religious assertions? This context of empirical verification seems to be the background Shipps uses to measure the contents of the Book of Mormon itself:

> Because the Book of Mormon's claim to historicity has been fully authenticated only in a fashion that does not lend itself to intellectual verification, it becomes a paradox whenever it is unquestionably accepted as a nineteenth-century translation of documents that had been buried for 1,400 years.[26]

Not allowing anyone to be more positivist than thou, Ashment makes the full range of positivist claims. He too asserts that historical knowledge must be empirically based: "While the historian seeks to base his conclusions empirically on the evidence, the fundamentalist apologist, having already arrived at his conclusions according to his faith, presumptuously admits as relevant only those facts that support his conclusions."[27] There is some irony in this claim because Ashment is the one who "presumptuously admits as relevant" only evidence that meets his positivist standard of empirical evidence. These claims that historical knowledge must be empirically verifiable (very little that historians do is empirical, by the way; most is textual in a way more similar to what the literary critic does than what the sociologist and pollster do when they act empirically) in order to pass as knowledge is quite venerable; these claims about the necessity for empiricism are intellectual shortcuts to depriving religion of any claim that it produces knowledge (they are primarily ideological, in other words):

> As the positivists used it, verification serves as something like a litmus test to discriminate the genuinely factual statements of scientific philosophers from what they consider the pseudo-factual variety put forth by metaphysicians, theologians, and other philosophically retarded types.[28]

What Jeffrey Alexander here says about sociology would be applicable to Mormon history also:

> In the more technical terminology I have introduced here, the "positivist persuasion" elaborated above may be viewed as including both positivism and the reductionist aspects of empiricism. With this qualification, I will refer to "positivism" and "empiricism" strictly considered as interchangeable with the positivist persuasion.
>
> In the light of the description I have made of the changing perspectives among leading historians and philosophers of science, it is revealing to note that after the consensus on the radical positivist perspective had long since crumbled, the leaders of the positivist persuasion in sociology continued to invoke the "discoveries" of "philosophers of science" as justification for their own position. Invariably, these references if actually specified, were to the radical positivist position that had already been sharply challenged by empiricism and was in the process of being even more radically confronted by the third, antiempiricist critique.[29]

3. Preconceptionless Positivism

The researcher's claim to approach the task of explanation free of ideology often takes the form of a claim to wipe his or her mind clean of all preconceptions. If the researcher can just divest him or herself of all preconceptions, then bias and other forms of ideology can be wiped clean from the slate. In response, hermeneutical theory has noted that bias and preconception are the very foundations of knowledge; prejudice against prejudice is an Enlightenment dead end. Without preconceptions, the process of knowing can't get started, even if those preconceptions are invalidated or modified later.

One of the elements Paul Edwards claims New Mormon Historians share (that is, what makes them New Mormon Historians) is that they have broad training in a number of fields, and therefore, "very importantly, they are not bringing in a lot of preconceived ideas from their graduate professors." Another common element is professional historical training: "most of them have been educated in historical methodology at universities in America and in Europe which support the germanic concepts of objective history."[30] This claim to lack preconceptions can only be believed by one who shares the ideological preconceptions of the historian in question. Another Community of Christ historian has made similar claims about approaching the Book of Mormon without preconceptions:

> Because the temper of our times is such that no movement nor institution nor book can forever remain impervious to the searchlight of scholarly inspection, our times demand that all the rudiments of religious faith be subjected to the scrutiny of reason and empirical research. As the *Book of Mormon* is examined without any intention solely to amass data to support preconceived notions about it, certain problems concerning traditional understandings of the book stand out.[31]

To my reading, it is this historian himself who uncritically applies preconceptions without analyzing them for ideological content.

In a book too little referred to by Mormon historians, Peter Novick denounces the idea that historians can approach any task without preconceptions:

> There were two views of the temporal relation of fact and theory, though both agreed on the authority of fact over theory, and agreed also that fact and theory were clearly distinguishable. In the older inductivist view, scientists, with an open mind, unclouded by preconceptions, first observed the facts, then devised theories based on these facts, and confirmed them. In the Popperian view, theory came first.[32]

More contemporary views (hermeneutical and postmodern) assert that preconceptions are the very grounding of any understanding—without preconceptions the researcher would not understand the past at all. A broad swath of the historical community in the United States has come to the conclusion that preconceptionless interpretation is impossible: "To think of truth-seeking as a matter of emptying oneself of passion and preconception, so as to become a perfectly passive and receptive mirror of external reality, has, for good reason, become notorious."[33]

In an irony that even positivists could appreciate, some historians now assert that claiming to be free of preconceptions is one way to ensure your ideology is applied to the interpretive task dogmatically and uncritically:

> The historian does not pose questions about the past in an intellectual vacuum, without preliminary assumptions. The very fact of posing a question assumes the possibility of looking for (and perhaps finding) an answer, and that requires some knowledge about the object of inquiry. Those assumptions may be treated by the historian more or less flexibly and more or less dogmatically.[34]

Every researcher has preconceptions. Those who claim to be outside the gravitational pull of preconceptions just orbit their ideologies uncritically.

4. Anti-Metaphysical Positivism, or I-Don't-Do-Metaphysics-the-Historian-Said-Metaphysically

The other side of the empiricist positivist coin is anti-metaphysical positivism. This version shows powerful dislike of large-scale conceptualization. Ideas about first causes (ontological foundations) and about what makes for knowledge (epistemological questions) are usually eschewed by historians. Historians instead usually adopt a common-sense ontology and epistemology whose foundations they use but feel no need to defend. Historians often claim that they don't deal with metaphysical ideas, which go beyond the physical evidence of the senses.

Ashment has denied that he or other Mormon historians are positivistic, yet he has made almost every positivistic claim I have explored so far. Here is another:

> Thus historiographically, the challenge is rendered specious, because it requires a presupposition on the part of the historian that would automatically disqualify any historical inquiry and thereby nullify conclusions that historical analysis would make. For it represents "an attempt to resolve a nonempirical problem by empirical means" by "framing . . . a question which cannot be resolved before the researcher settles some central metaphysical problem."[35]

Ashment believes that empirical evidence can somehow exist absent all ideas or concepts. This claim shows its ideological position when Ashment asserts that religious belief is hopelessly metaphysical so it can't count as genuine knowledge; science describes the empirical not the metaphysical; religious faith is metaphysical.[36]

Similarly, another Mormon historian, in a generally fine book, asserts this positivist claim about his own epistemology:

> In approaching the present study, I have tried to attain a proper level of objectivity. However, I do consciously accept a modern notion that absolute objectivity is unattainable—and perhaps only ambiguously desirable. Some recent studies have gone so far as to argue that historical "objectivity" not only is beyond human reach but is an incoherent construct. I do not follow them so far. The concept does retain meaning for me, and, because of the subject matter of this book, invites a brief explanation.[37]

Here Barlow connects his epistemological ideas with the objectivity ideology. He goes on to make metaphysical claims as he asserts his eschewal of them:

> I am convinced that reality has dimensions far transcending human capacities to ascertain. Perhaps those dimensions impinge on human activity. It may even be, as Richard Lovelace has said, that history, viewed without allowance for spiritual forces, "is as confusing as a football game in which half the players are invisible." If those forces are discernible at all, though, the discernment must come through private intuitions, or the vision of prophets, or the inspiration of poets, or the speculations of metaphysicians. They are not discernible through the tools of historians, strictly speaking, whose more modest task is to deal with things visible. Prophets or metaphysicians may, of course, point to matters of history. However, they are not by that motion acting essentially as historians, but as something else.[38]

Here, religious claims are banished to the realm of nonknowledge. This grouping of poets, prophets, and metaphysicians as people who speak non-sense is common among positivists.

James Clayton too couples the denial of metaphysics with the assertion that he adheres strictly to empirical evidence:

That is a theological statement, not a historical statement. Historians can say very little about the actual relationship between God and Christ, since there is virtually no historical *evidence* to deal with. All historians can do is to analyze what people say they think of that relationship. The same problem exists in the quotations from Herbert Butterfield. When Butterfield mentions the Incarnation, the Crucifixion, and the Resurrection, he is in the realm of metaphysics and well beyond the realm of history. One deals with these sorts of things on the basis of faith, not on the basis of empirical data. One asserts their ultimate truth, one does not calculate their probabilities.[39]

The difficulty with this assertion is that the researcher can't divide the world into empirical evidence and metaphysical nonsense without making a metaphysical distinction. Metaphysics is inevitable.

Specifically discussing positivism, Max Horkheimer notes these metaphysicians who deny being metaphysicians assert that science will be able to solve all questions for us sometime in the future. Outside the realm of science is the world of nonknowledge: "Besides science, there is art. In so far as metaphysics is not out and out nonsense, it belongs to poetry. Knowledge is the exclusive province of science."[40] Specifically for historians, historical knowledge must be constructed using some metaphysical ideas about what is to count as proper historical evidence and what can be discarded; some resort must be made to a philosophy of ideas:

> A metaphysical problem is that which cannot be formulated in the technical language employed by practitioners of the discipline to frame questions or provide answers to them. In a field such as history, then, the confusion of a metaphysical with a scientific question is not only possible but at some stage in a given investigation inevitable. And although professional historians claim to be able to distinguish between proper history on the one side and metahistory on the other, in fact the distinction has no adequate theoretical justification. Every proper history presupposes a metahistory which is nothing but a web of commitments which the historian makes in the course of his interpretation on the aesthetic, cognitive, and ethical levels differentiated above.[41]

Positivism is itself a metaphysical construct. So when a researcher makes positivistic claims to do without metaphysics, he or she is doing what others are being castigated for doing. But the positivist must suppress any awareness that the stance is hypocritical:

> Positivism does not come to grips with metaphysics but simply knocks the bottom out of it. It declares metaphysical assertions meaningless and, letting them stand as such, abandons them to a self-generating "disuse." Yet it is only through metaphysical concepts that positivism can render itself comprehensible. By being unreflectively put aside, they retain their substantial power even over their adversary.[42]

Like ideology, metaphysics is ineluctable. What even positivists

> have had to concede is that every science makes some presuppositions which are, themselves, neither empirical propositions, which are the substance of that science, nor analytic propositions, such as those of logic and mathematics, which give form to the relationships within and between empirical propositions.[43]

Not only historical knowledge, but all knowledge accepts a metaphysics: "All our knowledge of the external world actually rests on tacitly accepted metaphysical grounds."[44] To denigrate religious claims because they incorporate a metaphysics is to disadvantage the position for doing what all arguments do. Positivism makes this distinction between religion and empirical observation in order to dismiss religious claims a priori. The effect of this insistence that what isn't empirical isn't knowledge is to disenfranchise not only religion but philosophy, ethics, aesthetics and many other fields—even a great deal of what historians do:

> The effect of this [positivist] argument was extraordinary. Metaphysics, religion, aesthetics, and ethics, all ceased, virtually overnight, to be philosophically respectable. Since subjects like these simply throw around statements that can never be verified, it is no wonder philosophical progress is impossible

under a positivistic regime.[45] While is it true that ethics, aesthetics, and metaphysics are all put at a disadvantage by this positivist claim, religion suffers most through this approach to dismissing faith claims.[46]

5. Value-Free Positivism

A common version of positivism asserts that the historian must divorce him or herself from all moral and value commitments. *Should* and *ought* should have no intercourse. Only by achieving this level of objectivity can the historian see the world the way it really is.

In Mormon studies, Ashment cites approvingly the claim that the historian must be value-free. Elsewhere Ashment refers positively to a source that claims the "historian of religions acknowledges the existence of religious values and tries to understand that significance. But his method should be completely free from any value judgment." He then claims that those who defend the Book of Mormon fall into special pleading by trying to exempt the book from the same rigorous analysis they expose other systems to.[47] Another New Mormon Historian makes a similar claim as he defines the task of the historian who writes about the supernatural. The historian's goal is objectivity, which requires the separation of fact from "the predetermination of value based on divine intervention. They clearly state that polemics, uncritically presented, invalidate the objectivity of historical evidence and thus weaken the implied power of our narrative."[48] Here witness the positivist attempt to separate fact from value.

Just as with other positivist claims, historians and philosophers have concluded that value-free inquiry is an impossibility. One can't help but endorse some ordering of society or preferring one form of knowledge to another:

> Objectivity is not a fashionable term among historians today because of their sensitivity to the ideological implications of any position within a historical context. Once "value neutral" social science itself came under examination as a tool of domination, the universality of ideology came to be taken for granted. Yet this is not a disabling blow to historical writing; in fact, it has added to the feeling of security. Since ideological demystification of any given text or artifact is basic to both marxist and nonmarxist practice today, and since the position of the scholar within society is also continuously scrutinized ideologically, the "ideological skepticism" really becomes a confrontation between two or more reasonably knowable positions. . . . In fact the loss of willed objectivity that followed the ideologizing of all thought and action offers the sense of a firmer grasp on a "reality," however complex and elusive that reality may be.[49]

Claims to being value-neutral are a way researchers assert that their own values should be the predominant one within a society. Value neutrality is as impossible to achieve as freedom from metaphysics.

The commitment toward value-free analysis originated in a political context and has always had political consequences. It can no longer be believed, but is still widely held as an ideal by historians and others:

> At the level of advertisement, the tide has turned in favor of the debunkers. Especially in recent years, we hear a lot about the "myth of neutrality"; value-free research is described as "malignant nonsense," "logically incoherent," a mask for "liberal ideology." Abraham Edel in 1988 called the idea of value-neutrality "bizarre"; Sandra Harding in 1989 called it "a delusion."[50]

A large burden of argumentation falls on the shoulders of those who claim to do value-free inquiry considering how thoroughly the idea has been dismantled over the past twenty years. "The notion of value-free social science may itself be ideological, since it conceals the values with which we do operate."[51]

6. Anti-Particularity Positivism

Anti-particularity positivism asserts that the historian must withdraw from any commitment that makes him or her distinctive. Religious belief, patriotic attachment, gender identity, and hundreds of other individual locations of the historian: all are corrupting influences that must be eliminated in order to achieve the view from nowhere. These attachments to family, country, church, or any number of other associations are corruptions of objectivity. Of course, for the positivist religious association is a primary element that hinders proper objectivity.

For the positivist, religion turns one into an apologist for an ideology:

> Apologetics for this stance, such as those espoused by the Foundation for Ancient Research and Mormon Studies (FARMS), the Department of Religious Education at Brigham Young University, and the LDS Church Education System, occasionally employ limited critical perspectives but only to promote traditionalist assumptions of historicity.[52]

For the positivist, apologetics is something the opponent falls into, rather than being a general condition of humanity. Metcalfe doesn't consider that he has similar connections: he publishes in a journal with an ideological agenda, is anti-Mormon in a way that looks like religious belief, and attends certain conferences that look very much like ecclesiastical gatherings.

Similarly, another positivist approaches the study of Mormon texts uncritically by referring to the particularities of those he opposes without applying the same analysis to institutions that support his ideological position.

> Eight of the contributors to *RBBM* [*Reviews of Books on the Book of Mormon*] are employed by BYU, as are many of the frequent contributors to FARMS's other publications.... Perhaps through no fault of their own, the work of many FARMS researchers does not qualify as "critical" because they lack the essential ingredient of freedom.[53]

Leonard Arrington also provides his view of objectivity. He says to be objective is to avoid the contingencies of time and place, to avoid personal commitments, and to be unbiased: "No one would contend that Wilson's study was objective in the modern sense; it reflected the author's personal feelings and opinions, as well as the available literature and prejudices of the time."[54] Like other positivistic claims, this one begs the question about whether such freedom from contingency is either possible or desirable. These historians and would-be historians assume both uncritically.

The most straightforward of these claims comes from James Clayton when he states that "subservience to a particular religion is therefore incompatible with honest inquiry, whether by historians or by anyone else."[55] For some reason religious commitment is singled out from all other particularities as most damaging. Teaching at a secular university, being taught by positivistic professors, editing or publishing with a press or journal hostile to religious belief: none of these particularities seems to disturb these positivists. This position is best articulated by American philosopher Thomas Nagel: "A view or form of thought is more objective than another if it relies less on the specifics of the individual's makeup and position in the world, or on the character of the particular type of creature he is."[56] Nagel doesn't really think that particularity can be achieved, but he thinks it worth striving for. Others have expressed the idea that it isn't even worthy as a goal. This reflexive prejudice against particularity has more recently been attacked by historians and other researchers. Attempts to model history on science with its methodical approach as an escape from particularity are no longer plausible. In this positivist view,

> Science was both cumulative and progressive. Unlike other realms, in which particularist loyalties might produce partisan results, science was universalistic. Whereas findings in other fields might reflect the preferences of the investigator, science was value-neutral. Other disciplines suffered from the intrusion of ideological currents, but science proceeded in serene isolation from such distorting influences. Scholars in other fields might occasionally succumb to dogmatism, stubbornly clinging to cherished beliefs in the face of evidence, but the modern scientist was the sworn enemy of dogma of any kind.... Though few historians explicitly framed their understanding of historical objectivity in terms of this model, its assumptions permeated objectivist arguments in the historical community.[57]

Novick notes that this ethos was adopted by historians in America to explain their professional task. But such universalist aspirations are impossible to achieve, as an economist notes:

> Modernism promises knowledge free from doubt, free from metaphysics, morals and personal conviction. What it is able to deliver renames as scientific methodology the scientist's and especially the economic scientist's metaphysics, morals, and personal convictions. It cannot deliver what it promises. Probably it should not.[58]

That impossibility hasn't prevented historians from aspiring to this universalism:

> Over the last hundred years no component of the synthesis of ideas which went to make up the norm of historical objectivity has been more central and enduring than "universalism." Truth was one, the same for all peoples. It was, in principle, accessible to all and addressed to all. Particularist commitments—national, regional, ethnic, religious, ideological—were seen as the enemies of objective truth. They had to be transcended if unitary truth was to be approached. Ranke's commanding reputation rested in large part on the perception that he had risen above narrow nationalism and parochialism. American historians had taken from Francis Bacon not only their notions of the inductive method, but also his warnings about the "Idols of the Cave": particularistic commitments which blocked access to universal truth.... The close connection which historians saw between detachment and objectivity made them sympathetic to Mannheim's celebration of the vantage point of free-floating and socially detached observers, whose liberation from particularist loyalties allowed them to approach closer to objectivity.[59]

That version of modernity called biblical criticism saw religion as such a threat to the historian's objectivity that it insisted its practitioners act as though they didn't belong to separate churches and synagogues but as though modernity was their primary religion:

> For historical criticism is the form of biblical studies that corresponds to the classical liberal political ideal. It is the realization of the Enlightenment project in the realm of biblical scholarship. Like citizens in the classical liberal state, scholars practicing historical criticism of the Bible are expected to eliminate or minimize their communal loyalties,

to see them as legitimately operative only within associations that are private, nonscholarly, and altogether voluntary.[60]

But this very claim to have transcended particularity is a way of letting the historian surrender to his or her remaining particularity uncritically—it is the historian's way of exercising hegemony while disclaiming that power. The historian becomes the umpire in a game in which he or she is also a contestant.[61]

Literary critic Stanley Fish has articulated the most powerful refutation of this idea that one can shed all particularity. His point is that since such particularity is inevitable, faulting others for their location is problematical.[62] These claims to be free of faith or particularity are not supportable:

> What this means is that whenever Reason is successfully invoked, whenever its invocation stops the argument and wins the day, the result will be a victory not for Reason but for the party that has managed (either by persuasion or intimidation or legerdemain) to get the reasons that flow from its agenda identified with Reason as a general category, and thereby to identify the reasons of its opponents as obviously *un*reasonable. Like "fairmindedness," "merit," and "free speech," Reason is a political entity, and never more so than when its claim is to have transcended politics.[63]

These claims to be free of ideological and particularistic entanglements assert that their defenders are free of politics, but they operate politically and work only if their ideology is obfuscated:

> The traditions of the guild, reinforced by a positivist philosophy of history, forbid academic historians to position themselves regarding the present. A fetishism of the facts, premised on an antiquated model of the natural sciences, still dominates history and the other social sciences. It reinforces the view that any conscious positioning should be rejected as ideological. Thus, the historian's position is officially unmarked: it is that of the nonhistorical observer.[64]

If we are to be critical, we must begin to mark and unconceal the obscured ideology in these claims to universality.

Attacking someone else's position for its particularity works only if particularity can be overcome, which it can't:

> It is *because* all arguments owe their force to contingent historical factors that no meta-argument can make contingency a matter either of suspicion or of celebration; contingency is a given and can account neither for nor against an argument; any arguments must still make its way by the same routes that were available before contingency was recognized as a general condition.[65]

Rather than just assuming that belief in the Mormon tradition is a disabling handicap, the positivist must begin from the ground up to defend the idea that some particularities are more dangerous than others.

The Role of Ideology in Historical Explanation

The crux of all historiographical positivism is the assertion that the historian can transcend ideology. I have offered a few definitions of positivism in this essay as examples. All three of these bizarre definitions engage in ideology: all try to privilege one group at the expense of others. They are not objective in any way one might define objectivity. In this case, historians and amateur historians who want to decrease the role of religion in Latter-day Saint or American culture claim that their positions ought to be privileged because they offer a superior approach free of ideological bias. But these historians offer a bait-and-switch tactic, promising freedom from ideology while practicing a virulent and uncritical version of it. Positivist history privileges certain truth claims illegitimately and leads to pathological history, not to critical history.[66]

Postmodern versions of inquiry, and some that are frankly modern, insist that ideology is inescapable:

> It is therefore difficult to engage such critics [who claim to be free of ideology] in debate about ideological preconceptions, since the power of ideology over them is nowhere more marked than in their honest belief that their readings are "innocent."[67]

But no ideas are ideologically innocent. Ideologies, however, work best when their status as ideologies is concealed. Girard hints at the function of ideology when he suggests that "ideologies are actively engaged in furthering ends that are best furthered by not acknowledging their true natures."[68] The best gauge of ideological content is to see how willing the researcher is to admit his or her ideology and how it affects the resulting interpretation; the first step in mitigating the uncritical use of an ideology is to admit its presence. The positivist ideology denies its own ideological content even while exercising it. "Ideology, like halitosis, is in this sense what the other person has."[69] The first step toward critical appreciation of the past is to understand and explain to the reader the impact of the historian's own ideology. Positivism cannot survive such scrutiny because then it would be subject to history and to demonstrations that positivism itself is the product of a certain time and place:

> An important device by which an ideology achieves legitimacy is by *universalizing* and "eternizing" itself. Values and interests which are in fact specific to a certain place and time are projected as the values and interests of all humanity. The assumption is that if there were not so, the sectoral, self-interested nature of ideology would loom too embarrassingly large, and so would impede its general acceptance.[70]

As a rough rule of thumb, I suggest that the more insistent a historian is about his or her own objectivity, the more likely that historian is to be engaged in ideological warfare uncritically. Positivists have been successful at pointing to the ideologies of opponents, but they have been less successful at recognizing that "the method we use to criticize ideology can easily turn into an ideology itself."[71]

During its positivistic phase, history used to claim a scientific status with the attendant emphasis on objectivity, on freedom from ideology. But positivism was a false pretender; before the 1880s historians viewed themselves as part of the literary tradition. Since the 1960s the theoretically-informed part of the profession has returned to viewing history writing as continuous with literary writing rather than making assertions that history is a science.

In Graham Swift's 1983 novel *Waterland*, the protagonist is a historian and teacher. He lives in England's East Anglia region, the Fenland. The Fen country becomes the symbol of historical knowledge; history is a bog with constantly shifting rivers and buildings without firm foundations. Both marshes and history fit the following description: "For the chief fact about the Fens is that they are reclaimed land, land that was once water, and which, even today, is not quite solid."[72] The postmodern view of history sees the ground as watery, shifty, soft, insubstantial; modernity requires certainty, methodology, objectivity, solidity. But those dreams are denied the postmodernist.

> History, being an accredited sub-science, only wants to know the facts. History, if it is to keep on constructing its road into the future, must do so on solid ground. At all costs let us avoid mystery-making and speculation, secrets and idle gossip. And, for God's sake, nothing supernatural.[73]

What modernity requires of history is bound to lead to frustration and disappointment, for the historian can't avoid mysteries, speculation, interpretation. Objectivity is a dream denied, so one can begin a new defense of positivism from the ground up, making ideologies explicit if one wants to make positivistic claims (although to admit positivistic ideologies would be to engage in fatally oxymoronic behavior). When discussing the supernatural in issues of Mormon history, one ought not to dismiss deity by uncritically adopting positivistic assumptions about the world.

Henry Crick, the historian in Swift's story, at various times asserts that history is nothing but myth, but at other times he encounters history and realizes "that history was no invention but indeed existed."[74] That dialectical tension drives the novel. The more he discovers about the Fens, the more he comes to realize that history is less solid than he had been taught. As he explores history with his students, he learns

> that by forever attempting to explain we may come, not to an Explanation, but to a knowledge of the limits of our power to explain. Yes, yes, the past gets in the way; it trips us up, bogs us down; it complicates, makes difficult.[75]

Those positivists who in good faith believe they have found solid ground free of all metaphysics, grounded in empirical observation of brute facts free of interpretation, perceived without preconceptions, and independent of all values and historical contingency just haven't explored any of the recent work on historiography. History perceived this way is as unstable as water.

For Further Research

Alexander, Jeffrey C. *Positivism, Presuppositions, and Current Controversies.* Vol. 1 in Theoretical Logic in Sociology. Berkeley: University of California Press, 1982.

Alexander, Thomas G. "Historiography and the New Mormon History: A Historian's Perspective." *Dialogue* 19 (fall 1986): 25–49.

Arrington, Leonard J. "Scholarly Studies of Mormonism in the Twentieth Century." *Dialogue* 1 (spring 1966): 15–32.

Ashment, Edward. "Canon and the Historian." Paper presented at Mormon History Association meetings, June 1, 1991.

Ashment, Edward H. "Historiography of the Canon." In *Faithful History: Essays on Writing Mormon History.* Ed. George D. Smith. Salt Lake City: Signature, 1992. 281–301.

Ashment, Edward. "Making the Scriptures 'Indeed One in Our Hands.'" In *The Word of God: Essays on Mormon*

Scripture. Ed. Dan Vogel. Salt Lake City: Signature, 1990. 237–64.

Ball, Phillip. *Life's Matrix: A Biography of Water*. New York: Farrar, Straus, and Giroux, 1999.

Barlow, Philip L. *Mormons and the Bible: The Place of the Latter-day Saints in American Religion*. New York: Oxford University Press, 1991.

Clayton, James L. "Does History Undermine Faith?" *Sunstone* 7 (March–April 1982): 33–40.

Clayton, James S. "History and Theology: The Mormon Connection." *Sunstone* 5 (November–December 1980): 51–53.

Cohen, Percy S. "Is Positivism Dead?" *Sociological Review* 28 (1980): 141–76.

Diamond, Malcolm L. Review of James Edwards's *Wittgenstein and Religion* and Kai Nielsen's *An Introduction to the Philosophy of Religion*. *Religious Studies Review* 12 (January 1986): 17–22.

Dever, William G. *What Did the Biblical Writers Know & When Did They Know It? What Archaeology Can Tell Us about the Reality of Ancient Israel*. Grand Rapids, MI: Eerdmans, 2001.

Domanska, Ewa. *Encounters: Philosophy of History after Postmodernism*. Charlottesville: University Press of Virginia, 1988.

Eagleton, Terry. *Ideology: An Introduction*. London: Verso, 1991.

Eagleton, Terry. *Literary Theory: An Introduction*. Minneapolis: University of Minnesota Press, 1983.

Edwards, Paul M. "The New Mormon History." *Saints Herald* 133 (November 1986): 12+.

Fish, Stanley. *There's No Such Thing as Free Speech: And It's a Good Thing Too*. New York: Oxford University Press, 1994.

Geuss, Raymond. *The Idea of a Critical Theory: Habermas and the Frankfurt School*. Cambridge: Cambridge University Press, 1981.

Girard, René. *"To Double Business Bound": Essays on Literature, Mimesis, and Anthropology*. Baltimore: Johns Hopkins University Press, 1978.

Habermas, Jürgen. *Knowledge and Human Interests*. Trans. Jeremy J. Shapiro. Boston: Beacon, 1971.

Ham, Wayne. "Problems in Interpreting the Book of Mormon as History." *Courage: A Journal of History, Thought and Action* 1 (September 1970): 15–22.

Haskell, Thomas L. "Objectivity Is Not Neutrality: Rhetoric vs. Practice in Peter Novick's That Noble Dream." *History and Theory* 29 (May 1990): 129–57.

Hawkes, David. *Ideology*. New York: Routledge, 1996.

Hill, Marvin S. "Positivism or Subjectivism? Some Reflections on a Mormon Historical Dilemma." *Journal of Mormon History* 20 (spring 1994): 1–23.

Horkheimer, Max. *Critical Theory: Selected Essays*. Trans. Matthew J. O'Connell and others. New York: Continuum, 1992.

Hume, Robert D. "Texts within Contexts: Notes toward a Historical Method." *Philological Quarterly* 71 (winter 1992): 69–100.

Kellner, Hans. *Language and Historical Representation: Getting the Story Crooked*. Madison: University of Wisconsin Press, 1989.

LaCapra, Dominick. "On Grubbing in My Personal Archives: An Historiographical Exposé of Sorts (or How I Learned to Stop Worrying and Love Transference)." *Boundary 2* 13 (winter–spring 1985): 43–67.

Levenson, Jon D. *The Hebrew Bible, the Old Testament, and Historical Criticism: Jews and Christians in Biblical Studies*. Louisville: Westminster/John Knox, 1993.

Lincoln, Yvonna S., and Egon G. Guba. *Naturalistic Inquiry*. Beverly Hills: Sage, 1985.

Lukacs, John. *Historical Consciousness: The Remembered Past*. New Brunswick: Transaction, 1994.

McCloskey, Donald N. *The Rhetoric of Economics*. Madison: University of Wisconsin Press, 1985.

McLellan, David. *Ideology*. 2d ed. Minneapolis: University of Minnesota Press, 1995.

McMurrin, Sterling M. "On Mormon Theology." *Dialogue* 1 (summer 1966): 135–40.

McMurrin, Sterling M. *Religion, Reason, and Truth: Historical Essays in the Philosophy of Religion*. Salt Lake City: University of Utah Press, 1982.

Metcalfe, Brent Lee. "Apologetic and Critical Assumptions about Book of Mormon Historicity." *Dialogue* 26 (fall 1993): 153–84.

Nagel, Thomas. *The View from Nowhere*. New York: Oxford University Press, 1986.

Novick, Peter. *That Noble Dream: The "Objectivity Question" and the American Historical Profession*. New York: Cambridge University Press, 1988.

Partner, Nancy F. "Making Up Lost Time: Writing on the Writing of History." *Speculum* 61 (1986): 90–117.

Peterson, Daniel C. "Questions to Legal Answers." *Review of Books on the Book of Mormon* 4 (1992): vii–lxxvi.

Polanyi, Michael, and Harry Prosch. *Meaning*. Chicago: University of Chicago Press, 1975.

Poster, Mark. *Cultural History and Post-modernity: Disciplinary Readings and Challenges*. New York: Columbia University Press, 1997.

Proctor, Robert N. *Value-Free Science? Purity and Power in Modern Knowledge*. Cambridge: Harvard University Press, 1991.

Ricoeur, Paul. *The Reality of the Historical Past*. Milwaukee: Marquette University Press, 1984.

Rienstra, M. Howard. "History, Objectivity, and the Christian Scholar." In *History and Historical Understanding*. Ed. C. T. McIntire and Ronald A. Wells. Grand Rapids: Eerdmans, 1984. 69–82.

Ross, Stephen. "Positivism, Pragmatism, and Everyday Life." *Society* 28 (November–December 1990): 42–50.

Searle, John. "The World Turned Upside Down." Review of Jonathan Culler's *On Deconstruction*. *The New York Review of Books* (October 27, 1983): 74–79.

Shipps, Jan. *Mormonism: The Story of a New Religious Tradition*. Urbana: University of Illinois Press, 1985.

Swift, Graham. *Waterland*. New York: Vintage, 1992.

Thompson, Stephen E. "'Critical' Book of Mormon Scholarship," *Dialogue* 27 (winter 1994): 197–206.

Topolski, Jerzy. "A Non-Postmodernist Analysis of Historical Narratives." *Historiography between Modernism and Postmodernism: Contributions to the Methodology of the Historical Research*. Ed. Jerzy Topolski. Atlanta: Rodopi, 1994.

Trigg, Roger. *Understanding Social Science: A Philosophical Introduction to the Social Sciences*. New York: Basil Blackwell, 1985.

Trouillot, Michel-Rolph. *Silencing the Past: Power and the Production of History*. Boston: Beacon, 1995.

White, Hayden V. "The Burden of History." *History and Theory* 5 (1966): 111–34.

White, Hayden. *Tropics of Discourse: Essays in Cultural Criticism.* Baltimore: Johns Hopkins University Press, 1978.

Wilshire, Bruce. "Fifty Years of Academic Philosophy in the United States: Why the Failure of Nerve?" *Soundings* 67 (1984): 411–19.

Notes

1. Historians in general and New Mormon Historians in particular infrequently address these issues in a fastidious way. Mark Poster's comment is often heard among theoretically-sophisticated historians, that historians rarely have the intellectual tools and incentive to examine the philosophical underpinnings of their assertions about truth and the past, but instead assume a commonsensical and thin version of such philosophical ideas. Mark Poster, *Cultural History and Postmodernity: Disciplinary Readings and Challenges* (New York: Columbia University Press, 1997), 38.

2. Thomas Alexander, "Historiography and the New Mormon History: A Historian's Perspective." *Dialogue* 19 (1986): 31. Contrast this to Jerzy Topolski's claim that, at least by 1976, "the positivist way of thinking was still dominant in science and historiography." Ewa Domanska, *Encounters: Philosophy of History after Postmodernism* (Charlottesville: University Press of Virginia, 1988), 119.

3. Yvonna S. Lincoln and Egon G. Guba, *Naturalistic Inquiry* (Beverly Hills: Sage, 1985), 15.

4. John Lukacs, *Historical Consciousness: The Remembered Past* (New Brunswick: Transaction, 1994), xxviii–xxix.

5. Dominick LaCapra, "On Grubbing in My Personal Archives: An Historiographical Exposé of Sorts (or How I Learned to Stop Worrying and Love Transference)," *Boundary 2* 13 (winter–spring 1985): 48, 49.

6. Edward Ashment, "Canon and the Historian," paper presented at Mormon History Association meetings, June 1, 1991, 11.

7. Sterling M. McMurrin, "On Mormon Theology," *Dialogue* 1 (summer 1966): 136. See also Sterling M. McMurrin, *Religion, Reason, and Truth: Historical Essays in the Philosophy of Religion* (Salt Lake City: University of Utah Press, 1982), x, xii.

8. Edward H. Ashment, "Historiography of the Canon," *Faithful History: Essays on Writing Mormon History,* ed. George D. Smith (Salt Lake City: Signature, 1992), 289.

9. Marvin S. Hill, "Positivism or Subjectivism? Some Reflections on a Mormon Historical Dilemma," *Journal of Mormon History* 20 (spring 1994): 3 n. 5. I have looked up *positivism* in every edition of the *Webster's New Twentieth-Century Unabridged Dictionary* I can find, and I discover no way to derive Hill's definition from that dictionary.

10. John Searle, "The World Turned Upside Down," rev. of Jonathan Culler's *On Deconstruction* in *The New York Review of Books* (Oct. 27, 1983), 78.

11. Bruce Wilshire, "Fifty Years of Academic Philosophy in the United States: Why the Failure of Nerve?" *Soundings* 67 (1984): 414.

12. Nancy F. Partner, "Making Up Lost Time: Writing on the Writing of History," *Speculum* 61 (1986): 117.

13. Ashment, "Historiography of the Canon," 292–93.

14. Ashment, "Historiography of the Canon," 293.

15. Daniel C. Peterson, "Questions to Legal Answers," *Review of Books on the Book of Mormon* 4 (1992): liii–liv, italics added.

16. M. Howard Rienstra, "History, Objectivity, and the Christian Scholar," in C. T. McIntire and Ronald A. Wells, eds., *History and Historical Understanding* (Grand Rapids: Eerdmans, 1984), 70.

17. Hayden V. White, "The Burden of History," *History and Theory* 5 (1966): 131.

18. Even an archaeologist who calls himself a positivist denies this assertion. William G. Dever, *What Did the Biblical Writers Know & When Did They Know It? What Archaeology Can Tell Us about the Reality of Ancient Israel* (Grand Rapids, MI: Eerdmans, 2001), 70. Archaeology, like history, has been suffocated by a simplistic positivist orthodoxy, from which it is just now emerging.

19. Thomas L. Haskell, "Objectivity Is Not Neutrality: Rhetoric vs. Practice in Peter Novick's *That Noble Dream,*" *History and Theory* 29 (May 1990): 141.

20. Hans Kellner, *Language and Historical Representation: Getting the Story Crooked* (Madison: University of Wisconsin Press, 1989), 330.

21. Robert D. Hume, "Texts within Contexts: Notes toward a Historical Method," *Philological Quarterly* 71 (winter 1992): 84.

22. Wayne Ham, "Problems in Interpreting the Book of Mormon as History," *Courage: A Journal of History, Thought and Action* 1 (September 1970): 16.

23. James S. Clayton, "History and Theology: The Mormon Connection," *Sunstone* 5 (November–December 1980): 52.

24. Brent Lee Metcalfe, "Apologetic and Critical Assumptions about Book of Mormon Historicity," *Dialogue* 26 (fall 1993): 175.

25. Jan Shipps, *Mormonism: The Story of a New Religious Tradition* (Urbana: University of Illinois Press, 1985), 28.

26. Shipps, *Mormonism,* 29.

27. Edward Ashment, "Making the Scriptures 'Indeed One in Our Hands,'" *The Word of God: Essays on Mormon Scripture,* ed. Dan Vogel (Salt Lake City: Signature, 1990), 251.

28. Malcolm L. Diamond, Review of James Edwards's *Wittgenstein and Religion* and Kai Nielsen's *An Introduction to the Philosophy of Religion* in *Religious Studies Review* 12 (January 1986): 17.

29. Jeffrey C. Alexander, *Positivism, Presuppositions, and Current Controversies,* vol. 1 in *Theoretical Logic in Sociology* (Berkeley: University of California Press, 1982), 140 n. 74.

30. Paul M. Edwards, "The New Mormon History," *Saints Herald* 133 (November 1986): 14.

31. Wayne Ham, "Problems in Interpreting the Book of Mormon as History," 16.

32. Peter Novick, *That Noble Dream: The "Objectivity Question" and the American Historical Profession* (New York: Cambridge University Press, 1988), 524–25.

33. Haskell, "Objectivity Is Not Neutrality," 134.

34. Jerzy Topolski, "A Non-Postmodernist Analysis of Historical Narratives," *Historiography between Modernism and Postmodernism: Contributions to the Methodology of the Historical Research,* ed. Jerzy Topolski (Atlanta: Rodopi, 1994), 64.

35. Ashment, "Canon and the Historian," 4.

36. Ashment, "Historiography of the Canon," 291.

37. Philip L. Barlow, *Mormons and the Bible: The Place*

of the Latter-day Saints in American Religion (New York: Oxford University Press, 1991), xv.

38. Barlow, *Mormons and the Bible*, xvi–xvii.

39. Clayton, "History and Theology," 52.

40. Max Horkheimer, *Critical Theory: Selected Essays*, trans. Matthew J. O'Connell and others (New York: Continuum, 1992), 139.

41. Hayden White, *Tropics of Discourse: Essays in Cultural Criticism* (Baltimore: Johns Hopkins University Press, 1978), 71.

42. Jürgen Habermas, *Knowledge and Human Interests*, trans. Jeremy J. Shapiro (Boston: Beacon, 1971), 80.

43. Percy S. Cohen, "Is Positivism Dead?" *Sociological Review* 28 (1980): 149.

44. Michael Polanyi and Harry Prosch, *Meaning* (Chicago: University of Chicago Press, 1975), 188.

45. Stephen Ross, "Positivism, Pragmatism, and Everyday Life," *Society* 28 (November–December 1990): 43.

46. Raymond Geuss, *The Idea of a Critical Theory: Habermas and the Frankfurt School* (Cambridge: Cambridge University Press, 1981), 13–14.

47. Ashment, "Historiography of the Canon," 285.

48. Edwards, "The New Mormon History," 13.

49. Kellner, *Language and Historical Representation*, 206–7.

50. Robert N. Proctor, *Value-Free Science? Purity and Power in Modern Knowledge* (Cambridge: Harvard University Press, 1991), 9.

51. Roger Trigg, *Understanding Social Science: A Philosophical Introduction to the Social Sciences* (New York: Basil Blackwell, 1985), 204.

52. Metcalfe, "Apologetic and Critical Assumptions," 153.

53. Stephen E. Thompson, "'Critical' Book of Mormon Scholarship," *Dialogue* 27 (winter 1994): 205.

54. Leonard J. Arrington, "Scholarly Studies of Mormonism in the Twentieth Century," *Dialogue* 1 (spring 1966): 17–18.

55. James L. Clayton, "Does History Undermine Faith?" *Sunstone* 7 (March–April 1982): 34.

56. Thomas Nagel, *The View from Nowhere* (New York: Oxford University Press, 1986), 5.

57. Peter Novick, *That Noble Dream*, 525.

58. Donald N. McCloskey, *The Rhetoric of Economics* (Madison: University of Wisconsin Press, 1985), 16.

59. Peter Novick, *That Noble Dream*, 469.

60. Jon D. Levenson, *The Hebrew Bible, the Old Testament, and Historical Criticism: Jews and Christians in Biblical Studies* (Louisville: Westminster/John Knox, 1993), 118.

61. Paul Ricoeur, *The Reality of the Historical Past* (Milwaukee: Marquette University Press, 1984), 21.

62. Stanley Fish, *There's No Such Thing as Free Speech: And It's a Good Thing Too* (New York: Oxford University Press, 1994), 8.

63. Fish, *There's No Such Thing as Free Speech*, 18.

64. Michel-Rolph Trouillot, *Silencing the Past: Power and the Production of History* (Boston: Beacon, 1995), 151.

65. Fish, *There's No Such Thing as Free Speech*, 20.

66. A parallel to the way Phillip Ball defines pathological science is in *Life's Matrix: A Biography of Water* (New York: Farrar, Straus, and Giroux, 1999), 277–79.

67. Terry Eagleton, *Literary Theory: An Introduction* (Minneapolis: University of Minnesota Press, 1983), 198.

68. René Girard, *"To Double Business Bound": Essays on Literature, Mimesis, and Anthropology* (Baltimore: Johns Hopkins University Press, 1978), 74. See also Terry Eagleton, *Ideology: An Introduction* (London: Verso, 1991), 52.

69. Eagleton, *Ideology*, 2. See a similar statement in David McLellan, *Ideology*, 2d ed. (Minneapolis: University of Minnesota Press, 1995), 1.

70. Eagleton, *Ideology*, 56.

71. David Hawkes, *Ideology* (New York: Routledge, 1996), 81.

72. Graham Swift, *Waterland* (New York: Vintage, 1992), 8.

73. Swift, *Waterland*, 86.

74. Swift, *Waterland*, 62.

75. Swift, *Waterland*, 108.

Many Mansions:
The Postmodern Critique and a New Faithful History

Stephen C. Taysom

Introduction

Mormonism has always been controversial, and the study of its history reflects that controversy. As more Latter-day Saint historians have been trained in secular graduate schools and employed this training to critically examine their religious tradition, a divide has grown between "faithful" history and "faith-less" history. In a sense this dichotomy is misleading because it ignores a spectrum of approaches to the study of the Mormon past that blend elements drawn from the two extremes. In this paper, I will explore elements of "postmodernism" as they pertain to the study of the Mormon past. This will involve discussing the constructed nature of historical narratives and the inadequacy of scholarly methods to build faith. The discussion will eventually lead to my suggestion that more than one type of narrative may properly be considered "faithful." Historians have generally come to accept the fact that true objectivity is a "noble dream" that is simply beyond the grasp of human interpreters of the past. The types of scholarly approaches resulting from this reality range from those that strive for "functional objectivity" to those that abandon hope of writing a history that corresponds to an actual past because the past is essentially unrecoverable. The approach that I am advocating in this paper falls between these two approaches, and, I hope, will ease some of the tension that has come to hold sway within the Mormon historical community.[1]

Postmodernism and the Construction of Narrative

The idea of postmodernism has generated controversy within the historical profession for decades. Casting aside the extreme elements of the theory, which are those that suggest that any version of the past is as good as any other, one may recover a certain common-sense approach to the crafting of these narratives. I propose to suggest some ways that the postmodern critique may help to redefine the way we conceive of the Mormon past, the way we view the nature of historical "truth," as well as ways in which this approach may aid in the search for harmony between "faithful" and "academic" history. The term "postmodernism" itself is slippery. It may be said that this paper employs a selective reading of postmodernist thought. This is true, if for no other reason than no comprehensive statement exists about what constitutes postmodernism. For the purposes of this paper, postmodernism can be thought of as a way of thinking about the past which rejects positivistic, teleological, rationalist, and scientific ideas as they pertain to the construction of historical narratives. Historian of Christianity Robert E. Van Voorst defines postmodernism as consisting of any approach to historical study that "turns away from the overarching commitment to rationality and scientific approach characteristic of study from the Enlightenment through the twentieth century."[2] This paper explores an applied approach to postmodernism based on two key ideas. First, the postmodern rejection of the idea central to modernism that, as an outgrowth of the Enlightenment, presupposes that only those things amenable to "scientific" study and observation are "true" and that if something is "true" it is necessarily demonstrable through such observation and analysis. Historian Stuart Clark has pointed out that this postmodern approach is especially helpful when applied to religion because of the modernist tendency toward a "rationalism" which consists of the "dismissal as irrational any belief not warranted by correspondence to objective fact."[3] The irony of this position, as I will argue below, is that those "objective facts" are themselves determined by a rationalist agenda.

The second idea central to the role of postmodernism in this paper is the theory of "emplotment," or the notion that historical narratives represent intellectual constructs and that no recoverable normative discourse is available to the historian. I reject the more extreme postmodern position that no logic can or ought to be applied to the construction of these narratives. On the contrary, the extent to which the narratives are useful lies not in their ability to present ultimate "truth" but in their internal consistency and integrity. Some might argue that novels do this, and could, therefore, be considered the equals of historical narrative. I reject this notion on the grounds that historical narratives purport to represent a version of the past that, presumably, actually occurred. Novels do not aim to represent anything other than the author's own imagination. Saying that historical narratives are artificial and separate from the past that they claim to represent is absolutely not the same thing as arguing that they are fictional.

The Challenge of Faithful Scholarship in the Twenty-First Century

A brief time spent "surfing" the internet will provide any interested party with ample evidence of the conflict that rages among "liberal" and "conservative" Mormons and everything in between. It is a discouragement for a young scholar of faith to realize that phalanxes of critics with well-established agendas and considerable resources wait to pounce on any interpretation of Church history which may be labeled as "pro-Church" or "anti-Mormon." Testimonies are attacked on one side and academic professionalism on the other. What all of these efforts have in common is a belief that if one side piles up enough "facts," then any reasonable person could not fail to agree with them. The main problem with that approach is that certain matters of faith are not provable (or disprovable) in an academic sense.[4] As frustrating as that fact may be to believers, it is a fact nevertheless. Consider the hundreds of scholars familiar with the texts and sources of historical Mormonism that never decided to take up the cause. Clearly this evidence did not "prove" to these individuals the truth of Mormonism. Religious faith may be enhanced in some cosmetic fashion by historical evidence, properly interpreted, but it cannot be built upon such and function as it must. Likewise, testimonies based on faith, on a decision to believe in spite of the perpetually incomplete and contradictory historical record, are in no danger of being corroded or destroyed by "facts" about the Church that someone decides to interpret in a negative way.

Mormonism was born, grew, and continues to flourish in a world that is the product of the Enlightenment. The Enlightenment, like postmodernism, is not easily definable. The movement began in Europe in the seventeenth century and was heavily influenced by the scientific method. Adopting the Cartesian stance that doubt was the door to knowledge, Enlightenment thinkers "sought to unlock the mysteries of nature and reveal their logical, rational foundations in the laws of physics and chemistry," an attitude which brought about a "generalizing of the critical attitude."[5] More specifically, Peter Hamilton has provided a list of ten essential characteristics of Enlightenment thought that have influenced the development of Western intellectual culture. Of those ten, three seem particularly important to the task at hand. The first and most important is "the primacy of reason and rationality as a means for understanding and organizing knowledge about the human and natural worlds." The second is the rise of empiricism, "the philosophical doctrine that all human knowledge about the world is derived from empirical evidence accessible through the sense organs." Finally, the Enlightenment legacy of secularism, which "rejected religious knowledge of the world as ultimate" and which sought to reject "Christian dogma based upon a variety of humanistic, philosophical and scientific grounds," provided the context for long term tension.[6]

This tension between Enlightenment thought and the Mormon story begins much earlier, with Joseph Smith. Life in the "burned-over district," while often crude and difficult, nevertheless brimmed with Enlightenment beliefs and expectations. Whitney Cross, while trying to prove the opposite point, noted the "extreme gullibility" even among the social elites of the region and cited as evidence such commonly held beliefs as the danger of a drunken person bursting into flames through the ignition of alcohol in the stomach. Cross incredulously reports that "even a Universalist preacher" had engaged the services of a "glass looker" to search for hidden treasure. Despite the absurdity of such claims to a twentieth-century audience, one must take care not to confuse bad science with a non-scientific mindset. Cross himself acknowledges that the people involved in these activities viewed themselves as "scientific."[7] Clearly, they believed that empirical methods could be employed to achieve certain results. What makes this essentially scientific rather than superstitious is that the practitioners believed they were relying on natural laws rather than on supernatural powers to achieve their ends. Despite the argument made by some scholars that the revivals of the second Great Awakening and the movements that grew from them represented a reaction against the deistic merging of rationalism and theism, these religious enthusiasts continued to draw on Enlightenment ideas of "the rational." As Susan Juster notes, "the attempt to find a rational basis for Christian belief was not, after all, limited to Deists . . . evangelical theologians themselves often joined in such a task."[8] Joseph Smith's birth into this milieu meant that he too would be raised to believe in empiricism and in science, such as it was in this rustic setting. It is interesting to note that Joseph Smith came of age during a period of transition in America from the overtly Enlightened tone set by Thomas Jefferson to the more popular tone set by accessible ideas that drove the market revolution and Jacksonian democracy. It was between the decline of the sterile, deistic notions that set "reasonable" boundaries around appropriate religious experience and the advent some decades later of Darwinian science and "higher criticism" that the opportunity arose for religious seekers to accept both revival-style religious feeling and a commitment to a "rational" and "enlightened" mindset.[9] This opportunity resulted in an unprecedented surge in religious creativity, including an increase in interest in supernatural phenomena, which "appeared again in the ranks of college-educated Americans for the first time since . . . about 1680."[10]

From the mid-nineteenth century Mormon culture has exhibited tension between the world of faith and the world of modernist, post-Enlightenment rationalism. Nineteenth-century American culture, according to Henry May, was characterized by a "compromise between a belief in moral certainties and a belief in the desirability of change and progress."[11] The change and progress that May refers to is closely bound up with scientific empiricism. Until the mid-nineteenth century, these ideas of rationality and faith coexisted in relative harmony; a relationship Steven C. Harper describes as the coexistence of the "twin influences of the Bible and the democratization of rationalism."[12] In the broadest terms, it is safe to say that the advent of Darwinian ideas about the nature of human and animal evolution together with the advent of German "higher criticism" of the Bible made this relationship much less comfortable after the middle of the nineteenth century. While Darwin, and those whom he has come to represent, raised troubling questions about traditional interpretations of human origins, the higher critics concluded that "Abraham, Isaac, and the other tribal founders depicted in the book of Genesis were no more real than the heroes of Greek or Norse mythology."[13]

As the more stringent elements of European Enlightenment thought reasserted themselves in the middle of the nineteenth century, the quest for empirical knowledge came to be increasingly difficult for many to reconcile with previously held ideas about the literal, rational nature of the Bible and revealed religion in general. This tension has informed and, to a certain extent, is embodied in the ways that "faithful" and "faith-destroying" history have come to be defined. The late Eugene Campbell, himself no stranger to the struggle between faith and reason, once expressed the dilemma faced by faithful scholars when he asked this question: "How do I bring a fresh, new approach to a subject that has been heard many times before by church members without upsetting their faith or—better yet—while strengthening their faith?"[14] Embedded in this question is a system of assumptions which presents special difficulties for faithful students of the Latter-day Saint past. Central to this system of assumptions is that recoverable, historical "facts" exist and that they have the power to either upset or strengthen faith. Based on the modernist, Enlightenment view of faith and history, this is certainly true. If, however, we examine the relationship between the past and "history," as well as the true relationship between history and faith, some of these difficulties may begin to recede. To recast the way we think about these issues, we must consider the constructed nature of historical narrative.

Culturally Constructed Narrative

Perhaps the most important element of the postmodern critique is what it tells us about the nature of historical narrative. Postmodern thinkers like Hayden White have pointed out that written history is a likeness of the past created from bits of historical "fact" arranged in a particular pattern and order, depending upon the agenda of the writer. The historian, according to White, naturally assumes his or her perspective as normative and allows this perspective to influence the construction of the narrative. Much of this happens on a basic level, and thus transcends issues of conscious bias and objectivity.

Take as an example a historian writing a history of Gettysburg, Pennsylvania. For the month of July in the year 1863, we would expect that the narrative would focus on the famous battle that occurred between the Union Army and Lee's Army of Northern Virginia. We would expect more space to be dedicated to this event (or rather to the assorted microevents that made up the "battle") than to the birth of a child in the family of a local farmer just prior to the start of hostilities. All of these events occupied space and time; they all represent potential raw materials for the construction of a narrative. The battle wins out for a number of reasons: loss of human life, the importance of the battle in the development of our national institutions and culture, etc. This process is an example of what Hayden White has termed "emplotment": the act of taking a

> given set of events, arranged more or less chronologically and encoding them so as to appear as phases of a process with a discernible beginning, middle and end, and may be emplotted as a Romance, Comedy, Tragedy or what have you depending upon the valences assigned to different events in the series as elements of recognizable, archetypal story-forms.[15]

The "past" doesn't differentiate between the birth of a child, the death of a horse, a forest fire, a battle, a presidential election, or a theophany. History doesn't care, but the historian must. The choices the historian makes are the result of proclivities and idiosyncrasies influenced by untold experiences and conditions that collectively shape the historian's mind and thought processes. Many of these are widely held cultural biases so central to life as the historian and others in his world perceive it that they simply never come under scrutiny. In the example cited above, we unanimously assert that the death of thousands is historically more important than the death of a horse or the birth of one child. If, however, that child had become a historically important individual, his or her birth would take on historical significance and as such would find its way into the textbooks that previously paid no heed. Those things deemed historically relevant are culturally determined.

One such culturally determined idea that impinges on Mormon history is rooted, predictably, in the ideas of Enlightenment scientism. Western thought holds that time is progressing, moving from darkness to light, ignorance to knowledge. Implicit in this idea is that time is linear and that it matters when things happened, because that is an important way to gauge an event's relative importance.

Before exploring how this may be useful in constructing Mormon histories, it is necessary to re-establish some basic ideas. First, narratives consist of historical "facts" arranged in a specific order, in terms of time and importance, designed to make a larger point. The second point is a corollary of the first and holds that for any given set of "facts," any number of possible narratives may be created, depending upon cultural assumptions regarding the nature of time, the hierarchy of importance that sets some events above others, and the overall effect the author wishes to convey to the audience. Many people of faith, including Latter-day Saints, find such notions unsettling largely because they perceive, correctly, that such ideas ultimately rest upon relativism. It is absolutely crucial to emphasize however that an admission of relativism in the construction of historical narratives, the lack of an over-arching "meta-discourse" against which all historical knowledge must be measured, is certainly not the same as claiming that there is no ultimate reality. The historian's tools and insight are limited, sometimes painfully so. There is simply so much that the historian cannot know. This "methodological agnosticism," as some scholars have dubbed it, need not carry over into the worldviews of those who write and read history.

The final of the three foundational ideas is that ultimate truth is not, for Latter-day Saints, the result of historical study. It is not based on empiricism. That our culture is based on the principles of Enlightenment rationalism (and has been since the eighteenth century) tends to frame the way we interpret, perhaps erroneously at times, the nature of faith. Joseph Smith, as a man of his time, given to the notion (particularly early in his life) that physical evidence provided the most ready converts and calmed the most vociferous naysayers, received the following instruction from the Lord: "Behold, if they will not believe my words, they would not believe you, my servant Joseph, if it were possible that you should show them all these things which I have committed unto you"(D&C 5:7). Knowledge of the truth is derived from spiritual whisperings bestowed upon those who, as an act of faith, desire to know for themselves. If the historical "facts," as we have them, coincide with those spiritual impressions, fine. If they do not, so be it. To wait until the evidence is conclusive is, to borrow a phrase from philosopher Richard Sherlock, to "have placed your faith in hock to the historian."[16]

It is no accident that young missionaries are trained not in paleography, historical pedagogy or historiography but in faith and prayer. Harold B. Lee taught that testimony "didn't come from reading books . . . from studying theology or science or philosophy" but rather from "a witness in your heart that these things are true."[17] I would argue that testimonies must not rest on academic learning and that academic learning is not necessarily a threat to testimony. As a result, faithful history may be taken to mean history written by historians of faith, regardless of the narrative structure they choose to employ. An example may prove helpful at this stage. Let us consider the First Vision, an event central to Latter-day Saint tradition and an event that missionaries bear testimony of in the first discussion. From the perspective of the professional historian, the event's details, context, and reality are all foggy.[18] I may be able to scour documents for evidence of a revival in the vicinity of Joseph Smith's home in 1820. I would of course find a variety of accounts of the event, varying in details both large and small. I would also find that no mention is made of the First Vision for more than a decade after it was supposed to have happened and that it played no role in missionary work until quite a late date. Again, as a historian, I am not likely to proclaim that "I know" that it occurred, although I am free to emplot the events in the historical record in a number of narrative structures, depending upon what story I wish to tell. It is important to keep in mind that "facts" *never* speak for, interpret, or emplot themselves. As a person of faith, a believer in an ultimate reality that stretches beyond the limits of the archive, I can, and have, affirmed my knowledge of the event, but this knowledge ranges far beyond the analytical and textual tools provided by my historical training. The point is that a historian may not in good conscience (and frankly would not be allowed to) argue evidence from the point of view of personal faith in an academic setting and may just as easily ignore "facts" discovered in academic research in the realm of personal faith, if he so chooses. In either setting, and one is certainly more important than the other, he must apply different standards of epistemology, which may mean that there are times when his academic conclusions and his private faith are in conflict. Such conflicts do not indicate that a historian is either, faithless or gullible, but simply that two unequally important elements in ones' life do not follow the same rules of "knowing."

At issue is the question of whether or not an event may be both true and empirically unprovable simultaneously. Alma answered this when he wrote that faith consists of a "hope for things which are not seen, which are true" (Alma 32:21). Modernist interpretations, based as they are in scientific rationalism, abhor the ambiguity that such a proposition implies while postmodernism embraces the multiplicity of narratives that this allows. Constructed historical narratives are thus not pillars of faith, nor are they any great threat to it. They are, as we shall see, however, far from useless. The construction of narrative may be used to further a variety of goals, and fostering faith is one of them. It is important, however, to recognize that "faithful" narratives, like any intellectual constructs, are dependent upon a mercurial and fickle historical record and are subject to disruption and change. To base a testimony on such shaky ground is perilous indeed.

Triumphalism, Folly and Complexity

In an effort to demonstrate how our current ideas about "faithful" history may be unnecessarily narrow and overburdened with what should rightly be the work of faith itself, I would like to suggest three general narrative types into which most scholarship on Mormonism fits. The narrative of triumphalism refers to what many may term apologetic history. This narrative emphasizes continuity between the past and current interpretations of Latter-day Saint doctrine as well as continuity between the past and present cultures in which the historian works. A triumphalist narrative depends upon a traditional, linear view of history as a progressive force building to an ultimate climax. This is the kind of narrative we are asked to construct when leaders call for a history that acknowledges the "hand of the Lord in every hour and every moment of the Church from its beginning until now."[19]

Implicit in this request, and central to the structure of the triumphalist narrative, is the notion that a triumphalist narrative is very much a narrative of the moment. Put another way, telling the story of the Church through the use of this narrative structure depends upon what sorts of things are considered faith promoting by Church authorities at the time the narrative is constructed. This tendency is an example of what historian David Hackett Fischer refers to as "the fallacy of presentism," in which "the antecedent in a narrative series is falsified by being defined or interpreted in terms of the consequent."[20] Stories emphasizing the centrality of the doctrine of plural marriage and the heroic suffering endured at the hands of an intolerant government dominated nineteenth-century biographical and historical accounts of the triumphalist category. Today, this element of nineteenth-century Mormon history, as told in official publications, is peripheral to the story if it enters into it at all. Historians trying to reconstruct the plural marriages of Joseph Smith, or the deeply spiritual ordeals experienced by many Latter-day Saint leaders as they grappled with the Manifesto of 1890, for example, may even be deemed "faith destroyers." This points up the functional nature of triumphalist history while simultaneously belying the notion that "faith-promoting" history represents *the* normative discourse for people of faith. Far from being a timeless history for the ages, "faithful history" is in fact contingent upon current doctrinal interpretations and emphases as well as by cultural mores.

Insistence on continuity makes for some interesting dilemmas. Another example may serve to illustrate this point. Although Joseph Smith received the Word of Wisdom in early 1833, it was not until 1921 that adherence to certain selected portions of this law was required for a person to obtain a temple recommend.[21] Today it is a centrally important aspect of Mormon life. The difficulty comes when we attempt to read back into the past the same understanding of the Word of Wisdom that is common today. We should not be uncomfortable with the fact that such spiritually sensitive men as Brigham Young and Joseph F. Smith regularly used tobacco and alcohol at certain points in their lives. Nor should we have a problem with the presence of spittoons in early photographs of the various council rooms in the Salt Lake Temple. The triumphalist narrative, however, has no room for such discontinuities. To deal with the realities of Word of Wisdom adherence (or lack thereof) during the nineteenth century is often seen as an attempt to weaken or destroy faith, or to portray Church leaders as mere men rather than as prophets of God. This, of course, is a false dichotomy. In a church that is founded upon the idea of continuing revelation, it seems strange indeed that we should feel compelled to ignore the fact that such a process of continuing revelation *must* result in historical discontinuities. The attempt to emplot Mormon history without discontinuities is to "prune away the 'dead' branches of the past and to preserve the green buds and twigs which have grown into our contemporary world."[22] These very facts could be emplotted in a way that emphasizes the importance of revelation and living prophets, the ability of the Church to adapt to changing circumstances, and the powerful influence for good in the lives of diverse men and women the Church as it was measured in their own day.

On the other side of the ideological spectrum, although nearly identical in structure to the narrative of triumphalism, is the narrative of folly. The only structural difference between the two is that discontinuity is emphasized in the case of the latter in an effort to embarrass the Church. Like the triumphalist narrative, the narrative of folly relies on the idea that continuity is the mark of "truth" or legitimacy. Such works rely upon two faulty assumptions central to both of these narrative structures. The first faulty assumption is that historical inquiry holds the key to ultimate truth; the second is that both structures are based on "the fallacy of presentism" discussed above, in which the historical texts themselves undergo a "brutal impoverishment," an incarceration in the prison of presentism.[23] Each group thus finds it necessary to leave out large sections of historical source material to avoid endangering its activist agenda. It is also interesting that many authors that fall in to the folly category often had previous allegiance to the Church and express a subtle yet distinct sense of disillusionment in their work. As anthropologist James C. Scott has pointed out, "the disillusioned [believer] is always a greater threat to an established religion than the pagans who were never 'taken in' by its promises . . . the anger born of a sense of betrayal implies an earlier faith."[24] As an illustration of the structural similarities between these narrative structures and the people who produce them, consider the following example. If the Church decided tomorrow, through revelation, that plural marriage was again necessary, it would do no good to construct narratives that emphasize the importance of plural marriage to nineteenth-century Saints in an effort to embarrass the Church (because the discontinuity would be repaired). Similarly, the triumphalists would no longer need to ignore the importance of plural marriage for past generations of Saints because continuity between that element of the past and the present position of the Church had been restored. The most telling element of this scenario, however, is that both sides would simply swap emplotment points. Triumphalists would gravitate toward the old accounts of the centrality plural marriage theology, and those constructing a narrative of folly would publish post-1890 Church positions, which de-emphasized the importance of the principle, in an effort to illuminate the new discontinuity. This hypothetical is clearly exaggerated for effect, but it works to demonstrate the either/or situation that exists within these two narrative structures. Many members of the Church, as well as their most vociferous critics, have come to see this dichotomy as the only possible way to view the Mormon story. In the process, "faithful" history has come to be identified, unnecessarily in my opinion, with the triumphalist narrative. The theory of emplotment that figures so prominently in postmodern thought provides a different and broader definition for the possibilities of faithful history.

Ironically, the complex narrative represents the best attempt to date to explore the Latter-day Saint past without attempting to either prove or disprove its ultimate reality. This narrative structure emphasizes contextualization instead of continuity or discontinuity. Its name is drawn from the tendency of this type of scholarship to acknowledge the infinite number of potential narratives that may be fashioned from various parts of the historical record as well as the idea that no person or event is easily categorized. The complex narrative may also be used to nurture faith, promote rationalism, or to further any of a myriad of other agendas. The difference is that the author of a complex narrative recognizes the synthetic nature of his creation and allows that others may appropriate the historical record to craft other narratives that may be complementary or contradictory without endangering ultimate truth, which is beyond the power of the historian.

These narratives are essentially functionalist, although not necessarily designed to openly advocate a certain position (although they may do that as well). Writers and readers of such narratives must recognize that the narratives, intentionally or not, serve as "social authorizing practices" and as such may be used by a wide spectrum of individuals seeking to buttress certain positions.[25] In no case, however, should the author of such a narrative attempt to claim his or her version of the past is the only definitive and legitimate interpretation. Scholars of faith who employ this narrative technique can afford to take such a position because they acknowledge, as I discussed earlier, that "the reason for the hope within us" is not verifiable in the empirical sense. The historian of faith should not be discouraged then, by discontinuities of either a cultural or historical nature.

So how does one recognize a piece of scholarship based on the model of narrative complexity? Perhaps the most important characteristic is that of contingency. Both narratives of folly and of triumphalism share an essentially teleological structure. That is that they each conceive of history (in the case of triumphalism) or historiography (in the case of folly) as moving toward an ultimate goal. Because both are heavily presentist as well, the teleological endpoint is grounded in the moment the writing is performed. Thus the elements of the Church that survived to the present are seen as the important elements in the past as well. The result is that many elements that may have been of great importance in the past are ignored because they are of little or no importance to the present. The narrative of complexity, however, emphasizes contingency; it attempts to avoid reading into the past the eventual outcomes that inform the present. An example is an order here. A comparison of Latter-day Saint theology in 1832 and 1844 would yield a host of disparities. Most scholars of Mormonism on all sides would agree with that. If, however, an examination of 1832 theology alone occurred, the narrative of complexity would avoid reading back into the 1832 source material developments from 1844. Similarly, such a historian would not dismiss elements of that theology that would later be discarded.

One common example of the tendency to fail in this regard is the anachronistic reading many "faithful" Mormon historians give to section 132 of the Doctrine and Covenants. Evidence regarding the circumstances surrounding the writing of this revelation as well as sermons and writings of nineteenth-century Saints indicate that they understood the revelation in the context of plural marriage. Saints of this period routinely used the terms "celestial" and "plural" marriages interchangeably. It was from this text, in fact, that many nineteenth-century leaders argued for the centrality of plural marriage to Latter-day Saint theology. The document itself was consistently referred to as the revelation on the "eternity and plurality of marriage."[26]

In 1890, Wilford Woodruff declared that through revelation the Lord had ordered the practice of plural marriage discontinued. Since that time, Latter-day Saint exegesis of section 132 has stressed the importance of eternal monogamous marriage and routinely ignores both the historical context from whence the revelation sprang as well as the ways that nineteenth-century Saints interpreted the revelation. In the generally balanced *Story of the Latter-Day Saints,* this new emphasis is quite clear. The authors describe the revelation first as teaching the eternity of the marriage covenant, and they point out that "in Nauvoo, many husbands and wives were sealed by the power of the priesthood in the temple."[27] This is true, of course, but this is presented before the implications of the document regarding plural marriage are discussed. The resulting impression left with the reader is a thoroughly modern interpretation of section 132 as a revelation on eternal marriage with some mention of polygamy, when in fact in the nineteenth century it was understood as something close to the opposite of that. Given the Latter-day Saint belief in continuing revelation, the current interpretation of section 132 may be the more correct in an absolute sense, but this does not imply that an anachronistic, presentist construction of nineteenth-century Latter-day Saint thought on the matter is justified.

Conclusion

In 1986, professor Ronald Walker wrote that it was not until his involvement with the examination of the Hofmann documents that he "scrutinized" Joseph Smith in an academic sense.[28] Scholars of my generation, faithful believers in the mission of Joseph Smith raised in the shadow of the New Mormon history and the historiographical aftermath of the Hofmann affair, cannot readily identify with Walker's experience. For many of us, the innocence of the triumphalist narrative is inadequate to express the rich texture of the Mormon story as we have come to understand it from our earliest forays into the literature. Walker set the agenda for this new generation when he wrote that "apparent historical conflicts must be weighed, somehow harmonized, and molded into a new, more complex understanding."[29] The role of the new faithful historians is to do just that; not to create or destroy faith, because we cannot, but to create narratives of faith true to the sometimes conflicting stories that the past asks us to tell.

Notes

1. Some scholars have suggested that a dichotomy exists between facts that may be disturbing, such as the level of involvement of the Church in Mountain Meadows Massacre, and the way those facts are narrated. I believe that the issue is not really whether it is certain facts themselves or the way those facts are narrated that are potentially

damaging to faith, because I do not believe that these issues can be separated. We simply cannot know facts outside of some form of structured narrative.

2. Robert E. Van Voorst, *Readings in Christianity* (Stamford, Conn.: Wadsworth Publishing, 2001), 5.

3. Stuart Clark, *Thinking with Demons: The Idea of Witchcraft in Early Modern Europe* (Oxford: Oxford University Press, 1997), 5.

4. While this statement may seem obvious, even to the point of naiveté, to many scholars, it is certainly not obvious to scholars who assert, based on this historical record, that the Book of Mormon is, on the one hand, true and that "the evidence . . . strongly suggests that Joseph Smith was not, and could not have been, the author of the Book of Mormon" and validates "the spiritual conviction of millions of Latter-day Saints," and on the other hand scholars who, based on the same record, blithely conclude that "virtually all critical scholars agree that Joseph did not discover the Book of Mormon, but rather created it." Clearly these scholars believe that scholarship has the power to prove and disprove issues of faith. For the first quotation, see Daniel C. Peterson, "Not Joseph's, Not Modern," in Donald W. Parry, Daniel C. Peterson, and John W. Welch, ed., *Echoes and Evidences of the Book of Mormon* (Provo, Utah: FARMS, 2002), 219. For the second quote, see Robert M. Price, "Joseph Smith, Inspired Author of the Book of Mormon," in Dan Vogel and Brent Lee Metcalf, ed., *American Apocrypha: Essays on the Book of Mormon* (Salt Lake City: Signature Books, 2002), 324.

5. J. M. Roberts, *The Penguin History of the World* (New York: Penguin, 1976, 1992), 661. Roberts points out that while Enlightenment thinkers assumed their critical position to be the normative, neutral approach to knowledge, the Enlightenment itself "had its own authority and dogma," a point which postmodern thinkers base much of their theory upon.

6. Peter Hamilton, "The Enlightenment and the Birth of Social Science" in Stuart Hall and Bram Gieben, eds., *Formations of Modernity* (Oxford: Open University and Polity Press, 1992), 21–22.

7. Whitney R. Cross, *The Burned over District: The Social and Intellectual History of Enthusiastic Religion in Western New York, 1800–1850* (Ithaca, N.Y.: Cornell University Press, 1950), 80.

8. Susan Juster, *Disorderly Women: Sexual Politics and Evangelicalism in Revolutionary New England* (Ithaca, N.Y.: Cornell University Press, 1994), 195.

9. For a discussion of the various stages of the Enlightenment in America and how those stages shaped and were shaped by popular and religious culture, see Henry F. May, *The Enlightenment in America* (Oxford: Oxford University Press, 1976).

10. Jon Butler, "The Dark Ages of American Occultism, 1760–1848," in Howard Kerr and Charles Crow, eds., *The Occult in America: New Historical Perspectives* (Urbana: University of Illinois Press, 1983), 71. This perspective also helps explain both Joseph Smith's interest in folk magic as well as his desire to distance himself from it later in life; it wasn't because it was unbecoming of a prophet, it was embarrassing because by the 1830s and 1840s it was no longer considered "rational."

11. May, *The Enlightenment in America*, xi.

12. Steven C. Harper, "Infallible Proofs, Both Human and Divine: The Persuasiveness of Mormonism for Early Converts," *Religion and American Culture: A Journal of Interpretation* 10 (2000), 101. Harper provides an excellent and convincing argument for the coexistence of "supernatural origins and reasonable theology" among Mormon converts in the earliest phase of Mormon development. For an account of the shift away from the compatibility of religious experience and rationalism, see Leigh Eric Schmidt, *Hearing Things: Religion, Illusion and the American Enlightenment* (Cambridge, Mass.: Harvard University Press, 2000). Schmidt argues that the Enlightenment, as understood and explained by such prominent thinkers as Thomas Paine, ultimately held that "the divine could not possibly speak or call or intercede in a world of such predictable laws, such mathematical order, such perfect rationality," 7.

13. Daniel Lazare, "False Testament: Archaeology Refutes the Bible's Claim to History," *Harper's Magazine* (March 2002), 41. This piece embodies many of the arguments about modernist, "intellectual" approaches to religion that I make in this paper and which pervade popular intellectual thought.

14. Quoted in Clara V. Dobay, "Intellect and Faith: The Controversy Over Revisionist Mormon History," *Dialogue: A Journal of Mormon Thought* 27 (spring 1994): 97.

15. Hayden V. White, *Tropics of Discourse: Essays in Cultural Criticism* (Baltimore: Johns Hopkins University Press, 1978), 106. White argues that history is more similar to literature than science because "like literature, history progresses through the production of classics, the nature of which is such that they cannot be disconfirmed or negated, in the way that the principle schemata of the sciences are" (89).

16. Richard Sherlock, "The Gospel Beyond Time," in George D. Smith, ed., *Faithful History* (Salt Lake City: Signature Books, 1992), 51.

17. *Teachings of the Presidents of the Church: Harold B. Lee* (Salt Lake City: The Church of Jesus Christ of Latter-day Saints, 2001), 39.

18. I choose this example because it has been debated over for years among scholars of all beliefs and provides a clear case of a centrally important religious event that is extremely unclear in terms of the historical record.

19. Boyd K. Packer, "The Mantle is Far, Far Greater than the Intellect," *BYU Studies* 21 (summer 1981), 263.

20. David Hackett Fischer, *Historian's Fallacies: Toward a Logic of Historical Thought* (New York: Harper Torchbooks, 1970), 135. Fischer would doubtless bristle at the use of his work in an article lauding the selective use of postmodernism, but a key element of my argument is that the nonexistence of a normative metadiscourse in no way invalidates Fischer's assertion that historical narratives should exhibit internal consistency and logic for heuristic purposes.

21. Thomas G. Alexander, *Mormonism in Transition: A History of the Latter-day Saints, 1890–1930* (Urbana: University of Illinois Press, 1986), 264.

22. Fischer, *Historian's Fallacies*, 135.

23. Michael Adre Bernstein, *Forgone Conclusions: Against Apocalyptic History* (Berkeley: University of California Press, 1994), 2. Bernstein makes a fascinating argument about the lack of emphasis on human "free agency" in presentist and triumphalist narratives that should resonate with a Latter-day Saint audience.

24. James C. Scott, *Domination and the Arts of Resistance: Hidden Transcripts* (New Haven: Yale University Press, 2000), 107. Scholars that could, in my opinion, fit into this category include, among many others, Fawn M. Brodie, Dan Vogel, and Brent Lee Metcalf.

25. Susan E. Henking, "Does the History of Religion and Psychological Studies Have a Subject?" in Diane

Jonte-Pace and William B. Parsons, eds., *Religion and Psychology: Mapping the Terrain* (London: Routledge, 2001), 60.

26. For examples of how Mormons identified section 132 with plural marriage, see *Journal of Discourses*, 26 vols. (Liverpool: F. D. Richards, 1855–86), 6:362, 13:194, 16:166, 17:360–361, 21:10–11, 22:127, 25:309, 26:122, 26:340. Also see Stephen C. Taysom, "A Uniform and Common Recollection: Joseph Smith's Legacy, Polygamy and the Creation of Mormon Public Memory, 1852–2002," *Dialogue: A Journal of Mormon Thought* 35 (fall 2002), 113–44.

27. James B. Allen and Glen M. Leonard, *The Story of the Latter-day Saints*, 2d. rev. edition (Salt Lake City: Deseret Book, 1992), 184. Allen and Leonard's work was groundbreaking and bold when it appeared in the mid-1970s, and it remains today the only reliable synthesis of Church history. My mention of this work is intended to demonstrate that nearly thirty years later, it may be time to rethink some of the issues that Allen and Leonard dealt with in an earlier generation. This same idea is presented in the historiographical work *Mormon History*, of which James Allen is a co-author: "Since the writing of *The Story of the Latter-day Saints* . . . no similar work has appeared to take advantage of the new Mormon history's fecundity." Ronald W. Walker, David J. Whittaker, and James B. Allen, *Mormon History* (Urbana: University of Illinois Press, 2001), 96.

28. Ronald W. Walker, "Joseph Smith: The Palmyra Seer," *BYU Studies* 24 (fall 1984): 460.

29. Walker, "Joseph Smith: The Palmyra Seer," 462.

Telling the Story of Mormon History: The James Moyle Oral History Program

Matthew K. Heiss

My topic today is the Church Archives oral history program. Who better to tell the story of Mormon history than the people who are living it? I'd like to begin with a story from Malawi, Africa.

On May 20, 2000, three archivists from the Church Archives, including myself, and a professor from Brigham Young University were driven down a dusty road in central Malawi by a missionary couple from Salt Lake City, Dan and Berylene Frampton (fig. 1). Elder Frampton told us that the village we were about to visit is inaccessible during the rainy season. I understood why when we barely made it out of the first dry gully we had come to. The first time the Framptons were shown how to find the village, Sister Frampton, the navigator, took copious notes. She gave me a copy, which included such instructions as: "just before you come to the police barricade . . . there is a dirt road to the right. . . . Turn down that road and set your meter on 00. . . . At 3.68 kilometers you will pass through a small gully. . . . At 8.3 kilometers you will come to an intersection of trails with a large pointed termite mound at about 11:00 o'clock. Turn right."[1] The place we were going to is very remote.

After about forty-five minutes, we turned a corner and were met by a chorus of young people who were singing and standing off to the side of the road under a small baobab tree (fig. 2). A short time later, we saw a single dwelling with a bowery built to the side of it. People were milling around. We had reached our destination—Sitima Village. As we got out of the car, a group of women and children gathered around. They began singing. My co-worker Mike Landon turned on his tape recorder while I took pictures. The song they were singing is a Christian hymn. If you have a discerning ear, you can pick out the word *Yesu*, which means Jesus. Later that night, we played the tape for a young hotel worker, who said it was a Christian song sung in Chechewa, the local language.

Mike stopped recording, rewound the tape, and played it back for the women, who were thrilled to hear their voices. One sister grabbed the tape recorder and began to sing along. Soon, the youth choir entered the village, marching in formation and still singing, presumably to greet the white strangers.

That day it was our privilege to meet and interview McFarlane Phiri (fig. 3), the man who introduced the Church into the country of Malawi. Phiri's story is a great story of how he first learned about the Church in 1978 and waited fourteen years to be baptized, all the while preparing the people of his village to hear and accept the gospel. We recorded several oral histories with those who spoke English. We attended a special worship service. On this day, the first chapters of the Book of Mormon translated into

Fig. 1. Elder and Sister Frampton, May 2000.

Fig. 2. Malawian youth choir, May 2000.

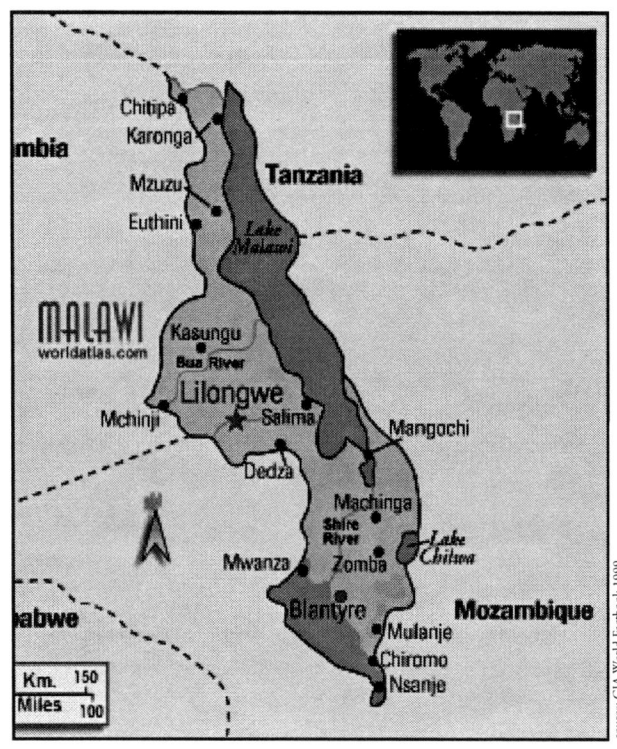

Map of Malawi, Africa.

Fig. 3. President McFarlane Phiri, May 2000. President Phiri played an important role in bringing the gospel to people in Sitima Village.

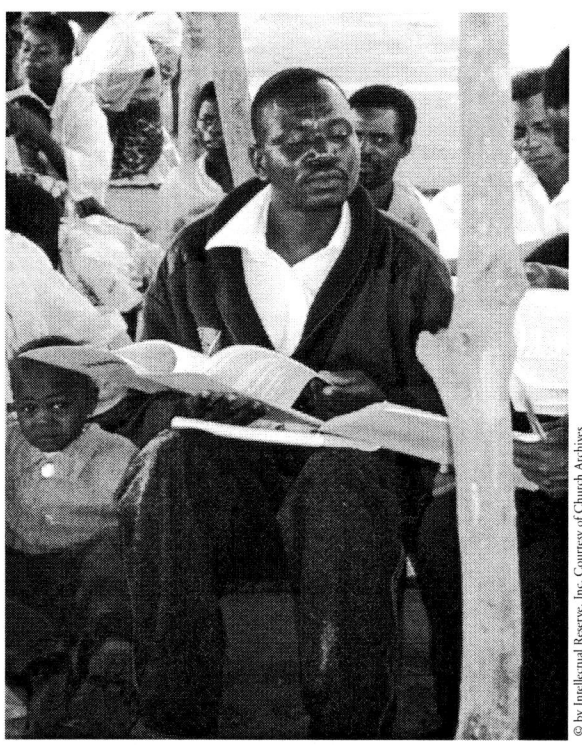

Fig. 4. Malawian Saints in Sitima Village receiving sections of the Book of Mormon, May 2000.

Chechewa were introduced (fig. 4). The branch presidency (fig. 5) took us to their future building site, where we saw the mound of bricks they had made for their chapel (fig. 6). The kids thought it was pretty cool when we stuck the stickers from our cassettes to their arms and heads (fig. 7). And we were treated to a traditional Malawian meal prepared by the branch Relief Society (fig. 8).

But we are not here to talk about the history of the Church in Malawi; rather, I was asked to tell you something about the oral history program of the Church Archives. This conference is about telling the story of Mormon history. Let me repeat the rhetorical question: Who better to tell the story of Mormon history than the people who are living it?

The year 2002 was the thirtieth anniversary of the Church Historical Department's use of oral history as a tool to capture Church history. In early 1972, Davis Bitton, who had just been appointed assistant Church historian, suggested that oral history be considered as a documentation tool to be used in the newly established History Division. The idea was accepted by the History Division, but then came the question: How do we organize an oral history program?

Wanting to do things in the right way, the History Division offered a fellowship to Gary Shumway, a history professor at California State University at Fullerton, who was a member of the Church with a vast oral history background. Shumway came to Salt Lake City for six weeks and gave a series of training seminars. He also recorded some of the first interviews in this newly established program. His interviewees included A. Theodore Tuttle, Delbert L. Stapley, and Spencer W. Kimball.

After the program was established, William Hartley of the History Division was given responsibility for oral history. Hartley was the director of oral history until late 1976. In November 1976, Gordon Irving was appointed as Hartley's successor. He served as director and coordinator of oral history until 1991. Since 1991, oral history has been under the umbrella of the Church Archives Collection Development.[2]

Finished oral history transcripts in the Church Archives bear the imprint of the James Moyle Oral History Program. Moyle was born in Cornwall, England, in 1835. He joined the Church in 1852 while living in Plymouth, and, with the help of the Perpetual Emigrating Fund,

Fig. 5. Sitima Village branch presidency, May 2000.

Fig. 6. Building site for the first LDS chapel in Sitima Village, May 2000.

Fig. 7. Children of Sitima Village, May 2000. These children show off the "cool" cassette stickers they were given by the Church archivists.

Fig. 8. Relief Society sisters of Sitima Village, May 2000. These sisters prepared a traditional Malawian meal for the Church archivists.

came to Salt Lake City in 1854. He worked as a stonecutter and mason on the Lion House and on the Salt Lake Temple grounds. Recognizing his construction skills, Brigham Young asked Moyle to be a construction superintendent for the Salt Lake Temple, which he was until 1890, the year he died. James Moyle was the father of James Henry Moyle.[3]

When James Henry Moyle died in 1945, he left a substantial financial legacy that led to the 1947 establishment of the James Moyle Genealogical and Historical Association. The association's purpose was to further family genealogical work and to do "any other worthy act, or perform any other worthy service by means of which the memory of James Moyle and his wives Elizabeth Wood Moyle and Margaret Cannell Moyle will be perpetuated."[4] By the early 1970s, members of the Moyle family were looking for other meaningful endeavors that could be supported by the association. They felt that the remainder of the money should somehow perpetuate history as well as the memory of James Moyle.

About this time, it became clear to members of the History Division that oral history was an expensive proposition. Additional funding was needed to facilitate transcription and editing of the interviews that were being recorded. Davis Bitton knew members of the Moyle family and became aware of the James Moyle Genealogical and Historical Association fund. After the History Division had worked with the family on other historical projects, including a biography of James H. Moyle, Bitton suggested that the family fund the Church's oral history program.[5]

The family agreed, and all our interviews since late 1976 have borne the Moyle name. The fund was vital to the survival of our oral history program, especially during its infancy in the 1970s and early 1980s. By 1980 we had recorded 1,530 interviews. That number had grown to 2,309 by the end of 1990. As of March 1, 2002, Church Archives employees have recorded 4,795 interviews in at least seventeen different languages, including Hungarian, Mongolian, Cantonese, Japanese, Dutch, Romanian, Finnish, and Russian.

Church Archives oral history interviews are transcribed in the Church Office Building by Church-service missionaries and secretaries. When interviews are recorded in foreign languages, Brigham Young University students with unique language and typing capabilities are hired to transcribe these interviews. After transcription, the texts are checked against the tape recordings to verify transcription accuracy. They are further proofread and edited to ensure readability. The finished transcripts, the audio recordings, and the electronic texts are all preserved in the Church Archives. Throughout this editorial process, we make it a priority to preserve the interviewee's voice and the feeling or spirit that was present during the interview.

The recording of oral histories is part of the Church Archives's overall mandate "to keep the church record and history" (D&C 47:3) of "things that transpire in Zion" (D&C 85:1) "which shall be for the good of the church, and for the rising generations . . . forever and ever" (D&C 69:8). But oral history is only one of the ways we document the story of Mormon history. We are actively developing the Church Archives collection by acquiring and preserving photographs, personal narratives, journals and diaries, letters and emails, and the official reports and files from Church departments and local units. The question naturally arises: If we are collecting all of these documents, why go out and record interviews, which are very expensive and time-consuming to process?

There are several reasons why we choose to use oral history as a documentation tool. Let me mention two. First, it has been my observation that very few first-generation Latter-day Saints are personal record keepers. (Since the passing of Spencer W. Kimball, how many of us who have been in the Church for generations are keeping good journals?) Often, these recent converts have their hands full planning sacrament meetings and holding presidency meetings, let alone doing home teaching, researching their family history, going to the temple, and reading scriptures that may or may not have been translated into their own languages. Our interviewing such people ensures that their voices and their stories will be preserved.

A second reason for recording oral history is that sometimes the written records that are sent to the Church Archives are inadequate. Oral history is a good way to fill in the gaps. Let me give you an actual example. The annual reports from a district in India for the years 1986 to 1988 read: "Historical Events: 1986. No historical

Fig. 9. Matt Heiss recording President Phiri's oral history, May 2000.

events." "Historical Events: 1987. Nothing." "Historical Events: 1988. No major historical events."[6] Now, I don't know about you, but I suspect that there was a lot more than "nothing" going on in this district during those three years. First and foremost, I would be interested to know what it meant and what it took to be one of the first Latter-day Saints in India. Luckily, during these years, Gordon Irving, a co-worker of mine, recorded an oral history with Raj Kumar, who was a counselor in the India North District presidency and had been president of the New Delhi Branch. Something from this important early period has been preserved because of oral history.

Selecting interview candidates is sometimes easy and sometimes difficult. When we are going into a nation where the Church is new, the selection is fairly easy. For example, a co-worker and I traveled to Moldova in June 1999. In five days, we had interviewed twenty-four of the forty-eight Latter-day Saints in that country. We concentrated on the earliest converts, the only returned missionary, and all the local leaders. In places where the Church is well developed and the pool of interview candidates is large, we have to make difficult decisions about whom to interview. We generally select a wide range of interviewees—people who represent all facets of the Church, from General Authorities and other priesthood leaders to auxiliary presidents, ordinary Church members, recent converts, old-timers, and even a few less-actives and members of other faiths who have been instrumental in helping the Church become established in a given area.

Conclusion

Earlier I said that one of our editorial goals was to preserve the spirit that was present at the interview and the voice of the person being interviewed (fig. 9). Let me conclude by returning to Malawi. I mentioned that McFarlane Phiri was baptized after waiting fourteen years. Following his baptism in 1992, perhaps because of the remoteness of his village, there was a period of about six years, from 1993 to 1998, when he had no contact from the Church. He felt abandoned and forgotten. One of the last things President Phiri asked me to do as I was leaving Sitima Village was to keep people from forgetting him and his village ever again. So, as partial fulfillment of the promise I made, let me have President Phiri conclude this presentation with his testimony:

> Especially in my testimony, I'm happy that I belong to this Church. I'm happy that the Lord loves me. I'm happy that I'm one of the persons, who, through the Lord's help, invited this church to come to Malawi. And I know that many people would be helped through the message which this church teaches. And I know that the Lord will continue to lead us, will continue to bring more to the understanding of the gospel, today, tomorrow, and forever. And I know that many people will be [baptized] in this country. And I know that if the Lord wills, we are going to have the temple in this country. And I know that we are going to have a stake sometime through the Lord's help. Amen.

Who better to tell the story of Mormon history than the people who are living it?

Notes

1. Dan Doxey Frampton collection, 1999–2000, Church Archives, Family and Church History Department, Salt Lake City, Utah.

2. Davis Bitton, oral history, typescript, 153–57, Church Archives, The Church of Jesus Christ of Latter-day Saints, Salt Lake City; Gordon Irving, oral history, typescript, preface, Church Archives; see also William Hartley, oral history, typescript, Church Archives.

3. See Alice Evelyn Moyle Nelson, *The Generations of James Moyle* (Salt Lake City, Utah: The James Moyle Genealogical and Historical Association, 1976), 27–29.

4. From the Moyle sheet in front of each Church Archives oral history.

5. See Bitton, OH, 154–55; Irving, OH, 126–30; and Hartley, OH.

6. New Delhi India District, Singapore Mission, annual historical reports, 1986–1988, 1990, 2001, Church Archives, Family and Church History Department, Salt Lake City, Utah.

Education in Pioneer Utah: A Quantitative Approach

Tally S. Payne

The education of children in pioneer Utah was an integral part of creating a viable frontier society. Though historians have told the story of The Church of Jesus Christ of Latter-day Saints or Mormon educational history using a number of different research techniques, the application of quantitative methods yields a unique view of this particular facet of Mormon history. By employing a large data set gathered from the 1870 U.S. Census to calculate school attendance rates and patterns, Mormon educational history can be dissected from a new perspective.

Early Church leaders vocally stressed the importance of education and set high goals for their territorial Utah school system. Joseph Smith was well known for his dictum: "The glory of God is intelligence" (D&C 93:36, 182). And Brigham Young said, "Learn! Learn! Learn! Continue to learn, to study by observation and from good books."[1] When the Latter-day Saints were camped on the Missouri River in 1847, Brigham Young issued an epistle counseling that the Saints

> should improve every opportunity of securing at least a copy of every valuable treatise on education . . . to gain the attention of children, and cause them to love to learn to read; and also every historical, mathematical, philosophical, geological, astronomical, scientific, practical, and all other variety of useful and interesting writings, maps, etc.[2]

In 1850, Utah's Secretary of State Willard Richards summarized the high goals for the Mormon education system when he spoke to the chancellor and regents of the University of Deseret:

> Raise the standard of intelligence so high that mortals cannot overreach you, and make the ascent so gradual and easy that all may attain unto it; for'ere long the world will be looking to you as the Queen of science, kings and nobles will become your patrons, their sons and daughters will be educated under your fostering care, and from hence the sun of science will impart its golden beams to earth's remotest bounds.[3]

Church leaders emphasized the importance of education from the earliest phases of their new society.

But the frontier was, after all, a tough place to start a school system with a "standard of intelligence so high that mortals cannot overreach you." In fact, Charles S. Peterson asserts that pioneering life did not necessarily agree with education and many "Mormons lived under conditions unconducive to learning until at least 1910."[4] The frontier, with its lack of textbooks, teachers, schoolhouses, school funding, and supplies, virtually prohibited a "Zion-like" education system. Thus, though education was emphasized and supported by the Church doctrine and leaders, schooling in pioneer Utah began under adverse circumstances.

The dichotomy between having extremely lofty educational goals pitted against almost insurmountable frontier challenges has drawn researchers into a fray. On one side, the "traditionalist" view holds that having lofty goals was the stronger force; the pioneers were dedicated to education and built a strong, exemplary school system in the territory of Utah. Representing the traditionalist position, Brigham Young Academy president George Brimhall claimed in a 1913 meeting of the National Education Association that Utah schooling had never known a "backwoods era."[5] Another traditionalist Mormon historian, Milton Lynn Bennion, believes that during the pioneers' "period of isolation and severe trial, they did not forget the education of their children, which they considered almost equally essential to their physical existence."[6] Edward Anderson also presents a traditionalist view: "The leaders of the Church have ever been firm friends of true education, and their efforts . . . have been nobly seconded by the Saints as a community."[7] Anderson's history, as well as other traditionalist histories, were written after the early 1920s when Utah schools surpassed many other states' educational attainments.[8] In sum, the traditionalist histories assume that Utah's high achievements by the 1920s resulted from educational excellence during the pioneer era.

The opposing, "non-traditionalist" view is expressed in more recent literature whose authors suggest that pioneer education was anything but ideal. These historians contend that territorial Utah schools and students lagged behind their eastern counterparts because frontier life simply did not support scholasticism. According to Frederick S. Buchanan,

> When we examine the development of public schooling in Utah during the half century which elapsed between the initial settlement by Mormon pioneers in 1847 and the granting of statehood in 1896, it is not obvious that a smooth developmental process of growth occurred.[9]

Another study by John Monnett also indicates that early Mormon education was not as exemplary as tradition holds. Monnett observes:

> In spite of Mormon rhetoric toward education, most early territorial schools were of low grade with few academic standards suggested and little central direction given. A constant lack of financial support to schools contributed to a lack of prestige among teachers and, consequently, to a lack of competent school personnel.[10]

Finally, Charles Peterson's non-traditionalist view of early Mormon schooling concludes that pioneer "teachers were poorly trained" and territorial Utah schools were taught only for short periods.[11]

This paper quantitatively tells the story of education in pioneer Utah and reveals that the empirical evidence does not fully support either of the polarized claims; Latter-day Saints had neither a picture-perfect school system nor a disorganized, unattended scattering of schools. Comparing quantitative findings to the Church leaders' high goals for education, studies of education in particular American communities, and the achievements of contemporary American students illustrates that although nineteenth-century Utah's school system was not flawless, the pioneers had overcome many frontier obstacles and made remarkable progress by 1870.

Data

The quantitative analysis of pioneer education relies on a data sample drawn from the manuscripts of the 1870 U.S. Census. The sample is a complete enumeration of several townships in the territory of Utah, including the following: Corinne, East Weber, Fillmore, Fountain Green, Logan Ward Four, Manti, Mill Creek, Nephi City, Payson, Richmond, St. George, and Salt Lake City Wards Four, Five, Seven, Eleven, Fifteen, and Nineteen. The townships represent nine different counties and are a geographically diverse sample of the rapidly growing population in the territory of Utah in 1870. The complete sample contains 13,491 individual observations and 5,191 children between the ages of five and twenty.[12] This group is considered to be "school age" for the study.

The census of 1870 recorded whether a child had attended school at any time during the preceding year. This school attendance measure does not indicate how long a child attended school nor the type of school attended. Despite its limitations, this variable—and its link to recorded personal, family, and household data—provides a comprehensive source of quantitative information about school attendance in the nineteenth century.[13]

TABLE 1

Territorial Utah School Attendance by Age and Gender

Age	Female Total	In School	%	Male Total	In School	%
5	217	17	7.8%	217	23	10.6%
6	211	48	22.7%	230	50	21.7%
7	194	74	38.1%	200	65	32.5%
8	174	63	36.2%	194	87	44.8%
9	200	99	49.5%	197	88	44.7%
10	212	159	75.0%	211	150	71.1%
11	179	133	74.3%	189	138	73.0%
12	196	153	78.1%	217	165	76.0%
13	197	146	74.1%	169	126	74.6%
14	145	101	69.7%	171	119	69.6%
15	138	88	63.8%	126	78	61.9%
16	130	70	53.8%	140	76	54.3%
17	108	39	36.1%	111	57	51.4%
18	93	28	30.1%	125	56	44.8%
19	73	13	17.8%	93	29	31.2%
20	46	6	13.0%	88	24	27.3%
Total	2513	1237	49.2%	2678	1331	49.7%

Source: 1870 U.S. Census Manuscripts

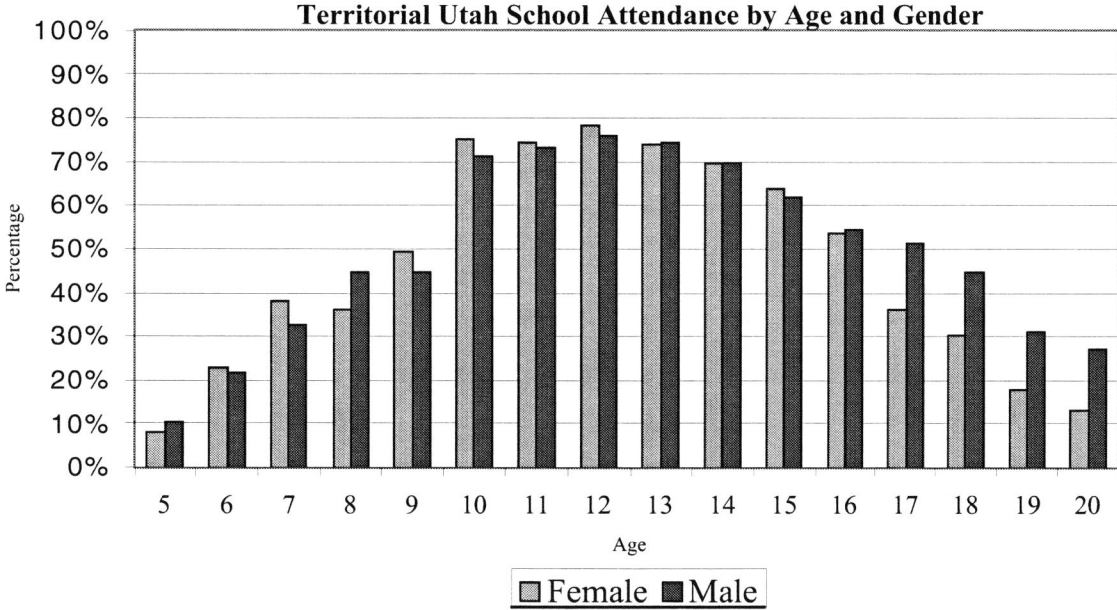

Fig. 1. Territorial Utah school attendance by age and gender. Taken from 1870 U.S. Census Manuscripts.

Attendance Rates and Patterns in Pioneer Schooling

The calculation of school attendance rates produces valuable information about nineteenth-century Utah education. Table 1 presents pioneer school attendance rates broken down by age and gender. Figure 1 depicts the same attendance rates graphically. Viewed graphically, the regular, bell-shaped pattern of the early Utah school attendance rates emerges. Before age ten, the majority of both males and females were not in school. Females did, however, attend school in slightly greater numbers than males prior to age twelve. The school attendance curve peaks within the middle age group, the children between ages ten and fourteen. Approximately 74.5 and 72.9 percent of females and males in the middle age group attended school in 1870. After age sixteen, the attendance rates of females declined more rapidly than males, leaving 13 percent of twenty-year-old females in school while 27.3 percent of twenty-year-old males attended school in 1870. Overall, just under half of the potential pioneer students in the sample data (49.2 percent of females and 49.7 percent of males) attended school at some point during the year of 1870; this preliminary statistical finding does not convincingly support the traditionalist or non-traditionalist position.

Figure 2 summarizes the patterns in school attendance rates according to the ethnicity and nativity of pioneer children. A child's ethnicity is considered the birthplace of his/her mother,[14] which is categorized in three groups: U.S.-born, foreign English-speaking, and foreign non-English-speaking.[15] Overall, almost 62 percent of the children had immigrant mothers. Of those immigrant mothers, over 80 percent spoke English while the other 20 percent emigrated from non-English-speaking countries, such as Sweden or Denmark. The nativity of a child is the child's birthplace, which is categorized similarly.[16] Both the ethnicity and nativity of a child affected school attendance rates in pioneer Utah.

In the sample, the total number of foreign-born mothers was substantially larger than the number of foreign-born children. Therefore, many of the pioneer children were first-generation Americans. Higher-generation American children, those with U.S.-born mothers, attended school in considerably higher proportions than children of foreign-born mothers. Children of foreign non-English-speaking mothers had an attendance rate of 41.9 percent while 45.5 percent of children whose foreign-born mothers spoke English attended school during 1870.

Less than a fifth of the school-age children in the sample data were foreign born. Of the

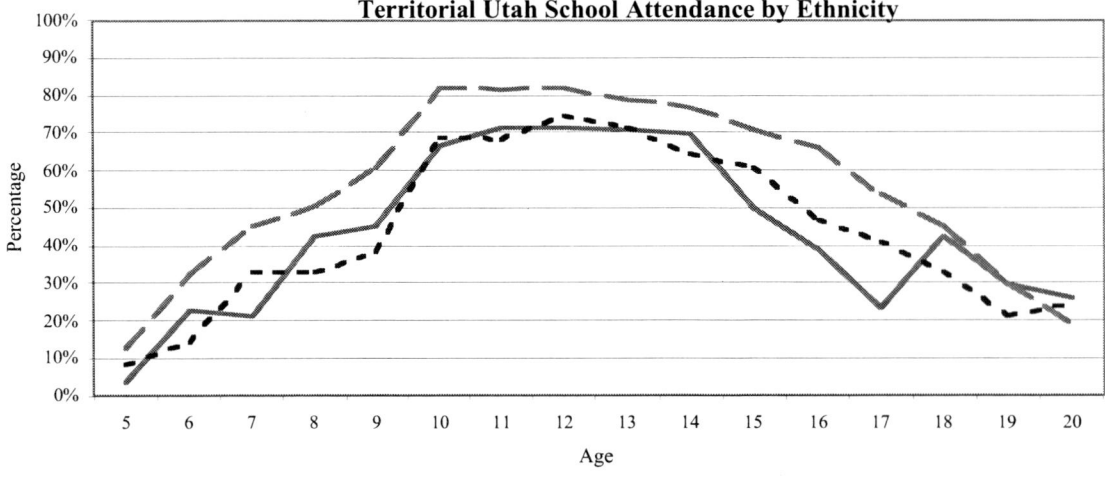

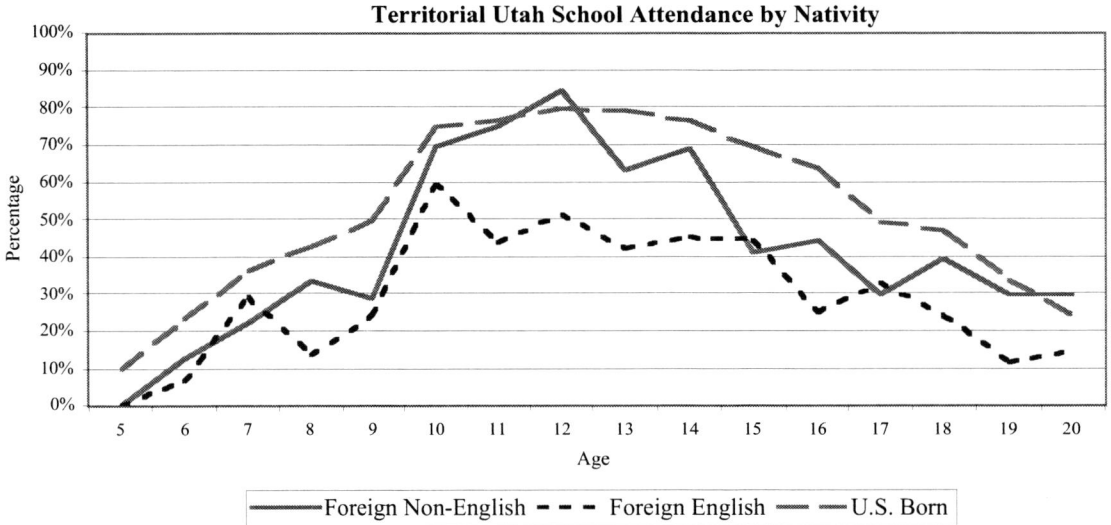

Fig. 2. Territorial Utah school attendance by ethnicity and territorial Utah school attendance by nativity. Taken from 1870 U.S. Census Manuscripts.

foreign-born group, less than a third of the children could not speak English. The three nativity groups—U.S.-born, foreign English-speaking, and foreign non-English-speaking children—attended school in different proportions. The U.S.-born children had the most regular pattern of school attendance and generally attended school in greater numbers than their foreign-born counterparts. However, at one point, the foreign-born children who could not speak English had the highest attendance rate of the three groups: 84.2 percent of foreign non-English-speaking twelve-year-olds attended school compared to 79.4 and 51.3 percent of U.S.-born and foreign English-speaking children, respectively. This foreign non-English-speaking bias towards school attendance is not apparent when considering a child's ethnicity. Yet, when considering a child's nativity, more foreign non-English-speaking children attended school at nearly all ages than those foreign-born children who could speak English.

Presumably, one of the primary motivations for these foreign children to attend pioneer schools was to learn English while the foreign children from England, Ireland, and other English-speaking countries abroad were far less likely to attend school in 1870. According to historian Carl F. Kaestle, "The presence of so many culturally alien people in antebellum America greatly reinforced the use of emerging public schools to teach children a common English language."[17] David B. Tyack indicates that the majority of school administrators and teachers "believed the schools should integrate the immigrant into American society."[18] This tendency to employ public schools in Americanizing foreigners extended to territorial Utah where schools also were used to bond the population together through a common English language. For example, Marin Kristin Nielson emigrated from Denmark with her husband Andrew. They settled in Sanpete County, and "[a]fter she learned English, . . . she decided to teach her children in her own home school."[19] Like the Nielsons, foreign non-English speaking children may have attended school in greater proportions than foreign English-speaking children to learn the language and adapt to their new life in Utah.

Many characteristics of a child's household tended to affect school attendance. For instance, literacy was recorded in the 1870 census as whether a person could not read, could not write, or could not do either.[20] Living in a household with an illiterate parent changed a Utah child's propensity to attend school in 1870. Table 2 summarizes pioneer school attendance by the literacy of parents. Note that the vast majority of Utah children had literate parents; just 11 percent of the children sampled were in households with an illiterate mother or father. That 11 percent of children, however, was far less likely to attend school than children of literate parents. While there was one anomaly in which the ten-year-old children of an illiterate parent had an impressive school attendance rate, parent illiteracy generally curbed school attendance in pioneer Utah. This table lends some strength to the traditionalist point of view. Because the literacy rate in Utah was extremely high, and because parent literacy contributes positively to school attendance, Utah schooling had a boost from the types of pioneers who settled the area.

Household wealth was also correlated to nineteenth-century school attendance due to both direct and indirect schooling costs. Many of the early Utah schools operated through direct fees to students. Territorial School Superintendent Robert L. Campbell related in the 1865–66 school report that

> [t]uition fees range from four to six dollars per quarter for teaching the common branches. . . . School-houses have been (with few exceptions) built by voluntary contribution. There being no school fund available, fees for tuition are paid by the parents or guardians of the pupils, except in a few districts, where, in conformity with the provisions of last year's school bill, a tax was assessed for that purpose.[21]

Although the initiation of a school tax came with a territorial law in 1852, schools were not truly free or common until a free school law was passed in 1890.[22] Since there was a considerable direct cost to schooling in territorial Utah, the level of household wealth played a role in determining whether a child could attend school.

Indirectly, there was a large opportunity cost to attending school on the frontier. Children of wealthier households were spared more easily from farm work while children in poor households often needed to work to survive the

TABLE 2

Territorial Utah School Attendance by Parent Literacy

	Have Literate Parents			Have an Illiterate Parent			
Age	Total	In School	%	Total	% (of Total Children)	In School	%
5	383	37	9.7%	51	12%	3	5.9%
6	387	95	24.5%	54	12%	3	5.6%
7	341	128	37.5%	53	13%	11	20.8%
8	333	141	42.3%	35	10%	9	25.7%
9	349	169	48.4%	48	12%	18	37.5%
10	377	271	71.9%	46	11%	38	82.6%
11	326	244	74.8%	42	11%	27	64.3%
12	364	282	77.5%	49	12%	36	73.5%
13	333	250	75.1%	33	9%	22	66.7%
14	277	196	70.8%	39	12%	24	61.5%
15	236	149	63.1%	28	11%	17	60.7%
16	237	131	55.3%	33	12%	15	45.5%
17	198	89	44.9%	21	10%	7	33.3%
18	196	77	39.3%	22	10%	7	31.8%
19	146	38	26.0%	20	12%	4	20.0%
20	124	28	22.6%	10	7%	2	20.0%
Total	4607	2325	50.5%	584	11%	243	41.6%

Source: 1870 U.S. Census Manuscripts
Note 1: A child is considered to be in the "parent illiterate" category if either his/her mother or father was illiterate.

challenges accompanying the frontier lifestyle. One Mormon historian takes the relationship between wealth and schooling further and suggests that there was an anti-intellectual movement in territorial Utah related to the direct and indirect costs of schooling. Arthur Bassett notes,

> This anti-intellectual thrust generated from many sources, not the least of which was the problem of frontier economics. Children, who were viewed as a valuable economic resource, were needed in the fields and in the shops more than they were needed in the schools, where they were thought to while away their time, absorbing seemingly impractical information. The cost of schools, both in terms of time and money, seemed prohibitive to many of those who daily struggled to make a living on the frontier, men and women who placed more emphasis on work than education.[23]

Given this "frontier economics" argument, one would expect the empirical evidence to show that children in increasingly wealthier households attended school in greater numbers because the direct and indirect costs of school attendance were less prohibitive.

The calculations in Table 3 reinforce the expected positive relationship between household wealth and school attendance rates. After accounting for the children whose household heads did not list any amount of wealth in the census, the household head's wealth for the school-age children is categorized in quintiles. The lowest quintile contains households with a combined value of real estate and personal property between $1 and $500. The most wealthy quintile of households valued their real estate and personal property at over $2200 in 1870. The attendance rates by age and household heads' wealth range from a low of 2.9 percent to a high of 90.1 percent. The discrepancy in attendance rates by household wealth is especially noticeable with fifteen-year-old children for whom school attendance rates varied nearly 53 percent between the children in the lowest and highest wealth categories. At age fifteen, just 27.3 percent of children in households without any wealth attended school while 80 percent of children in the wealthiest households attended school at some point during the year. Beginning with children in the households without any wealth, the overall school attendance rates by quintile were 31.0, 44.8, 49.3, 51.7, 58.1, and 61.1 percent. The steady increase in attendance rates across quintiles is consistent with the expected relationship between household wealth and school attendance, and the

TABLE 3

Territorial Utah School Attendance by Household Head's Wealth
School-age Children's Household Heads' Wealth by Quintile

Age	No Wealth Listed Total	% In School	$1–$500 Total	% In School	$501–$700 Total	% In School	$701–$1100 Total	% In School	$1101–$2200 Total	% In School	$2201 and over Total	% In School
5	55	5.5%	107	8.4%	69	2.9%	70	11.4%	62	9.7%	71	16.9%
6	54	13.0%	95	22.1%	85	22.4%	79	24.1%	59	27.1%	69	23.2%
7	49	22.4%	95	36.8%	60	28.3%	82	37.8%	50	46.0%	58	37.9%
8	55	20.0%	78	32.1%	58	43.1%	49	51.0%	69	47.8%	59	52.5%
9	50	30.0%	91	40.7%	55	47.3%	79	51.9%	61	54.1%	61	57.4%
10	50	50.0%	92	68.5%	68	72.1%	67	83.6%	60	73.3%	86	83.7%
11	44	52.3%	83	74.7%	55	76.4%	68	69.1%	60	78.3%	58	86.2%
12	62	54.8%	89	71.9%	59	76.3%	69	82.6%	70	87.1%	64	89.1%
13	53	52.8%	62	64.5%	53	69.8%	67	79.1%	60	83.3%	71	90.1%
14	56	50.0%	60	66.7%	51	76.5%	49	69.4%	53	69.8%	47	89.4%
15	33	27.3%	58	62.1%	23	52.2%	49	67.3%	51	72.5%	50	80.0%
16	51	31.4%	50	46.0%	38	57.9%	38	50.0%	45	68.9%	48	72.9%
17	43	20.9%	46	32.6%	31	58.1%	32	40.6%	29	58.6%	38	63.2%
18	28	14.3%	45	31.1%	31	41.9%	42	38.1%	32	46.9%	40	55.0%
19	39	15.4%	31	16.1%	12	50.0%	29	17.2%	28	39.3%	27	33.3%
20	26	11.5%	25	28.0%	15	26.7%	18	11.1%	22	45.5%	28	14.3%
Total	748	31.0%	1,107	44.8%	763	49.3%	887	51.7%	811	58.1%	875	61.1%

Source: 1870 U.S. Census Manuscripts

pattern makes it impossible to dismiss the non-traditionalist, "frontier economics" theory.

Along the same lines, whether a child was employed outside the home also influenced 1870 school attendance rates. Naturally, the number of children with occupations increased with age, yet overall only 10.6 percent of sampled children had a job listed in the census records. Though the sample size of "occupied" children is relatively small compared to "not-occupied" children, comparing the school attendance rates between the two groups reveals large differences. Table 4 illustrates that within every age group except the twenty-year-old children, the unemployed children had higher attendance rates than those with occupations. Almost 15 percent of fourteen-year-olds were working at some job in 1870. Forty-five percent of eighteen-year-olds were employed. And, by age twenty, the majority of children sampled were employed. School attendance trends by employment follow a very regular, predictable pattern, excluding age twenty. Whether children were required to work because of "frontier economics" or chose to work, those with occupations attended school in smaller percentages than pioneer youth who were "at home" or "at school," which bolsters the non-traditionalists' arguments.

Figure 3 presents school attendance rates by residential location. Of the nine counties represented in the sample data, Weber had the lowest attendance rate. Weber County's school attendance of 14.1 percent compares unfavorably with the attendance rates of all the other counties. Interestingly, Salt Lake County, which was the most urbanized county in the sample, had the next lowest attendance rate at 41.2 percent. Cache and Washington Counties led in school attendance with 66.5 and 68 percent of children attending school in those locations.

One might expect that the extent of urbanization in certain areas would account for differences in school attendance by county. An "urban effect" might exist if children in more populated areas had greater opportunity to attend school because (1) more schools were built in urban areas, (2) urban children lived within reasonable travel distance to schools, or (3) urban children were less likely to live in subsistence farming households that required children to work. One test for an urban effect is to compare school attendance in Salt Lake County to attendance in the other counties.[24] However, as Salt Lake County does not have the largest school attendance rate, urbanization is probably not driving the residential differences in attendance.[25]

An alternative explanation for the vastly different residential location attendance rates is the duration of settlement for each township sampled. In this case, one would expect that counties settled the earliest would have the most widespread and successful school systems by 1870. In theory, those counties that had been settled recently in 1870, on the other hand, might not have had time to develop extensive school systems. This duration of settlement explanation is explored in Figure 4. The nine counties in the data set are first ranked according to their settlement dates, starting with the earliest.[26] Then, the counties are ranked by the magnitude of their school attendance rates. The ranks are then plotted against each other to see the relationship between a county's settlement date and school attendance in 1870.

Figure 4 illustrates that, in contrast to the expected relationship, counties that had been settled for fewer years exhibited greater propensities to school children. Though the relationship is not tight, Figure 4 suggests that school attendance did not increase as a settlement endured. Weber

TABLE 4

Territorial Utah School Attendance by Child's Employment

	No Occupation			Occupied		
Age	Total	In School	%	Total	In School	%
5	434	40	9.2%	0	0	--
6	441	98	22.2%	0	0	--
7	394	139	35.3%	0	0	--
8	368	150	40.8%	0	0	--
9	396	187	47.2%	1	0	0.0%
10	422	309	73.2%	1	0	0.0%
11	362	268	74.0%	6	3	50.0%
12	403	315	78.2%	10	3	30.0%
13	347	264	76.1%	19	8	42.1%
14	269	195	72.5%	47	25	53.2%
15	214	149	69.6%	50	18	36.0%
16	193	116	60.1%	77	30	39.0%
17	143	68	47.6%	76	28	36.8%
18	119	47	39.5%	99	37	37.4%
19	91	24	26.4%	75	18	24.0%
20	44	7	15.9%	90	23	25.6%
Total	4640	2376	51.2%	551	193	35.0%

Source: 1870 U.S. Census Manuscripts

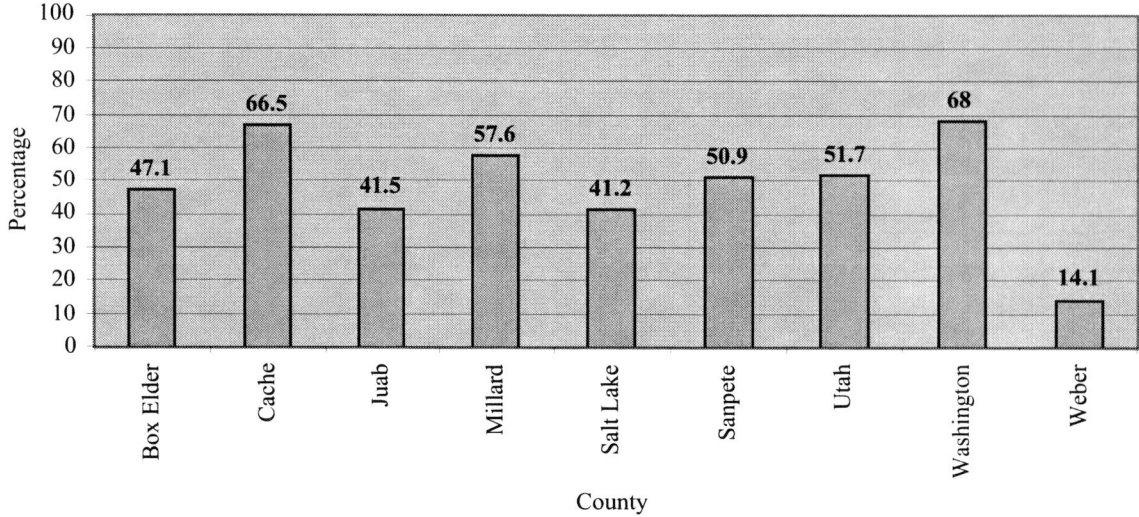

Fig. 3. Territorial Utah school attendance by county. The school attendance rates depended heavily upon the townships sampled withing the county. For example, Washington county could have different attendance rates if towns other than St. George were sampled. Taken from 1870 U.S. Census Manuscripts.

County, although it was one of the first areas settled in territorial Utah, had the lowest attendance rate. The more recently settled townships in Cache and Washington Counties had the highest school attendance rates. The pattern indicates that children in the newer settlements were more likely to have attended school in 1870.

Neither the urban effect nor duration of settlement effect explains the variation in school attendance by location. It is reasonable to suppose that schooling differences among the counties may be explained by the predominance of localism in territorial school governance and development. Small administrative units developed early Utah's school systems; local leaders passed laws or changed schooling procedures in their respective places.[27] Thus, the effectiveness of school systems in 1870 could have varied considerably depending upon the local leadership and local support for schooling.

Washington County is a good example of how school effectiveness could fluctuate because of local leadership. The data sample includes the inhabitants of St. George, Washington County, Utah in 1870. The settlement was fairly new as it was settled by a large group of families called to the "Cotton Mission" in 1861. Though the St. George population grew quickly and was over eleven hundred in 1870,[28] it was still no match for Salt Lake City in terms of urbanization. Yet, St. George had the highest school attendance rate of the sampled areas in 1870. Because of the "small school district pattern that was common in Utah for more than half a century," the remarkable progress of St. George's schools could be attributed to the school-supportive leadership in that area.[29] The company called to settle St. George "left Salt Lake City early in November [1861] with George A. Smith, Erastus Snow and Orson Pratt, three stalwarts, as their leaders."[30] In addition, St. George was settled under a very deliberate plan by Brigham Young: "families were selected so as to insure the communities with the right number of farmers, masons, blacksmiths, businessmen, educators, carpenters, as needed."[31] As St. George was settled carefully under the leadership of "stalwarts" who also were known to be great supporters of education,[32] the new town developed an extensive education system rapidly.

Other locations, despite being more urban or settled earlier than St. George, did not have educators called to the settlement under stalwart leaders who emphasized the importance of education. Thus, given the case of St. George, the county attendance rates calculated for 1870 may not vary

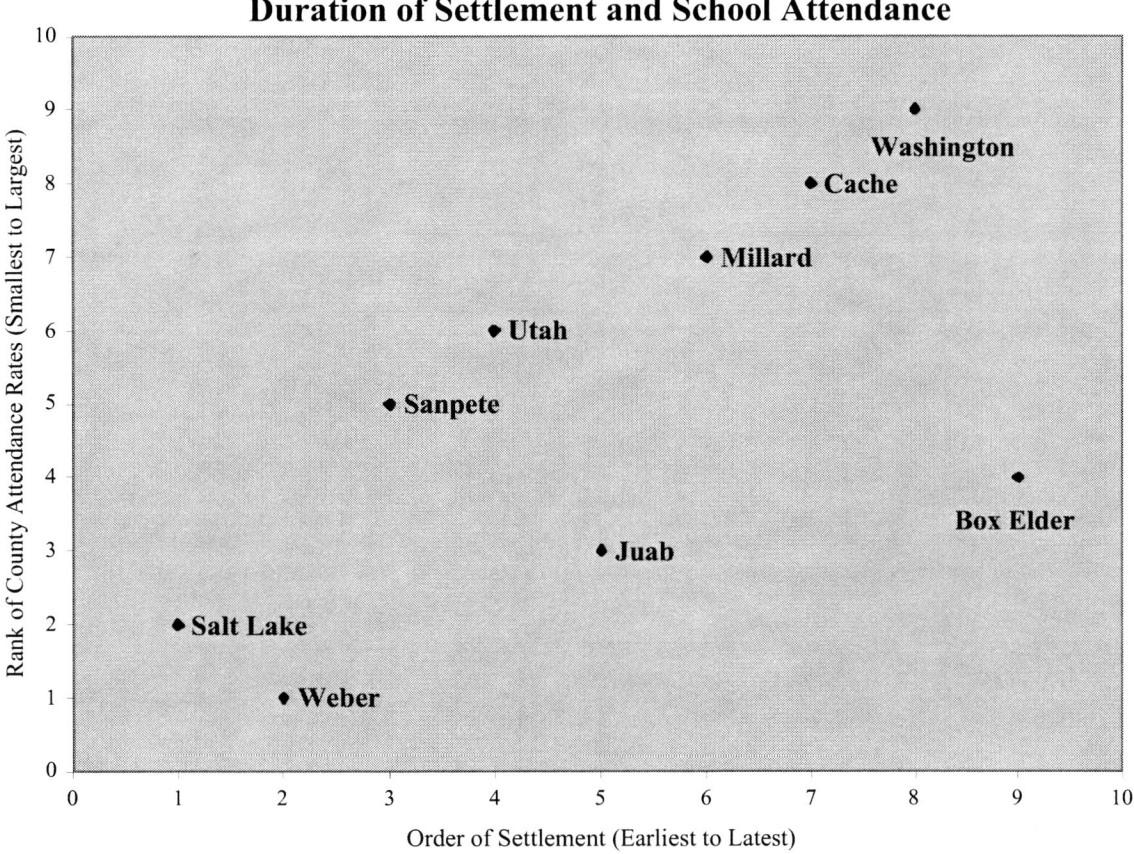

Fig. 4. Duration of settlement and school attendance. Taken from 1870 U.S. Census data; James B. Allen and Glen M. Leonard, *The Story of the Latter-day Saints* (Salt Lake City: Deseret Book, 1992); and Richard H. Jackson, ed., *The Mormon Role in the Settlement of the West* (Provo, Utah: Brigham Young University Press, 1978).

due to urbanization or settlement dates; the differences may result from the diverse personalities involved in schooling on the local level. Families, teachers, and school administrators in the settlements could have varied greatly in their support for schooling, which is difficult to quantify. In this case, the lack of a quantifiable explanation for the large variance in county attendance rates actually lends credence to the traditionalist position. Lofty goals, aggressive personalities, and the pioneering spirit created a foundation for territorial Utah's education system.

Benchmarking Pioneer School Attendance Rates and Patterns

The story of historical pioneer schooling cannot be told quantitatively without a contextualization of the statistics. Knowing that just under half of the potential pioneer students (49.2 percent of females and 49.7 percent of males) attended school at some point during 1870 is virtually meaningless without also knowing whether the Utah attendance rates were less than, equal to, or greater than the attendance rates of other nineteenth-century students. Benchmarking the statistical results from the territory of Utah against several different standards shows how Utah measured up to its own goals and how it compared to other contemporary locations. The pioneer school attendance rates and patterns discussed above are compared to (1) the lofty educational goals of Latter-day Saint prophets and leaders, (2) the results from quantitative studies of select American communities' schools, and (3) the educational attainments of contemporary American students.

Lofty Educational Goals of Latter-day Saint Prophets and Leaders. The historical empirical evidence shows that early Utah schooling did not meet the idealistic schooling goals of

Church leaders. By 1860, Brigham Young said of the educational progress among the pioneers:

> I give it as my opinion that . . . you will find more schools in the midst of this people, notwithstanding their poverty, their drivings, sufferings and persecutions, and more persons that can read and write, in proportion to our population, than in any other place on this earth.[33]

Brigham Young's statement is overly optimistic. Economist Claudia Goldin reports that 57 percent of the five- to seventeen-year-old American population enrolled in school during the 1869–70 school year.[34] Using the census data, 51.4 percent of the five- to seventeen-year-old Utah population attended school at some point during the same year. Although the Utah attendance rate is commendable for the frontier, the 51.4 percent is below average; there were certainly many "place[s] on this earth" with more schooling.

Some evidence supports Brigham Young's claim about literacy. Of the 13,491 Utah people sampled from the 1870 census manuscripts, 9.6 percent indicated they were illiterate. Territorial Utah's 90.4 percent literacy rate is extremely respectable given that America's white population had only 88.5 percent literacy and just 80 percent of the total population was literate in 1870.[35] In addition, America's literacy rate compared favorably with nations around the world. According to economist Albert Fishlow, the first available literacy statistics of 1840 show that "only Scotland and Germany are comparable [to the United States], with England and France much farther behind."[36] Territorial Utah did have high literacy rates, although, like school attendance, the rates may not have been as high as Brigham Young claimed.

Brigham Young also asserted that the territory of Utah had "more schools . . . in proportion to [its] population" than other places. Though Brigham Young did not clarify his statement precisely, his assertion can be evaluated from a few different angles. If President Young was referring to Utah's having more schools in proportion to its student population, his statement was inaccurate. In 1870, the *Report of the Commissioner of Education* indicates that even other frontier territories had more schools in proportion to their student populations than the Utah Territory. Idaho and Montana each had 15 schools compared to Utah's 243. However, those 15 schools in Idaho and Montana served approximately 23 and 12 pupils per school, respectively. While Utah's number of schools seems impressive, it had far more students than these other territories; there were over 61 pupils per pioneer Utah school in 1870.[37]

On the other hand, Brigham Young's claim is more accurate if he was referring to Utah's having more schools in proportion to its total population. Of the four organized frontier territories that reported school statistics completely in 1870, Utah led in the number of schools in proportion to total population.[38]

In addition, Brigham Young simply may have been implying that the accessibility of Utah's schools was superior to school accessibility in other places. If this were the case, one would expect Utah's school attendance to surpass other locations' attendance rates. For the 1869–70 school year, Massachusetts reported that, on average, 75 percent of the school-age population attended.[39] In comparison, just 44 percent of the school-age Utah children were in "average daily attendance."[40] The discrepancy in average school attendance suggests that schools may not have been as easily accessible in Utah as they were in Massachusetts and other places.

Willard Richards's 1850 statement about raising "the standard of intelligence so high that mortals cannot overreach you" also embodies the optimistic view towards the newly-created education system to which many Utah leaders subscribed.[41] Unfortunately, the educational idealism and high standards of Willard Richards for the University of Deseret went unrealized. The University of Deseret operated only four terms, ceasing its operations for almost twenty years while the Latter-day Saints were isolated in the Utah Territory.

At other times, the Church leaders were more realistic about the shortcomings of their frontier education system. Historian Ronald Walker states, "[Brigham Young] acknowledged that the Saints stood in need of intellectual improvement. Many were ignorant and mean in manner, and Utah in fact could boast of only 'a few learned men and a few good scholars among the women.'"[42] Though empirical evidence does not reveal how many pioneers could be considered "learned," the data suggest that many frontier youth "stood in need of intellectual improvement" largely because many were not attending school.

Results from Quantitative Studies of Select American Communities' Schools. Utah's school attendance rates are less than stellar when compared to attendance rates calculated for select American communities. Several historical studies have focused on school attendance rates in eastern United States cities, using similar data from census manuscripts. Pioneer Utah's rates are below most of the school attendance rates presented in these studies, which implies that frontier education may have lagged behind eastern American education because of the unique challenges to educating children in the West.

Carl F. Kaestle notes that enrollments for "eight towns in Massachusetts in 1860, for Washtenaw County, Michigan, in 1850, and Chicago in 1860 [were about] 85 to 90 percent at the prime common-school ages, seven to thirteen, for all ethnic and occupational groups."[43] The attendance rate for twelve-year-old children in territorial Utah, the group with the largest attendance rate, was approximately 77 percent. Utah attendance for the other ages fell significantly below the 85 to 90 percent witnessed in more settled areas.

David W. Galenson performed economic analyses with historical census data from Boston and Chicago. For school-age males in Boston in 1860, Galenson discovered three features:

> high attendance at early ages, with one quarter of boys in school at age 4, and three fifths attending at 5; high peak attendance, with more than 90 percent in school from 7 through 12; and a sharp decline in the mid-teens, with attendance falling from more than 80 percent at 14 to less than 20 percent at 17.[44]

These figures on school attendance from Boston not only surpass the Utah school attendance rates, they are also from a decade earlier. Utah boys in the younger age groups attended school in much smaller numbers than the boys Galenson analyzed (See Table 1). However, for the oldest age group, the sharp decline in attendance rates is a visible trend for both Utah and Boston boys.

Galenson's Chicago education study produced school attendance trends for the "urban frontier" of America.[45] He estimates that

> [b]oys began to enter school in large numbers at age 5, when just over a third attended, and two thirds were in school at 6. Enrollment rates reached 80 percent at age 7, and remained between 80 and 90 percent through age 12. A gradual decline occurred at older ages, as more than half of the boys were still in school at 16, and one fifth at 18.[46]

While the "urban frontier" school attendance trends are a closer match to Utah's trends, pioneer children were schooled in smaller numbers than Chicago youth. At age six, just 21.7 percent of boys attended school in Utah compared to the two thirds who attended Chicago schools. Enrollment rates were about 80 to 90 percent for seven- to twelve-year-old Chicago boys while Utah school attendance rates peaked at just 76 percent for twelve-year-old males. The school attendance for Chicago and Utah sixteen-year-old males is comparable: more than half of the boys were still in school in both places. Though Utah's schooling trends are somewhat similar to Chicago's, a large gap in attendance rates is apparent at nearly all ages. Furthermore, an even larger gap between the Chicago and Utah attendance rates could exist if Galenson had used 1870 data for Chicago.

Carl F. Kaestle and Maris Vinovskis studied schooling in eight Essex County, Massachusetts, towns from 1860 to 1880. They calculated attendance rates as a proportion of persons under twenty years old, whereas the Utah attendance rates consider only children ages five to twenty. The five Essex rural communities had an attendance rate of 70.4 percent in 1870 and the three urban communities sampled had an attendance rate of 53.3 percent.[47] The authors calculated attendance rates by age for 1860; in that year, attendance rates reached 100 percent for some ages in the rural areas of Massachusetts and over 95 percent in the urban communities.[48] The attendance rates for early Utah are consistent with Kaestle and Vinovskis's discovery of a rural bias towards school attendance. However, Utah's general attendance rates are significantly below the attendance rates in nineteenth-century Essex County, Massachusetts.

Though more precise comparisons of pioneer Utah's school attendance rates are not possible, the comparisons that are available imply that pioneer Utah's schooling was not on par with education in eastern nineteenth-century communities.

Educational Attainments of Contemporary American Students. Despite not measuring up to Church leaders' standards nor schooling children

Table 5

Pioneer Utah Schools in Comparison: Territories, States, and the Nation in 1871–72

State	Public School Enrollment (%)	Average Attendance (%)1	Average School Term (Days)2	Pupil-to-Teacher Ratio3	Expenditures Per Pupil ($)4
Alabama	36.5	27.8	68.5	41	3.96
Arkansas	59.1	NA	NA	47	3.76
California	56.9	48.9	130	39	21.34
Connecticut	88.4	61.9	172.5	39	13.18
Delaware	39.8	NA	122	NA	NA
Florida	22.3	NA	93.2	42	NA
Georgia	9.4	6.3	55	NA	NA
Illinois	75.0	37.4	147	32	11.30
Indiana	72.7	45.3	116	38	7.75
Iowa	73.7	46.0	134	23	11.57
Kansas	64.3	37.1	108	28	6.70
Kentucky	NA	29.0	NA	NA	NA
Louisiana	37.2	28.4	130	NA	5.81
Maine	55.7	43.0	106.5	21	6.72
Maryland	41.9	20.4	180	51	10.50
Massachusetts	97.9	72.7	188	33	20.48
Michigan	73.2	44.4	150	25	10.19
Minnesota	66.9	34.5	138	26	8.23
Mississippi	36.6	26.2	110	42	7.79
Missouri	52.0	29.5	90	37	5.30
Nebraska	56.3	NA	74	19	18.55
Nevada	68.1	47.9	170	44	29.20
New Hampshire	94.1	63.7	84	19	6.44
New Jersey	63.7	32.6	178	58	14.02
New York	68.4	32.9	175	36	9.35
North Carolina	31.8	NA	80	26	NA
Ohio	66.0	38.1	152	32	9.62
Oregon	NA	41.1	90	NA	NA
Pennsylvania	85.5	55.0	120	45	9.99
Rhode Island	66.0	52.8	172	37	16.80
South Carolina	36.5	NA	120	35	3.70
Tennessee	NA	NA	NA	NA	NA
Texas	66.8	42.7	NA	57	9.57
Vermont	83.5	NA	120	17	8.11
Virginia	40.9	23.4	115	44	5.50
West Virginia	42.3	30.8	85	29	8.18
Wisconsin	63.2	NA	140	29	7.26
Territories					
Arizona	NA	20.6	120	NA	NA
Colorado	60.2	34.7	114	36	25.93
Dakota	50.0	NA	70	18	17.34
District of Columbia	49.1	36.7	200	59	30.86
Idaho	75.4	NA	103	24	12.16
Montana	NA	NA	NA	NA	NA
New Mexico	NA	NA	NA	NA	NA
Utah	59.1	44.6	147	47	NA
Washington	46.0	NA	120	22	NA
Wyoming	NA	NA	NA	NA	NA
Minimum	9.4	6.3	55	17	3.70
Maximum	97.9	72.7	200	59	30.86
Average	58.3	38.6	125	35	11.68
St. Dev.	19.2	13.5	36	11	6.96

Source: United States. Department of the Interior, Bureau of Education, Report of the Commissioner of Education for the Year 1872 (Washington, D.C.: GPO, 1873), 608–13. The data mostly corresponds to the 1871–72 schoolyear, although in a few cases 1870 data is reported. Earlier national education reports do not contain sufficient data to make comparisons.

Note 1: This figure is the average attendance per total number of school-age children.

Note 2: The commissioner reported length of school term in months and days. The conversion to days assumes one month is twenty school days.

Note 3: The pupil-to-teacher ratio is calculated as the total number of students enrolled per teacher.

Note 4: The expenditures per pupil are the expenditures per student enrolled.

in as great of numbers as eastern American communities, early Utah's education system was still progressing against the odds on the frontier. Table 5 presents several school quality measures that benchmark territorial Utah against other states, other frontier territories, and the nation around 1870.[49] Of the six territories that reported, Utah Territory had only the third highest school enrollment rate, although Utah's enrollment was greater than the national average. However, Utah actually had a higher attendance rate than the national average and the other territories that reported in 1870. Utah also offered a school term longer than the average school term in the United States. In contrast, the territory of Utah had a pupil-to-teacher ratio that was much worse than the national average and the other territories' class sizes. Unfortunately, Utah did not report its school expenditures that year, although in subsequent years its expenditures did not compare favorably to the national average or the other territories.[50] These measurements put pioneer Utah's education system in perspective.

Conclusion

The empirical evidence from 1870 illustrates that 49.2 and 49.7 percent of potential female and male pioneer scholars attended school during that year. School attendance increased with age and peaked at about twelve. After age twelve, the likelihood of attending school declined with each additional year. A child's gender did not affect school attendance significantly until after age fifteen, when female attendance fell off rapidly.

The U.S.-born children had the most regular pattern of school attendance and generally attended school in greater numbers than their foreign-born counterparts. However, at nearly all ages, non-English-speaking foreign children had a higher school attendance rate than those who could speak English. Having a foreign-born mother, whether English- or non-English-speaking, significantly reduced school attendance for the potential pioneer scholars. Higher-generation American children had the highest school attendance rates in territorial Utah. In addition to a child's ethnicity and nativity, other characteristics of a child's parents and household affected pioneer schooling. For example, having an illiterate parent negatively impacted school attendance in early Utah.

Household wealth and "frontier economics" played into 1870 school attendance as children in poorer households attended school in fewer numbers than children from wealthy households. The direct and indirect costs of school attendance were prohibitive. Furthermore, the frontier lifestyle often required children, especially the older children of Utah's households, to work outside the home. Those children with occupations attended school in smaller percentages than unemployed pioneer youth.

Residential location was another significant factor in the pioneer Utah schooling equation. Neither the urban effect nor duration of settlement effect explains the variation in county attendance rates; the differences probably are due to the prevalent localism and other non-quantifiable aspects of territorial school governance and development.

Benchmarking the statistical results from the territory of Utah against the high-reaching goals for Mormon education, the economic studies for different locations, and the education of contemporary American students reveals that the nineteenth-century pioneer education system was neither "Zion-like" nor inferior. Rather, the Latter-day Saints in territorial Utah started an education system from scratch in 1847 that by 1870 was better than the American average in school enrollment, school attendance rates, and length of school terms, though the Utah "standard of intelligence [was not] so high that mortals [could not] overreach" it.

In some ways, then, the non-traditionalists are correct: Utah education did have a backwoods era. The pioneer school system could not be characterized as ideal when the University of Deseret ceased operations, just 30 percent of five- to nine-year-olds attended any school, and when potential scholars like young Ellen Burton, instead of going to school, had to "help clear the farmland of oak brush, fight crickets, and plant and tend a garden and orchard" out of necessity.[51] This quantitative evidence supports the non-traditionalists and their claims that the Utah Territory had schools "of low grade with few academic standards."[52]

Yet other data substantiate the traditionalist view. The Latter-day Saint leaders and many pioneers were dedicated to education and built a strong education system. In 1870, Utah Territory had higher enrollment and attendance rates than the national average. In addition, Utah reported a school year that was longer than the average school year in the United States. Utah also boasted correctly about having extremely high literacy rates. These facts provide quantitative evidence favoring the traditionalist view of historical schooling in Utah.

Though in certain instances the evidence may point in one direction or the other, taken as a whole, the quantitative study of pioneer education is a story of two opposing forces essentially meeting in the middle. The traditionalists cannot ignore "frontier economics" and other equally challenging aspects of frontier life that hindered the building of an exemplary education system in pioneer Utah. The non-traditionalists cannot dismiss the powerful effect of having lofty goals and stalwart, school-supportive leadership. The data do not support fully the traditionalists who claim early Utah settlers built a picture-perfect school system nor the non-traditionalist historians who argue that Utah schools lagged behind their eastern counterparts. Utah's pioneer schools and students did not trail far behind educational developments in eastern United States. On the other hand, not even a majority of young pioneer children were learning their "three R's" in romantic schoolhouses on the frontier. Although early Utah's school system was not perfect, the hardworking pioneers made remarkable progress with their school system by 1870, considering that they molded it from the dry dust of the American frontier.

Notes

1. Ronald W. Walker, "Brigham Young on the Social Order," *BYU Studies* 28, no. 3 (1988): 41.
2. Brigham Young, quoted in M. Lynn Bennion, *Mormonism and Education* (Salt Lake City: Deseret News Press, 1939), 38–39.
3. Willard Richards, "Address: To the Chancellor and Regents of the University of the State of Deseret," April 17, 1850 (Salt Lake City: n.p., 1850), 12.
4. Charles S. Peterson, "The Limits of Learning in Pioneer Utah," *Journal of Mormon History* 10 (spring 1983): 66–67.
5. George Brimhall, quoted in Frederick S. Buchanan, "Education Among the Mormons: Brigham Young and the Schools of Utah," *History of Education Quarterly* 22 (1982): 436.
6. Bennion, *Mormonism and Education*, 38.
7. Edward H. Anderson, *A Brief History of The Church of Jesus Christ of Latter-day Saints*. 4th ed. (Independence, Mo.: Press of Zion's Printing and Publishing, 1928), 147–48.

8. A 1925 study ranked Utah second among the states using literacy rates, Army Alpha Scores, per capita circulation of prominent magazines, production of present leaders, and per capita income. See Buchanan, "Education Among the Mormons," 437.
9. Buchanan, "Education Among the Mormons," 439.
10. John D. Monnett, "The Mormon Church and its Private School System in Utah: The Emergence of the Academies, 1880–1892" (Ph.D. diss., University of Utah, 1984), 15–16.
11. Peterson, "The Limits of Learning in Pioneer Utah," 67.
12. After paring the sample down to include only the individuals between ages five and twenty, household heads and wives were taken out of the sample of potential school-age children. This reduced the sample from 5,443 to 5,191.
13. Many scholars have relied on this school attendance measure to study historical schooling. For example, see Steven Herscovici, "Ethnic Differences in School Attendance in Massachusetts: 1850–1860," *Social Science History* 18 (winter 1994): 471–96.
14. The child is linked to its mother whenever possible to avoid complications from polygamy, though polygamy is not a large factor in this sample. Of the 2,593 households sampled, just 152 (5.9 percent) were female-headed households with school-age children. Note that if those mothers were widows, the household information is correct. Less than 12 percent of the children lived in homes where the household head's occupation was "Keeping House" or "Housekeeper." Results from two separate regression analyses using this data indicate that polygamy did not affect dramatically the data and school attendance study. See Tally S. Payne, "Education on the American Frontier: The Territory of Utah in 1870" (master's thesis, Brigham Young University, 2000).
15. Foreign-born mothers were divided into English and non-English-speaking groups based on birthplace. This categorization is employed because the 1870 census did not record language ability.
16. Children were divided into three groups—U.S.-born, foreign English-speaking, and foreign non-English-speaking—using the same process described for grouping mothers.
17. Carl F. Kaestle, *Pillars of the Republic: Common Schools and the American Society, 1780–1869* (New York: Hill and Wang, 1983), 71.
18. David B. Tyack, *The One Best System: A History of American Urban Education* (Cambridge: Harvard University Press, 1974), 232.
19. James B. Allen, "Everyday Life in Utah's Elementary Schools," in *Nearly Everything Imaginable: The Everyday Life of Utah's Mormon Pioneers*, ed. Ronald W. Walker and Doris R. Dant (Provo, Utah: Brigham Young University Press, 1999), 360.
20. The census considered people who could read or write in any language, not necessarily in English, to be literate. See Herscovici, "Ethnic Differences in School Attendance," 491. I assume that because the same literacy standard was enforced in all census enumeration, the measure is a valuable variable related to school attendance even if it does not necessarily equate with true literacy (or with literacy in the English language). See Kenneth A. Lockridge, *Literacy in Colonial New England: An Enquiry into the Social Context of Literacy in the Early Modern West* (New York: Norton, 1974).
21. Robert L. Campbell, quoted in John Clifton Moffitt, *The History of Public Education in Utah* (Salt Lake City: Deseret News Press, 1946), 122.

22. Moffitt, *History of Public Education,* 120.

23. Arthur Ray Bassett, "Culture and the American Frontier in Mormon Utah, 1850–1896" (Ph.D. diss., Syracuse University, 1975), 32.

24. The multivariate logistic regression analysis of the data illustrates more decisively than simple attendance rates the lack of any "urban effect" since all of the other potential correlates to school attendance are held constant while calculating a child's propensity to attend school given his or her residential location. See Payne, "Education on the American Frontier."

25. Economic historians find a similar rural school attendance bias in a study of Essex County, Massachusetts, children in 1860. See Carl F. Kaestle and Maris A. Vinovskis, "From Fireside to Factory: School Entry and School Leaving in Nineteenth-Century Massachusetts," in *Transitions: The Family and the Life Course in Historical Perspective,* ed. Tamara K. Hareven (New York: Academic Press, 1978), 149–53.

26. This paper uses the settlement dates for the townships sampled within the county. For example, Nephi City is the township sampled from Juab County. Because Nephi was settled in 1851 after settlements in four other counties were established, Juab County is ranked "5."

27. Bennion, *Mormonism and Education,* 56.

28. Hazel Bradshaw, ed., *Under Dixie Sun: A History of Washington County* (Panguitch, Utah: Garfield County News, 1950), 437.

29. Moffitt, *History of Public Education,* 200.

30. Bradshaw, *Under Dixie Sun,* 294.

31. Bradshaw, *Under Dixie Sun,* 293–94.

32. For example, Orson Pratt had served as a Deseret University regent from 1850 to 1853, a university chancellor from 1859 to 1860, and was a professor of mathematics, astronomy, and moral science. He also held some of the early St. George classes in his home. See Martha Cragun Cox, "Autobiographical Sketch of Martha Cox, 1852–1932 [photocopy]," L. Tom Perry Special Collections Library, Harold B. Lee Library, Brigham Young University, Provo, Utah. Also see Paul B. Porter, "Psychology at the University of Deseret: A Century of Progressive Struggle," *Journal of the History of the Behavioral Sciences* 24 (January 1988): 41.

33. Brigham Young, quoted in John Clifton Moffitt, *A Century of Public Education in Provo, Utah* (Provo, Utah: n.p., 1944), 13.

34. Claudia Goldin, "A Brief History of Education in the United States," NBER Historical Working Paper 119 (Cambridge, Massachusetts, 1999), 29.

35. U.S. Bureau of the Census, *Historical Statistics of the United States: Colonial Times to 1970.* Bicentennial Edition, Part I. (Washington, D.C.: GPO, 1975), Series H 664–68, 382.

36. Albert Fishlow, "Levels of Nineteenth-Century American Investment in Education," *Journal of Economic History* 26 (December 1966): 418.

37. U.S. Department of the Interior, Bureau of Education, *Report of the Commissioner of Education Made to the Secretary of the Interior for the Year 1870* (Washington, D.C.: GPO, 1870), 28.

38. U.S. Department of the Interior, *Report of the Commissioner, 1870,* 28.

39. U.S. Department of the Interior, *Report of the Commissioner, 1870,* 504.

40. U.S. Department of the Interior, *Report of the Commissioner, 1870,* 331.

41. Richards, "Address: To the Chancellor and Regents," 12.

42. Walker, "Brigham Young on the Social Order," 41.

43. Kaestle, *Pillars of the Republic,* 107.

44. David W. Galenson, "Ethnicity, Wealth, and Urban School Attendance in the Mid-Nineteenth Century: The Case of Boston" (Unpublished paper, University of Chicago, 1995), 4.

45. David W. Galenson, "Educational Opportunity on the Urban Frontier: Nativity, Wealth, and School Attendance in Early Chicago," *Economic Development and Cultural Change* 43 (April 1995): 551.

46. David W. Galenson, "Determinants of the School Attendance of Boys in Early Chicago" (Unpublished paper, University of Chicago, 1995), 3.

47. Kaestle and Vinovskis, "From Fireside to Factory," 149.

48. Kaestle and Vinovskis, "From Fireside to Factory," 152.

49. U.S. Department of the Interior, Bureau of Education, *Report of the Commissioner of Education for the Year 1872* (Washington, D.C.: GPO, 1873), 608–13. Data in earlier reports are insufficient for comparisons.

50. U.S. Department of the Interior, Bureau of Education, *Report of the Commissioner of Education for the Year 1880* (Washington, D.C.: GPO, 1882), XXIV.

51. Allen, "Everyday Life in Utah's Elementary Schools," 359.

52. Monnett, "The Mormon Church and its Private School System in Utah," 15–16.

African Converts without Baptism: A Unique and Inspiring Chapter in Church History

E. Dale LeBaron

I wish to speak about a unique and inspiring chapter in Church history. It took place in recent years among the beautiful people of Africa. Too often we have misconceptions about Africa and its people. The media usually portrays Africans as primitive, starving, or at war with each other. One African official observed that the darkest thing about Africa is America's ignorance of it.[1]

There is much we can learn from our African brothers and sisters, who are among the great pioneers in this Church. President Gordon B. Hinckley said, "The days of pioneering in the Church are still with us; they did not end with covered wagons and handcarts."[2] Pioneers are those individuals who help establish the Church all over the world.

In 1853, nine years after the martyrdom of the Prophet Joseph Smith, missionaries were sent to Africa for the first time, but they only proselyted among the white people of South Africa. It was not until 125 years later, following the revelation on the priesthood in 1978, that the gospel was preached to *all* people of Africa.

However, thirty years before the revelation, Church leaders became aware of other Africans who were interested in the Church. By the 1950s, many letters were sent to Church headquarters from the West African nations of Nigeria and Ghana requesting literature and membership in the Church. The letters were written by devout Christians who had gained a testimony from the Book of Mormon or other Church literature.

What began as a comparative trickle of requests in the early 1950s became a flood by the 1960s. More letters requesting literature were received from Nigeria and Ghana than from all the rest of the world combined.[3] The Church responded by sending literature, but the demand for Church literature was so great that some Africans even established Latter-day Saint bookstores. However, since there were no priesthood holders to preside and provide priesthood ordinances, those asking for baptism were told, "The time is not yet. You must wait."

As they waited, they shared their knowledge and testimony of the gospel with others and organized congregations. It was reported that in the 1960s there were more than sixty congregations in Nigeria and Ghana, with more than sixteen thousand participants—none of whom were baptized.[4]

This was a paradoxical situation for the Church. With an army of missionaries eager to go to the ends of the earth to teach and baptize, there were thousands in Africa pleading to join the Church whom they were not able to baptize. As far as is known, nothing like this had occurred in this or in any other dispensation.

In 1960, President David O. McKay assigned South Africa mission president Glen G. Fisher to be the first Church representative to visit some of these unbaptized converts. He met with several groups in Nigeria, one of which had more than 5,600 participants in many congregations. President Fisher told the First Presidency that he received a royal welcome; they had been preparing themselves and their congregations for baptism for years. Their continued plea was, "We want the true church."[5] President Fisher was also impressed with their sincerity.

The intensity of their pleadings continued to increase, as reflected in this letter to President David O. McKay from a pastor in Nigeria who had made previous requests for baptism. He wrote:

> I have to say that my heart will not rest . . . until I achieve my objective to be a baptized member of The Church of Jesus Christ of Latter-day Saints, to receive the gift of the Holy Ghost, . . . and to be fully instructed in the gospel as restored [through the] Prophet, Joseph Smith . . . , in order to be able to preach the true gospel to my people and win for my Savior hearts that should otherwise perish in the darkness.[6]

In 1961, President McKay assigned LaMar Williams, secretary to the Church Missionary Department, to go to Nigeria on a month-long fact-finding mission to determine if the people were sincere and willing to accept the Church without holding the priesthood.[7] Although Brother Williams had been responding to the flood of letters from Africa, he was not prepared for what he found there. He was met at the airport in Lagos, Nigeria, by ten pastors with whom he had been corresponding. He, too, was treated like royalty, and was surprised to discover that not only did each pastor operate independently, they had not even been aware of each other.[8]

The first official Church meeting in black Africa was held on October 22, 1961, in a small mud hut in Opobo District, Nigeria, where Brother Williams met with a pastor and 110 followers. No one came by car. Many, including eight mothers with small children, had begun their day before 4:00 A.M. and walked twenty-five miles or more to be there. After teaching them for two hours, Brother Williams prepared to end the meeting. He recorded:

> It was hot as blazes. . . . My suit was wringing wet. . . . When I turned the meeting back to [the pastor], I heard a murmur all through the congregation . . . and [the pastor] said to me, "They don't want to go home. They have something to say."
>
> Then for three hours . . . these people were standing up bearing testimony to the truthfulness of the Church and how they believed in the prophets. I could not believe what I was hearing.[9]

One elderly gentleman said:

> I keep hearing you say, "if we are sincere." Elder Williams, I want you to know that I am sincere. I am an old man . . . I am sick. But when I heard you were going to be here, I walked 16 miles this morning to see you and to hear what you have to say. I still have to walk 16 miles to get back home, and I am not well. I want you to know that I am sincere or I would not be here. I have not seen President McKay. I have not seen God. But I have seen you. And I will hold you personally accountable to tell President McKay that I am sincere.[10]

Brother Williams reported to President McKay that he felt thousands were ready for baptism.[11]

Three months later, on February 26, 1962, President McKay called Brother and Sister Williams to preside over the first mission in black Africa, but the Nigerian government refused to issue the necessary visas. This was primarily due to media attacks against the Church because of its position in denying blacks the priesthood, and at this time civil rights was an explosive issue. After four years of intense effort, one day Brother Williams was at the embassy in Nigeria hoping to finally obtain the visas. While there he received a telegram from the First Presidency stating, "Discontinue negotiations in Nigeria and return home immediately." Shocked and confused, but obedient, he returned home.[12]

Upon his return to Salt Lake City in November 1965, President N. Eldon Tanner assured Brother Williams that the Church would yet go to Nigeria, and they would both live to see it.[13] He further said, "We don't know why we called you back. We only know it was urgent. There is a reason, and we will know [what it is someday]."[14] Within three weeks Africa's most devastating civil war, the Biafran War, exploded in Nigeria, with much of the fighting in the area where the unbaptized congregations of believers were located.[15] Brother and Sister Williams were released from their mission call, and in June 1966, LaMar Williams turned over fifteen thousand names and addresses of unbaptized African converts to Elders Spencer W. Kimball and Gordon B. Hinckley, both of whom were on the Church Missionary Committee.[16]

It is important to note that the Church made every effort to establish itself in West Africa but was prevented from doing so. However, the Lord has promised that his eternal blessings will come "in his own time, and in his own way, and according to his own will" (D&C 88:68). The Lord's "own time" for black Africa came in June 1978. "His own way" was a revelation given to his prophet, President Spencer W. Kimball, making all gospel blessings available to all worthy members. The Lord's "own will" regarding the priesthood restriction and the removal of it has been stated by prophets, seers, and revelators.

President Spencer W. Kimball—whose clarion call during his ministry was to take the gospel to every nation, kindred, tongue and people—was particularly aware of many under priesthood restriction throughout the world, and he pleaded long and earnestly with the Lord in their behalf (see D&C Official Declaration 2). Also, in numerous temple meetings, President Kimball met with his counselors and the Twelve to discuss this issue. In such a meeting on June 1, 1978,

President Kimball asked the Brethren to express their feelings regarding this matter. Elder David B. Haight recalled that as each one spoke, there was "an outpouring of the Spirit which bonded our souls together in perfect unity."[17]

How important was this revelation? It has been said that "the greatest events of history are those which affect the largest numbers for the longest periods."[18] By this criteria, when we consider those affected by this revelation—which includes millions on the earth and billions on the other side of the veil—we can see why President Kimball said that it brought "one of the greatest changes and blessings that has ever been known."[19] Floodgates were now open for the gospel to go to Africa and to African ancestors.[20]

When this revelation was announced, my wife and I were presiding over the only mission on the continent of Africa. The announcement brought feelings and stirrings impossible to describe. As inspiring as it was, I felt a great concern because Africans do not traditionally keep written histories, and I felt their unique experiences needed to be preserved. The desire to help preserve that history was later realized. Since coming to BYU I have been blessed by the Lord and helped by others in obtaining oral histories from more than six hundred African pioneers.

Prior to the revelation on the priesthood, the unbaptized converts in Africa were guided and strengthened by the Lord according to their faith in him. The Lord used two types of disciples to help accomplish this.

First, the Lord guided many Latter-day Saint expatriates from North America to Africa on professional assignments, many of whom provided much-needed support and encouragement for these pioneers. Elder Alexander B. Morrison of the First Quorum of the Seventy said in general conference:

> In every corner of Africa, there are faithful expatriate members of the Church. . . .
>
> I testify they are not there by chance. As part of God's great and grand design for growth, they have been placed on the frontiers of the Church by divine providence. . . . They are the right people at the right place and at the right time in history.[21]

Second, the Lord raised up Eliases to prepare people for the gospel so the infant Church could grow quickly and withstand Satan's fury. John the Baptist was the Elias who prepared people at the Savior's time. In this dispensation the Lord raised up various Eliases. For example, Sidney Rigdon, a Campbellite preacher in Ohio, prepared many for the gospel, including future counselors in the First Presidency, apostles, and presiding bishops. In black Africa, a loving Heavenly Father raised up many Eliases to prepare the people for the revelation on the priesthood, which was, in effect, the restoration of the gospel for them.

With the extraordinary initial success the Church had in Africa, growth has been a continuing and major challenge to the institution in Africa. Limiting baptisms, so membership did not outgrow leadership, was like trying to contain an explosion. The spiritual hunger of the people and the dedicated efforts of the Eliases brought such rapid growth that Presiding Bishop Victor L. Brown said to Elder Mabey, "I think you are on the frontier of one of the greatest historical events in Church history as far as growth is concerned."[22]

In both Nigeria and Ghana the missionaries found hundreds who had testimonies of the Book of Mormon, the Prophet Joseph Smith, and the Restoration of the gospel. All they needed was baptism. And so they were baptized. In one 24-hour period, 149 people were baptized.[23] Within one year there were more than 1,700 members in 35 branches in West Africa.[24]

After only nine and a half years of missionary work, Elder Neal A. Maxwell organized the Aba Nigeria Stake on May 15, 1988—the first stake in which all priesthood leaders were black—and he noted that this was "a historic day in the Church in this dispensation, and in any dispensation."[25]

Presidents Harold B. Lee and Gordon B. Hinckley have said that the strength of the Church is not in our numbers, our buildings, or the amount of tithes and offerings. Our strength is in the testimonies that burn in the hearts of the members.[26]

Notes

This information was drawn from a devotional address given by E. Dale LeBaron. It's published as "African Converts without Baptism: A Unique and Inspiring Chapter in Church History," in *1998–99 Speeches* (Provo, Utah: Brigham Young University, 1998), November 3, 1998.

1. See James H. Robinson, in *African American Quotations*, ed. Richard Newman (Phoenix, Arizona: Oryx Press, 1998), 18.

2. "Many Are Still Blazing Gospel Trails," *Church News,* published by *Deseret News,* July 24, 1993, 6.

3. Edwin Q. Cannon, Jr., interview by Gordon Irving, January 10, 1980, Church Historical Department, Salt Lake City.

4. LaMar Williams, interview by E. Dale LeBaron, Salt Lake City, February 12, 1988. All interviews, letters, and tapes are on file with the author unless otherwise noted.

5. Glen G. Fisher, *Glen G. Fisher: A Man to Match the Mountains,* ed. E. Dale LeBaron (Edmonton, Alberta: Fisher House, 1992), 147–48.

6. Letter to David O. McKay, July 29, 1961, Church Historian's Library; Williams, interview.

7. Williams, interview, 10–11.

8. Williams, interview, 11–12.

9. Williams, interview, 10–12.

10. Letter on file.

11. Williams, interview, 25–27.

12. Williams, interview, 4, 22–24; LaMar Williams, journal, "Nigerian Mission," Church Historical Library, 64.4.

13. See Williams, journal, 64.1.

14. Williams, journal, 64.4; Williams, interview, 4, 22–24.

15. See *Encyclopedia of Africa South of the Sahara,* ed. John Middleton (New York: Charles Scribner's Sons, 1997), 4:357.

16. Williams, interview, 7, 20–21, 35.

17. Lucile C. Tate, *David B. Haight: The Life Story of a Disciple* (Salt Lake City: Bookcraft, 1987), 279–80.

18. "The First Presidency Easter Message," *Church News,* March 26, 1994, 1.

19. Edward L. Kimball and Andrew E. Kimball Jr., *Spencer W. Kimball: Twelfth President of The Church of Jesus Christ of Latter-day Saints* (Salt Lake City: Bookcraft, 1977), 451.

20. See Bruce R. McConkie, "All Are Alike unto God," CES Symposium, Brigham Young University, August 18, 1978.

21. "The Dawning of a New Day in Africa," *Ensign* 17 (November 1987): 26.

22. Rendell N. Mabey and Gordon T. Allred, *Brother to Brother* (Salt Lake City: Bookcraft, 1984), 140.

23. See Mabey and Allred, *Brother to Brother,* 143.

24. See Mabey and Allred, *Brother to Brother,* vii.

25. "Nigerian Stake," *Church News,* May 21, 1988, 7.

26. See Harold B. Lee, "Strengthen the Stakes of Zion," *Ensign* 3 (July 1973): 6; Gordon B. Hinckley, "The True Strength of the Church," *Ensign* 3 (July 1973): 49.

The Historiography of Latter-day Saints in the Pacific

Grant Underwood

The Prophet Joseph Smith concluded his stirring April 1843 remarks to the Quorum of the Twelve with this challenge: "Don't let a single corner of the earth go without a mission."[1] Less than a month later, the Quorum met in the Prophet's Nauvoo office and called Addison Pratt, Noah Rogers, Benjamin F. Grouard, and Knowlton F. Hanks to the first Pacific Islands mission in this dispensation. All realized that such an endeavor would entail sacrifice and unforeseen hardships. Addison Pratt's wife, Louisa, wrote, "when it was first announced to me that his mission was the South Pacifick Ocean, and for an absence of three years, a weeping spirit came upon me which lasted for three days." Then, in a spirit of consecration, Louisa added, "by degrees we became reconciled to the separation."[2]

On June 1, 1843, without fanfare but not without feeling, Pratt and the others quietly commenced their journey to Massachusetts. In October they set sail on the whaler *Timoleon* bound for the Pacific Ocean. Nearly seven months would elapse before Pratt disembarked on the island of Tubuai, commencing his mission in what is now French Polynesia. Pratt, who knew some Hawaiian from his whaling days, and Grouard learned the local tongue quickly and began teaching the gospel to the islanders.[3] It was the first mission of The Church of Jesus Christ of Latter-day Saints in which proselyting was systematically carried out in a language other than English. It was also the first Latter-day Saint mission outside North America to a non-European people.

From that small beginning, great things have come. As of 2003, there are over four hundred thousand Pacific Islander Latter-day Saints, and their faith is legendary in the Church. Samoa was the first country in the world to be completely covered by stakes, and before the surge in temple building in the late 1990s, there were more temples per capita in the Pacific Islands than in any other area of the Church. Sixth-generation Latter-day Saints can be found in a number of places around the Pacific. Church schools have been built in various countries in the Pacific Islands, as well as in the state of Hawaii, where Church College of Hawaii has grown into Brigham Young University–Hawaii, a highly regarded four-year liberal arts institution. As with any human history, the story of the Church in the Pacific is not only a remarkable tale of triumph, but it is also a narrative of tragedy, of fits and starts, of sinners as well as saints. Out of the surviving relics of this rich and variegated past, a history can be pieced together that is quite as engaging and poignant as the Mormon saga in the mainland United States. The purpose of this article is to introduce readers to the surprising number of published studies, large and small, that tell this story.

One can gain a sense of the scope of archival as well as published materials pertaining to Church history in the Pacific by consulting the now twenty-plus-year-old book Russell T. Clement, *Mormons in the Pacific: A Bibliography* (Laie: Institute for Polynesian Studies, 1981). It contains 2,877 entries! Of course, the vast majority of entries are unpublished primary sources, ranging from diaries and letters to mission histories and manuals. The monumental bibliography James B. Allen, Ronald W. Walker, and David J. Whittaker, *Studies in Mormon History, 1830–1897: An Indexed Bibliography* (Urbana: University of Illinois Press, 2000), though incomplete for Pacific Mormon history, still lists several hundred pertinent publications. This includes articles in Church magazines, which occasionally publish pieces on the Church outside North America. Accounts in the earlier magazines in particular are historically valuable because many of their authors were the pioneering missionaries themselves.

Crucial details on the early history of the Church among the New Zealand Maori, for instance, come from a series by Alma Greenwood published in the *Juvenile Instructor* in 1885 and 1886, and similarly invaluable information on the early Samoan mission can be found in an 1893 *Juvenile Instructor* series by Edward J. Wood.[4]

Of the books on the subject, first and foremost is R. Lanier Britsch, *Unto the Islands of the Sea: A History of Latter-day Saints in the Pacific* (Salt Lake: Deseret Book, 1986). Retired in 2002 from Brigham Young University, Britsch has devoted decades to researching and writing the history of the Church in the Pacific. For much of this time, he has been the subject's sole academic practitioner and is by far its most productive one, making him the field's premier authority alive today. Originally commissioned to write the Pacific volume for the Church's 1980 sesquicentennial history, which for a variety of reasons never appeared as a series, Britsch published his work in 1986 as *Unto the Islands of the Sea*. Given the book's vast, Pacific-wide scope, its pathbreaking narrative depth in most places, and its solid academic foundation, the volume stands as the standard work on its subject.

A repository that should be a leading research source for students of Pacific Mormon histories, particularly those pertaining to Hawaii, is the series of annual conference proceedings produced by the Mormon Pacific Historical Society (MPHS). The MPHS was founded in 1980, and since then its annual conference has provided a venue where both academic and islander genres of telling history, as well as their harmonization, is welcome. Part of the success of the MPHS has been its ability to provide a place where wise local elders, seasoned family historians, and students apprenticing in various scholarly disciplines participate side-by-side with professional historians and university professors. From the beginning, the MPHS has recognized that Pacific cultures generally preserve their heritage through oral tradition and performative lore. These "sources" have been as respected and as readily utilized by conference presenters over the years as have the missionary diaries and Church periodicals that academic historians tend to favor. It has been the tacit conviction of the MPHS that traditional and academic perspectives on the Church's past in the Pacific can mutually invigorate each other.

Over the years, nearly two hundred presentations have been made at MPHS annual meetings. Each year the Society has rounded up those that were written down and photocopied and collated them. It has distributed a hundred or so bound copies of the proceedings to Society members and other interested individuals. While enjoyed by this handful of primarily Hawaii-based readers, the distribution procedure meant that some fine historical work received limited circulation. In 2000 it was decided that a fitting way for the MPHS to celebrate its twentieth anniversary (and the Church's sesquicentennial in Hawaii) as well as introduce its work to a wider audience would be to publish a commemorative volume showcasing some of the meetings' more significant presentations. Grant Underwood, ed., *Voyages of Faith: Explorations in Mormon Pacific History* (Provo, Utah: Brigham Young University Press, 2000) was the result. The two dozen articles selected for inclusion in *Voyages of Faith* underwent full editorial revision before being formally published. The unpublished remainder should be used with the awareness that the unedited nature of the informally reproduced proceedings means that, despite their sometimes sophisticated sensitivity to different worlds of knowledge, many are still unrefined, early-stage pieces.[5] Since only two-thirds of the presentations from 1980 to 1992 (and none since) were indexed in *Studies in Mormon History*, an appendix is included here with a complete listing through 2003.

It is important to stress that, true to its MPHS origins, *Voyages of Faith* operates at the nexus of the traditional and the academic. This blend is well illustrated in BYU–Hawaii President Eric B. Shumway's chapter, "Tevita Muli Kinikini: Portrait of a Tongan Pioneer," 311–38. It is one of the lengthiest and most carefully crafted in the book, but it contains only a single footnote. On one hand, this level of documentation is inevitable when dealing with peoples and places where most sources are spoken or performed. Yet the piece is more than that. Eric Shumway is an acknowledged authority on Tongan language and culture and one of the few *palangi* (non-islanders) to have received a chiefly title. He draws on numerous oral interviews, on his own experience, and on a profound mastery of the Tongan language and culture to produce a portrait of

Kinikini's life that was applauded for its authenticity by those who knew Kinikini and Tongan culture. Peer review in Tonga takes place around the kava circle, but mastering the details and subtleties of cultural protocol is no less demanding than mastering the literature of an academic field. Though such mastery is not cited in footnotes, it is abundantly evident to the cultural connoisseur. As too often happened in the past with Pacific Studies generally, scholarly narratives that were insufficiently attentive to culture prompt islanders to remark, "We do not recognize ourselves in this book."

If *Voyages of Faith* and MPHS proceedings generally try to bridge the divide between academic and islander genres of telling history, most other histories of the Church in the Pacific (and elsewhere) know and follow only the cultural protocols of academia. It is to be sincerely hoped that this imbalance will be redressed in the future. The increasing prominence of islander voices and perspectives, together with the postmodern shift within Western academic disciplines, has opened up Pacific Studies to a whole new array of possibilities and opportunities. Future Mormon history in the Pacific should capitalize on this openness to different ways of knowing and different ways of telling history. As one scholar has pointed out, "This does not imply a suspension of critical judgment, but avoiding [the presumption that] Western scholars have the truths and Pacific [islanders] are perpetrating illusions or self-delusions."[6] Readers and writers of history accustomed to purely academic approaches are invited, when engaging Pacific Islander history in the future as well as *Voyages of Faith* and the MPHS proceedings presently, to respect a different culture of knowledge and to trust its legitimacy.

What follows now is a region-by-region review of select, significant publications, generally of a solely academic character, that pertain to the history of the Church in the Pacific. These regions are presented roughly chronologically according to when the Church was first introduced in each.

French Polynesia

The Church in French Polynesia is fortunate to have had two couples—George and Maria Ellsworth and Yves and Kathleen Perrin—who devoted much of their adult lives to researching and writing its history. The late S. George Ellsworth was one of the most respected Mormon historians of the second half of the twentieth century. Though perhaps best known as founding editor of the Western Historical Quarterly and author of a widely used textbook on Utah's history, Ellsworth completed his University of California, Berkeley dissertation in 1951 on missionary work in the early Church and thereafter maintained an ongoing interest in the subject. In the 1950s, Ellsworth acquired the diaries of Addison Pratt, to whom his wife, Maria, was related, and these diaries became the basis for his 1959 Utah State University Faculty Honor Lecture, "Zion in Paradise: Early Mormons in the South Seas" (Logan: Utah State University Faculty Association, 1959). This was a milestone publication—the first academic treatment of Pacific Church history anywhere in print.

The Ellsworths' love affair with the story of Addison Pratt and his wife, Louisa, who joined him in French Polynesia during his second mission there, led to the eventual publication of two priceless historical records—S. George Ellsworth, ed., *The Journals of Addison Pratt* (Salt Lake City: University of Utah Press, 1990); and S. George Ellsworth, ed., *The History of Louisa Barnes Pratt: Being the Autobiography of a Mormon Missionary Widow and Pioneer* (Logan: Utah State University Press, 1998). Nearly four hundred pages in the *Journals of Addison Pratt* deal with the period from 1843 to 1852, when Addison spent most of his time in French Polynesia. The *History of Louisa Barnes Pratt,* consciously written with an eye to publication, offers a woman's and a wife's perspective on mission life there during some of the same time period. The felicitous convergence of the Pratts' pioneering personalities, extraordinary experiences, and literary aspiration with the Ellsworths' passion to publish the Pratts' writings has produced an unparalleled glimpse, through the eyes of two American protagonists in this drama, of the beginnings of the Church in French Polynesia specifically as well as early Mormon missionary work generally. These books greatly amplify the one previously published missionary memoir covering some of the same ground—James S. Brown, *Life of a Pioneer: Being the Autobiography of James S. Brown* (Salt Lake City: George Q. Cannon & Sons, 1900).

Some of the material from George Ellsworth's earlier articles was published in the rich editorial essays of the two Pratt volumes. Most of his articles, though, have been combined and expanded into a fully fleshed-out narrative that, along with the excellent coverage of the post–World War II years by Kathleen Perrin, became *Seasons of Faith and Courage: The Church of Jesus Christ of Latter-Day Saints in French Polynesia; A Sesquicentennial History, 1843–1993* (Sandy, Utah: Yves R. Perrin, 1994). It is a sad commentary on market economics that such a pathbreaking work, the only book-length history in English of the Church in French Polynesia, had to be privately published. A decade before, Yves R. Perrin, former Tahitian Mission President, had written in French a similar mission history covering the same period— *L'Historie De L'Eglise Mormone En Polynesie Francaise De 1844 a 1982* (Papeete, Tahiti: Imprimerie CES-STP, 1982).

Maria Ellsworth made a noteworthy contribution to French Polynesian Latter-day Saint historiography with "The First Mormon Missionary Women in the Pacific, 1850–1852," in *Voyages of Faith,* 33–48. This might profitably be read in conjunction with the more broadly based and richly contextualized Carol Cornwall Madsen, "Mormon Missionary Wives in Nineteenth Century Polynesia," *Journal of Mormon History* 13 (1986–87): 61–85. Overlapping work already mentioned but offering a convenient sample of George Ellsworth's historical craftsmanship is "New Wine and Old Bottles: Latter-day Saint Missionary Work in French Polynesia, 1844–1852," in *Voyages of Faith,* 13–32. Thanks to the Ellsworths' concern for future study, four decades worth of their extensive and meticulous research is now preserved in the S. George and Maria S. Ellsworth Collections at the Utah State University Library in Logan. For this topic, only the Church Archives offers a richer resource.

Several other fine studies of the Church in French Polynesia need to be mentioned. The chapters covering French Polynesia in *Unto the Islands of the Sea* stand on the shoulders of George Ellsworth, but here and there offer new details and added insights.

When pressure from the French led to the expulsion of the American missionaries in the 1850s, islander Latter-day Saints were left without direction from Church headquarters. Only forty years later were missionaries again sent to French Polynesia. In the interim, however, Reorganized Church of Jesus Christ of Latter Day Saints (RLDS, now Community of Christ) missionaries visited the islands and converted many former Latter-day Saints to the Reorganization. When Latter-day Saint missionaries returned to French Polynesia in the 1890s, they found that the RLDS church was one of the largest in the country. The RLDS story is told in F. Edward Butterworth, *Roots of the Reorganization: French Polynesia* (Independence, Miss.: Herald Publishing House, 1977); and *The Adventures of John Hawkins* (Independence, Miss.: Herald Publishing House, 1963).

Hawaii

In 1850, the same year that Addison Pratt returned with his family and several others to French Polynesia, another group of men, including George Q. Cannon, sailed to open the work in Hawaii. Though some of the men grew discouraged with their lack of success among the small white population in the Sandwich Islands, Cannon felt impressed that their primary mission was among the native Hawaiians. Persistence paid off, and within a very few years, thousands had been baptized and the Book of Mormon was translated into Hawaiian. The ensuing history of the Church in Hawaii is a fascinating one, with tales of that "rascal in paradise" Walter Murray Gibson; of the subsequent establishment and flourishing of a Mormon gathering place in Laie, Oahu; and of periodically close relations with Hawaiian royalty, including the eventual baptism of Queen Liliuokalani. Twentieth-century milestones included construction of the Church's first temple in the Pacific, of the first Latter-day Saint post-secondary school in the Pacific, and of the Polynesian Cultural Center. Unlike some Protestant groups, the Church has eventually come to support rather than suppress the appropriate expression of indigenous culture where it has established itself. The story of the Church in Hawaii is also the story of how the gospel was taken to thousands of Chinese and Japanese immigrants in Hawaii, who by the twentieth century outnumbered the native Hawaiians.

The Church's history in Hawaii has been far more extensively studied than its history in any other part of the Pacific. While not the first group of islands to receive the restored gospel, for a variety of reasons Hawaii became the Church's most important center in the Pacific. The most comprehensive history of the Church in Hawaii is R. Lanier Britsch, *Moramona: The Mormons in Hawaii* (Laie: Institute for Polynesian Studies, BYU–Hawaii, 1989). *Moramona,* as a stand-alone monograph on the Church in Hawaii, expands Britsch's already seminal work in *Unto the Islands of the Sea.*

George Q. Cannon, Joseph F. Smith, and even Samuel E. Woolley may be well known to many Church members today, but who outside of Hawaii has heard of Kaleohano, Kahumoku, and Keanu? Unfortunately, Hawaiian Saints, like most Pacific Islanders, generally did not keep diaries, and virtually no personal written records have survived. Longtime BYU–Hawaii faculty member Joseph H. Spurrier, however, spent many years culling from the dozens of mainland missionary diaries and letters any reference to nineteenth-century Hawaiian Saints. From such material, he wrote *Sandwich Island Saints: Early Mormon Converts in the Hawaiian Islands* (Oahu: J. H. Spurrier, 1989). Critics have noted the absence of scholarly footnotes (though Spurrier did provide a bibliography), but *Sandwich Island Saints* is the volume to go to for an impressive and inspirational reconstruction of the lives of Hawaiian Saints in the 1800s. Readers interested in a detailed recounting of the activities of the American Latter-day Saint missionaries and mission presidents during this period, as well as those interested in the twentieth-century Church in Hawaii, should consult Britsch's *Moramona.*

One other major figure in the historiography of Latter-day Saints in Hawaii needs to be mentioned—Lance D. Chase. Like Spurrier, Chase for many years was on the BYU–Hawaii faculty. Throughout his career he produced a number of significant article-length studies on a variety of topics pertaining to Mormon history in Hawaii. Most were delivered at the annual meetings of the MPHS, of which Chase was the co-founder. A baker's dozen of Chase's studies were collected for a volume which, due to his untimely death from cancer, ended up being published posthumously as *Temple, Town, Tradition: The Collected Historical Essays of Lance D. Chase* (Laie: Institute for Polynesian Studies, 2000).

Aside from these three major figures in the Latter-day Saint historiography of Hawaii, other contributors have written significant articles or graduate theses on a particular topic. In the latter category are Margaret C. Bock, "The Church of Jesus Christ of Latter Day Saints in the Hawaiian Islands" (master's thesis, University of Hawaii, 1941); and Richard C. Harvey, "The Development of The Church of Jesus Christ of Latter-Day Saints in Hawaii" (master's thesis, Brigham Young University, 1974); as well as the more specialized Raymond Clyde Beck, "Palawai Basin: Hawaii's Mormon Zion" (master's thesis, University of Hawaii, 1972).

There are other areas in which Britsch's writings have been supplemented by more recent work. This is particularly true for the early period. Authors have mined an unusual number of detailed missionary diaries (see lists in the bibliographies of *Moramona* and *Sandwich Island Saints*). Several of these journals can be readily accessed through biographies that rely on them to reconstruct their subjects' experiences in Hawaii. Chief among these is Davis Bitton, *George Q. Cannon: A Biography* (Salt Lake: Deseret Book, 1999). The chapter on Cannon's years in Hawaii draws heavily on his journal (heretofore only available to family members), as well as on *My First Mission* (Faith Promoting Series, Book 1 [Salt Lake City: Juvenile Instructor, 1879]), an inspirational summary that Cannon himself prepared and published in the 1880s based on his journal. In the 1990s, the Church Historical Department received permission to publish the entirety of his significant and extraordinarily detailed journal, which spans the second half of the nineteenth century. The first, slender volume, covering Cannon's pre-Hawaii year in California, has already been published. Next out will be the hefty tome containing all his 1850s Hawaii diaries which, when it finally appears, will be a milestone in the historiography of the Church in Hawaii.

Other biographies that likewise rely on missionary diaries for their accounts of the early Church in Hawaii include M. Guy Bishop, *Henry William Bigler: Soldier, Gold Miner, Missionary, Chronicler, 1815–1900* (Logan: Utah State University Press, 1998); and E. Dale LeBaron, *Benjamin F. Johnson: Friend to the*

Prophet (Provo, Utah: Grandin Press, 1997). Shorter, specialized studies of significance that cover the early period include Donald R. Shaffer, "Hiram Clark and the First LDS Hawaiian Mission: A Reappraisal," *Journal of Mormon History* 17 (1991): 94–109; Scott G. Kenney, "Mormons and the Smallpox Epidemic of 1853," *Hawaiian Journal of History* 31 (1997): 1–26; Jeffrey S. Stover, "'Wars and Rumors of Wars': The Perceived Threat of the 'Mormon Invasion' of Hawaii," in *Voyages of Faith,* 49–58; and Lance D. Chase, "The Hawaiian Mission Crisis of 1874: The Awa Rebellion Story," in *Voyages of Faith,* 59–70.

For most of the Church's history in Hawaii, the three major books mentioned above plow new ground. The paucity of specialized studies that ordinarily undergird volumes of such chronological sweep means that the narratives these books provide can be found nowhere else. Several topics have been fairly thoroughly explored. Treatment, for instance, of Walter Murray Gibson, that colorful confidant of both Church President Brigham Young and members of Hawaiian royalty, is a good example. Historians and romantics alike have been fascinated with this eccentric individual for decades. Popular writers of historical fiction from James A. Michner to Paul Bailey and Samuel Taylor have taken a turn at telling Gibson's story. An important historical study is Jacob Adler and Robert M. Kamins, *The Fantastic Life of Walter Murray Gibson: Hawaii's Minister of Everything* (Honolulu: University of Hawaii Press, 1986) which focuses on his later political life after he was excommunicated from the Church. For his Mormon years, the range of assessments of his character and contribution can be sampled in two articles: Gwynn Barrett, "Walter Murray Gibson: The Shepherd Saint of Lanai Revisited," *Utah Historical Quarterly* 40 (1972): 142–62; and R. Lanier Britsch, "Another Visit with Walter Murray Gibson," *Utah Historical Quarterly* 46 (1978): 65–78.

The Church's Polynesian Cultural Center (PCC), created in the 1960s, has also drawn considerable attention. Brief treatments worth consulting are Vernice Wineera and Rubina Rivers Forester, "The Polynesian Cultural Center: Reflections and Recollections," in *Voyages of Faith,* 209–38; and James Whitehurst, "Mormons and the Hula: The Polynesian Cultural Center in Hawaii," *Journal of American Culture* 12 (1989): 1–5. Full-length studies include the "official" twenty-year history Robert O'Brian, *Hands Across the Water: The Story of the Polynesian Cultural Center* (Laie, Hawaii: Polynesian Culture Center, 1983); and several graduate theses: Craig Ferre, "A History of the Polynesian Cultural Center's 'Night Show,' 1963–1983" (Ph.D. diss., Brigham Young University, 1988); Douglas Terry Webb, "Mormonism and Tourist Art in Hawaii" (Ph.D. diss., Arizona State University, 1990);[7] Ann Marie Robinson, "The Polynesian Cultural Center: A Study of Authenticity" (master's thesis, California State University—Chico, 1991); and the long-awaited Vernice Wineera, "Selves and Others : A Study of Reflexivity and the Representation of Culture in Touristic Display at the Polynesian Cultural Center, Laie, Hawaii" (Ph.D. diss., University of Hawaii, 2000). Wineera, who heads the Institute for Pacific Studies in Laie, Hawaii, and has been intimately associated with the PCC for years, has written a masterful work, well-deserving of careful attention. As of 2003, R. Lanier Britsch is in Laie to complete the official fortieth anniversary history of the center.

The very existence of the PCC testifies to the close association that many Pacific Islanders feel between cultural performing arts and the gospel. Hawaiians, like other islanders, tell their history more through songs, chants, and dances than written texts. Hawaiian hula, for instance, is far more than the form of entertainment that people from beyond the Pacific typically assume it to be. Hawaiian Latter-day Saints have been significant actors in the field of preserving and perpetuating this important aspect of their culture. In the twentieth century, a disproportionate number of leading Hawaiian-culture performers in the twentieth century have been Church members. Latter-day Saint missionaries and mission presidents in the nineteenth century tended to be less antagonistic to hula and other Hawaiian cultural performances than their Protestant counterparts. At times Mormons were positively supportive, as evidenced by the incorporation of performances and competitions in some of the annual mission conferences. Those familiar with the music scene in Hawaii today acknowledge a significant Latter-day Saint presence. That intimate association is detailed in Ishmael W. Stagner, Victoria Kekuaokalani, and Midge Lanihuliokauahaao Oler, "The Gospel and the Hawaiian Performing Arts," in *Voyages of Faith*, 239–54.

William Kauaiwiulaokalani Wallace III, Director of the Ka Halau Nui A Hawai'iloa (Center for Hawaiian Language and Cultural Studies) at Brigham Young University–Hawaii is a devout Latter-day Saint who grew up on the island of Moloka'i. His piece, "Mo'olelo Kahiko o Moloka'i, or Stories from Moloka'i's Past," in *Voyages of Faith*, 357–70, draws on oral histories to tell about Church history in Moloka'i. In so doing, Wallace and his associates remind us that Hawaiian Mormon history is more than what happens in Laie or on the Big Island of Hawaii.

Part of the Molokai story has been the impressive influence of Latter-day Saints with Hansen's disease (leprosy) who for a century have lived in the island's "leper colony" at Kalaupapa. The Kalaupapa experience has been told in a few popular magazines, but the best account is by Lance D. Chase and Kuulei Bell, herself a resident, "Faith, Hope, and Hansen's Disease: The Saints at Kalaupapa," in *Voyages of Faith*, 371–86.

Hawaii is often called a "melting pot" and a "salad bowl," where a variety of ethnic groups have dwelt in reasonably peaceful co-existence for years. Two fine studies that probe the ethnic dimension of Mormon history in Hawaii are Max E. Stanton, "Samoan Saints: Samoans in the Mormon Village of Laie, Hawaii" (Ph.D. diss., University of Oregon, 1973); and Russell T. Clement and Sheng-Luen Tsai, "East Wind to Hawaii: History and Contributions of Chinese and Japanese Latter-day Saints in Hawaii," in *Voyages of Faith*, 89–106. The most detailed study of the earliest Japanese converts is Shinji Takagi, "Tomizo and Tokujiro: The First Japanese Mormons," *BYU Studies* 39 (2000): 73–106.

Throughout the world, Latter-day Saints engage in sharing faith-promoting stories. This activity may be even more common among Mormons in traditionally oral societies. Academic historians tend to want to "get to the bottom of" the stories they encounter, and several pertaining to the Church in Hawaii have been thoroughly investigated: Harold S. Davis, "The Iosepa Origin of Joseph F. Smith's 'Laie Prophecy,'" *BYU Studies* 33 (1993): 81–108; Lavina Fielding Anderson, "Prayer Under a Pepper Tree: Sixteen Accounts of a Spiritual Manifestation," *BYU Studies* 33 (1993): 55–78; and Kenneth W. Baldridge and Lance D. Chase, "The Purported December 7, 1941, Attack on the Hawaii Temple," in *Voyages of Faith*, 165–90.

Twentieth-century Mormon history in Hawaii was profoundly influenced by the Church's four "entities" (as they are locally called) in Laie. Aside from the PCC, they are the temple, Church College of Hawaii (now BYU–Hawaii), and Zion Securities (now Hawaii Reserves). Treatment of these entities in Britsch, *Moramona* may be profitably supplemented with Paul L. Anderson, "A Jewel in the Pacific: The Art and Architecture of the Hawaii Temple," in *Voyages in Faith*, 147–64; and Richard O. Cowan, "Temples in the Pacific: A Reflection of Twentieth-Century Mormon History," in *Voyages of Faith*, 129–33. For CCH–BYU–Hawaii, see the accounts of inaugural president Reuben D. Law, *The Founding and Early Development of the Church College of Hawaii* (St. George, Utah: Dixie College, 1972); and subsequent president Alton Wade, "BYU–Hawaii: A Promise in the Pacific," *Brigham Young Magazine* 48 (1994): 34–39. Kenneth W. Baldridge offers a fascinating, behind-the-scenes glimpse at the deliberations that went into deciding what kind of Church school should be built in Hawaii and where it should be located in "Search for a Site: Selection of the Church College of Hawaii Campus," in *Voyages of Faith*, 191–208. This is part of a full-scale history of the college that Baldridge has made his labor of love for more than two decades. As of 2003, he will be receiving extra help under the auspices of BYU–Hawaii President Eric Shumway to see that the manuscript is published in some form for the school's fiftieth anniversary in 2005. Over the years, Lance Chase boldly essayed several studies of the somewhat checkered career of principal Laie landowner Zions Securities. Its history can be traced through several chapters in Chase's *Temple, Town, and Tradition*.

A final subject of importance to Latter-day Saint Hawaiian history actually did not take place in Hawaii at all. It occurred in Utah, where for a quarter century a gathering place for Polynesians was designated in the late 1800s. The story of

Skull Valley's Iosepa (the Hawaiian word for "Joseph"), located seventy-five miles west of Salt Lake City, is one of the most fascinating chapters in Mormon history. Iosepa was founded in 1889, after much of the Great Basin had already been colonized, and was disbanded in 1917, after virtually all its several hundred inhabitants had returned to Hawaii to assist with the building of the recently announced temple in Laie. Dennis Atkin has studied Iosepa over a longer period of time and has written more on it than anyone else. His "A History of Iosepa, the Utah Polynesian Colony" (master's thesis, Brigham Young University, 1958) is still the baseline study. For an accessible summary of his research, see Atkin, "Iosepa: A Utah Home for Polynesians," in *Voyages of Faith,* 71–88. For a different perspective, see Tracey E. Panek, "Life at Iosepa, Utah's Polynesian Colony," *Utah Historical Quarterly* 60 (1992): 64–77.

New Zealand

The first Latter-day Saint baptisms in New Zealand occurred in the 1850s among European, primarily British, settlers. These settlers were called *Pakeha* by the Maori. For a quarter century, a handful of Pakeha Latter-day Saints kept the church alive in the Wellington and Christchurch areas, but their numbers never amounted to more than a few dozen. Prior to the 1880s there was no concerted outreach to the Maori. Within a few short years, however, thousands of New Zealand Maori had been baptized. By the turn of the twentieth century, the Church counted nearly a tenth of the total Maori population as members, with a significantly higher percentage in certain *pa* (settlements) along the east coast of the North Island from the southern Wairarapa to Poverty Bay and beyond. From the 1880s to the 1950s, the Church in New Zealand was overwhelmingly Maori in composition. After midcentury, however, the number of Pakeha members increased significantly as missionaries more aggressively sought them out and emphasized the universal character of Mormonism rather than its compatibility with Maori culture. Today, though Church membership more closely reflects the national population with a majority of the members being Pakeha, a sizeable minority are Maori, and a residual respect for the Maori-Mormon connection remains.

The story of Mormon beginnings in New Zealand can be found in several general histories: Brian W. Hunt, *Zion in New Zealand: A History of the Church of Jesus Christ of Latter-day Saints in New Zealand, 1854–1977* (Temple View, New Zealand: Church College of New Zealand, 1977); and R. Lanier Britsch, *Unto the Islands of the Sea: A History of the Latter-day Saints in the Pacific* (Salt Lake: Deseret Book, 1986). A thematically organized though historically detailed revisionist work is Marjorie Newton, "Mormonism in New Zealand: A Historical Appraisal" (Ph.D. diss., University of Sydney, 1998). Still helpful in some aspects is Ian R. Barker, "The Connexion: The Mormon Church and the Maori People" (master's thesis, Victoria University of Wellington, New Zealand, 1967).

A shorter, specialized study valuable for its focus on the beginnings of the Church among the Maori is Peter Lineham, "The Mormon Message in the Context of Maori Culture," *Journal of Mormon History* 17 (1991), 62–93. Offering some new details on the early history is Grant Underwood, "Mormonism and the Shaping of Maori Religious Identity," in *Voyages of Faith,* 107–26. More theoretically oriented exploration of the Maori embrace of Mormonism is Underwood, "Mormonism, the Maori and Cultural Authenticity," *The Journal of Pacific History* 35 (September 2000): 133–46.

Carrying the story of Mormon-Maori cultural interaction into the twentieth century is Ian Barber, "Between Biculturalism and Assimilation: The Changing Place of Maori Culture in the Twentieth-Century New Zealand Mormon Church," *The New Zealand Journal of History* 29 (October 1995): 142–169. A fine specialized study is Eric G. Schwimmer, "Mormonism in a Maori Village: A Study in Social Change" (master's thesis, University of British Columbia, 1965). A brief, personal memoir is Harold T. Christensen, "The New Zealand Mission during the Great Depression: Reflections of a Former Acting President," *Dialogue: A Journal of Mormon Thought* 24 (fall 1991): 69–76.

One of the most important figures in Church history in New Zealand is Matthew Cowley. Given his outsized importance in the Pacific, particularly in New Zealand, where he served as a missionary and mission president for more than a decade, two volumes pertaining to Matthew Cowley may be profitably consulted: Henry A. Smith, *Matthew Cowley, Man of Faith* (Salt Lake City: Bookcraft, 1954); and [Glen L. Rudd], ed., *Matthew Cowley Speaks* (Salt Lake City: Deseret Book, 1954).

Because historically Pacific Islanders were voyaging peoples, intra-Pacific migration has long been a common phenomenon. In the past half-century, however, Auckland, New Zealand, one of the largest metropolises and port cities in the South Pacific, has experienced a huge influx of diverse peoples from all over the South Pacific. How this has imparted a multi-ethnic character to the Church is studied in Ruby Welch, "Ethnicity Amongst Auckland Mormons" (master's thesis, University of Auckland, 1989).

Samoa

One of the ironies of Pacific Mormon history is that the wayward Walter Murray Gibson was responsible for seeing to it that the restored gospel was carried to Samoa. In the early 1860s, he sent two Hawaiian elders, Samuela Manoa and Kimo Pelio, to Samoa to spread the good news. A quarter century later, when American missionaries Joseph Harry and his second wife, Florence Ridges, arrived there, they found Manoa and a small group of converts still faithful to the gospel after years of isolation. So began the fascinating story of the Church in Samoa. That history includes accounts of the conversion of entire villages; the establishment of special gathering places in the islands such as Sauniatu, which Church President David O. McKay called the most beautiful spot on earth; and the construction of schools, chapels, and eventually a temple. To local Samoans, it is often the story of missionary service in a distant village, participation in the mid-twentieth-century labor mission, or personal acts of faith like that of Maliatoa Fitisemanu, who turned down a prominent position to which he was entitled by his chiefly lineage with the famous remark, "I would rather be a deacon in the Mormon Church than the king of Samoa." Such faith, as well as their significant numbers—60,000 out of a population of just over 160,000—make the Church in Samoa a force to be reckoned with.

The only book-length history of the Samoan Church presently available is the privately produced *Samoa Apia Mission History, 1888–1983* (Pesega, Upolu, Western Samoa: Samoa Apia Mission, 1983), put together under the direction of BYU Professor and then Samoan Mission President R. Carl Harris. More inclusive of nonecclesiastical matters, and the only formally published account that essays to be comprehensive in its coverage, is Britsch, *Unto the Islands of the Sea*, 347–428. This fine study continues to be the best documented and most accessible account to date. It also incorporates most of the material found in Britsch's earlier "The Founding of the Samoan Mission," *BYU Studies* 18 (1977): 12–26.

As is typical of LDS historiography, interest in beginnings is dominant in Samoan Church history. Several privately produced compilations that offer excellent detail are Jennie M. Hart, John W. Hart, and R. Carl Harris, *The Expanded Samoan Mission History, 1888–1900, Vol. 1.* (n.p.: 1988); and Bill Hart, *LDS Voices from the Past: A Collection of Newspaper & Magazine Articles about Samoa, 1889–1917* (Downey, Idaho: Ati's Samoan Print Shop, n.d.). A number of other unpublished studies focus on individual missionaries: Melvin S. Tagg, "The Life of Edward James Wood, Church Patriot" (master's thesis, Brigham Young University, 1959), which focuses on one of the first American missionaries in Samoa; Ruth R. Yeaman, "Women From Zion in the Samoan Mission: 1888–1900," in *1990 MPHS Annual Conference Proceedings* (Laie, Hawaii: Mormon Pacific Historical Society, 1990), 54–80; and R. Wayne Shute, "The Life and Times of Early Latter-day Saint Missionaries in Polynesia: Samoa," in *World Conference on Records: Preserving Our Heritage, August 12–15, 1980* (Salt Lake City: The Church of Jesus Christ of Latter-day Saints, 1980), 1–6, which provides a brief overview.

An important early convert and patron of the Latter-day Saint missionaries, who donated land to the Church in the 1890s on or near which stands the mission home today, a Church school, and the temple in Pesega, is Rubina Rivers (Ahmu) Forester, "Ahmu: an Early Samoan Latter-day Saint," *1984 MPHS Annual Conference Proceedings* (Laie, Hawaii: Mormon Pacific Historical Society, 1984), 27–30. The impressive life of renowned first-generation convert Opapo Fonoimoana is discussed in Carl Fonoimoana,

"Opapo: The Power of his Faith," in *Voyages of Faith*, 305–10. In 1904, Opapo helped found Sauniatu, the famed Samoan Latter-day Saint gathering place. The history of that famous spot is detailed in Kenneth W. Baldridge, "Sauniatu, Western Samoa: A Special Purpose Village, 1904–1934," *Journal of the Polynesian Society* 87 (1978): 165–92. Incidentally, Baldridge's study is one of only two articles on Mormons in the Pacific ever published in this top-tier journal.

Two missionary accounts cover the years just before World War I: William A. Moody (who was mission president), *Years in the Sheaf: The Autobiography of William Alfred Moody* (Salt Lake City: Granite Publishing, 1959); and Dean B. Farnsworth, "Missionary Service in Samoa: 1910–1912," in *1984 MPHS Annual Conference Proceedings* (Laie, Hawaii: Mormon Pacific Historical Society, 1984), 21–26. This latter paper was based on the diaries of missionary Burton K. Farnsworth. Missionary work and Church life in Samoa following World War I is explored in the autobiographical W. Karl Brewer, *Armed With the Spirit: Missionary Experiences in Samoa* (Provo, Utah: Brigham Young University Press, 1975).

Beyond these studies pertaining to the first quarter-century of Mormon history in Samoa, little specialized work has been done. Thus, for the bulk of Samoan Church history, Harris, *Samoa Apia Mission History* and Britsch, *Unto the Islands of the Sea* break new ground and are virtually the only published sources of information. One important exception is Jennie Hart, ed., *Autobiography of Percy John Rivers* (Downey, Idaho: Ati's Samoan Print Shop, 1996), which is the story of Ah Mu's grandson, who was the first Samoan Stake President and Regional Representative. One other study worth noting, which offers a Samoan perspective, though not a Latter-day Saint perspective, on the Church in Samoa, is Tafailematagi Muasau, "The Appeal of the Mormons in Samoa," *Pacific Journal of Theology* 2 (1991): 35–41.

Tonga

The first Latter-day Saint missionaries to Tonga were sent in 1891 by the president of the recently founded Samoan mission. They arrived just after a religious controversy over whether all Tongans could be compelled to belong to the Methodist-based Tongan Free Church. Though religious freedom was on the books, the perception that loyalty to the king and loyalty to the Tongan Free Church were one and the same led to the termination of the Latter-day Saint mission before decade's end. Ten years later, in 1907, missionaries were once again sent to the Tongan islands. This time the mission persisted, and, though growth was slow, by 1916 it was decided that Tonga should no longer be a part of the Samoan Mission, and the Tongan Mission was founded. Again in the 1920s, the Church in Tonga would face dissolution when the government passed a "passport act" preventing the entry of any more Latter-day Saint missionaries. Once the act was repealed a few years later, the Church grew slowly but steadily. The visit of Elder George Albert Smith in the late 1930s, the translation and publication of the Book of Mormon in Tongan in the 1940s, and the construction of Liahona College (equivalent to an American high school) in the 1950s all had a strengthening impact on the Church. As in Samoa and elsewhere in the world, beginning in the late 1950s the rate of growth began to intensify. Stakes were organized and by the 1980s a temple, symbolizing Church maturation, was constructed. Today some 40 percent of the Tongan population is Latter-day Saint.

For the full sweep of Tongan Mormon history, Britsch, *Unto the Islands of the Seas* shares the spotlight with two other valuable histories. Former Tongan missionary and founding principal of Liahona College, Ermel J. Morton, who also translated the Book of Mormon as well as the Doctrine and Covenants and Pearl of Great Price into Tongan, prepared a *Brief History of the Tongan Mission of the Church of Jesus Christ of Latter-day Saints* (Suva: Fiji Times Print, 1968) for the mission's jubilee anniversary. The other crucial work is the culturally sensitive history *Tongan Saints: Legacy of Faith* (Laie, Hawaii: Institute for Polynesian Studies, 1991) by Eric B. Shumway, former Tongan missionary, mission president, and master linguist. Shumway's volume reflects his sophisticated analysis of both Tongan oral tradition and missionary diaries articulated earlier in "Problems in Oral History in Tonga," *1980 MPHS Annual Conference Proceedings* (Laie, Hawaii: Mormon Pacific Historical Society, 1980), 20–26; and "A Tongan

Missionary Journal: History As Anecdote," *1982 MPHS Annual Conference Proceedings* (Laie, Hawaii: Mormon Pacific Historical Society, 1982), 3–11.

Specialized studies of particular aspects of Tongan Mormon history are few. Britsch contributed "Mormon Intruders in Tonga: The Passport Act of 1922," in *Mormons, Scripture, and the Ancient World,* ed. Davis Bitton (Provo, Utah: Foundation for Ancient Research and Mormon Studies, 1998), 121–48. Veteran administrator of Church schools Harvey L. Taylor, produced a two-volume unpublished study that is vital for understanding not only the history of Liahona College but all other Church schools in the Pacific as well. See Taylor, "The Story of LDS Church Schools," 2 vols. (Provo, Utah: Prepared for the Church Commissioner of Education, 1971). On Liahona specifically, see Delworth Keith Young, "Liahona High School, Its Prologue and Development to 1965" (master's thesis, Utah State University, 1967).

After the release of the big-screen production *The Other Side of Heaven,* arguably no aspect of Tongan Mormon history is better known than the mission experiences of John H. Groberg, member of the First Quorum of the Seventy. Groberg's mission memoirs—*In the Eye of the Storm* (Salt Lake City: Bookcraft, 1993), reprinted as *The Other Side of Heaven* (Salt Lake City: Deseret Book, 2001), on which the movie was based, and *The Fire of Faith* (Salt Lake City: Bookcraft, 1996)—provide an unforgettable portrait of the intersection of Tongan culture and Latter-day Saint missionary and Church life in the late 1950s. A somewhat contemporary Tongan memoir is Fa'aki Kihelotu 'Alatini Richter, *From Tonga to Zion: The Story of Fa'Aki Kihelotu 'Alatini Richter or Faith and Prayer,* ed. Ella Mae Judd, (Phoenix, Ariz.: Polynesian Publications, 1991).

Mormonism in Tonga has also been the subject of two topically focused graduate theses that are worth consulting. First in importance—though controversial within the Tongan Mormon community—and soon to be published by a university press is anthropologist Tamar Gordon's provocative "Inventing Mormon Identity in Tonga" (Ph.D. diss., University of California, Berkeley, 1988). One can sample her interpretations in "Inventing the Mormon Tongan Family," in *Christianity in Oceania: Ethnographic Perspectives,* ed. John Barker (Lanham, Md.: University Press of America, 1990), 197–217. A master's thesis that examines the Church's impact as the largest external contributor to the Tongan economy is Sosaia H. Naulu, "Incidental Effects of Church Activity on Development, Landscapes and Culture: An Example From Tonga" (master's thesis, Brigham Young University, 1990).

Melanesia

Melanesia ("black islands," in reference to the color of the inhabitants) designates that group of islands that lie to the north (Papua New Guinea) and northeast (Solomon Islands, New Caledonia, Vanuatu, and Fiji) of Australia. In large part because of the similarity in appearance (although there is no genetic connection) between Melanesians and Africans, the Church stayed away from these islands until the mid-twentieth century because of the priesthood issue. In 1955, on his return visit to the South Pacific, after a stopover in Suva, Fiji, President David O. McKay decided that Melanesians were not under the priesthood ban and that the work should go forward in Fiji. In an inspired move similar in intent to the popular punch line of the movie *Field of Dreams,* "if you build it they will come," Pres. McKay commissioned the building of a full-sized chapel complex in Suva, Fiji. As Britsch notes in the only extant, reasonably detailed account of the beginnings of the Church in Fiji, "For many years the little branch rattled around in the structure, and even they wondered whether President McKay had made a mistake" (*Unto the Islands of the Sea,* 505). But the Fijians came, and as of 2003, there were more than 12,000 Latter-day Saints, four stakes, and a temple in Fiji.

It should be pointed out that approximately 50 percent of Fiji's current population are Indians, brought from the subcontinent in the nineteenth century to work the plantations. In the twentieth century, however, they moved into business and commerce and today they provide the economic backbone of the country. A significant number of Latter-day Saints in Fiji are Indians, some of whom were among the first missionaries to re-open the work in India toward the end of the twentieth century.

To date, aside from Britsch's fine study, which, because of its 1980s publication date covers barely half of Fiji's total Mormon history, the only other published histories are a handful of brief pieces that have appeared in Church periodicals during the past twenty years. Of these, Shirleen Meek, "Fiji: Islands of Faith," *Ensign* 20 (December 1990): 32–37 is the most informative and accessible, though English-speaking readers should not overlook *Tambuli,* the Church's periodical for portions of the South Pacific. Not all the articles appearing there appear in the *Ensign.*

Coverage of the Church in the rest of Melanesia is even more sparse. *Unto the Islands of the Sea* offers only pages instead of chapters, as the Church was either very new or not yet established in these areas when Britsch's book was published. For example, though several Latter-day Saint Tongan families had lived in the capital of Vanuatu, Port Vila, since the 1950s, missionary work commenced in earnest in Vanuatu (New Hebrides) in the early 1970s when two Tongan missionaries were sent there to further the work. Growth has been slow in the country, with a Latter-day Saint population numbering less than 1,500 in 2003. On the other hand, the Church in Papua New Guinea, where the first branch was organized in 1979, stands at nearly 11,000 members, almost as many as in Fiji and more than half the membership in French Polynesia, where the Church has been since 1844.

Tahitian migrant workers took the gospel to New Caledonia in the 1950s. In the 1960s, the first branch was formed in the capital Noumea and the country was officially dedicated for preaching the gospel. Like in Vanuatu, the Church in New Caledonia is still too small to have a stake, numbering just over 1,500 members.

The most recent Melanesian country to receive the gospel is the Solomon Islands. Though earlier attempts had been made, missionary work only became a permanent fixture in the Solomon Islands in the 1990s. Missionaries have served continuously in the capital Honiara on the island of Guadalcanal since 1994. Most of the two hundred Solomon Islands Saints belong to the Honiara branch.

Aside from the brief account in *Unto the Islands of the Sea,* published historical pieces of note include Connie and Ralph Andersen, "Vanuatu: Gospel Growth in the Islands of the Sea," *Ensign* 31 (October 2001): 73; R. Val Johnson, "Islands of Light," *Ensign* 30 (March 2000): 31–35 for New Caledonia; and Michael Morris, "'One Talk' in Papua New Guinea," *Ensign* 25 (February 1995): 22–29. Nothing has yet appeared on the ten-year-old history of the faithful few hundred Saints in the Solomon Islands. A significant, if unpublished, resource deserving special notice is the Pioneers in the Pacific Sesquicentennial Celebration Archives located at BYU–Hawaii. During a week-long celebration at BYU–Hawaii and the PCC held in October 1997, a number of sessions (nearly all of which were successfully recorded) featured personal accounts from pioneers in the history of the Church in Melanesia. This included Vaiba Rome, president of the first stake in Papua New Guinea, and Benson and Ethel Ariembo from Papua New Guinea; Teahumanu Manoi (discussed preciously in Johnson, "Islands of Light") from New Caledonia; Edwin Basil from Vanuatu; and Joseph Sokia and Jesse Maiwiriwiri from Fiji. In addition, BYU–Hawaii sent a representative to Melanesia to videotape oral interviews of Church pioneers. Sixty hours of such interviews and video recording of Church sites of historical importance throughout Melanesia are preserved in the BYU–Hawaii Archives. This should provide an invaluable resource for writing the history of the Church in Melanesia.

Micronesia

Micronesia (small islands) refers to islands in the northwestern quadrant of the Pacific Ocean, roughly situated between the Philippines and Hawaii. This includes Kiribati (Gilbert Islands), the Federated States of Micronesia, the Republic of Belau, Guam, the Republic of the Northern Mariana Islands, and the Republic of the Marshall Islands. With the exceptions of Guam and of limited contact with Latter-day Saint G.I.s during World War II in other areas, these are countries that have known the gospel only since the 1970s. With some 10,000 members representing 10 percent of the country's population, the Church in Kiribati is numerically larger than in all the rest of Micronesia put together. The early part of its impressive story is told in Britsch, *Unto the Islands of the Sea.* As with Melanesia, however, significant advances to the emerging historiography of Micronesia were made at the 1997 Pioneers in the Pacific conference in Laie, Hawaii, and can be consulted in the BYU–Hawaii

Archives. Of particular note with regard to Kiribati was W. James Jacob's presentation, drawn from his extensive in-country research and oral interviews. In terms of published Micronesian Mormon history, readers can glean from *Unto the Islands of the Sea* as well as from a few, short pieces in Church periodicals: Val R. Johnson, "The Seabirds of Kiribati," *Ensign* 30 (December 2000): 40–44; and Val R. Johnson, "Charting a New Course in Micronesia," *Ensign* 26 (July 1996): 38–42. One notable exception pertaining primarily to the Federated States of Micronesia and Guam is the privately produced William W. Cannon, *Beachheads in Micronesia* (Salt Lake City: W. W. Cannon, 1997), which offers excellent detail from Cannon's service as an early Micronesia-Guam mission president.

Pacific-Wide

A few significant studies do not fit comfortably in the regional organization followed in this article. Thumbnail sketches of the Church's history in many of the areas just discussed can be found under each country's entry in the *Encyclopedia of Mormonism*, ed. Daniel Ludlow, 4 vols. (New York: Macmillan, 1992). A fine, interpretively rich essay originally given as the annual Mormon History Association Tanner Lecture is Laurie F. Maffly-Kipp, "Looking West: Mormonism and the Pacific World," *Journal of Mormon History* 26 (spring 2000): 40–63. A valuable pan-Pacific study that includes comments on the Church is Manfred Ernst, *Winds of Change: Rapidly Growing Religious Groups in the Pacific Islands* (Suva, Fiji: Pacific Conference of Churches, 1994). A similarly Pacific-wide overview of Church education in the Pacific is R. Lanier Britsch, "Latter-day Saint Education in the Pacific Islands," in Davis Bitton and Maureen U. Beecher, eds., *New Views of Mormon History* (Salt Lake City: University of Utah Press, 1987), 197–211.

An aspect of the Latter-day Saint experience in the Pacific that for a variety of reasons looms large in Pacific Islanders' own minds is the labor mission program. From New Zealand to Hawaii during the 1950s and 1960s, young Polynesian men were called to donate time and muscle to carrying out an ambitious building program within their own countries and sometimes elsewhere in the Pacific. They learned skills and developed friendships that have persisted over the decades. Presently the only lengthy study of the labor missions is the very outdated David W. Cummings, *Mighty Missionary of the Pacific: The Building Program of The Church of Jesus Christ of Latter-Day Saints, Its History, Scope, and Significance* (Salt Lake City: Bookcraft, 1961), which now functions more as a primary rather than a secondary source.

Inter-island migration is a prominent part of life in the Pacific. Aspects of the Mormon experience along these lines are discussed in Max E. Stanton, "A Gathering of Saints: The Role of the Church of Jesus Christ of Latter-day Saints in Pacific Islander Migration," in *A World Perspective on Pacific Islander Migration*, ed. G. McCall and J. Connell (Sydney, Australia: University of New South Wales, 1993), 23–37. Though not printed publications, two video documentaries meriting mention are the BYU-produced "Islands of Love, People of Faith" (1993) and the KSL-produced "The Polynesian Cultural Center" (2003). Finally, readers should watch for a forthcoming volume to be published by the BYU Religious Studies Center that will contain highlights from the 1997 "Pioneers in the Pacific" Sesquicentennial Conference held in Laie, Hawaii.

Frontiers in Pacific Latter-day Saint Historiography

Though many important and fascinating studies in Pacific Mormon History have been produced in the past, there is still considerable room for more to be done. The following are areas that need more information or fresh interpretations:

(1) "Interregnum" Mormonism. Whether in French Polynesia or in Hawaii, there have been periods after the gospel was first brought to the islands when the local Saints were left on their own. In some instances, it was decades before the "Zion Elders" returned. What happened during the years Church members were on their own? For instance, during the forty-year period from 1852 to 1892, in French Polynesia various groups emerged known as Israelites, Whistlers, Abraham's Church, the Sheep, and Darkites. We know very little about them. How did the experience in French Polynesia compare with, say, the aberrations introduced by Walter Murray Gibson in Hawaii or with what happened to the first generation of Samoan Saints, converted by Manoa and Pelio.

(2) Missionary Techniques. We need a good history of missionary techniques used throughout the Pacific both as they developed in response to directions from Salt Lake City and to local need.

(3) Pacific Prophets. More detailed studies of Pacific Islander "prophets," whose prophecies are construed to predict the arrival of Mormon missionaries. This phenomenon is known from Hawaii to New Zealand.

(4) Biographies of Local Leaders. Many more biographies of local islander Saints who played prominent roles in the history of the Church in their own locales should be produced. Here one thinks of Maihea and Mapuhi in French Polynesia, or Pelio and Manoa in Samoa, or Wiremu Duncan in New Zealand, just to name a few.

(5) Comparative Studies. Interweaving Pacific Mormon studies with other "contact" and religious syncretism studies in the region would be most enriching. Full and nuanced histories of the interaction between indigenous culture and Mormonism would situate Mormon Studies in the center of current Pacific Studies. These histories would include comparative study of the appeal of Mormonism in various places. What were the customs, ideas, and values that made the Church seem attractive at the various times and places?

(6) World War II. A sophisticated and comparative study needs to be done on the World War II years and how they impacted the Church around the Pacific. Sorely needed is a detailed and comprehensive study that presents oral histories and personal narratives of World War II veterans in this regard before too many pass away. Some comments are found in Robert C. Freeman and Dennis A. Wright, *Saints at War: Experiences of Latter-day Saints in World War II* (American Fork, Utah: Covenant Communications, 2001).

(7) The Labor Missionary Program. As mentioned before, a comprehensive history of the labor missionary program would address what Pacific Islander Latter-day Saints feel is one of the most important chapters in their twentieth-century Church history.

(8) Gathering Places. Given the importance of the doctrine of "gathering" in Church history, a full and comparative history of the various "island zions" and why they were created in lieu of gathering to the mainland United States, would be most illuminating.

(9) Folk Mormonism. The distinction between official and popular religion is prominent in religious studies. Attention to a comparative study of "folk Mormonism" in various Pacific cultures would be helpful.

(10) Localization. We need a better understanding of the chronology and dynamics of the localization of Church leadership in each of the areas of the Pacific.

Paraphrasing the words of the famous missionary hymn "Ye Elders of Israel," the harvest of Mormon history in the Pacific is great but the laborers are few. There is room for all to thrust in the sickle with their might and to recruit others to do likewise. Research on Mormon history in the Pacific is just beginning, and there is much work that can be done. So doing will help preserve a rich history well worth recounting.

Notes

1. Joseph Smith Jr., *History of The Church of Jesus Christ of Latter-day Saints*, ed. B. H. Roberts, 2d ed., rev., 7 vols. (Salt Lake City: Deseret Book, 1971), 5:368.

2. S. George Ellsworth, ed., *The History of Louisa Barnes Pratt: The Autobiography of a Mormon Missionary Widow and Pioneer* (Logan: Utah State University Press, 1998), 65.

3. Hanks died at sea, and Rogers would return home early.

4. Alma Greenwood, "My New Zealand Mission," *Juvenile Instructor* 20 (1885): 71, 82–83, 100–102, 114–15, 139–41, 146–47, 171–72, 190–91, 206–07, 222–23, 238, 251, 258, 278, 301–02, 325, 349–50, 356, 371; 21 (1886): 6–7, 48, 66. The series abruptly ends on page 66 with promise of continuation, but no further installments appear, most likely because they had moved from detailing the history of the Church to a providing details of New Zealand's natural beauty.

Edward J. Wood, "My Samoan Experience," *Juvenile Instructor* 28 (1893): 85–87, 131–33, 191–94, 209–11, 326–28, 347–49, 407–9, 489–91, 537–40, 700–703, 772–76.

5. Given the informal nature of their production, it is understandable that the proceedings of the Mormon Pacific Historical Society have carried slightly different titles over the years. For purposes of standardization in *Voyages of Faith* they were referenced as *MPHS Annual Conference Proceedings*, a procedure followed here in the appendix. Thus, a given presentation would be cited like the following example: Joseph H. Spurrier, "The Hawaii Temple: A Special Place in a Special Land," in *1986 MPHS Annual Conference Proceedings* (Laie, Hawaii: Mormon Pacific Historical Society, 1987), 28–34.

6. Margaret Jolly, "Specters of Inauthenticity," *Contemporary Pacific* 4 (spring 1992): 63.

7. Douglas Terry Webb published several chapters from his dissertation in scholarly journals in the 1990s, but the sense of cultural experts in the PCC–BYU–Hawaii community was that his interpretations were more imaginary than imaginative.

Appendix
Twenty Years of Mormon Pacific Historical Society Proceedings

Compiled by Grant Underwood

1980

Leonard J. Arrington, "On Writing Latter-day Saint History"

Donald Johnson, "It Is *Not* All Cut and Dried"

Agnes C. Conrad, "Sources for Family History in Hawaii"

Eric B. Shumway, "Problems in Oral History in Tonga"

R. Lanier Britsch, "The Establishment of the Church in French Polynesia, 1844–1917"

Leonard J. Arrington, "The LDS Hawaiian Colony at Skull Valley, Utah 1889–1895"

Joseph Spurrier, "Family Life in Hawaii During the Hawaiian Monarchy"

Ishmael Stagner, "Na Makua Mahalo I'a—Mormon Contributions to Hawaiian Music"

Carl Fonoimoana, "Opapo—Man of Miracles"

Vernice Pere, "The Story Behind the Legend of the Seven Maori Canoes and the Descending Maori Chief"

Albert Like, "Preservation of the Hawaiian Identity in the Present Day Hawaiian Family"

Lance D. Chase, "The Hawaiian Mission Crisis of 1874: Character as Destiny"

1981

S. George Ellsworth, "New Wine and Old Bottles: The LDS Conversion Experience in French Polynesia"

Russell Clement and Sheng-Luen Tsai, "East Wind to Hawaii: Contributions of Chinese and Japanese Mormons in Hawaii"

Max Stanton, "Samoan Saints: Settlers and Sojourners"

William K. Wallace, "LDS Homesteaders–Hoolehua: 1923–25"

Joseph Spurrier, "Early Missionaries to Hawaii"

Faaki Richter, "Missionary Work in Tonga"

Edwin Kamauoha, "Malae O Le Alofa (The Village of Love)"

LeRuth Tyau, "My Genealogy and History Experience"

Lance Chase, "Life in Early Laie, 1850–80"

S. George Ellsworth, "My Voyage from Zion in Utah to Zion in Paradise, or What Treasures Do You Have in Your Attic?"

Barbara Elkington, "A Unity of Many Islands: The Building Mission Program in Hawaii"

Elizabeth Lim, "A Mormon Family in Hawaii"

Ishmael W. Stagner, II, "Hawaiian Hula Genealogies: The Laie Connection"

1982

Eric B. Shumway, "A Tongan Missionary Journal: History as Anecdote"

C. J. Fox, "Clio and Calliope: Writing Imaginative Histories of the Pacific"

Glenn Lung, "Statistical Growth of the LDS Church in Samoa and Tonga"

Edward Clissold, "Assignment Kona, 1921"

Howard Lowe, "Walter Murray Gibson: Renegade or Saint"

Marvalee Tahauri, "Memories of Rose Naaieono Young"

Ishmael Stagner, "Hawaiian Music and Dance: Some Mormon Influences"

1983

Kenneth W. Baldridge, "Search for a Site: Selection of the CCH"

Lance Chase, "Horse Soldiers and the Spaulding Manuscript: Hawaiian Missionary Life a Century Ago"

Jerry Loveland, "Polynesian Origins and Migrations"

Glenn Lung, "Statistical Growth of the LDS Church in Samoa and Tonga"

Kurt Richter, "Origins of the Polynesians"

Marvalee Tahauri, "The Singing Ruau of Tahiti"

Leruth Tyau, "History Recorded Through Art Work: A Personal Experience"

Emil Wolfgramm, "Tonga: Receptacle of New Concepts"

1984

R. Lanier Britsch, "On the Pacific Frontiers: Recent Church Growth in the Non-Polynesian Areas"

David Chen, "The Lost Tribes of Israel and Our Mission in the Pacific"

Lela Dalton, "A Glimpse into the Early Hawaii Mission and Oahu Stake Relief" (A Slide Presentation)

Dean Farnsworth, "Missionary Service in Samoa"

Rubina Forester, "Ahmu: An Early Samoan Latter-day Saint"

Robert O. Joy, "The Historical Origins of the Goals of BYU–Hawaii Campus"

Glenn Lung, "LDS Pacific Update"

1985

J. Frank Woolley, "Reminiscences of the Construction of the Honolulu Tabernacle"

Joseph K. Whitford, "Persecution in Fiji: The Story of Three LDS Couples"

Dennis Atkin, "Iosepa, A Utah Home for the Polynesians"

Victoria K Kekuaokalani, "Sally M. Wood Naluai: A Story of My Life"

Eric Shumway, "Tevita Muli Kinikini, Missionary, Poet, Man of Faith"

Donene Olmstead, "A Bell Rings in Paradise: Eli Bell's Mission to Hawaii"

Glenn Lung, "Pacific Update"

Lance Chase, "John Stillman Woodbury and the Battle Against Prejudice, Ignorance, and Superstition in Hawaii"

1986

Kenneth Baldridge, "Tour of Historic Laie"

Joseph Spurrier, "History of Laie" (Hawaii LDS Temple)

Ruth Austin, "Our Lei to You: A Biography of Samuel Edwin Woolley"

Dale Berge, "The Laie Sugar Mill (1868–1900)"

Russ Clement, "Apostle in Exile: Joseph F. Smith's Third Mission to Hawaii (1885–1887)"

Rubina Forester, "History of the Polynesian Cultural Center"

Kenneth Baldridge, "History of BYU–Hawaii: Search for Academic Excellence"

1987

Lance Chase, "Voice of the Waves of the Sea"

Jim Kaanaana, "Historical Highlights of Kahana"

Midge Oler, "Sam Pua Ha'aheo"

Robert Stauffer, "The Hui of Kahana"

1988

Paul L. Anderson, "A Jewel in the Gardens of Paradise: The Art and Architecture of the Hawaiian Temple"

Justin F. Fairbanks, "Restoration of the Hawaii Temple Friezes"

R. Lanier Britsch, "The Conception of the Hawaii Temple"

Dorothy L. Behling, "Love for Ohana Helps Bring the Temple"

Lance D. Chase, "The Attempted Attack on the Hawaii Temple"

Kenneth Baldridge, "In Search of a Tale: A Personal Account"

Mark Augustine, "Exploding an LDS Myth"

1989

Kenneth W. Baldridge, "George Q. Cannon: A Look at a Giant"

Joseph Spurrier, "Sandwich Island Saints"

Gloriann Akau, "The Maui Moikeha's: An Extended Family"

Frank A. Bruno, "Faith like the Ancients: The Church on Maui and in Pulehu"

Adren J. Bird, "Koolau District, Maul: Beginning of a Successful LDS Mission"

Evan Larsen, "The Formation and First Ten Years of the Kahului-Hawaii Stake"

Jubilee Moikeha, "Chapels on Maui"

1990

Sharlene B. C. L. Furuto, "Japanese Saints in Hawaii and Japan: Values and Implications for Baptism"

Lavina Fielding Anderson, "Prayer Under a Pepper Tree: Five Accounts of a Spiritual Manifestation"

Ruth R. Yeaman, "Women from Zion in the Samoan Mission: 1888–1900"

Ambrose Don Kameakaulana Velasco, "Chiasmus in Ancient Hawaiian Prophecies, Prayers, and Chants"

Richard O. Cowan, "Temples in the Pacific: A Reflection of Twentieth Century Mormon History"

Maria S. Ellsworth, "The First Mormon Missionary Women in the Pacific, 1850–1852"

1991

Kenneth W. Baldridge, "Report on the Kahana Chapel Restoration"
Eric Shumway, "Tongan Saints: Legacy of Faith"
Ruth Austin, "I Would That Ye Should Remember Me, Mosiah 1:6"
Lance Chase, "Samuel Edwin Woolley: A Valet's Hero"
Kathy Creager, "From Kapu to Christianity"
Bob Stauffer, "Miriam Kekuku: An Early LDS Resident of Kahana and Laie"
Dale Beecher, "Zion in the Pacific: Polynesian Gathering Places"
Leda Kalilimoku, "Early Church History of Waimanalo"
Eunice McElroy, "Church History in Waimanalo: 1946–47 to Present"
Midge Oler, "LDS Composers, *Kumu Hula* and Musicians"

1992

Kuulei Bell, "A Servant of God: A Story of Jack Sing Kong"
Alexander Bishaw, "Molokai Temple Excursion"
Lance Chase, "Mormons and Lepers: The Saints at Kalaupapa"
Mokihana Davis, "LDS Chapels on Molokai"
Betty Jean (BJ) Fuller, "Mary Lee: Charity Never Faileth"
Martha Kalama, "How My Molokai Childhood Experiences Led Me to the Church"
William Wallace, Jr., "Mo'olelo Kahiko"

1993

Albert N. Like, "Kalihi Chapel"
Dorothy L. Behling, "In Search of Early Hawaiians"
Steven R. Lee, "The Impact of Hurricane Iniki on the Life of an Island and its People"
Glenn Lung, "Hawaii Physical Facilities, Church of Jesus Christ of Latter-day Saints"
May Leinani Parker Au, "History of the Latter-day Saint Church in Kane'ohe Hawai'i"
Lance Davis Chase, "The Meek Did Not Inherit the Earth: The 1927–1928 Laie Beach Front Sale and Lawsuit"

1994

"The Coming of Christianity to Waialua"
"The "Mormons" Come to Waialua"
Henry Sin Kui Ah nee and Esther Kawaiola Takauya-Ah nee, "Family Organization"
David Grandy, "Glass Balls as Artifacts and Archetypes"
Roy Kakulu Alameida, "Aina Kaulana o Waialua"
Cynthia D. Woolley Compton and D. Chad Compton, "What Is Going on Here? Making Meaning of Life in a Global Information Society."
Grant Underwood, "Frontiers in Mormon Pacific History"

1995

Herman Paleka, "Hurricane Iniki Experience"
Kenneth Baldridge, "A Very Personal History"
Lance Chase, "If At First You Don't Succeed: The Beginnings of Mormon Missionary Work on Kaua'i 1850–54"
David Grandy, "Mormonism and Native Hawaiian Religion: It's a Small World After All"
Delia Ulima, "A Comparison Between the Ancient Hawaiian Ho'oponopono Process and the Repentance Process"
Rex Frandsen, "The National Personnel Records Center Fire of July 12, 1973"

1996

Brian O'Brien, "History of LDS in Kailua"
David Grandy, "An Attempt at Reconciliation"
Inoke Funaki, "Sione Malu'amaka Tupolo: His Conversion and Pioneering Efforts Toward Establishing the Mormon Church on the Islands of Niua Fo'ou and Eua"
William Wallace II, "The Hawaiian Studies Program at BYU–H"
Glenn Lung, "Kaneohe Stake Center and LDS History in Kaneohe"
Jeffrey Stover, "Not All is Obvious: The Political Reason For King Kamehameha V Not Wanting the Mormon Colony to Preach"
Adren Bird, "Priesthood Power"
Merlin Waite, "History of the Oahu Stake"
Grant Underwood, "Mormonism and the Shaping of Maori Religious Identity"

1997

MPHS co-sponsored the PIP Sesquicentennial Conference

1998

Sanford Okura, "Early Missionary Experiences on the Island of Hawaii"

Riley Moffat, "The Return of Sam Brannan"

Olani Durrant, "Stewart A. Durrant: Missionary Assignment Hilo 1935–36"

Carol Helekunihi, "Minerva Eliza Fernadez: A Life of Service"

Brian O'Brien, "The Architecture of Harold Burton"

Grant Underwood, "The Cowley Correspondence: A Behind-the-Scenes Glimpse at Matthew Cowley"

Dennis Atkin, "Utah's Iosepa: Polynesian Beauty in the Desert"

Lance D. Chase, "The Purported Attempt to Bomb the Hawaii Temple: Dec. 7, 1941"

1999

Tribute to Lance D. Chase

E. Dale LeBaron, "Benjamin F. Johnson and the Early Hawaiian Mission"

2000

Business meeting and publication celebration for the twentieth anniversary volume *Voyages of Faith: Explorations in Mormon Pacific History*

2001

22nd Annual Conference, March 24–26

2002

Annual meeting held in New Zealand with various informal site papers/presentations

2003

No proceedings

Selected Bibliography: Historiography of the Church in Eastern Europe

Compiled by Kahlile B. Mehr

General

Benson, Ezra Taft. *A Labor of Love: The 1946 European Mission of Ezra Taft Benson.* Salt Lake City: Deseret Book, 1989. Account of Ezra Taft Benson's relief effort in war-torn Europe.

Babbel, Frederick W. *On Wings of Faith.* Salt Lake City: Bookcraft, 1972. Account of Ezra Taft Benson's relief effort in Europe including Poland, Czechoslovakia, and Germany after World War II as told by his traveling companion.

Hickman, Martin Berkeley. *David Matthew Kennedy: Banker, Statesman, Churchman.* Salt Lake City: Deseret Book, 1987. Contains several accounts of Kennedy's experiences trying to obtain recognition for the Church in various countries of eastern Europe.

Jardine, Leo A. and Judith C. N. Jardine. *Out of Obscurity, Out of Captivity, Out of Darkness: The Church and Humanitarian Services in Former Yugoslavia and the Russian Empire.* [Salt Lake City]: By the authors, 1998. Account of experiences of missionaries who directed humanitarian services in eastern Europe, 1995–96. Contains otherwise unavailable statistics.

Mehr, Kahilie B. *Mormon Missionaries Enter Eastern Europe.* Provo, Utah: Brigham Young University Press, 2002. History of Latter-day Saint presence in eastern Europe from 1865. Includes reminiscences of Elder Mischa Markow, first Latter-day Saint missionary in eastern Europe.

Van Orden, Bruce A. *Building Zion: The Latter-day Saints in Europe.* Salt Lake City: Deseret Book, 1996. Includes a comprehensive look at eastern Europe. Based heavily upon published sources.

Czechoslovakia

Campora, Olga Kovářová. *Saint Behind Enemy Lines.* Salt Lake City: Deseret Book, 1996. Compelling and touching account that describes the pulse of life in a socialist country in contrast with gospel light.

Loscher, J. Peter. *J. Peter Loscher.* Salt Lake City: By the author, 1976. Account of Loscher's experiences in Czechoslovakia, 1964–65, while serving as president of the Austria Vienna Mission.

Anderson, Martha Sharp Toronto. *A Cherry Tree Behind the Iron Curtain: The Autobiography of Martha Toronto Anderson.* Salt Lake City: By the author, 1977. Compelling account of a mission president's wife in Czechoslovakia before and after World War II through the communist takeover in 1950.

East Germany

Davis, Garold N. and Norma S. Davis. *Behind the Iron Curtain.* Provo, Utah: BYU Studies, 1996. Primary accounts of those who lived the gospel in a hostile political and social environment.

Monson, Thomas S. *Faith Rewarded: A Personal Account of Prophetic Promises to the East German Saints.* Salt Lake City: Deseret Book, 1996. Account of experiences of the Apostle concerning eastern Europe, 1968–85.

Hungary

Hill, Ivy Hooper Blood. *John Ensign Hill: Diaries and Biographical Material.* Logan: J.P. Smith, 1962. Personal account of the first missionary to learn Hungarian in order to teach in that country, 1909–1910.

Romania

Ball, DeAnna and Terry Ball, eds. *Each One a Miracle.* Orem, Utah: Grandin Book, 1994. Touching stories of adopting Romanian orphans with a few references to the humanitarian service missionaries serving in Romania during 1990–91.

Clifton, Carmin. *Come Lord, Come: A History of The Church of Jesus Christ of Latter-day Saints in Romania.* San Jose, Calif.: Writers Club, 2002. Written by a returned missionary who did extensive interviewing to compile a comprehensive history including activity during the communist period.

Russia

Browning, Gary. *Russia and the Restored Gospel.* Salt Lake City: Deseret Book, 1997. Detailed stories of experiences and conversions. Important primary material.

Rogers, Thomas F. *A Call to Russia: Glimpses of Missionary Life from the Journal of a Mission President in the Russia St. Petersburg Mission.* Provo, Utah: BYU Studies, 1999. Reminiscences on experiences and gospel principles.

Ukraine

Biddulph, Howard L. *The Morning Breaks: Stories of Conversion and Faith in the Former Soviet Union.* Salt Lake City: Deseret Book, 1996. Good history of early missionary work in Ukraine.

Historic Sites as Institutional Memory

Steven L. Olsen

It is not a trivial question to ask how necessary the historical enterprise of The Church of Jesus Christ of Latter-day Saints is to the Church's lofty spiritual mission. Compared with other Christian religions, the Church devotes an amazing amount of resources to preserve its past via libraries, archives, museums, historic sites, publications, curriculum materials, internet sites, research aids, audio-visual media, pageants and other performances, and the preservation and decoration of noteworthy ecclesiastical buildings such as temples, tabernacles, and meeting houses. The Church also encourages its members to create family and personal histories, establish family associations and traditions, study the history of the Church in ancient and modern times, preserve mementos of the past, and in other ways keep a record of the past "for the good of the Church and the rising generations" (D&C 69:8). On a per capita basis, Latter-day Saints likely devote more time and money and more interest and expertise to preserving their individual and institutional pasts than do members of other sizeable religions, Christian or otherwise.

Why should this be so? Why should a vibrant and deep-seated historical consciousness be so essential to Latter-day Saints? From the perspective of my formal training in cultural anthropology and my nearly quarter-century career in Church history, I speculate on this seeming necessity in this article. These thoughts are my own; they do not represent any official position of the Family and Church History Department. I suggest three possible reasons why the Church's historical enterprise, and in particular the Church's historic sites program, is central to Mormon religious identity. The Church currently maintains nearly two dozen sites or site complexes, from Vermont to southern California, to document essential events, lives, and values connected with the gospel's restoration in this dispensation.

The Nature of Latter-day Saint Theology

The belief systems of most Christian religions are expressed in formal terms—that is, as logical deductions from metaphysical or supernatural premises which are organized in a systematic manner. By contrast, the core religious tenets of the Church are largely defined in terms of spiritual experiences and expressed in terms of narratives. That is, the Church's theology is more experiential than propositional. For example, the standard works are for the most part structured as narratives or have clear and direct reference to a historical context; personal testimonies are often expressed as spiritual experiences or events; and moral and ethical principles are often taught by actual or metaphorical examples. This experiential emphasis has more than simple heuristic or pedagogical value. Rather, it seems to partake of the very essence of Latter-day Saint religious identity.

This is not to say, as some scholars have said, that the Church is fundamentally anti-intellectual and has not produced profound religious thinkers. Nor does this point of view necessarily engender pessimism about the future of Mormon thought, as expressed by such notable scholars as Thomas O'Dea and Mark Leone.[1] However, this perspective does acknowledge that in Mormon epistemology and ontology, knowledge of the truth results more from spiritual experiences that occur in real time and space, that involve real people, that respond to real circumstances, and that affect both the mind and the heart (see D&C 8:2) than from logical inferences, reasoned abstractions, or other formal philosophical or rational processes alone.

For Latter-day Saints, the process of getting to know God—the ultimate goal of theology and the essence of eternal life as defined by Christ in his great intercessory prayer (see John 17:3)—is similar to that of getting to know an earthly loved one. The process is contingent upon a lifetime of experience and is motivated by devotion, tempered by service, and refined by reflection. In short, Latter-day Saint doctrine is ultimately based on revelation and other spiritual experiences and not on reason per se.

From this perspective, Latter-day Saint belief cannot be separated from Mormon experience. The dichotomy of history and doctrine that exists in much of Christianity is an artificial and largely unsatisfactory construct in Mormonism. The noted historian of religion, Martin Marty, addressed this point when he traced the ultimate truth claims of the Church to two experiences: Joseph Smith's First Vision and the coming forth of the Book of Mormon. Said he:

> if the beginning of the promenade of Mormon history, the First Vision and the Book of Mormon, can survive the [historiographical] crisis, then the rest of the promenade follows and nothing that happens in it can really detract from the miracle of the whole. If the first steps do not survive, there can be only antiquarian, not fateful or faith-ful interest in the rest of the story.[2]

From this perspective, Church historic sites are more than just attractive destinations for family vacations or user-friendly proselytizing platforms. In a very real sense, they are the public places where the "work and . . . glory" of God (Moses 1:39) have been most explicitly manifest in this dispensation. Historic sites document the most significant events and key personalities of the gospel's restoration, and hence are among the most important physical and visual representations of the Kingdom of God on the earth. Such tangible, empirical, and intimate dimensions of faith are essential for a religion that claims that God is a distinct physical being, that mankind are His spiritual offspring, that the true history of the earth is the unfolding of God's plan of salvation, and that earth will eventually become a heaven for those worthy enough to live with their loved ones in the literal presence of God.

The Nature of Mormon Covenants

The Church's historical enterprise is essential for Latter-day Saints to keep their baptismal covenants. The most frequently quoted scriptural passage in the Church is not James 1:5, Moses 1:37, 1 Nephi 3:7, nor Moroni 10:4–5. It is Doctrine and Covenants 20:77, 79. The sacrament prayers are recited verbatim weekly, as a renewal of baptismal covenants for millions of Church members in tens of thousands of congregations in sacrament meetings throughout the world. In the ordinance of the sacrament, Latter-day Saints promise to do certain things in response to and in anticipation of divine blessings. The two verbs that characterize the Saints' promises in this covenant are "witness" and "remember." Both verbs and their respective cognates appear at least once in each prayer.

We often don't think of "remembering" and "witnessing" as essential obligations of Church membership; nevertheless, a quick review of the scriptures reinforces the central religious importance of these two mandates. For example, the verb "remember" and its cognates appear more than two hundred times in the text of the Book of Mormon, making "remembering" one of its most frequently repeated messages. In addition to the frequency, the usual placement of these words in the narrative should leave no doubt of the importance of the message. In nearly every instance, the message appears as a spiritual imperative, as in the plea, "And now, O man, remember and perish not" (Mosiah 4:30).

Similarly, the importance of witnessing finds numerous applications in the scriptures. For the purpose of this article, I confine my inquiry to three general categories of witness: human, physical, and historical.

Most often, witnesses are selected people, who, because of their unique relationship to a gospel truth, can testify to the world of its eternal veracity. But the law of witnesses is not restricted to the oral or written testimony of holy men and women. The scriptures are replete with examples of places or things that serve as physical, tangible witnesses of spiritual experiences or other divine realities. Among the most noted material and spatial witnesses in the Bible story are Jacob's well, Joshua's altar at Shechem, Abraham's tomb at Hebron, Mount Moriah, Mount Sinai, the Mount of Transfiguration, the Garden of Gethsemane, Golgotha, and the Garden Tomb. All of these sacred places helped to preserve an identity of divine chosenness and physical and social continuity among biblical peoples.

Historical events also serve as witnesses of sacred truths. Included in the pattern of the many covenants that have been established between

God and man over the centuries is the frequent rehearsal of key historical events that provide an effective prelude to the covenant and a compelling statement of the willingness of the divine and human parties to be so united.[3]

Likewise, in the present dispensation, a cryptic rehearsal of historical events integral to the gospel's restoration accompanied the formal organization of the Church and was canonized in one of its revelations most important to Church organization. Early in the current section 20 of the Doctrine and Covenants (vv. 5–12), reference is made to the First Vision, the coming forth of the Book of Mormon, the restoration of the priesthood, and the beginning of missionary work as essential prerequisites for Joseph Smith to serve as "First Elder" of the Church (v. 2). Immediately following this review of these events, the revelation continues:

> Thereby, having so great witnesses, by them shall the world be judged, even as many as shall come to a knowledge of this work. And those who receive it in faith, and work righteousness, shall receive a crown of eternal life; But those who harden their hearts in unbelief, and reject it, it shall turn to their own condemnation. (D&C 20:13–15)

This passage suggests that the restoration of the gospel in this dispensation is clearly signaled by certain critical historical events which serve as witnesses to the world of the restoration and as a means by which many can avail themselves of its eternal blessings.

Church historic sites use all three types of witnesses—human, physical, and historical—to help individuals accept or strengthen their faith in the restored gospel and to help the Church stay focused on its core mission. That is, official missionaries conduct tours of restored sites which are the settings for the key events of the gospel's restoration. This central purpose lies at the heart of decisions about which sites should be restored by the Church, to what degree they are restored, and how they are interpreted.

The Nature of Effective Pedagogy for Communicating the Gospel's Message

Church historic sites provide a complete and effective context for preserving the story of the gospel's restoration in this dispensation. A recently published and brilliant distillation of numerous learning theories in western civilization suggests that learning, or the making of meaning, results from the interplay of three complementary contexts. First, the personal context for learning is determined by individuals' prior knowledge and experience, their values, motivations and expectations for learning, and their biological and physical capacities to learn. Next, the social/cultural context for learning involves the numerous social relationships, interpersonal activities, and man-made features of the learning environment that are directly and indirectly abundant in every educational experience. Finally, the physical context for learning recognizes that learning can be enhanced or inhibited by many features of the physical environment and that elements of the physical environment are often more easily remembered by the learner than are the more abstract aspects of the educational activity.[4]

Church historic sites take conscious and extensive advantage of this contextual model for learning. The personal context of learning at historic sites assumes that most visitors have been prepared by personal experience, spiritual desires, and other compelling motivations to receive the complementary human, physical, and historical witnesses to the gospel's restoration that are ever present at these settings. The social/cultural context takes advantage of missionary guided tours, audio-visual presentations, interpretive exhibits and markers, and the groups in which most visitors come to the sites. The physical settings of sites are restored to be both accurate and appropriate to the targeted events of the gospel's restoration and conducive to learning by the visitors who come there.

In conclusion, Church historic sites not only take advantage of the burgeoning cultural tourism industry, in which millions of persons spend billions of dollars annually to receive authentic educational experiences at a wide range of cultural venues, but more importantly, these sites constitute an essential program for communicating the gospel's message to the world and for preserving the divinely revealed identity of the Latter-day Saints and the Church to which they belong.

Notes

1. Thomas F. O'Dea, *The Mormons* (Chicago: University of Chicago Press, 1957), 224–40; Mark P. Leone, *Roots of Modern Mormonism* (Cambridge, Mass.: Harvard University Press, 1979), 167–93.

2. Martin E. Marty, "Two Integrities: An Address to the Crisis in Mormon Historiography," *Journal of Mormon History* 10 (1983): 9.

3. Delbert R. Hillers, *Covenant: The History of a Biblical Idea* (Baltimore: Johns Hopkins University Press, 1969), 30–32.

4. John H. Falk and Lynn D. Dierking, *Learning from Museums: Visitor Experiences and the Making of Meaning* (Walnut Creek, Calif.: Alta Mira Press, 2000).

Nineteenth-Century Latter-day Saint Immigration: Lessons from Sea Trek 2001 for Telling the Story Better

William G. Hartley

Francis Parkman's history of the Oregon Trail is a classic because he went out on the trail and wrote from firsthand experience. Likewise, Samuel Eliot Morrison's study of Christopher Columbus is outstanding because of Morrison's sea experiences.[1] Stanley Kimball is *the* expert on the Mormon Trail because he has walked it, camped on it, flown over it, ridden on it, and searched for its swales and ruts. Parkman, Morrison, and Kimball stand in the front ranks of historians who have demonstrated that, although much history is written from sources in libraries and archives, some histories are best written by those who have "been there" and "done that." Knowing that hands-on experience can enhance histories, and being engaged in research about nineteenth-century Latter-day Saint immigration, I grabbed the once-in-a-lifetime opportunity that Sea Trek 2001 provided me to cross the Atlantic on a tall sailing ship—a hands-on workshop to experience something of what those immigrants experienced. My fifty-nine days with Sea Trek gave me several insights that can help us tell the immigration story better.

Before sailing, I had published articles about Latter-day Saint immigrant voyages on the sailing ships *International, Olympus, Monarch of the Sea,* and *Yorkshire*.[2] For a book I am writing about Latter-day Saint emigration in 1861, I had done extensive research reading library and archive records—diary, letter, and reminiscent accounts by or about sail-immigrants and Church emigration records and ledger books—and visiting docks in Liverpool and New York City. But, being a Stan Kimball Mormon Trail protege, I knew I needed to go to sea, even if by ocean liner or freighter, to better understand what it meant for Saints to cross the Atlantic. So when I learned that Sea Trek had chartered sailing ships to commemorate that era of sail and was asked to be a teaching historian on board one of those ships, I went without hesitation.

While designed to commemorate—not replicate or recreate—the nineteenth-century immigrant experience, Sea Trek did provide a chance to cross the ocean on a square-rigger similar to ones that carried those immigrants.

The Era of Latter-day Saint Immigration by Sail

Latter-day Saint immigration by sail spans a clearly defined time period from 1840 to 1868, after which Church companies used steamships. Conway Sonne has shown that during that period approximately 50,000 Latter-day Saint immigrants traveled on at least 173 different sailing ships during more than three hundred voyages. Coming from the British Isles, Scandinavia, and western Europe, they sailed primarily from Liverpool to New Orleans (until 1855) or New York (until 1868). Sonne calculated that the average voyage length to New Orleans was fifty-four days and to New York, thirty-eight days.[3] Of ships used during the 1840s the average size Latter-day Saint company on board was 157; in the 1850s, 266; and in the 1860s, 424. The largest company, 976 passengers, sailed in 1864 on the *Monarch of the Sea*.[4] That was the largest ship used by the Saints, measuring 223 feet long and 44 feet wide.[5] Amazingly, that ship was shorter than one of the three Sea Trek ships that crossed the Atlantic.

Sea Trek 2001: An Overview

To commemorate the European Saints' immigration, the Sea Trek Foundation[6] chartered eight tall sailing ships and recruited paying passengers (about $150 per day) to fill them. The ships were training ships used by various countries and companies to teach the basics of sail navigating. Three ships were Norwegian; one, Russian; one, German; and three, Dutch.[7] These ships, like their nineteenth-century counterparts, had tall masts and yards and systems of square-rigged and other sails, and were built primarily to be wind-powered. Crews, with help from the passengers (we were officially trainees), unfurled and furled the sails and repositioned the yards by hand and rope. Trainees, not crew members, steered with the on-deck captain's wheel and compass much like crews on old sailing ships did. To meet modern safety standards, Sea Trek's ships had steel hulls, radar, radios, electricity, navigational computers, modern kitchens, simple bathroom facilities, and technology to make drinking water from the sea.

Sea Trek 2001 had two main purposes. First, in European ports it generated publicity and awareness of the historic Mormon migration by sail. Sea Trek sought to prime those countries for the 2002 Winter Olympics by showing their individual connections, through immigration, to far-off Utah. Sea Trek attracted good television, radio, and print media coverage through the stately arrival and departure of the ships, dock displays, dockside concerts, genealogy tents, dignitaries' dinners, presentations of statues, a powerful Sea Trek–commissioned cantata in respected music halls, and spectacular dockside fireworks. For example, some 200,000 Swedes watched Sea Trek's dockside activities at Gothenburg. When our ships sailed into and out of Hull, England, an estimated 10,000 onlookers lined the shores to wave and watch, and some 50,000 toured the docked ships.

Second, Sea Trek provided an opportunity for people to travel on tall sailing ships in order to experience something of what their immigrant ancestors did. About 1,700 people became Sea Trek passengers for one or two days or more. Twenty-two of us made the entire fifty-nine-day journey between August 6 and October 4, 2001.

Sea Trek had two stages. The first, called "The Gathering," lasted seventeen days and involved six ships and seven European ports—Esbjerg and Copenhagen, Denmark; Gothenburg, Sweden; Oslo, Norway; Hamburg, Germany; and Hull and Portsmouth, England. Two other Sea Trek ships went from Gothenburg to Greenock, Scotland, to Liverpool, England, and then to Portsmouth to join the others. Passengers chose a departure port and arrival port, which determined how many days they would be at sea. "The Gathering" stage allowed people to board a sailing ship in a port where perhaps their ancestors had boarded a century and a half ago.

Sea Trek's second stage was "The Crossing." Three of the eight ships (*Statsraad Lehmkuhl, Christian Radich,* and *Europa*) left from Portsmouth to cross the Atlantic. For wind purposes, our route made a big U-shape, taking us due south to the Canary Islands (only one or two Latter-day Saint ships took this route in the nineteenth century), west with the trade winds that carried Columbus to the New World, and northwest to Bermuda and New York City. Our "grand entry" into New York harbor, concert, and fireworks, all designed to be a media event in the media capital of the world, turned into a barely noticed arrival and no festivities. This hurt Sea Trek, not only in terms of its PR mission, but financially because events were canceled and sales of souvenirs, soundtrack CDs, and clothing never happened, because of the 9/11 tragedy, which happened while the three ships were in mid-ocean, five days beyond the Canary Islands.

Insights and Lessons from Sea Trek

Before leaving for the voyage, I listed several "realities" those immigrants experienced that I wanted to encounter, at least partially, during my voyage. For example, I wanted to sail into and out of the particular ports of Hamburg and Hull. I wanted to see how passengers, strangers at first, gelled into a company; how a Mormon company interacted with a non-Mormon ship crew; and how weeks isolated at sea, always rocking, impacted people who were not used to sea travel physically, mentally, emotionally, and spiritually. Sea Trek corroborated and reinforced many aspects of the immigrant voyages as I understood them from written records. But I gained several new insights that were not explicit in immigrants' records.

Ship Sizes and Riggings Are Historical Clues to Travel Conditions. Our generation cannot appreciate the fragility of some ventures described in diaries without knowing the ship's parts and how ships worked. For example, can the armchair historian grasp what Wilford Woodruff wrote in this 1841 diary entry on board the square-rigged *Rochester*?

> May 1st A fine beautiful pleasant May's morning. A fair northeast wind or light breeze. Water smooth. We have 19 pieces of canvass spread. A jib, flying gib, 8 pieces upon the foremast, 5 upon the main mast, & 4 upon the mizzen mast including the spanker. It was truly a beautiful sight.[8]

To verbalize that our immigrants boarded sailing ships and came to America fails to convey the realness of that experience. Once on board they lived in a new and strange world, one of ships, barques, brigs, and brigantines, of foremasts, mainmasts, mizzenmasts, of topgallant sails and jibs, and of buntlines and sheets and halyards.

Reference books provide raw facts about ship lengths and widths and heights. But without being on a ship, we can't know how those dimensions affected the experiences of the immigrants. When full, the Sea Trek ship *Christian Radich* could carry about 100 passengers and crew. It measured 205 feet long and 29 feet wide. By comparison, my ancestor Edward Bunker left Liverpool in 1856 on the *Caravan,* which was ten feet shorter than the *Christian Radich* but carried 357 more Saints.[9] Being on and below deck, we were amazed how many people those nineteenth-century ships carried, given such small deck and steerage space. Sea Trek's biggest ship on the Atlantic, the *Statsraad Lehmkuhl,* was nearly 100 feet longer than the biggest ship the Saints ever used, the *Monarch of the Sea,* but its passenger maximum was 140 compared to the *Monarch*'s 976. I traveled on the *Europa,* and when all forty-eight passengers were topside, the main deck was fairly crowded, so I marvel how the *Caravan*'s 457 passengers could move around at all when on deck.

Each Voyage Was Unique. Certainly companies of Saints that sailed weeks or months or years apart had different experiences due to weather, wind, and technology changes. But the three Sea Trek ships that participated in "The Crossing" were not very far apart (although they did not sail near or with each other) on the same days, so that their weather and sea conditions were similar. Nevertheless, how we on the Dutch *Europa* slept, ate, worked, and filled time differed considerably from how passengers on the Norwegian *Christian Radich* and *Statsraad Lehmkuhl* did. Each ship had a unique mix of facilities, crew, passengers, practices, and systems. It is easy for the armchair historian to presume the main differences between the 173 ships used by the immigrating Saints involved size. But Sea Trek demonstrated that each ship was a unique organism and each voyage differed from the rest.

Company Presidents Were More Than Figureheads. Sea Trek assigned me to be the company or passenger president for the *Europa*. Ship captain Klaas Gaasta had supreme authority over the ship's operations, crew, and passengers. Through the first mate, he informed passengers of the ship rules, but he expected the passengers to have their own officers to organize them and communicate the ship needs and assignments. I was the company president, responsible for the passengers' well-being, group activities, and their Church functions (although I had no authority to handle Sea Trek business matters or policy problems). I was authorized by the European West Area Presidency and by a blessing from my stake president to conduct Church services and prayer meetings and to be an ecclesiastical advisor.[10]

I thought that being company president would be a perfunctory assignment, that I would be mostly a token official. But once on board, I discovered that company presidents were essential. I was responsible, personally or by delegation, to make and change work assignments for three watches or work periods daily, to make sure people fulfilled those assignments, to set times for morning devotional, evening social events, and Sunday meetings—which times shifted depending on sea and port situations—and to designate people to be in charge of those events. I chose two counselors, a Relief Society president, and a chaplain, who helped with these activities.[11] Passengers looked to us to organize and carry out daily activities to help them pass time and socially interact. Given the many conveniences our generation enjoys, communication on board should have been simple, but it was not. Because we were divided into three groups, each having a different watch or work shift, the company never was all together at the same time, except for the sacrament hour on Sundays. Because people in the same cabin (four to six persons in bunkbeds per cabin) had different watch assignments, I was not able to knock on cabin doors to give messages to anyone. We had no photocopy machine, so I had to hand print any announcements or messages. I posted notices in the main cabin, but not everyone bothered to check the bulletin board. The Captain could ring the ship's bell to communicate—five bells meant "all hands on deck"—but I had no such system. So getting out new information about meals, laundry, special activities, and changes in routine required more work than one public announcement.

If someone had problems with the ship, laundry, food, cabins, work assignments, or a particular crew member, the chain of command required that person to go to me, not to the captain directly. Likewise, if the captain or a crew member had a problem or concern relating to one of the passengers, that person, too, went through me. That system kept order on the ship. I had to settle some complaints and differences among passengers, but not many.

On our first Sunday at sea, the captain wanted the watch groups to do ship maintenance work—varnishing, sanding, painting ropes, cleaning, and other chores. I talked with him about Saints wanting to keep the Sabbath Day holy, so he informed the crew that on Sundays the passengers would do normal watch duties but not maintenance work.

On Sea Trek's two other Atlantic ships, historians Dean May and John Peterson served as Latter-day Saint company presidents.[12] Each of us had our own unique leadership style and passenger matters to deal with, so passengers on one ship had a different group experience from those on another ship. This variety of experience was also the case in the nineteenth century.

The Simplest Daily Activities Became Hard. Those ship diarists who noted daily activities listed them but rarely reacted to them or assessed how they impacted the passengers. We know they prayed, ate, and used chamber pots. In galleys below or on deck they cooked or had someone cook for them. They congregated in clusters for singing, English classes, talking, playing, walking, sewing, and prayers.[13] But, how smooth or difficult was it for them to do those activities?

For Sea Trek passengers, and no doubt for nineteenth-century immigrants, the ship's constant rocking and swaying made everything a physical challenge. One day I noted in my diary that everything was hard—standing up, picking something up, going to the bathroom, taking a shower, walking below or on deck, going upstairs and downstairs, getting something in or out of the closet or drawers, getting into bed, sleeping, eating, reading. *Hard* might be too strong a word, but the ship's constant motion made simple actions a challenge. When winds were up or waves were busy, people fell, objects slid off tables and stands, and food and drinks spilled. We administered the sacrament water in little cups on a flat silver tray, and while men blessed the bread and water, I kept one hand under the tray to raise and lower one edge to keep the tray level when the ship tipped so that the cups did not fall over. When winds and waves were high, even my little muscles became weary by bedtime because of being kept tense nearly all day long.

This reality of being unable to relax, coupled with many nights when the ship's rocking ruined our sleep, made me realize that such a condition must have drained nineteenth-century immigrants and could explain why some of them stopped when they got to port and quit traveling until they stabilized themselves again.

Good Hygiene Was Not Possible. Diaries mention shipboard seasickness, diarrhea, measles, consumption (tuberculosis), and general debility. While noting hygiene problems, perhaps thankfully for us, diarists rarely gave much detail. During Sea Trek, although we were on modernized ships, we had limited laundry facilities, modest toilet facilities, and limited use of showers. Something as simple as getting out a change of clothes and putting away the ones we took off was difficult enough that during the last two-thirds of the voyage many quit changing clothes daily (laundry limitations contributed to this lifestyle change as well). I could not shower when the shipped tipped to port side because the shower water then ran away from the floor drain. Our ship produced drinking water from the sea, but at times we had to reduce our water use. During weeks of hot weather, for daily dress we skimmed down to bathing suits and tee shirts. Halfway across the Atlantic, I had good cause to worry that my deodorant stick might wear out before the next port.

So, when considering the jam-packed sail immigrants, we need to recognize that personal cleanliness for everyone, not just the slothful, was next to impossible during those five to eight weeks at sea. Coupled with their unbalanced food fare, the close quarters caused health problems on board the ships and debility and sickness after the voyage during trips upriver on steamboats and in wagon trains rolling west.

Poor Nutrition Probably Contributed to Health Problems Then and Later. Nineteenth-century immigrants ate food provided for them as part of their ticket purchase. They cooked their own food or arranged for someone to do it. Some Latter-day Saint companies "called" a few men to be cooks at the ship's cooking galleys, which were located below deck or sometimes on the deck. Passengers brought food with them to supplement the ship provisions. Our situation on Sea Trek was similar, in that we ate what the ship's cooks concocted. They fixed what their tastes and talents said we should have. Our ship was Dutch, and Marianne van der Staay, our cook, fixed food somewhat strongly seasoned. Like anyone else, I have my likes and dislikes, and as the weeks passed, some foods I ate and some I avoided. Even with my own stash of nuts and small candies, I lost about twenty pounds during Sea Trek. By the time I landed, I was physically weak.

That experience makes me believe we have underestimated the role that poor diets might have played in the lives of our immigrants, not only during the voyage but during the rest of their lives. An unbalanced diet, by our better understandings of nutrition, probably contributed directly to sickness along the five-to-six-month journey and trek to Zion and to deaths on the journeys upriver to outfitting posts, at the posts, and during the physically taxing trek across the plains, if not after they reached Utah. Historians may need a nutritionist or two to examine what records say about the ship diets and then project what physical problems could or should have resulted from that long-term deprivation. Did eight weeks at sea cause malnutrition that gave the travelers troubles then and later on?

Long Atlantic Voyages Were Debilitating. Halfway through the voyage I discovered I was losing body strength. True, we helped the crew pull ropes to work the sails and yards, but mostly we stood, sat, or laid down. Two of our passengers[14] took up walking, but their only route was a small rectangle of space around the perimeter of the main deck, which one could cover in eighty paces. They walked that tiny route, dodging ropes and crew at work, forty or fifty times daily. But aerobics, calisthenics, and other exercises performed while standing were dangerous because of the ship's constant motion.

When I reached port in New York City after fifty-nine days, most of them at sea, I was physically weak, mentally dulled, and emotionally discouraged. Clearly, immigrants must have struggled, like I did, with maintaining physical strength, keeping the mind busy, and enduring long stretches of prison-like confinement. I believe historians need to look hard at how the long voyages might have debilitated people by the time they reached port and how those weakenings worked against them during long and demanding treks from port to Utah.

Distance, Isolation, and Loneliness Probably Caused Depression. As noted, on average the sail immigrants had fifty-four days at sea to New Orleans or thirty-eight days to New York. Such long voyages meant people had many hours to fill. Company officers sometimes provided group activities, but by and large the passengers had to keep themselves busy. On Sea Trek, four-hour watch shifts twice daily gave passengers something to do every day. But nineteenth-century immigrants had no such duties to perform. Certainly they spent much time just handling personal needs, such as cooking, cleaning berths, simple personal hygiene, caring for children, and moving about the ship. But when those basics were done, what else did they do to prevent boredom?

It became essential that we five *Europa* company officers provide activities for our passengers and encourage them to participate. We saw it was unhealthy for passengers to stay below in their cabins or just sit around doing nothing. So every evening we held a one-hour program of entertainment in which passengers participated. Even some of the crew joined in—they, too, needed such diversions. We sang, played group games, held readers' theater and skits, took turns performing dramatic readings and poems, had a quiz show with prizes, and performed musical numbers. Passengers and crew members from European countries told us about their native lands. Nearly every day I taught one or more history classes for anyone interested. And Church Humanitarian Services arranged materials for us to sew school bags for them. I also provided parlor games for passenger use—*Yahtze, Scrabble, Battleship, Pit*—and dominoes and card games. Except for occasional storms, squalls, or total calm, and for occasional sightings of whales, dolphins, or flying fish, our days and nights developed a sameness. We lost track of what the date was and even what day of the week it was. Mid-ocean we went for days without seeing another ship or anything other than endless ocean and sky and clouds. We saw no airplanes. Monotony caused some to tire of being at sea and a few to become discouraged.

Slowly crossing that vast ocean we felt isolated, a reality we shared with nineteenth-century immigrants. Unlike the other two Sea Trek ships, ours had no passenger email. We had no way to make telephone calls. Mid-ocean, we thought more and more about loved ones at home. We longed for contact, for news from home. We worried about family situations—babies being born at home, operations, sick relatives. We felt cut off from life. We felt imprisoned with no escape possible. Sociability—talking with others—was our lifeline to sanity. Based on that experience, I feel that when studying nineteenth-century immigrants, we need to find out what psychologists can tell us about the long-term effects of being uprooted and cut off from our normal living conditions and relationships. Clearly, this discouragement factor needs scrutiny, particularly when we look at those immigrants who stopped heading for Zion between the arrival port and the wagon train outfitting posts and especially those who opted never to continue on to Zion.

Latter-day Saint Emigration Agents Played a Major Role. During Sea Trek I got off the ship in seven different countries—five of which were non-English speaking. With less than one day in port I badly needed quick guidance about four matters: (1) where to exchange money so I could buy a few items—an ATM if not a bank, (2) where to buy stamps so I could mail letters, (3) where to find a grocery store, and (4) where to find a phone on which I could make international credit card calls. In most ports, no one from Sea Trek met us and helped us, so we fanned out on our own, wasting much time and energy and even money. On those few times when someone did meet us with a map that had key places marked, our short stops in port were much better. In each country where we docked, the ship's first mate rounded up our passports to gain clearance for us to go ashore.[15] In the Canary Islands, one of my fellow passengers[16] lost her passport, and we had a frightening and rushed scramble to locate a U.S. State Department person to authorize port authorities and ship officers to let her continue. How vital for us, and with that perspective how vital it was for nineteenth-century Latter-day Saint immigrants, to have agents in ports and transfer points to assist and to solve travel problems for the passengers.

Our immigration studies overlook the crucial work performed by the Latter-day Saint immigration agents in the ports and transfer points. New Orleans is a good example. When a company of Saints arrived there, they had to go through inspections and then disembark. At that point an assigned agent needed to be there to greet them and tell them what to do next. He needed to have made arrangements ahead of time for their tickets on a river steamer and for vehicles to transport their luggage to that steamboat. He had to help those who did not speak English with exchanging currency, shopping, mailing letters, and filling out paperwork. If some had health problems, he needed to find medical help for them. He had to help them reach the proper wharf or dock and then to board the river steamer. He had to be sure the luggage went on board and that boat officers had tickets for everyone. At each transshipping point these agents were vital. But how many of them are noted in our histories? In fact, no one yet has compiled a list of who these Latter-day Saint agents were at the each of the main ports.[17]

Money Shortfalls and Numerous Currency Exchanges Were Constant Problems. A few nineteenth-century immigrants wrote in detail about trip costs, but most merely mentioned or listed some of them. However, as anyone knows who travels abroad today, on Sea Trek or otherwise, money is a major challenge during the entire trip. You leave hoping what money you take will last. But unexpected costs can drain the funds away before the journey ends. Some on our ship had to borrow from fellow passengers. Not only must money last, but money, to be usable, must be changed into the currencies of the countries you enter. In the immigrant days, Latter-day Saint Swedes went to Copenhagen, then Hamburg, then England, and then to the United States, requiring at least three currency exchanges. I gained new respect for our immigrants who disembarked in New Orleans or New York City without American currency. Thank goodness Latter-day Saint agents could help them or steer them to where currencies could be traded.

Voyages Became Gospel Workshops. Today's missionaries go to missionary training centers to be immersed in gospel study and discussions. Based on Sea Trek, I now sense that the long sea voyages served nineteenth-century converts in a similar way—providing them a time-out period and groups for gospel study, discussion, and reflection.

On the ship we held Sunday meetings because we were supposed to—that's what good Latter-day Saints do. Besides, it gave us something to do on Sunday, something to break the monotony of the days of sailing. But the meetings achieved an importance well beyond those perfunctory purposes. Starting with our first sacrament meeting and priesthood lessons at sea, I sensed something very powerful at work. Talks and lessons, while on familiar topics, conveyed new perspectives because they came from Saints not from our own countries. Like nineteenth-century companies, ours was a mix of strangers sharing the same gospel. From Portsmouth to the Canaries, our group included European Saints from Switzerland, Spain, Denmark, and England.[18] Their explanations about Church operations in their countries and challenges to gospel living in them, made us rethink our lives as Saints in our home wards.

Ours was a tiny ship in a vast ocean, with a 180-degree sky in daytime and that same sky blackened at night but bejeweled by thousands of brilliant stars. Day and night, God's grandeur seemed overwhelming. We had no television, radio, or computer distractions, so our minds had time and freedom to contemplate and wonder. Ocean and outer space were so immense and we were so tiny that it astounded me to realize that during meetings and gospel discussions we could feel the Holy Ghost—that God knew where we were and his Spirit could find us way out there. Feeling that immense love from the Creator caused many of us to reconsider scriptural statements and stories relating to the oceans and seas—Noah's experience, Lehi's voyage, the Jaredite barges, Jonah, Jesus calming the sea, and promises that during the Resurrection the sea would yield up its dead. We came to understand how much God loves the ocean and the islands of the sea. While on night watch in pitch darkness except for the canopy of brilliant stars, in the immense quiet, with nothing nearby, I was alone with my thoughts, surrounded by God's creation, and nothing of man's except our puny, fragile ship. We could not help pondering what life and creation was all about. Many serious gospel discussions took place among our passengers, especially during long watch assignments at night or in the privacy of tight cabins below deck.

If we had such time to ponder and stimuli to consider the universe, and felt the touch of the quiet and loving Holy Spirit, certainly those choice nineteenth-century converts immigrating because of religious fervency felt similar impressions and enlargements. People on those voyages had a forced period when, removed from normal everyday concerns about houses and property and jobs and associates, they pondered what gathering to Zion meant, spiritually. Two months at sea provided a valuable training period and setting that, like a mission training center, prepared the immigrants for their mission to settle in and build up Zion in the Rocky Mountains.

At sea we not only beheld God's wonders and felt drawn to him, but we had occasions to seek his help because we had no other recourse. We had several small storms during those many days at sea and one major one. I didn't allow our group to sing "Master the Tempest Is Raging" until the big one, and we sang with sincere intensity.[19] Another situation when we wanted divine help came when one passenger[20] became violently ill far from port. We had no nurse or doctor on board. The captain had authority to radio the Doctor of the Sea, an international radio-based emergency medical operation, and get permission to prescribe medicines from his locked medicine cabinet, but only if we knew what the problem was, and we did not. On land we could have taken him to a doctor, but at sea we had no such option. Our precarious situation compelled us to reach out to God. Those with faith in God and priesthood power gave him a priesthood blessing, and fellow passengers prayed and fasted for him. He recovered. In nineteenth-century Latter-day Saint immigrant accounts, we read of similar appeals for God's help. Sea Trek underscored for me how pressing such matters must have been for them.

Diarists back then mentioned church meetings and prayer meetings and preaching services on deck. Sea Trek showed me that those were more than perfunctory meetings. They were intense learning experiences that produced strong contemplations and deeper understandings of the gospel. Some of their company presidents, who preached during the voyages, included men who then were, or later became, outstanding Church leaders and teachers.

Conclusion

Telling the story of Mormon history involves diligent research in existing documents and records found in libraries, archives, and people's homes. But some studies require that the historian experience what he or she is writing about, go to where it happened, and to do, when possible, some of the activities written about. Sea Trek gave several historians, including myself, hands-on experience with sailing ships, ports, captains and crews, companies of passengers from a variety of backgrounds, storms and waves, seasickness, currency exchange, and long stretches of isolation at sea, such that we can tell the stories of nineteenth-century Latter-day Saint immigration with more insight and in more informed ways than we otherwise could.

Notes

1. Francis Parkman, *The Oregon Trail* (1849); Samuel Elliott Morrison, *Admiral of the Ocean Sea* (1942).

2. William G. Hartley, "Voyage on the Ship *International*," *New Era* 3 (September 1973), 6–9; William G. Hartley, "Atlantic Crossing of the Ship *Olympus*," *New Era* 8 (June 1978), 33–36; William G. Hartley, "Aboard the *Monarch of the Sea*," chap. 19 in *Kindred Saints: The Mormon Immigrant Heritage of Alvin and Kathryne Christenson* (Salt Lake City: Eden Hill, 1982); William G. Hartley, "Broken Sails Off Cuba: LDS Immigrants and the Voyage of the *Yorkshire*," *Mormon Heritage Magazine* 2 (May/June 1995), 9–11.

3. Regarding nineteenth-century Latter-day Saint immigration by sail, see Conway B. Sonne, *Saints on the Seas: A Maritime History of Mormon Migration, 1830–1890* (Salt Lake City: University of Utah Press, 1983); Sonne, *Ships, Saints, and Mariners: A Maritime Encyclopedia of Mormon Migration, 1830–1890* (Salt Lake City: University of Utah Press, 1987); Sonne, "Under Sail to Zion," *Ensign* 21 (July 1991), 6–14. For general Latter-day Saint migration studies see Philip A. M. Taylor, *Expectations Westward: The Mormons and the Emigration of Their British Converts in the Nineteenth Century* (Ithaca, N.Y.: Cornell University Press, 1966); William Mulder, *Homeward to Zion: The Mormon Migration from Scandinavia* (Minneapolis: University of Minnesota Press, 1957, reprint co-published with Brigham Young University Press, 2000); Andrew Jenson, "Church Emigration," 30 vols., *Contributor*, vols. 12–14 (May 1891–Sept. 1893); and William G. Hartley, "Coming to Zion: Saga of the Gathering," *Ensign* 5 (July 1975), 14–18.

4. Sonne, *Ships, Saints, and Mariners*, 146–47.

5. Sonne, *Ships, Saints, and Mariners*, 148–159, 168, 169.

6. The Sea Trek foundation was a private, nonprofit organization that had no affiliation with The Church of Jesus Christ of Latter-day Saints. It was funded by generous donors and by ship passenger fees. Its founders were William and DeAnn Sadleir of Salt Lake City. Sea Trek's advisory board included Michael K. Deaver of Edelman Public Relations Worldwide; Larry King of CNN and his wife Shawn Southwick-King; Retired Coast Guard Admiral Paul A. Yost; Jane Clayson of CBS TV; U.S. Senator Gordon H. Smith of Oregon; former Secretary of the Navy James Webb; Stephen J. Solarz, former congressman from New York; David Checketts, former president and CEO of Madison Square Garden; Rick Burns, Director of the Danish Immigration Museum in Iowa; and David Baxter, British Telecom executive.

No history of Sea Trek has been written. Founders Bill and DeAnn Sadleir are helping the author create a Sea Trek archive and assisting him to write a history of the Sea Trek voyage. Participants did, however, receive a handbook that explained much about Sea Trek's organization, purposes, itinerary, ships, and passenger requirements. See Dayna D. Sadleir and Candice Beckwith, *Sea Trek 2001: Participant's Guide Book* ([Salt Lake City]: Sea Trek Foundation, 2001).

7. The eight vessels were the *Statsraad Lehmkuhl*, *Christian Radich*, and *Sorlandet* (Norwegian); *Europa*, *Antigua*, and *Swan Fan Makkum* (Dutch); *Mary-Anne* (German); and *Mir* (Russian). Depending on mast numbers and sail types, sailing vessels are categorized as ships, barques, barquentines, brigs, brigantines, and other categorizations. Sea Trek had three ships (*Christian Radich, Mir,* and *Sorlandet*), 2 barques (*Europa* and *Statsraad Lehmkuhl*), 1 brigantine (*Swan Fan Makkum*), and 2 barquentines (*Antigua* and *Mary-Anne*). An excellent coffee-table-type book about present-day sailing ships, with photographs and facts about scores of them, is Thad Koza, *Tall Ships: The Fleet for the 21st Century* (East Hartford, Conn.: Tide-Mark Press, 2002).

8. Wilford Woodruff Account, *Rochester* Voyage Accounts, May 1, 1841, on *LDS Immigration Index* CD ROM (Salt Lake City: The Church of Jesus Christ of Latter-day Saints, 2000).

9. Sonne, *Saints on the Seas*, 36.

10. In Sea Trek communications with Elder Rolf Kerr of the Europe West Area Presidency concerning ship presidencies, he advised that Sea Trek invite individuals to be ship presidents and that those individuals seek a blessing, but not a setting apart, from their stake presidents before departure. DeAnn Sadleir to William G. Hartley, June 10, 2001, copy in author's file.

11. My counselors in the *Europa*'s company presidency were Fred Mortensen of Morgan Hill, California, and Paul Toone of St. George, Utah. Becki Toone served as Relief Society president. Neal Southwick, a BYU–Idaho professor, was our chaplain.

12. Dean May, a University of Utah history professor and former Latter-day Saint bishop, was company president on the *Christian Radich*. John Peterson, an instructor at the LDS Institute of Religion at the University of Utah, was president on the *Statsraad Lehmkuhl*. I, too, had been an Latter-day Saint bishop.

13. For generalizations about life aboard ship for Latter-day Saint immigrants, see Sonne, "Under Sail to Zion."

14. Julie Molen and Neal Southwick.

15. To Portsmouth the *Europa*'s first mate was Daan Jaeger. His replacement for the Atlantic crossing was Hank Mijnlieff.

16. Bethany Benac.

17. Brigham Young University professor Fred Woods is working on such a list, as part of his studies of the port and transit points of importance in Latter-day Saint emigration history.

18. Passengers included Jean-Michel Gillet-Mahrer (Geneva, Switzerland), Eric Andersen (Denmark), Paul Hector (England), Josef Othmar Kempf (Austria and Spain), Britt-Marie Kempf (Denmark and Spain), Carlos Garcia Hiniesto (Spain).

19. Leaving Bermuda, we dodged storm systems for two days but had high winds and waves of fifteen to twenty feet. When I polled the company later, we found that only fifteen of our forty-five passengers did not get sea sick during that stormy stretch.

20. Neal Southwick.

An Extraordinary Influence: Church History in the Classroom Setting

Susan Easton Black

Knowing something of the inherent power of successful teachers or those gifted with the ability to speak and influence others, Governor Thomas Ford in his *History of Illinois* wrote, "It is to be feared that in course of a century, some gifted man like Paul, some splendid orator, who will be able by his eloquence to attract crowds of the thousands who are ever ready to hear . . . [may] make the name of the martyred Joseph ring . . . loud and stir the souls of men."[1] Did Governor Ford have a premonition that B. H. Roberts, T. Edgar Lyon, Ivan J. Barrett, and Milton V. Backman Jr. would pause in the course of scholarly writings to raise their voices in praise of the Prophet Joseph Smith?

Ford fantasized that gifted speakers might elevate obscure place names like "Sharon, Palmyra, Manchester, Kirtland, Far West, Adamon Diahmon, Ramus, Nauvoo, and the Carthage jail, . . . [to] holy and venerable names, places of classic interest, in another age; like Jerusalem, the garden of Gethsemane, the Mount of Olives, and Mount Calvary to the Christian, and Mecca and Medina to the Turk."[2] Did Ford know that LaMar C. Barrett, Keith W. Perkins, and Larry C. Porter would search land records in these agrarian communities so that they, too, could speak in sacred remembrance of the Prophet Joseph?

Ford's final fear was personal and was the most worrisome to him. It was that "the humble governor of an obscure state, who would otherwise be forgotten in a few years, stands a fair chance like Pilate and Herod, by their official connection with the true religion, of being dragged down to posterity with an immortal name."[3] President Gordon B. Hinckley, Elder Dallin H. Oaks, and Marvin S. Hill have made his final fear a stinging reality. The name of Governor Ford has been leagued with mobocrats, Carthage Greys, and other unscrupulous villains. So well known are his misdeeds that on April 18, 1997, when Gordon B. Hinckley was introduced to Illinois' thirty-eighth governor, President Hinckley skipped formalities and simply stated, "I trust that you are a better man than Governor Thomas Ford." The late-twentieth-century governor didn't hesitate or ask the question: "Who was Governor Ford?" Instead, he immediately retorted, "Of course I am! I am a Republican!"[4]

I am grateful for gifted leaders, scholars, and teachers who have given meaning to Ford's expressed fears. I am also grateful for the seeming endless host of speakers and teachers who testify with power and heartfelt conviction in meetinghouses, seminaries, institutes, and classrooms throughout the world.

I express gratitude for the exceptional faculty members at Brigham Young University who advance the cutting edge expected of bookish scholars, yet take valuable moments from their whirlwind of literary pursuits to share precious moments in the classroom. It was in the classroom that I witnessed disciple scholars, whose hours in the library were as evident as their hours in prayer. They unabashedly spoke well-chosen words that pierced my heart and confirmed that Joseph Smith was a Prophet of God.

As a tribute to my colleagues—my betters, my friends, the master teachers of Church history—I present glimpses of why I believe the Church history professor has an extraordinary influence upon students.

1. The Professor Reads and Digests Edifying Content

The professor loves and has an abiding passion for any and every truth surrounding The Church of Jesus Christ of Latter-day Saints. An obscure fact about Joseph Smith or even Governor Thomas Ford is never viewed as trivial. Instead, it is prized—as one cherishes a valuable antique—and saved for years in a bulging file cabinet only to be discovered anew years later.

The ardent scholar plans purposeful vacations, even family vacations, to the sacred sites of Palmyra, Kirtland, Nauvoo, and Independence. Although family members may become disenchanted with souvenir shopping or even frequent visits to restoration sites, the professor is not distracted by their verbal or nonverbal duress. Historic presentations and conversations with local "history buffs" alleviate any family discomfort. When children's longing tugs attempt to shorten the professor's visit, it is not unusual for the scholar to express hopes of seeing more exciting sites—graveyards, out-of-the-way libraries, or nearby homes in which a historic artifact may be sequestered.

Speaking assignments within driving distance of sacred Church history lands are rarely rejected by the professor. An opportunity to speak in Richmond or Liberty, Missouri, is viewed as being of more worth than the opportunity of speaking at major universities on either coast. "For to walk a day where Joseph walked is always a better day than a day spent elsewhere," the devoted professor exclaims.

The scholar becomes immersed in the discipline. Those who choose not to vacation in Church history lands, do not speak of Joseph Smith at every occasion, or seem to lack interest in the Latter-day Saint legacy are viewed by the scholar as missing the great joys of life. Although some people mistakenly view the professor as imbalanced for missing sunsets, sandy beaches, and a round of golf just to study Church history, the true scholar counters such negative impressions with an assurance that the pearl of great price has been found. The pursuit of the pearl has been nurtured by hours of reading old books and manuscripts with bespectacled friends in libraries, archives, and cramped quarters and has been renewed with each illuminating discovery in these poorly lit rooms.

It can easily be said that few quests in life provide a euphoria comparable to searching the past for one's colleagues. It is not unusual to see the aging professor emerge from a library, finding that the day has passed and that the evening has captured the sky, and then to hear the exclamation, "Joy, another great day."

The reason the days and hours of scholarly pursuit are so great is, of course, the personal joy found only from discovering light and truth. But for the classroom professor, the joy of those hours is doubled because the discoveries made today will not await a future manuscript or a publisher's delay. Instead, the discoveries will soon be shared with students in a classroom setting. Students, whose professions and lifestyles will take a different path from the professor's, need the scholar's learning to strengthen their testimony of Joseph Smith and the history of The Church of Jesus Christ of Latter-day Saints.

2. The Professor Loves All the Students

The success of the classroom professor can not be based on scholarship alone. Although there is no substitute for meticulous scholarship, for surely the Lord can not draw from a listless mind, love for each student is just as important. Without heartfelt love, the professor can not experience joy in the classroom even though scholarly pursuits may be impeccable.

The love required to be a classroom success is a gift from God, for it is an ability to see beyond the current situation—the student who is late, uninterested, or distracted. The professor has sought this gift on bended knee and has received the gift with gratitude. Possessing unrestricted love enables the teacher to reach the students on the front rows, whose well-marked scriptures reveal their dedication, and to ignite the latent fire of the trapped senior seated in the back.

This type of love permits the professor to see beyond the obvious and reach out with enthusiasm, laughter, and hope to captivate the mind and heart of each student. And in so doing extends the classroom far beyond the four walls. Some students may even tape the classroom presentations so that family members, sweethearts, and roommates can experience the wonder they have felt under the tutelage of a master teacher. Still others speak of the classroom presentation long after the bell has rung.

It comes as no surprise that the student evaluations for such a professor are punctuated with complimentary phrases: "Church history is my favorite class," "My testimony grew leaps and bounds in the class," and "I wish that all my instructors could be like my Church history teacher." These written comments expand through the years as former students become more grateful for the opportunity of learning about the Latter-day Saint legacy from such a noble teacher.

As the years pass, the professor may occasionally review the laudatory comments and listen to expressions of gratitude by former students, but in so doing, always feels inadequate and surprised by the adulation. The scholar didn't choose to be a teacher in order to enjoy such praise or to be recognized as a classroom favorite. In fact, the professor often has been known to speak of personal imperfections rather than contributions and recognitions.

3. The Professor Organizes Scholarly Material into a Clear and Logical Presentation

Scholarship and love combine to form the foundational beginning for the successful professor of Church history. The combination, however, is neither the means to the end nor the end itself. A major task—a task as vital as the hours of scholarship and as pertinent as the love of each student—remains. It is the task of organizing scholarly material into a clear presentation that will have a lasting benefit for the students.

With the same precision used to gather scholarly data, the professor organizes truth "for the benefit of the children of God" (D&C 46:26). In so doing, the professor follows the divine directive to prepare "for the benefit of those who love [the Lord] and keep all [his] commandments" (D&C 46:9). The professor knows that the design and construction of presentations is as critical to the classroom success as patterns are to a seamstress and blueprints are to an architect.

In the construction process, the professor is ever vigilant to ensure that the prepared lessons never become a forum to exhibit minutia that overwhelms the student and pretends to elevate the teacher above the learner. Instead, the professor stays true to the succinct advice uttered by B. H. Roberts: "Back to Bedrock."[5] Teaching the basics of Church history and constructing classroom presentations from the bedrock up is the norm for successful classroom preparation.

Although it is tempting to tantalize students with the mysteries of the kingdom, the professor knows that the classroom format is not designed for speculation but for learning, and learning demands a logical, fundamental approach. To achieve the logical approach, the professor memorizes principal themes and gripping phrases, humorous one-liners, and descriptive stories that illustrate precepts. The teacher is willing to "sacrifice anything, everything, [even] seeming eloquence" or a favorite illustrative story to be understood by the students in the classroom.[6] To achieve the needed convincing power, the theme, key points, lines, and precepts must be as clear as the interesting asides that dot the presentation with memorable human-interest stories, attention-stimulating humor, and visual aids.

Once the preparation process reaches a clear and logical format, the professor practices delivering the classroom presentation again and again. For a few scholars, the practice is a rehearsal that invites staging, props, and criticism. For others, it is a preview sprinkled with flaws, stuttering, twitches, and even lapses of memory. But this doesn't matter, for the professor and the critical listeners know that the rehearsed delivery is a rough stone that is being polished and will prove wonderful in the hour needed.

From the many late night or early morning practice sessions emerge a unique teaching style—a professional persona in the classroom—a persona that is riveting in nature and tone, and that becomes a noted trademark of the professor. And what is so interesting about the process is that the developed persona has as much to do with the lasting influence of the scholar as does passion for the subject and love of the student. For Richard O. Cowan the persona is visual in nature, for Donald Q. Cannon it couches Church history in the broader American scene, and for Richard E. Bennett it places the student in the library.

As vital as the persona is to the professor's ability to influence students, there remains a greater influence that must be humbly sought—the Spirit of the Lord. The classroom delivery or teaching moment of Church history can never be a solo event, an event without the Spirit. As scholar Truman Madsen wrote, "[If] the Spirit is not granted, not given, the words spoken are stillborn."[7] And as C. S. Lewis so aptly reminds us all, "We are nothing without God."[8] The professor knows that the divine promise, "It shall be given you in the very hour, yea, in the very moment what you shall say," must be prayerfully sought before entering the classroom (D&C 100:6).

4. The Professor Presents the Well-Rehearsed Lesson in the Classroom

Armed with the Spirit of God, scholarship, love of student, and a much practiced presentation, the professor enters the classroom. The students observe that the professor is wearing Sunday attire to show respect for them and the subject of the classroom presentation. The visual appearance bespeaks the importance of the hour for the professor as well as the student. From attire to facial expressions and from carefully chosen words to visual aids, the professor knows that any untoward display will detract from the message the Lord wants given. To do so causes a setback that is very painful, for the teaching experience will then be solo as the Spirit of God will not abide in the classroom.

Thus, under the microscope of watchful eyes that probe into the mind and heart of the scholar, the fifty-minute class begins. Although the time allotted for classroom delivery is brief in comparison to the hours of preparation, the preparatory hours are worth it because the professor "speak[s] from a fullness of information under the inspiration of the Holy Ghost." And what becomes apparent even to the professor is that "the works of God, or those which he inspires, far outshine" the capability of the scholar.[9] The professor fulfills what Alma envisioned: "O that I were an angel, and could have the wish of mine heart, that I might go forth and speak with the trump of God" (Alma 29:1).

The professors who achieve this type of classroom teaching have paid the price—the price of scholarship, the price of love, the price of preparation, and the price of living a life that invites the Spirit of the Lord. In attempt to not embarrass my beloved colleagues who have and do pay that price, I share from the past one whom I believe was this type of teacher. "From the first ten words to the last paragraph you knew that Brother [B. H.] Roberts had thought that thing through," wrote David W. Cummings,

> It was nothing of your lazy habit of standing on your feet without a thought to say and then taking 30 minutes just to prove it. He never used to waste other people's time. He was there to do the best that God would permit him to do in the preaching of the Gospel and he did it, and what he told you, you remembered. He thrilled you, he held you, he fascinated you. You could feel the result of those nights of work.[10]

Another student recalled the occasion of a gathering of Latter-day Saints in Logan, Utah, when Roberts gave a sermon in which he described Jesus Christ raising Lazarus from the dead. "So vivid were his images and so moving his presence that the audience was carried with him. When in a loud voice he repeated the Master's words, 'Lazarus, come forth,' the entire congregation involuntarily came to their feet."[11]

So powerful a teacher was B. H. Roberts that Heber J. Grant encouraged his family to hear Roberts "whenever and wherever he spoke, even if it means a half day's travel." President Joseph F. Smith, after hearing Robert's classic discourse entitled "Has Missouri Paid?" exclaimed, "I thank God for the truth and for someone able to teach it."[12]

5. The Results of Good Teaching

Do professors of Church history at Brigham Young University receive such praise today? I have heard students exclaim, "My roommate had Alex Baugh's class and said it's great." Another shared, "My family and I took a vacation last summer in Nauvoo after I took a Church history class taught by Paul Peterson." One student selected Ensign Peak to ask his girlfriend to marry him after taking a class from another professor. Still other students are naming children Joseph, Brigham, and Taylor because of what they have learned from my colleagues. I have yet to hear of a baby named Wilford or Lorenzo, so we still have some work to do.

To those who are presently teaching and to those who have taught Church history in yesteryears, I express gratitude. They have paid the price of scholarship and shared that scholarship in the classroom, and by so doing they have created an extraordinary influence that will not soon end. As if casting their bread upon the water, their former students in meetinghouses, seminaries, and institutes worldwide recall anecdotes, stories, and facts spoken by their favorite professors. And through this process, classrooms of yesteryear live on across the globe as learners become teachers.

If Governor Ford could have seen the number of faithful faculty members at Brigham Young University who lift their voices in praise of a Prophet of God, he would have hid his face in shame. For he would know that his expressed fears of Mormonism have become a reality and that the professor has had an extraordinary influence.

Notes

1. Thomas Ford, "Downfall of Joseph Smith 1844–1845," ch. 11 of *A History of Illinois from its Commencement as a State in 1818 to 1847* (Chicago: S. G. Griggs, 1854), as cited in Joseph Smith Jr., *History of the Church of Jesus Christ of Latter-day Saints,* ed. B. H. Roberts, 2d. ed., rev., 7 vols. (Salt Lake City: Deseret Book, 1971), 7:40.

2. Ford, "Downfall of Joseph Smith," 7:40–41.

3. Ford, "Downfall of Joseph Smith," 7:41.

4. Conversation between Gordon B. Hinckley and Governor Jim Edgar, April 18, 1997, Seventies Hall, Nauvoo, Hancock County, Illinois.

5. Truman G. Madsen, *Defender of the Faith, The B. H. Roberts Story* (Salt Lake City: Bookcraft, 1980), 348.

6. Madsen, *Defender of the Faith,* 348.

7. Madsen, *Defender of the Faith,* 352.

8. Jean Peerenboom, "Does God Exist? C. S. Lewis Says Yes," *Lifestyle,* March 9, 2002.

9. *Liahona* 5:209, as cited in Madsen, *Defender of the Faith,* 352.

10. David W. Cummings in a tribute to B. H. Roberts, delivered in Hollywood Ward, September 1933. Manuscript in possession of Truman Madsen, as cited in Madsen, *Defender of the Faith,* 355.

11. Reid Nibley to Truman Madsen, as told to him by a family member, as cited in Madsen, *Defender of the Faith,* 355.

12. *Conference Report,* October 1926, 125, as cited in Madsen, *Defender of the Faith,* 356.

T. Edgar Lyon:
Teaching LDS History by Faith and by Fact

Thomas E. Lyon Jr.

Editor's Note: A teacher at the Salt Lake Institute of Religion for three decades, T. Edgar Lyon Sr. regularly drew more students than could squeeze into his classroom. Lyon's gift as a vivid storyteller made Church history "come alive." Thomas E. Lyon Jr.'s rich biography, *T. Edgar Lyon: A Teacher in Zion* (Provo: Utah, Brigham Young University Press, 2002), debuted at the "Telling the Story of Mormon History" conference. Revealed through engaging narrative, the biography explores Lyon's mission and mission presidency in the Netherlands, University of Chicago studies under renowned biblical scholars, contributions to seminary and institute programs during the Church Educational System's formative years, and work with the Nauvoo Restoration project.

Thomas Edgar Lyon was born at home in 1903, in the Avenues area of Salt Lake City as the seventh son of a Scottish pioneer family. His mother expected that he take up medicine; Lyon made other choices! He attended public grade schools in Salt Lake and then enrolled in the Church's LDS High from 1917 to 1921. He studied at the University of Utah for two years before accepting a mission call to the Netherlands. After the mission he and two other released missionaries toured through Europe, Greece, Egypt, and Palestine for three months. In 1927 he completed a B.A. degree in history and political science at the University of Utah (the "U"), married Laura Hermana Forsberg, and accepted his first teaching job at the high school in Rigby, Idaho. Here he came to the attention of a strong-willed stake president who helped Lyon land a job in the Latter-day Saint seminary system in Midway, Idaho. From 1928 through 1933 he taught in the expanding seminary program in Idaho. The recently standardized seminary curriculum was heavily oriented toward history; only three courses were taught: Old Testament History, New Testament History, and LDS Church History.

One of the creators of this program, M. Lynn Bennion, affirmed that religious education was "vital to character training, and no textbook has yet appeared to replace the Old Testament as a source of inspiration."[1] This historical emphasis in seminary harmonized well with his academic preparation; he also used pictures and stories from his post-mission travels to the Holy Land to foster interest.

Between 1928 and 1933, Lyon attended summer schools at the "U," at Brigham Young University, at U.C. Berkeley, and also spent an entire year at the Divinity School of the University of Chicago. In 1933, President Heber J. Grant called Lyon, who was barely thirty, to preside over the Netherlands Mission. Upon returning to the United States in 1937, he was assigned, quite to his surprise, to serve as temporary director of the LDS Institute at the University of Utah while the previous director, Lowell L. Bennion, was on assignment to the University of Arizona. From 1937 to 1975 his professional life was the 'Tute at the "U." In September 1978, at age seventy-five, just three years after retiring from teaching, T. Edgar Lyon died of cancer.

Inviting the Outside World In

During the late 1920s and early '30s, Commissioner of Church Education Joseph F. Merrill, Ph.D., encouraged his seminary teachers to seek advanced degrees. So during summer 1929, Lyon attended summer school at BYU and immediately fell under the spell of Sidney Sperry's exciting teaching. At that time Sperry held an M.A. degree from the University of Chicago and would complete his Ph.D. in 1931. His own teaching mirrored the methods of his world-famous Old and New Testament mentors at that institution. Sperry ignited a fire in the seminary teachers, using critical approaches of close textual criticism, archeological investigation, and historical exegesis. Lyon was amazed at these approaches and lapped them up. He found them excitingly different from the simple memorization of names and dates which he had experienced with Levi Edgar Young and George Fellows at the University of Utah. Sperry's classes and methods also "converted [Commissioner Merrill] to the idea that we Church education teachers ought to have more education at the University of Chicago."[2]

For the next summer, 1930, Sperry and Merrill contracted Chicago's Edgar J. Goodspeed to teach at the "Y." Goodspeed had already published more than a score of books on religion, including his own translation of the New Testament from the original. His classes were so stimulating that Merrill, with the approval of President Grant, invited him to lecture in the Salt Lake Tabernacle. This was indeed an exciting time in the Church. General Authorities like Merrill, James E. Talmage, John A. Widtsoe, and B. H. Roberts were reaching out, bringing scholars and new ideas to Utah. These Latter-day Saint scholar-leaders viewed it as both possible and wise to embrace serious secular scholarship and apply it to Latter-day Saint theology and history. Their own writings and lectures exemplified the open, inquiring attitude of the early '30s. From them, Lyon felt great promise for his future in Church Education.

Sending the Inside Out

In fall 1930, Commissioner Merrill "called" three of the system's teachers to study at the University of Chicago. George S. Tanner, Russel B. Swenson, and Daryl Chase accepted the assignment, were granted a leave of absence at half pay, and completed degrees in the Divinity School.[3] Lyon received reports of their academic successes and created his own plan to study in Chicago. The expanding depression eliminated any Church funding for his studies, but he was granted a year's leave from the system. Once in Chicago, in the summer of 1931, he began to recognize his own inadequacies:

> We [Latter-day Saint students] went back there as a group of ignoramuses because none of us knew Greek or Latin. . . . We were not Hebrew scholars and we didn't know Aramaic and Syriac and things of that sort . . . . We'd get in a class and they'd start talking about a lot of literature in the Christian field that we were just ignorant of . . . [so] we kept our mouth shut. But at the same time we learned.[4]

Lyon took classes from William W. Sweet and John T. McNeill, both world-renowned scholars. He also studied with Shailer Matthews and Shirley Jackson Case. Matthews, dean of the Divinity School, informed his students that the college had "no interest in producing dilettantes. It seeks to train students for spiritual leadership . . . trained in a sense of reality, in efficiency, and in contagious faith."[5] The Divinity School's goal was "to harmonize faith with intellect and to do so with serious scholarship." Matthews taught with the fire of socio-historical criticism. Goodspeed insisted on linguistic exactness and accepted no private interpretation of scripture. Sweet, Lyon's thesis adviser, taught what he called "modern" criticism and demanded that all Christian history be explained with logical facts and deep analysis. Emotionalism was rejected. Yet despite the fame of his instructors, Lyon harbored some doubts about their faith and the methodologies he was experiencing. In a letter to his parents he confided:

> Down in their hearts they [these professors] are all either infidels or agnostics. . . . The University of Chicago is noted as being the most liberal school (and that means Modernism) in America. All religion is taught as a product of social growth, and anything supernatural is looked upon as merely a betrayal of one's own ignorance and primitive mind. . . . Of course they merely feel sorry for us when they hear that we are so ignorant and primitive that we still believe in a personal God. Their God . . . is "the cosmic force of the Universe."[6]

These approaches challenged Lyon's faith but did not destroy it; on the contrary, he emerged much stronger in his own beliefs. And despite the criticism of modern tools used in the Divinity School, Lyon learned methods that demanded rigor, detailed research, use of original sources whenever possible, mistrust of emotion, an understanding of the times in which a document originated, close analysis, logic, and a lot of common sense. This approach infused all his later teaching and writing.

By the end of spring quarter 1932, Lyon had completed a thesis titled "Orson Pratt—Early Mormon Leader." This, the first detailed biography of one of Mormondom's early theologians, caused him to confront conflicts in Church history among some of the inspired individuals who created that history. The deep research necessary to resolve these conflicts strengthened Lyon's conviction of his own spiritual heritage and assured him that Latter-day Saints need not fear their own history. He learned that a faith-filled Latter-day Saint could indeed confront all issues and not lose testimony in the process. Years later he recalled that "some of the Brethren were fearful about this higher criticism coming into the Church [and] being applied to the Book of Mormon [and] the Pearl of Great Price, fearful that it might destroy the faith of the people."[7] Such was not his experience. He believed in rigor and authenticity as the only valid approach to researching and teaching Mormon history.

The Chicago experience, or experiment, was a very positive venture for the Church; it drew the Church nearer to the "outside" world and helped form scholars who would be credible beyond the valleys of the mountains. None of the ten men who received money or released time to study at the Divinity School left the Church. Some left the seminary or institute system after returning to the Intermountain West, but most continued to make positive and lasting contributions to education and the Church. Lyon evaluated the results in these words:

> It appears to me that the securing of graduate degrees . . . represents a landmark in an educational outreach which the Church had never known before, and which has profoundly influenced the teaching in the seminaries and institutes since that day. The importation to the BYU summer school for teachers of religion of Doctors Goodspeed, Graham, McNeill, and Bower . . . is reflected in the lessons and textbook written for use in the Church schools and auxiliaries since that time. It was a time of an intellectual and spiritual awakening which was the entering wedge that put the Church educational system in contact with the ongoing mainstream of Christian scriptural and historical research. This outlook has aided in the metamorphosis of the L.D.S. Church from a sectionally oriented to a worldwide Church in less than forty years.[8]

So positive was the Chicago experience for Lyon, his wife Hermana, and their two children, that he began course work for a Ph.D. during the summer quarter of 1932. He continued for several summers until World War II caused many of the Divinity School's programs to close, but he did not complete his Ph.D. until 1962.

Despite the difficult economic times, the early 1930s was a period of intellectual outreach and academic awakening in the Church. Jeffrey E. Keller has examined a 1931 conflict among some of the Church leaders regarding science and religion, specifically the never-ending discussion of creation and evolution.[9] Duane E. Jeffrey also notes the importance of dialogue and intellectual stimulation that suffused even the highest councils of the Church in the 1930s.[10] The amazing publication of B. H. Robert's multivolume history of the Church, coinciding with the 1930 centennial, was a landmark in the collection of original historical documents and analysis. But the death of Roberts and Talmage, both in 1933, limited the intellectual debate among Church leaders. John A. Widtsoe was called to serve as president of the European Mission from 1927 through 1933 and hence missed much of the public debate of the era; Joseph F. Merrill replaced Widtsoe in Great Britain, from 1933 to 1936. The death and prolonged absence of these four academically oriented General Authorities left a gap that was not filled for many years. Then, in 1938, J. Reuben Clark delivered a well-known speech entitled, "The Charted Course of the Church in Education," pointedly directed at the higher criticism that had come from Chicago and that was being introduced into some Church teaching.[11] A college student of that era, Edward Hart, later a Rhodes scholar and BYU professor, recalled that "there was an intellectual awakening [in the 1930s] and many drifted away from the Church [as a result]."[12] But Hart also observed that many academically oriented students found answers to their concerns by participating in the LDS Institutes.

Institute Teacher

In 1937, after returning from nearly four years as mission president in the Netherlands, Lyon began his thirty-eight year teaching career at the Institute at the University of Utah. During that time he taught at least sixteen thousand students. In the first years, he usually taught fourteen to sixteen sections of six different classes.[13] He was able to use both the information as well as the methodology gleaned in Chicago to teach courses in:

1. Mormonism: An Interpretation and Way of Life (7 sections)
2. History and Religion of Early Christianity (2 sections)
3. Missionary Training (2 sections)
4. Seminar in Religion and Modern Thought (2 sections)
5. Doctrine and Covenants (2 sections)
6. History of the Church (1 section)

The missionary training class was Lyon's own creation; he later recalled that he was the first teacher in the entire Church to develop and teach this course.[14] Many of his classes allowed him to push his students deeper into his love of Christian and Church history.

In the 1930s there was no set curriculum for LDS institutes; teachers enjoyed a surprising latitude to develop courses according to their own spiritual and academic preparation. Franklin L. West, the commissioner of education (but not a General Authority), insisted on a high level of academic freedom for all his teachers and encouraged innovation in each institute's curriculum. Over a period of four years, in summer "retreats" at West's mountain cabin, institute instructors (including those trained at the Chicago Divinity School), aided by BYU's Sidney Sperry, discussed spiritual needs of their students and created twelve courses for the rapidly expanding Church institute system. The group assigned Lyon to develop two of these courses—"Joseph Smith and the Restoration" and "Doctrine and Covenants and the Pearl of Great Price"—quite obviously recognizing him as the authority on restoration history. Not only did he prepare course outlines and teaching aids for these classes, he also wrote a complete textbook for each.

Like his close friend and colleague Lowell Bennion, Lyon taught courses in courtship, marriage, family life, the meaning of Mormonism, the Book of Mormon, and much more. His teachings and techniques are legendary; his creative ideas and approaches stimulated thousands of inquiring students from 1935 through 1962.[15] Lyon was the designated history teacher of this dynamic pair. Their methods varied greatly, but their goals were singular and similar—to instill a lasting faith in the hearts of questioning and capable university students.

This ideal required not only classroom contact, but regular hours of personal counseling, one-on-one discussions, spiritual firesides, worship services, social activities, and direct involvement in the lives of their students. The names "Lyon and Bennion" became synonymous with the institute at the University of Utah during the 1930s, '40s, and '50s.

Lyon also taught outside the institute. Shortly after his return from the Netherlands, President Grant called him from the audience to speak in general conference in October 1937. Now he was immediately known to many, and in a day when "outside speakers" were much more common in the Church than at present, Lyon was invited to speak many times in a single week. His Sundays were always full. He spoke in sacrament meetings, firesides, study groups, priesthood quorums, Sunday School classes, and family gatherings. He addressed General Authorities and international visitors. He also delivered scores of radio talks and baccalaureate addresses, and he spoke at more than three hundred missionary farewells and in several "Religious Emphasis Weeks" at universities throughout the West. His own diaries indicate that he delivered at least 4,700 formal talks from 1937 to 1978, and reached an estimated audience of more than 750,000 listeners. And the topic was usually history, Latter-day Saint history, faith-filled history.

He also published books, manuals, and numerous articles, all dealing with Christian and Latter-day Saint history. For many years all LDS institutes used his book *Introduction to the Doctrine and Covenants and the Pearl of Great Price* (1948, 1955). His *Apostasy to Restoration* was the Melchizedek Priesthood manual for the entire Church in 1960 and was translated into twelve foreign languages. His frequently revised and often translated *We Believe* (1947, 1951, 1959) served as a manual for youth and new members all over the world. Most of his forty-one articles appeared in Church publications and appealed to a broad, general audience for whom he interpreted the uniqueness of Church history. A meaningful article that illustrates Lyon's approach to teaching history, entitled "Is it Hearsay or History?" published in the *Instructor* in April 1957, calmly challenges the tendency to repeat faith-promoting myths, inaccuracies, and exaggerated stories from Church history. He provides wise guidelines to help the lay Mormon distinguish between myth and historical reality. Lyon spent his life trying to de-mythify the Latter-day Saint past. The real story, he often argued, was better than the myth and built testimonies that would not be challenged if the myths were shattered. But such true stories only came after rigorous research.

Lyon's lasting influence in telling the story of Mormon history will likely not be his publications, although some are very good, but rather his stimulating teaching and the powerful effect his teaching had on two generations of students and would-be historians. Obviously only a few of his 16,000 students have pursued the professional field of history, but thousands gained an appreciation of the amazing story of Mormonism from his well-researched words and prodigious memory.

A Master Teacher

Lyon will be remembered as a master teacher, whether in the classroom, the front room, behind the pulpit, or walking the dusty streets of Nauvoo. A few examples will demonstrate some of his unique techniques.

He seldom displayed deep emotion and usually did not venture openly into the realm of feeling in the classroom, though passion underlay all of what he taught. On the surface his orientation was more practical. In discussing how the pioneers crossed the plains, he might ask a class of city-dwelling students to think about how they would move pigs, or geese, or chickens almost 1300 miles. Most had never thought of the daily challenges of pioneers whom history often describes only in terms of virtues such as sacrifice, dedication, and testimony. "How do you herd pigs?" he would query. "Have you ever tried it?" He had, and he wanted his students to think about this simple but very real problem which their pioneer ancestors experienced. Or he might ask why Brigham Young chose oxen instead of horses or mules to move wagons westward. On this point he would describe the differences between the two animals—oxen could survive on poor grass without the need for supplemental grain, and oxen ate much less in comparison to the weight they could pull. "Better gas mileage," he would say, "better fuel economy." And he would describe the hundreds of apparently temporal decisions that brought about spiritual ends, an exercise which implicitly or explicitly raised the interconnection between spiritual and temporal decisions made by Church leaders ever since. "One's testimony is in the details," he would affirm. He used history as a means of challenging his students to think more deeply about what underlay their faith.

In courses on Church history, he might tell of Edson Whipple, a carpenter who left Nauvoo with finished planks stowed on top of the wheels and axles of his wagon, which meant considerable extra weight and slower travel. He asked his students to think why he might make this sacrifice. After he had listened respectfully to several answers, he then told them that the reason was to build coffins. This surprised some students, but that explained that Brigham Young had promised that the Church would take anyone who wanted to get to Zion, including the elderly and sick, and that some were sure to die along the way. What kind of burial would they receive? A shallow grave that wolves and coyotes could dig up? Absolutely not! Brigham wanted them to be buried deep, in a good coffin if possible, and the graves were marked. Then he would ask students to think about what this meant in everyday terms: delayed arrival, increased risk of winter storms, extra energy expended to dig graves, and someone who had to work far into the night by firelight to build a coffin. The spiritual process began months earlier when Edson compassionately laid planks on the running gear of his wagon in Nauvoo. Lyon then made the spiritual connection between the way people treated their dead—with respect and expecting a real resurrection—and its meaning for their professed faith. The lessons drawn from a simple, unvarnished story about a carpenter who left Nauvoo probably taught Lyon's students more about faith, devotion, and sacrifice than dozens of formal sermons.

When teaching about the Latter-day Saints' departure from Nauvoo, he helped his students to recognize the detailed planning that followed the spiritually confirmed decision to leave. He told of a meeting in the small east wing of Brigham Young's red brick home—"This tiny room was effectively *the* Church office, and all important decisions were made there," he noted. "On September 30, 1845," he stated, "the Brethren were already preparing for the move west. And what preparations they were!" Then he might write on the board—"3,285 LDS families in and around Nauvoo; 1,505 wagons available at that time, and another 1,892 additional ones under construction—a total of 3,397 to move the 3,285 families." But Heber C. Kimball made a survey and found that many of the wagons were too fragile and run-down to make the long journey. The old farm wagons that each family had would not suffice—they simply weren't sturdy enough. "You wouldn't start a trip from Salt Lake to New York City in a 30-year-old jalopy would you."

According to him, Church leaders wisely and with great foresight stressed that wheel rims must be at least two inches wide, that the front wheel had to be three feet high, and the rear four, so as not to bog down in the inevitable mud of the prairie. "How are your tires; will they make it to New York?" Then he praised the leaders for their detailed planning, which he considered to be a confirmation of their inspired calling. He further taught of their foresight in adding another ninety wagons to haul mill stones, mill irons, construction tools, looms, books, scientific apparatus, Church and Nauvoo City records, and so on. And to complete the journey successfully they would need 53,635 livestock, and he emphasized that they must be healthy and truly *live stock*. He broke down this prodigious number into specifics:

14,000	oxen, mules, or horses (4 animals for each wagon)
3,500	extra draft animals (for the likely case of accidents, disease or death)
6,570	milk cows (for milk and cheese along the way)
6,570	beef cattle
3,285	saddle horses (for herd and guard duty, also for the hunters)
9,855	hogs (3 per family)
9,855	sheep
Total:	53,635 livestock animals[16]

"Dogs and cats were optional," Lyon would explain. "Now, where would they get all these animals and wagons?" he asked. The student quickly understood the magnitude of the enterprise—basically moving the whole city of Nauvoo to the Great Basin!

Ronald K. Esplin, a former student and now director of the Joseph Fielding Smith Institute for Church History at BYU, observes that his teaching did not bog down in facts: "His detailed knowledge was not that of an antiquarian. He analyzed, integrated, interpreted, and shared his knowledge in a way that made it comprehensible and come alive for the rest of us. He made his students feel that he knew the people of whom he spoke."[17]

Lyon's command of Church history sometimes left his listeners in awe. One former student remembered that "he had more facts in his head than any person I have ever known."[18] But he was far more than a lecturer who merely transmitted facts. Sometimes he became so absorbed in his subject that students had to remind him when class was over. Fred Buchanan, a former student, recalls that "he was not simply a dispenser of information; he helped students probe beneath the facts to determine what they all meant. He took time in and out of class to raise questions, promote discussion, and above all to get students thinking critically and creatively about Church history and its implications for the religious life." Buchanan also recalls Lyon's "infectious enthusiasm for history, the twinkle in his eye when he got students involved in thinking about difficult historical issues, and his ability to communicate the human dimension of . . . divine events."[19]

Another former student, Truman G. Madsen, an emeritus professor of philosophy at BYU, illustrates the depth of his knowledge and his prodigious memory with this example: "In his class we used to play a game—we'd just give him any date in [LDS] Church history, say 4 January 1841, and he'd be able to tell us something that happened that day. . . . Since the death of Joseph Smith no other man has taken so much knowledge of early Church history to the grave." Madsen "took every class that T. Edgar and Lowell offered—most of them twice, because he [Lyon] was constantly preparing by everything that he read; and he seemed to remember it all." Lyon often brought notes to class but rarely used them. Rather, "the class came from his head." And despite dealing with sensitive and difficult issues, "he did it with candor, and he was always sweet-spirited."[20]

With vast historical knowledge grounded in deep conviction, Lyon attracted students at the University of Utah who often were challenged and disoriented by the secular learning they were receiving. Over the years many of them have claimed that were it not for his ability to reconcile problems and questions in Church history that challenged them, they would not be in the Church today. Their statements seem to confirm Lyon's conviction that accurate, unvarnished Church history was ultimately more faith-promoting than glorified versions not grounded in fact. Years later, Elder Neal A. Maxwell, who attended Institute classes at the University of Utah in the early 1950's, echoed this view when he wrote:

> We must be careful . . . not to canonize [our role] models as we have some pioneers and past Church leaders—not to dry all the human sweat off them, not to put ceaseless smiles on their faces, when they really struggled and experienced agony. Real people who believe and prevail are ultimately more faith-promoting and impressive than saccharine saints with tinsel traits.[21]

Lyon would not have stated it so colorfully, but it summarizes his view that to build faith through the presentation of Church history, that history needed to be ground in fact, not hearsay or myth.

Notes

1. Milton Lynn Bennion, *Mormonism and Education* (Salt Lake City: The Department of Education of The Church of Jesus Christ of Latter-day Saints, 1939), 215–17.

2. Cited in Russel B. Swenson, "Mormons at the University of Chicago Divinity School: A Personal Reminiscence," *Dialogue* 7 (1972): 47.

3. Swenson, "Mormons at the University of Chicago," 33–47. In total, ten seminary and institute men received degrees from the Divinity School, from 1931–1938. They were all cautioned that "re-employment in the Church school system would depend upon our faith and continued loyalty" (40).

4. T. Edgar Lyon, *Oral History*, 94, Church Archives, Family and Church History Department, The Church of Jesus Christ of Latter-day Saints, Salt Lake City (hereafter cited as Church Archives) and L. Tom Perry Special Collections, Harold B. Lee Library, Brigham Young University, Provo, Utah (hereafter cited as Perry Special Collections).

5. Shailer Matthews, cited in Charles H. Arnold, *Near the Edge of the Battle* (Chicago: The Divinity School Association, 1966), 18.

6. T. Edgar Lyon to parents, August 21, 1931, Church Archives and Perry Special Collections.

7. Lyon, *Oral History*, 100.

8. Letter to Russel B. Swenson, cited in "Mormons at the University of Chicago Divinity School: A Personal Reminiscence," *Dialogue* 7 (1972): 47.

9. Jeffrey E. Keller, "The 1931 [B. H.] Roberts—[Joseph Fielding] Smith Controversy," unpublished paper in possession of Ted Lyon.

10. Duane E. Jeffrey, "Seers, Savants and Evolution: The Uncomfortable Interface," *Dialogue* 8 (1973): 65.

11. J. Reuben Clark, "The Charted Course of the Church in Education."

12. Edward L. Hart, interviewed by Ted Lyon, January 23, 1996, Provo, Utah; taped interview in Perry Special Collections.

13. Institute Records, University of Utah LDS Institute, Salt Lake City, 1937–1937.

14. T. Edgar Lyon to E. LV Richardson, January 9, 1970, Church Archives and Perry Special Collections.

15. See Mary Lythgoe Bradford, *Lowell L. Bennion: Teacher, Counselor, Humanitarian* (Salt Lake City: Dialogue Foundation, 1995).

16. T. Edgar Lyon to Mark E. Peterson, copy of letter in Church Archives and Perry Special Collections.

17. Ronald K. Esplin, interview by Ted Lyon, August 28, 1995, Provo, Utah.

18. Ruth Fetzer Carr, interview by Melinda Silver, September 2, 1991, Salt Lake City.

19. Frederick S. Buchanan, interview by Ted Lyon, June 14, 1991, Salt Lake City.

20. Truman G. Madsen, interview by Ted Lyon, May 14, 1992, Provo, Utah.

21. Cited by Bruce C. Hafen, *A Disciple's Life: The Biography of Neal A. Maxwell* (Salt Lake City: Deseret Book, 2002), xv.

Author Biographies

MELVIN L. BASHORE is a senior librarian at the Church History Library in Salt Lake City. He received a B.F.A. from the University of Utah, M.Ed. from University of Missouri–St. Louis, and M.L.S. from Brigham Young University. He has published historical articles on topics ranging from the Mormon Trail to prisons and pro football.

RICHARD E. BENNETT is professor of Church History and Doctrine in Religious Education at Brigham Young University. He is author of a number of articles and books including *We'll Find a Place: The Mormon Exodus, 1846–1848* (Salt Lake City: Deseret Book, 1997) and *Mormons at the Missouri, 1846–1852: "And Should We Die"* (Norman: University of Oklahoma, 1987).

DAVIS BITTON is emeritus professor of history at the University of Utah. He received a B.A. from Brigham Young University, and a M.A. and Ph.D. from Princeton University. His graduate training at Princeton University and thirty-six years of university teaching were in the field of early modern European history. But he early became interested in Mormon history and for ten years served as assistant Church historian. He was also a president of the Mormon History Association. His most recent major publication is *George Q. Cannon: A Biography* (Salt Lake City: Deseret Book, 1999).

SUSAN EASTON BLACK joined the faculty of Brigham Young University in 1978. She is currently a professor of Church History and Doctrine and an Eliza R. Snow Fellow. She is a past Associate Dean of General Education and Honors and Director of Church History in the Religious Studies Center. Dr. Black was the recipient of the Karl G. Maser Distinguished Faculty Lecturer Award in 2000.

ROBERT H. BRIGGS received a B.A. in political science from Brigham Young University in 1974 and a J.D. from Pepperdine University School of Law in 1977. As an attorney, he has been in private practice in southern California for twenty-five years. Besides his professional activities he has pursued studies in anthropology and western and Mormon history. He presented the 2002 Juanita Brooks Lecture on the Mountain Meadows Massacre. His research interests include the Utah War, the Mountain Meadows Massacre, the John D. Lee trials, and the curtailment of Negro and Mormon civil rights in late nineteenth century America due to racial and religious discrimination.

DORIS R. DANT has an M.A. in American literature and another M.A. in counseling psychology, both from Brigham Young University. In 1990 she became executive editor of *BYU Studies,* a post she has held ever since. Doris has written several articles for *BYU Studies* publications and various English and technical journals. With John W. Welch she coauthored *The Book of Mormon Paintings of Minerva Teichert* (Provo, Utah: BYU Studies, 1997).

JESSIE L. EMBRY is assistant director of the Charles Redd Center for Western Studies and an instructor of history at Brigham Young University. She has a B.A. and M.A. in American history from BYU. She is the author of numerous history books and over seventy articles on western American oral history and Mormon history topics including a history of Wasatch County, North Logan, and *Mormon Wards as Community.* In 2002 she received a Friends of the Humanities award from the Utah Humanities Council for her research and writing on Utah and Mormon history. Her most recent book is *Asian American Mormons: Bridging Cultures* (Provo, Utah: Charles Redd Center for Western Studies, 1999).

ALAN GOFF is professor of General Education at DeVry University in Phoenix, Arizona, and teaches writing, literature, and humanities. He has M.A.s in political science and English, and a D.A. in humanities. A major research concern is how historians, novelists, and literary critics draw the boundary between literature and history; this research takes him deeply into the literature of contemporary historiography.

BRUCE C. HAFEN is a member of the Quorum of the Seventy of The Church of Jesus Christ of Latter-day Saints. He received his B.A. in political science from Brigham Young University and his J.D. from the University of Utah.

WILLIAM G. HARTLEY is an associate professor of history at Brigham Young University and a research historian for the Joseph Fielding Smith Institute for Latter-day Saint History. He has served as president of the Mormon History Association and is on editorial boards for the *Journal of Mormon History* and *Mormon Historical Studies*. He is one of twenty-two people who did the entire fifty-nine days of the Sea Trek 2001 experience. He is writing a book about 1861 Latter-day Saint emigration (Sea Trek 2001 was part of his research).

MATTHEW K. HEISS received his B.A. at Brigham Young University in humanities. He earned his M.A. from the University of Virginia in history of religion. In 1987 he began working at Church Archives, where he is responsible for documenting Church history in Europe and Africa. He edited the journals of Mischa Markow, which were published in *Mormon Missionaries Enter Eastern Europe* by Kahlile Mehr (Provo, Utah: Brigham Young University Press, 2002).

E. DALE LEBARON is professor emeritus of Church History and Doctrine at Brigham Young University. He has spent more than eight years in Africa on Church and professional assignments. He has collected more than seven hundred oral histories from African Latter-day Saint pioneers, from which he has published a book titled *All Are Alike Unto God* (Orem, Utah: Granite Publishing, 1998).

THOMAS E. LYON JR. is professor of Latin American literature at Brigham Young University. He earned his Ph.D. from the University of California–Los Angeles and has taught at universities in the United States and Scotland. He has written a biography of his father, *T. Edgar Lyon: A Teacher in Zion* (Provo, Utah: Brigham Young University Press, 2002).

CAROL CORNWALL MADSEN is emeritus professor of history and senior research historian at the Joseph Fielding Smith Institute for Latter-day Saint History at Brigham Young University. She holds a Ph.D. in American history from the University of Utah and specializes in the fields of American and Utah/Mormon women's history. She is author of *Journey to Zion: Voices from the Trail* and *In their Own Words: Women and the Story of Nauvoo* (Salt Lake City: Deseret Book, 1994), and is currently working on a biography of Emmeline B. Wells.

KAHLILE B. MEHR holds both an M.A. in family and local history and an M.A. in library science from Brigham Young University. He works at the Family History Library in Salt Lake City, where he helps develop the collections of Eastern Europe, the Iberian Peninsula, and the Pacific Islands. He has received the Mormon History Association's T. Edgar Lyon Award three times, once for best article of the year and twice for excellence. His most recent publication is *Mormon Missionaries Enter Eastern Europe* (Provo, Utah: Brigham Young University Press, 2002).

STEVEN L. OLSEN is Associate Managing Director for Church History, The Church of Jesus Christ of Latter-day Saints. He earned a Ph.D. in anthropology at the University of Chicago. He has published widely, most recently his dissertation, "The Mormon Ideology of Place: Cosmic Symbolism of the City of Zion, 1830–1846" (Ph.D. diss., University of Chicago, 1980; BYU Studies and the Joseph Fielding Smith Institute for Latter-day Saint History, 2002), was added the Smith Institute's series Dissertation Reprints in Latter-day Saint History.

TALLY S. PAYNE received B.A.s in economics and American studies from Brigham Young University in 1997. After working for Ernst & Young's economics division in Washington, D.C., she returned to BYU for an M.A. in American studies. She has published in economics and educational history, and her master's thesis received the Reese History Award in 2000. She resides in Casper, Wyoming, and teaches American government at Casper College.

STEPHEN C. TAYSOM holds a B.A. in history from Brigham Young University and an M.A. in religious studies from Indiana University, where he is a Ph.D. candidate and associate instructor. His research interests include American religious history and religious historiography, and he has published articles in these fields in *Dialogue: A Journal of Mormon Thought* and elsewhere. He and his wife, Shawny, live in Bloomington, Indiana.

GRANT UNDERWOOD is Professor of History at Brigham Young University and Research Historian at BYU's Smith Institute for Latter-day Saint History. He is author of the prize-winning *Millenarian World of Early Mormonism* (Urbana: University of Illinois Press, 1993), and editor of *Voyages of Faith: Explorations in Mormon Pacific History* (Provo, Utah: Brigham Young University Press, 2000). He has also authored dozens of articles on Mormonism and delivered papers at more than sixty scholarly conferences.

JOHN W. WELCH is Robert K. Thomas Professor of Law at the J. Reuben Clark Law School, Brigham Young University, and editor-in-chief of *BYU Studies*. He serves as director of publications for the Joseph Fielding Smith Institute for Latter-day Saint History at BYU and also on the board of the Institute for the Study and Preservation of Ancient Religious Texts, which oversees the Foundation for Ancient Research and Mormon Studies. He has authored numerous books and articles and sits on the executive committee of the Biblical Law Section of the Society of Biblical Literature. He earned a J.D. from the School of Law at Duke University.

CROOKS & NANNIES
The Charmed Inn Mysteries 2
Misty Simon

This is a work of fiction. Names, characters, places, and incidents either are the product of the author's imagination or are used fictitiously, and any resemblance to actual persons living or dead, business establishments, events, or locales, is entirely coincidental.

© COPYRIGHT 2025 by Misty Simon

All rights reserved. No part of this book may be used or reproduced in any manner whatsoever without written permission of the publisher except in the case of brief quotations embodied in critical articles or reviews.

AI was not used to write this book, to create the cover art, or in formatting.

NO AI TRAINING: Without in any way limiting the author's and publisher's exclusive rights under copyright, any use of this publication to "train" generative artificial intelligence (AI) technologies to generate text is expressly prohibited. The author reserves all rights to license uses of this work for generative AI training and development of machine learning language models.

Warning: Not intended for persons under the age of 18. May contain coarse language and mature content that may disturb some readers. Reader discretion advised.

Cover Art Design by: Kelly Moran/Rowan Prose Publishing
Photo Credit: Adobe Images/Deposit Photos
First Edition
ISBN: 978-1-961967-58-8
Rowan Prose Publishing, LLC
www.RowanProsePublishing.com
Published in the United States of America

PRAISE FOR MISTY SIMON:

"Cozy fans will be charmed."
-Publishers Weekly
"A mystery like no other I have read."
-Lisa K's Reviews Blog
"You'll be cheering as the clues pile up in this creative cozy mystery."
-Lynn Cahoon, *New York Times* bestselling author
"A down-to-earth heroine."
-Kirkus Reviews
"An amusing new series with an engaging, spirited sleuth."
-Library Journal
"A cast of entertaining characters."
-Kings River Life Magazine
"Simon has you laughing out loud."
-Cozy Mystery Book Reviews

Chapter 1

There was nothing quite like a huge to-do list to make you feel like you were just about ta-done. I sighed into the phone and covered it up as a laugh as I gave one more family the directions to The Charmed Inn. Directions that were not only on our website--down to the last turn into the U-shaped drive out front that led to the wide front porch and the front door--but also on any app, on any phone that gave specific turns. I'd even gone to each app and made certain it was correct last month. Because my boyfriend Dean was out of town, I'd had a little downtime and nothing better to do.

Yes, you read that right. Dean was now my boyfriend. It had been a truly wonderful six months since that first kiss. Let me tell you. I, Roxanne Gleason, was the luckiest girl in the world because the guy who I had harbored a secret crush on, the one who had listed me in his phone months before as Hottie instead of Roxy, was now eating dinner with me in the evenings as often as he could, and we were actually going out to do couples things instead of just best friend things. It had been a little weird at first, but I wouldn't have traded that weird for anything.

Anyway...

I sincerely wished I'd taken that time while he was away doing family business to just relax in my room, to give myself a reprieve before the summer onslaught, but I hadn't, and so now here I was.

Actually, I should have asked my books with my dubious but growing "talent" as a bibliomancer if I should have relaxed. Maybe it would have come through with the big letters again to say *YES*. Although, that talent hadn't been doing much lately. Still, it would have been worth a try. But I hadn't, and so here I was instead, trying not to lose my cool while also fielding the questions that were also answered on the website--if only people would have chosen to read through my very-well-put-together FAQ sheet at the bottom of *every single page* of the website. But no.

Fourth of July weekend was always a big holiday here in our small town on the Susquehanna River in Central Pennsylvania. People came from all around the state to watch the fireworks that launched from a tiny island in the middle of the river and shimmered with brilliance on the surface of the slower-moving water. The town had entertainment set up on the waterfront. The ferry would run up until sunset. And food trucks lined the paved path I normally used to do my daily walks so that my wristwatch wouldn't constantly beep at me that I wasn't being active enough.

Today, however, there would be no beeping since I'd hit my target by ten in the morning. And I still had so much left to do before guests arrived over the next two days to begin their vacation at my inn.

I had to swing by and talk to Glennis in the kitchen to make sure she had everything she needed to feed the guests this weekend, as well as make the special Independence Day cakes I'd asked for. I had thought I would hear from her already. The delivery truck had pulled up about an hour ago. Maybe she'd gotten distracted and had forgotten to let me know, even though I'd asked her to. She was like that sometimes. We had an ongoing battle over who was actually the owner here, but it was one I was willing to be a little softer on because I couldn't run the inn without her, and she knew it.

It wasn't a hardship to stop by in the kitchen and check. If anything, it meant that I got to sneak a bite or two of the potato salad I'd asked Glennis to prepare for the staff lunch and also check in on my new employee, Nell, who'd been here for about a month. She was a friend of a friend, and I was happy to have her, but I needed to keep an eye on her progress.

With so many guests coming in, the whole staff would be running their rear ends off. If I made a point to thank everyone before the onslaught for all the work, I knew they'd be doing over the next few days, it usually helped immensely. Especially since they were going to have to do it around the two guys, I'd had to call in for a water pipe emergency and replumb, along with electrical work. My normal, little jobs, handyman Dean, had said that was out of his wheelhouse for repairs.

Something had been going wrong almost every day for two weeks, and I had finally had to give in and call the professionals. After checking the damage, they gave me an estimate. I'd thought we'd be in the clear with having everything done before the new guests arrived since I'd scheduled them for last weekend. However, only the apprentice electrician had shown up without his dad, and things had continued to go haywire. Out of pure desperation, I'd tried the other local handyman, but he'd turned me down because he was out of town. I had about given up hope when the father, who was the actual professional, finally showed up this morning.

It was Tuesday, and I had been assured everything would be fixed no later than Friday. I was counting on them to be right as that was when the house would be full of the final set of guests arriving. Some were due over the next few days, but we were sold out come Friday.

As I approached the kitchen door, I walked and wrote to add to my list of things I needed to check on after lunch, while also adding a few to my current list of things to do before lunch. When I had to turn the page in my notebook to start listing even more things, I felt my blood pressure spike with the lack of checkmarks next to the many items.

Being in my head was the only excuse I could give for not registering the raucous laughter coming from the kitchen until I swung the door open and was hit right in the face with all the noise.

The laughing was the first thing that sent me right back to nights, hiding under my blankets with my younger sister and a flashlight as we tried to tell each other scary stories. I'd often been left shaking and suffering with waking nightmares. And she'd be laughing like a loon and topping herself, even though I had been pretty sure she couldn't have gotten any creepier if she'd tried.

But she always had, without fail. The girl had a horror imagination in a Barbie body.

And in case you were wondering, I adored her for it, even if I had neither the imagination nor the Barbie body.

"Well, look who the cat dragged in," I said, leaning in the door frame with the door slightly ajar behind me. "Do you have a reservation?"

Philomena Carthwright Gleason launched herself from her seat at the butcher block in the huge kitchen, and I was certain she'd knock us both out into the hallway with her enthusiasm. I was only five-foot-one inch and slightly plumper than her, but her five-foot-seven height and slender frame could and had taken me down many times once she'd outgrown me when she'd turned thirteen and shot up like a tree.

She stopped short, though, right before she hit me with the full force of her body and instead gently wrapped her arms around my neck and then rested her forehead on top of my head. I felt her breath catch in her throat and stutter in her chest. Briefly, I wondered what was going on with her to make her react like that with me when she'd just been laughing like a loon two seconds earlier. But I didn't have time to ask because she backed away, shaking her head and putting the biggest smile on her face, one that would even outshine Barbie on her best day.

Grabbing my hand, she dragged me over to the butcher block and forced me down onto the bar stool next to her and her cup of something that didn't exactly smell like just coffee. In fact, it was very close to being a blond bombshell, and I wondered how much Irish cream she'd talked Glennis into letting her pour into the mug.

That was probably a question for another time. She pushed my knees so that the stool rotated to face her.

"I'm here working, and my boss rented the room for me."

Immediately, my mind whipped through who was renting and who that boss might be. Was she talking about the banker who was here for the weekend, supposedly with his wife? That could be…awkward. What about the three couples who were coming in for the fireworks as they did every year?

I was pretty sure they wouldn't be the boss of my sister. And beyond that, I wasn't even aware she had a job. Usually, she house-sat for dozens of people, working her way across and around Europe and the United States to watch dogs or make sure the house didn't burn down. I couldn't imagine being that much of a nomad, but if it worked for her, I wasn't going to judge her.

Unless whoever she was working for was setting up a hotel, and she was here to scope things out. That I might have an issue or two with.

"Are you even listening to me?" she asked, clamping her hand on my knee, which tickled far more than hurt, and she knew it since she used to do it all the time, very deliberately.

I jumped and screeched louder than she had been with her laughing, which just set her off into more guffaws.

Glennis chuckled, and Aunt Hellen came rushing in from the front desk. I saw her quick walk through the dining room on the flat-screen television hanging in the kitchen to keep an eye on things and shut my eyes. Had Mena walked in without saying hello to her? She had often snuck in the back and knew right where the key was.

"Tell me you said hi to…" I stopped talking when Aunt Hellen whipped the door open and stood with her arms crossed and a scowl on her beautifully aging face. Technically, she was my great aunt, but I didn't call her that because she would deliberately take the word great wrong and let it blow up her ego a little more than I was ready to handle.

"Philomena Carthwright Gleason, what on earth are you doing here, and when did you arrive?"

Since I wanted those answers, too, I didn't step in to try to save my younger sister from that scowl. She knew better.

"Aunty Hell, I was just coming out to see you in a moment. I caught a glimpse of you through the front window when I pulled up in the taxi, and you looked super busy, so I didn't want to interrupt you. I figured I would bother Glennis first and then come bother you right after. Promise."

Of course, that scowl on the older woman's face went to a smile when our aunt opened her arms and Mena jumped off her chair to tackle hug Hellen. She could take it more than I could and was ready for it. There was some squealing and a little jumpy dance. I took the time to smell the mug Mena had been drinking out of to see how much of the contents was alcohol.

Glennis caught me getting a whiff and shook her head at me. Was it just milk? Quite possibly. Huh.

What was that job she said she was doing again?

I waited through the chatter of how they each looked awesome, and it was so good to see each other. There was that little screech from Mena that was much cuter than mine, and then she came back to her chair while Aunt Hellen leaned against the counter next to Glennis.

"So, what are you doing here?" I asked before they could get rolling again. "I love that you're here, but what are you doing here?"

"Roxy, Roxy, Roxy, always so inquisitive. Don't you already know? Can't you answer that question on your own?"

I did not roll my eyes or sneak a quick glance over at Glennis. She was talking about my talent for being a bibliomancer, supposedly able to answer any question posed to me by looking at a passage in a book and answering correctly. It was a total crapshoot and definitely not one of the cooler talents that ran rampant in our family. But we also weren't supposed to discuss the weird things we could do in front of people who were not related to us or also talented. Which meant she shouldn't have said anything with Glennis in the room.

Typical Mena.

And then I didn't have to nail her to her chair with a lethal side-eye because Aunt Hellen took care of it.

"Of course, Roxy is happy that you're here. We all are. But it would have been a lot nicer of you if you had given us a heads-up before finding you in the kitchen. We could have set up a dinner with everyone or at least have made your favorite bed up with your favorite sheets."

"Fair enough." Mena smiled, and all was right in the world. Of course. "I still want the sheets, but I can put them on myself.

And to answer your other question, I'm a nanny now," Mena said, popping a piece of an apple crisp into her mouth.

"A what?" That was the very last thing I would have expected her to say. "I don't remember you being a big fan of kids." She had never liked when someone younger than her was in the room before becoming a teenager, and then once a teenager, anyone younger than her was to be ignored because she was now a big girl and only did big-girl things. That could have changed now that she was in her mid-twenties, but who knew?

"This kid is adorable, and her parents are a true joy to be around." She took a sip from her mug and then smiled at me again. "Very plain, very quiet, very wealthy, very generous. I met them in Greece, and when I said I didn't know where I was going next, they asked if I'd accompany them to the US. They wanted to find somewhere quaint to have a quick vacation before diving back into their busy season. I recommended here, of course, and they loved the idea of it being in a small town over the fourth of July, and especially the fireworks, so here we are."

"Why didn't you let us know?" Aunt Hellen tapped Mena on the nose, and it reminded me that everyone used to call Mena by the nickname Philly, thinking it was cute to use the nickname as a shorthand for Philomena. She'd grown out of that, too, when she moved into her teens. From then on, she absolutely hated that people would not only call her a horse, but also boop her on the nose, just like our aunt had done not two seconds ago.

This time, there was no screech, no anger, no huffing and puffing. Mena just smiled and then finished off whatever it was she had in her mug. I made a note to ask Glennis later for confirmation. I couldn't always trust her head shakes.

"Is your family just meeting you here then? I haven't checked anyone in early." I cocked my head to the side to take Mena's measure. "Better question is, are you even checked in?" I asked, thinking that was probably what I should have asked first.

"Not yet. I was getting there. Besides, it's early, and I know how militant you can be about your check-in times. I've seen the reviews online."

"They're not bad. I look at them every day."

"Oh no, dear sister, they're not bad at all. People love the way you run things, but they often comment on how very punctual you are. I'd call it anal retentive, but I guess punctual works too." She snickered, and I groaned. I adored my sister, but she never passed up the opportunity to needle me.

It was going to be a fun week while she was here. It had to be.

But then she gave me that cheeky smile, and I couldn't deny that I enjoyed her needling. It kept me on my toes, and since I was the older one—for once in this house—I could have the upper hand if I chose to. I'd save that for later, though.

"So, you're here for the week with a family as a nanny. I'm not sure I can wrap my head around that."

"It's not that difficult, actually," Mena said, taking another apple turnover under Glennis's watchful eye. "I like this kid. I'm not always a fan of all kids, but this one is adorable. And the parents are super low-key, which speaks to my need to not be overwhelmed with rules and regulations. I keep the kid happy and safe, and the parents leave me to it. Win-win as far as I'm concerned. Not to mention they're paying for my stay here, and my salary is..." She puckered her lips and gave the chef's kiss universal symbol.

Okay then.

"When are they getting here?" I asked as I broke off half of her turnover and popped it in my mouth.

She scowled at me, but she knew the rules, so she kept her griping to herself. My kitchen, my food, especially with a younger sister. "Tomorrow. In the meantime, I thought I'd get my room ready the way I like it, catch up with everyone I can, and then settle in to begin the business of enjoying my time here as a guest instead of a grunt worker." There was that smile again.

"Well, guests don't get to eat in the kitchen and snatch food. That isn't part of the package. Just saying."

Glennis laughed and whisked the empty plate out from under Mena's hand.

Loud banging started above us, and I sighed out a breath of resignation. I'd made every effort not to have the work done while I would have guests just because of this very thing. People paid to come here and relax, to enjoy a carefree weekend or week without loud noises or distractions. And now we had this. I really hoped they'd be gone by the weekend.

At least they knew what they were supposed to do and had just gotten straight to work, but I was not a happy camper that they were going to be making so much noise, just as I was expecting a full house.

"I need to go make sure that Rand and his son are doing what I asked them to do. Enjoy the last of your non-guest amenities until it's time to check in," I said to Mena and then hugged her before leaving her with Aunt Hellen and Glennis.

I could have taken the back stairs from the kitchen to the second floor and emerged from behind the floor-to-ceiling painting where the door was hidden. However, the front steps made more sense, and from the racket, it sounded like Rand might be right where the door opened. I didn't want to start out our working relationship by smacking him in the head or knocking him over. No matter how tempting that seemed at the moment.

The third stair creaked like it always did. I thought about asking the guys if they could possibly take a look at that, too. But I stopped myself because the creak was under the carpet runner that spanned the middle of the staircase, which meant that it would all have to be taken up in order to get to the possible damage. That was not happening this week. It had waited for probably all of my nearly thirty years. It could wait a little longer.

Arriving at the top of the stairs, I found that I had made the right decision by not taking the back stairs. Rand was sitting squarely in front of where it would have opened out, fiddling with the electric socket directly to the right.

"Hey," I said, chuckling to hopefully start our conversation out in a better way than I felt at their tardiness. "I thought you were the plumbing guy."

He glanced up at me and then immediately went back to whatever it was he was doing. "This is what happens when I let the welp do anything. He just came back to town recently. I've been trying to help him get his life in order, but I'm not sure that's going to be happening anytime soon. I'm sorry we were late. I didn't find out when he'd scheduled the job until just this morning. He told me it was sometime next week, and I've been dealing with some family issues over the last few days. I had no idea we were supposed to be here last week." He grunted and kept his eyes down, which left me staring at the top of his thinning gray hair.

"It's okay." Not really, but what else could I say? "Ty has been here over the last week, though not a lot has been fixed. At least you're here now. Do you still think it will take three days to do everything? I have guests coming in. Should we move it to a different week?" I really did not want to do that. The circuits had shorted a few times in the upstairs hallway and two of the rooms. The last thing I wanted was for a fire to break out because I'd waited too long to fix things. I did try to get things fixed in a timely manner, to be fair to myself, but today was the first day Rand had shown up, and I really hoped it meant that things would move along swiftly now.

My grandfather, who I affectionately called Poobah, had given me the inn over a year ago. And it would be the ultimate betrayal of his trust if I was to burn down over two hundred years of our family's legacy because I hadn't been anal-retentive enough.

"I'm relatively certain we can be done in a timely manner."

That sounded a lot like a non-answer, but I left it and him alone after thanking him.

I had no idea where his son was or what he was doing, but I hoped it was work and fast work at that. I turned back around a few steps from the top.

"Is Tyler working on something else?" I asked, wanting to know where everyone was and what they were doing. Okay, maybe Mena had a point.

His answer was drowned out by a scream from downstairs.

Chapter 2

What on earth was that? Like a banshee with a megaphone, the noise zoomed up the stairs and seemed to shatter on the ceiling, then fall all around me and Rand.

He merely rolled his eyes, and I wondered how that could be his reaction. Mine was to clamp my hands over my ears and start running down the stairs. My balance was thrown off by my posture on my descent, though, and I stumbled down the last three stairs and then fell into waiting arms.

Dean's arms, to be exact. And I was not mad about that, especially since the scream had cut off to be replaced by laughter.

"Hello there," Dean said with a smile that melted my heart and made me forget all about anything but looking directly into his gray eyes.

"Hi." I would have tucked my hair behind my ears if my arms weren't wrapped around his waist. Six months in, and I still wasn't completely used to being able to call this very awesome man my boyfriend. The fluttering of my heart in my chest was a wonderful feeling. And I hoped it would never dull or slow down.

"Were you running toward something?" He removed his hand from my hip and swept my bangs away from my eyes.

"Even if I was, I think I've forgotten all about it."

As he chuckled, I felt the reverberation throughout my body. There was no containing the smile on my lips. It grew as he leaned forward and rested his forehead against mine. Because of our height difference, it moved my chest away from his, but I didn't regret that as he kissed me. Just a quick one, since I was working and there were people walking around in my place of business, but even that two seconds was enough to send the flutter into overdrive. Oh, my.

He leaned back. "What's going on? You're practically vibrating with this energy that I can't quite put my finger on."

It was not easy to have a boyfriend who you could not share your whole self. It was a rule within our family and the heritage we shared that we were not allowed to share our talents with anyone who was not also within the group of mancers––people who had special talents. I had been doing research on it, though, because there had to be someone within our line who had married someone who was not talented. We wouldn't have been able to continue the line without coming too close to those we were already related to if no one ever married outside our heritage.

But I hadn't come across anything yet. That didn't mean I was stopping. I wasn't willing to give Dean up without continuing to look into things and find a way around the rule. There had to be.

But until I found it, I would enjoy every second of every day that I could spend with him. I smiled up at him, and he kissed me again.

Someone cleared their throat behind me, which had me closing my eyes.

No privacy, such was the life of an inn owner.

"You didn't tell me you hired Nell," Mena said with her arms crossed under her chest and one hip cocked. It was a classic "how dare you" stance, but I had no idea why she would be throwing that out now over a new employee.

Turning in Dean's arms, I rested back against his chest and faced my sister, who did not look happy. "Dean, my younger sister, Mena. Mena, Dean." I flipped my hand back and forth between them. "I never tell you anything about who I hire. We don't talk that much, anyway, because you're usually on the road or in a completely conflicting time zone. And even when we do manage to connect, it's almost never about inn business, except when we had that death here six months ago." Even then, I hadn't told her all the details, like how it had affected Aunt Hellen and her relationship with our uncle.

"Right, right, right. But Nell was my best friend in high school, and of course, I would want to know if you'd decided to hire her. That makes my stay even better! We can catch up while she's working, and now I don't have to arrange to meet her after work or try to make our schedules line up. I thought she was traveling abroad, so it's awesome to see her here."

I barely resisted groaning. "She does need to work while you're here. We can't have the two of you screaming every time you see each other and then running off to put your heads together and gossip."

Mena had the gall to laugh, even though I was serious. "So, you do remember that we were friends."

Truthfully, I didn't remember that at all. However, I would have been at the inn pretty much all the time as soon as I'd turned eighteen and could start helping Poobah. I was almost never home when Mena was a high schooler. But I wasn't going to admit that if I didn't have to, and honestly, that was her M.O. with every friend she'd ever had, so I'd taken a calculated guess.

"I have to work, too," she said. "I just meant we could talk when we pass each other during our jobs or whatever."

"Sure."

When she squinted at me, I realized I had not carried that off the way I had thought I could. Story of my life.

"I'm serious," she said.

"I know that, and I appreciate it, but Nell is newer and still learning her job, so I want to make sure she is also focused on what she's doing here. We've had a few issues with her training and overuse of earbuds when she should be listening for guest requests." I probably shouldn't have said that since it was private. But this was my sister. "Keep that between us."

"Of course," Mena said.

I sighed. "Okay, I'm fine with minor conversations when passing each other through the halls or whatever, but I can't have her distracted catching up with you." That didn't come out much better from the stormy expression on her face.

"You really think I'd jeopardize my job and hers by standing in the hall forever and just yapping our heads off?"

I sighed again and wished I could have just gone back to enjoying the feeling of Dean's arms around me and listening to the sound of his heartbeat as I rested my head against his chest. "No, I don't think you would deliberately do that, and I know you're a responsible person. But I also know you like to talk. I saw your report cards when Mom would have to meet with the school about your chatter and always getting in trouble for doing your little monologues instead of sticking with the assignment."

That got her to laugh, and it was the real kind, straight from her belly. "Fair enough, and you have a point. I love my job this time, and it's been a lot of fun to hang with people instead of always being on my own in a new place where I know no one. What if I promise to keep a clock on myself and not go full-on Gossip Girl? I won't even soliloquy. I'll watch myself, promise, but I really am happy she's here. This way, we can just talk in passing instead of having to plan an afternoon for coffee. You know those can turn into three solid hours for me without even a hint of the conversation faltering." She took my hand and squeezed it. "I like being here with you, too. Any chance of taking Aunt Hell up on her idea and talking Glennis into making a big old dinner for everyone since my family isn't coming in until tomorrow? It'll be my last night without a child to look after."

Dean chuckled from behind me, and I felt the rumble in my back. "I'm sure we can work something out. And I like you being here, too. Just don't distract my employees."

"So noted. And with that, I should go get things ready in my room so that I can be the best employee when my family shows up. Which room am I in? Can I have the one on the third floor that our cousin Murphy says has a ghost? I may need someone else to talk to if I have to curb myself throughout the day."

And there she was, my wonderful, frustrating, out-there, and so in my heart sibling. I hadn't realized how much I'd missed her until just now. I stepped away from Dean to pull her into a hug that caged her arms against her sides. She laughed again and then broke my hold to wrap her arms around me. "Love you, too. Now let me have my room. You're taking up a lot of my time, and I don't want to keep you from your work. I've heard you have a tough boss."

"I'll add that to the anal retentive. Thanks so much." We smiled at each other, and then she kissed me on the cheek and left.

"You know, Caper is the same way with me." Dean lifted my hand and brushed his lips over my knuckles.

"I've seen the interactions between you and your brother and have been relieved sometimes that I don't have to deal with it on the daily like you do now that he lives in the cottage out back. I guess I'll have to weather the storm over the next few days. What could go wrong?"

I groaned as soon as I had the thought and let it come tumbling out of my mouth. As with most things, the moment I said something like that, the Universe took it as a challenge and threw the gauntlet back in my face. I paused, waiting to see if anyone would run out of the kitchen saying something was on fire, or maybe another electrical outlet had gone out, or the plumbing had backed up again. But nothing happened in the immediate area, so I let myself relax, just a little bit, back into Dean's arms.

"Any chance you want to come to dinner tonight with all the family? You know most of the characters in mine anyway, and if anyone new shows up, you at least have the lay of the land around here." Well, except for the part where we all carried some form of magic. But we knew enough to put a lid on it when there were others around who didn't have any talents. That could be both a curse and a blessing, depending on the timing and what was happening.

My talent had been a blessing for once when I'd found one of our guests dead six months ago. I hadn't been able to activate it like it had been active during that time, but that was okay as long as there were no more deaths.

"Sure." He shrugged. "I was planning on having dinner with just you, but I don't mind a bigger crowd."

That Dean is always so easy-going about any changes or pivots in the road. I envied his ability to flow with things like that, but I didn't envy why he was able to do it so effortlessly. Especially since it had a lot to do with his family being a little on the shady side. He'd gotten out of their way and their sphere by moving here about a year ago, but then the trouble had followed him, namely his brother. But that also included his niece and nephew, who were gems. It was complicated, but when wasn't life complicated?

"Do you think Caper and the kids would want to join us, too? Get everyone in the same room at the same time to get it out of the way in one shot?"

Dean laughed, and I loved to hear the noise. "It doesn't have to be like a showdown at the OK Dinner Table, Roxy. I'm sure everyone will be on their best behavior."

I was glad one of us thought that.

"Well, I should go let Glennis know the table needs to be extended by about ten then, and I should get back to work. I can't exactly tell anyone that they're lollygagging if I'm doing the very same thing."

"Fair to a fault, that's my Roxy."

Let me tell you, I did not, at all, mind being called his anything and everything.

We parted ways with one more quick kiss. Dean was going out back to talk to Caper about the dinner invitation and then heading off to work. Having him right down the road at the ferry launch meant he could come up for lunch every day if things weren't too busy down at the dock and shed. We were in peak season now, though, so I took him whenever he could get away. Whenever he still stopped by, I loved it. For someone who'd always played whatever role was needed at whatever time it was needed, it made a huge impression on me that I was a top priority for him.

Okay, I'll stop fawning now. Seriously.

But that didn't stop me from strolling by the bay window facing the backyard to watch him walk along the brick path to the house his brother was currently staying in to get his life back on track and keep his kids safe.

Dean's height and how wide his shoulders were normally kept my attention, but when I saw Mena bolt out from the kitchen door, I couldn't stop myself from following her with my eyes. When she flew across the lawn and jumped onto the white gazebo with her arms spread, my full attention was diverted from Dean to what on earth she was doing.

And then I saw a man's head pop up, and I remembered something I had not thought of in years—Ty, the son of Rand, the guy working on my inn, had been a forbidden love interest when Mena was fifteen and he was twenty.

Uh oh. Why hadn't I thought of that when he'd done the estimate? Then again, it was seeing the two of them together that sparked the memory. And I wouldn't have been thinking of her or high school when I was facing some serious money-spending to get things working correctly around here.

The memory of them hit me in the forehead. The two of them talking out at the river, sitting on the very edges of a bench, five feet between their bodies, not touching at all. Mena had clenched her arms around her middle and bent her head. I couldn't hear what she was saying because I'd been hiding behind a bush, watching without her knowing it. My books had told me she needed to be protected. Well, actually, I had read a passage in a fantasy book where swords were drawn, and the fate of the world was in the balance. The message I'd taken from it was that she needed protection. I was also about nineteen, so don't judge.

He'd reached a hand out to touch her shoulder. She'd scooted farther along the bench and ended up tipping herself over the edge. In a flash, he'd crouched by her, keeping his hands to himself. After a few seconds, she'd sat up and brushed herself off, but stayed on the ground with her arms wrapped around her knees.

My parents had told her earlier that afternoon she was not allowed to see him anymore. They'd found out that he was five years older than her fifteen. The age gap was too much, legally, and for her level of maturity. She'd been crushed, but had listened to them.

I hadn't really been there to spy on her, at least I would never admit to that, just to protect her.

A few seconds later, he had dropped his head, grabbed the back of his neck, and then walked away. He didn't see me because I made my small self smaller, plus he wasn't paying attention to anything but the ground right in front of him and the tips of his sneakers.

I'd assumed at the time that she'd told him they couldn't see each other, and I had never seen them together again. Rand had said Ty had only recently come back to town. Wasn't it weird that Mena showed up at the same time? I hadn't been joking when I said we didn't talk much. Every time we did, it was as if it had only been a day or two, but our conversations were mainly about what she was doing while she traveled all over the world.

Escaping a romance that had never happened, and then they had both gone their separate ways only to meet up again as if the stars had aligned for them?

Was she going to interrupt his work schedule, too?

Man, I wished I had a book on me right now so I could ask if this was coincidence or kismet. I was very much going to ask my dear sister later, that was for sure. But it was also for a different time.

And speaking of time, I was paying him per project, not per hour, so he was more than welcome to talk to my sister all he wanted as long as he got things done.

After another couple of seconds, I turned from the window because whatever they talked about was not my business. And darn it, I'd missed Dean walking into the small cottage in the backyard that his brother and his brother's children were currently inhabiting.

Such was life, and I needed to move on. I had things to do and people to get ready for.

I made my rounds, stopping in the kitchen to snag that snack I'd thought about earlier and also make sure Glennis was doing all the things she did so well.

She gave me a pinched look, and the thought crossed my mind that we might have to have a conversation sooner rather than later about who was the boss around here. It was true she had been in the employ of the inn under my grandfather for longer than I'd been alive, but I was the one whose name was on the deed. I didn't want her to leave because she and her talents were way too valuable to walk out the door, but we also needed to come to an understanding that while she was totally the dowager Duchess of the Kitchen, I was the Duchess of the house overall. I didn't like that particular image. Believe me, I'd rather we just be able to work together as partners. But I'd received a warning from Aunt Hellen that Glennis had something on Poobah that might have made him allow her to have a little more leeway than I was willing to give. That meant I had to keep an eye on her, too.

Along with Nell, who seemed enthralled with whatever podcast or music she was filtering through those earbuds that never seemed to be anywhere but in her ears. At this point, I was going to have to channel being a spider to keep all my ducks in a row.

"Hey, Nell?"

She hummed to something I couldn't place.

"Nell?" I said it a little louder this time, and she took one earbud out. "Everything going well?"

She frowned and then cleared that with a smile. "Yeah, sorry, just listening to a documentary on the life and times of Joan of Arc. Fascinating stuff."

It must have been very fascinating since she immediately replaced her earbud and went back to wiping a counter while staring out the window into the backyard.

Maybe after lunch, I'd corner Glennis and see if Nell was pulling her weight around here or not.

An hour later, I was back in the dining room when the lights flashed in the overhead chandelier and the sconces that gave the room an intimate and beautiful ambiance. And then they went out altogether. I groaned. Another outage, or had Rand hit a wire that had tripped the fuse box?

"Rand, was that you?" I called up from the bottom of the staircase.

"Was what me?" he asked, way closer than I had expected. I stumbled back a step since I had thought he was above me, not behind me.

"The lights just went off in the dining room."

He wiped his hands on a rag and shrugged. "Better check the fuse box then. I didn't touch anything that would have tripped anything. I was in the bathroom down the hall." He hooked a thumb over his shoulder as if I might not know where my own guest bathroom was down here.

"I..." Was cut off.

"I'd do it for you, but I have to get back up there and check some glue to make sure that it didn't dry incorrectly." He stepped past me. When he hit the third stair, it creaked like it always did and stopped him in his tracks. He rocked back and forth on it, making it squeak again and again. "You want me to look at that?"

"Maybe later. I have a lot of people coming in over the next few days, and I'd like the runner to stay in place until after they're gone."

"Your choice," he said, shrugging and mounting the rest of the stairs, then disappearing at the top.

Girding myself for the steep stairs and close quarters on the staircase to the basement, I set myself on the course to the wine cellar where the fuse box was located.

Even though this place was mine, I was not a big fan of the basement. I wasn't a big fan of basements in general, but mine was particularly not my favorite. I'd heard from one of my cousins that a not-so-good mancer had previously used it for some shady stuff, and those shady things had left a particular feeling in the area. Per Poobah, it was incredibly safe, and Aunt Hellen had also confirmed that fact, but I still didn't like it very much.

I had to see if I could get the lights back on, though. I'd already sent some texts and made some calls about everyone coming over for dinner, and I couldn't expect them all to eat by candlelight.

Although, actually, I could, I thought as I stood at the top of the stairs down to the basement and considered turning around and not dealing with this right now. I could also find Nell and ask her to go down and check things out. Or I could ask Glennis to go for wine for dinner and ask her to stop by the fuse box along the way.

I could also stop being such a nincompoop and just go do the thing. I'd taken longer hanging out up here, dillydallying about what to do or not do, than if I'd just gone down and done the thing. And I was totally relying on old words to distract myself.

After straightening the neckline of my blue silk shell, I smoothed down the hips of my A-line skirt and made myself take the steps carefully in my kitten-heeled shoes.

Nothing to be afraid of. Residual energy was absolutely a thing, but I did not have to be scared of it. And if I was so concerned about it, then I could ask Uncle Vince to come down and do some kind of cleansing ritual. In fact, I could ask Mena to come down with her pyromancy and burn out any darkness.

Was it another coincidence that when I turned the corner into the wine cellar, she was already there? I could ask her to take care of it now before her family showed up and she had to do normal job-type things.

That completely fled my mind when I realized she was standing over a very dead Ty. He was not breathing, and his hair looked singed. His eyes were wide open and didn't blink at all.

CROOKS AND NANNIES

His face was frozen in a shocked, silent scream. I wasn't going to say I was a pro at dead bodies, but this time, I knew.

Uh oh.

Chapter 3

Mena and I stared at each other in the softly lit basement. There were rows and rows of shelves stocked with all brands and vintages and flavors of wine. Years and years of collecting bottles of wine from abroad, from nearby wineries, from gifts to the inn. We had a whole section of wines that Poobah's father had brought with him after his trip to Italy and another set that his mother had brought back from France.

It was rare that anyone ordered any of the truly vintage stuff since it was incredibly costly. We kept it on hand for special occasions like someone coming into their powers or anniversaries. We hadn't had one of those in the last five years onsite since my grandmother, Poobah's wife, had died. My parents tended to travel for their anniversaries, so they celebrated on their own without any of us. Maybe someday soon someone in our family would have a baby, and we could look forward to a new generation of mancers. But at the moment, Mena was our youngest family member and way past her initial talent coming out.

Mena. I continued to stare at her as these inane thoughts went through my head, allowing me to not look down at the floor again.

A bare bulb hung from the ceiling with the pull chain vibrating slightly from the harsh way Mena was breathing. No matter how much I tried not to look, I could not keep the view of Ty out of my peripheral vision field. His normally slightly tousled sandy-colored hair was sticking straight up off his head and looked slightly singed. That look of horror etched on his face was frightening. Had he electrocuted himself? That would have been an accident and far better than where my brain was going, that Mena had somehow killed a man in my cellar, and I'd just caught her in the final act.

"What..." I cleared my throat and tried again. "What are you..." Another throat clearing. I needed to get at least one complete sentence out. I could do this. "What are you doing down here?"

Simple enough. Open enough to have a dozen different answers I could think of right off the top of my head. And they all ran through my brain like a train going off the rails.

"I don't know." Mena wrapped her arms around herself and shook. "I have no idea." And then she started crying.

Damn.

I quickly wrapped my arms around her and pulled her gently but firmly away from the body at our feet. He wasn't going anywhere, so he could wait just a minute or two while we sorted some things out. I would not hide a crime, and if something had happened while my sister was in his presence, like he did indeed get electrocuted, then we could explain it to the police and make sure they knew she had nothing to do with it. Unless she did...

Double damn.

"Let's start from the beginning." I couldn't get her to look me directly in the eyes, even when I bent down to make eye contact from below, so I gave up and just held on to her. "What made you come down to the wine cellar? It isn't a place you would normally be, and I didn't ask you to pick out any wine. Did someone else?" Had that someone killed Ty and then tried to blame it on my sister?

My mind also jumped to what happened last time with the cursed necklace, and I shuddered. "You haven't accepted anything from anyone recently, have you?"

"Only a text from Ty. I put my number in his phone when I saw him out at the gazebo. He sent me a text to confirm who he was. I had to get something from the house, and he had to get back to work, so we agreed to meet up later. But then his later was earlier than my later. He texted about five minutes ago and let me know he was in the basement. And since he was going to be down here for a bit, did I want to come down and keep him company? We could talk while he worked."

I held on as she drew in a deep breath. I was afraid the dam was about to break, but she kept herself together.

"He jokingly called me Philly in the text, and I thought, if nothing else, it would be good to just hang out for a few minutes and see how he's been doing. Like I said, he got called away when we were in the gazebo, so we didn't really get a chance to do anything more than say hi and then bye. I don't hate the cellar as much as you do, and at least we wouldn't be out in the open in front of anyone who might pass by if we decided to have a conversation we should have had a lot of years ago."

So much to unpack there, but still no definitive denial that she'd killed the guy at our feet, which was starting to worry me.

"So, you were down here to talk with him. Was he like this when you arrived?" I wanted to add the words, *or had she done this*, but did not want to be the one to say that out loud.

"Roxy!" She didn't quite yell the word, but the look on her face was pure horror.

"It's a valid question. Just answer it."

"I came down the stairs and was calling his name. I didn't know exactly where he was as he only said that he was in the basement, not in which room. I wandered a little, and then the lights flickered, and I stopped in my tracks to make sure they weren't going to go out altogether. I heard you've been having some serious trouble around here with malfunctions, and I didn't want to get caught in the back recesses of the basement with nothing but the flashlight on my phone."

I held my tongue even though I wanted to remind her again that she still hadn't answered my question and was instead seeming to dance around it.

"But the lights came back on, and when I rounded the corner into the wine cellar, I found him on the floor, just like this." Tears glistened in her eyes again.

Finding a dead body on a ferry six months ago had been rough. I'd known the victim to the extent that he had been here every year for his annual writers' weekend. But I hadn't had any feelings for him other than a casual acquaintance kind of softness.

This was different.

"Was he moving at all? Did you check for a pulse?"

She immediately ducked away from me and went straight for Ty's throat. I grabbed her hand and yanked her back before she could touch him.

"Don't. Don't do anything you haven't already done." I bit my lip. "We need to call the police. Since I own the inn, I'll be the one to check for a pulse. I was seen in the hallway before coming down here, and I couldn't have in been two places at once. It will look better if I'm the one to touch him."

Those glistening tears began raining down her cheeks like a waterfall and were accompanied by a low but intense keening that did not bode well for me, being able to use my phone in the same room with her.

"Why don't you go upstairs? Head to the kitchen and get something to drink, and then just stay there until I can get the cops out here, okay? Do you need me to take you up? I don't really want to leave the scene of the accident until someone is here to check things over." And I really hoped it was not my nemesis Norm, who seemed to hate everything about me, even though, as far as I knew, I hadn't done anything wrong to him since the ninth grade. And even then, it was small potatoes.

"I don't want to leave him." She reached out a hand again, and I gently moved her farther away from the body. I was almost sure he was dead. With his hair sticking up like that and the fact that I hadn't seen his chest move in the last three minutes, I felt it was a pretty safe bet that he was gone.

"He already left us, Mena. I need you to go upstairs and wait in the kitchen with Glennis. She'll take care of you until someone arrives to help. You might have to come back down here at some point with the police, so give yourself a chance to breathe and regroup before that happens."

She drew in a sharp breath and then fled through the hallways. I heard her clatter up the stairs a moment later. I did not breathe out a sigh of relief because things were about to get dicey. And I was not happy that I was in the basement in the first place, but also that there was a dead body down here with me.

When had my life turned from mundane and inn-keeperish to this strange stage of bodies showing up unannounced? For the record, I did not like it. This was most certainly not going to be my dead-person era.

Taking my phone out of my pocket because all skirts should come with pockets, I called the non-emergency line to the police as I swiftly knelt next to Ty and checked his wrist for a pulse. I felt nothing and still hadn't seen his chest move, so I was pretty sure he was gone. But why and how?

Those were questions for the police.

"Didn't I just talk to you last week?" Shirleen, at the front desk of the police station, said as soon as she picked up the phone. "You were having some issues with vandalism or something, right?"

"Um, no, that wasn't me. We talked at the grocery store about Mrs. Lincoln calling in bird droppings on her car roof as vandalism."

"Right, now I remember. I never did get my strawberry milk, even though that's precisely what I had gone into the store for in the first place. I should put that on my list."

I should have just called 911, even if I was pretty confident this was no longer an emergency.

"Shirleen, we've had an accident at the inn. It appears someone electrocuted themselves in the basement. Can you please send an officer out to handle this? I don't want to touch anything, but I did feel for a pulse and couldn't find one."

"Oh, my goodness! You should have led with that, Roxy. Oh, my goodness! Electrocution? That's horrible! We'll have someone right out."

And then she hung up on me. Which meant I was going to have to make another call to warn the inn staff that the police were about to infiltrate us.

I considered a couple of options and finally decided on my Aunt Hellen. She was the most dependable of the people here, even if she wasn't technically staff. She lived here for room and board and helped out around the inn with anything I asked.

She'd also recently been teaching me how to use this gift that I'd had for years with no real guidance on how to use it.

Fortunately, she picked up on the first ring. "I just saw Mena in the kitchen. Glennis is taking care of her, and I'll be right down. Where are you?"

It was a valid question since the square footage of the basement reflected the square footage of the first floor of the inn, which was a lot. We had rooms down here for decorations, furniture, and random supplies, along with antiques I couldn't use, but also couldn't get rid of. And then, we also had the racks and racks of wine.

"I'd rather you stay up there and greet the police at the front door. We can then meet at the entrance to the wine room. I don't want to move too far from the victim of the accident."

"You're sure it was an accident?" She'd dropped her voice and sounded a little scared. Join the crowd, Aunt Hellen.

"Positive. The cops should be here any minute. Just take care of things, and if it's Norm, make sure it's not just him because I can only handle so much right now, and he is not on that list at all."

"Got it."

I heard sirens in the background of her phone and shut my eyes. This was not an emergency. It was an accident. They did not have to make a spectacle of the whole inn just because something not-so-good had happened here.

"Where is he, and what happened?" Norm was talking loud enough that I could almost hear him through the floorboards and definitely over the line. I shut my eyes because this was not going to go well, but I also couldn't avoid it. I ended the call with Aunt Hellen and then texted Mena to stay where she was. Finally, I braced myself for the onslaught.

I didn't have long to wait. Footsteps clattered down the wooden staircase, and then there was a staccato rhythm of about four people running along the concrete hallways. No way was Aunt Hellen running, so I peeked around the corner to prepare myself.

She had her arms out, almost touching each wall, and holding the three people in uniform behind her like she was the leader of the band. The clattering footsteps were them trying to dodge around her, but she kept her arms out, and I was almost sure she was using just a little bit of her magic to make sure the barrier held.

She and I made eye contact, and I pulled back to the wine room, taking up a position at the door, making my own barrier to Ty's body.

"Why didn't I automatically assume you'd be the one to find something like this?" Norm said, still standing behind Aunt Hellen. He was struggling to break free from her hold, but he wouldn't be able to do anything until she let him. Because of her kind of magic, he also wouldn't be able to realize she was the reason he couldn't get through. When the spell was over, he wouldn't realize anything untoward had happened at all. She had awesome power, and I was jealous that all I'd gotten stuck with was the ability to read answers from random books.

But that was not an issue for the moment. I nodded at her, and when she nodded back, Norm nearly fell head-first into the wine room and stumbled toward the body at my feet. He righted himself at the last second, or Hellen righted him, and he straightened his gun belt before clearing his throat and squinting at me.

"Neither Hellen nor I were the one to find him, and this is not anything more than an accident."

"We'll see about that. Seems that lately, you are having all kinds of trouble with dead bodies."

It was only one other one, and I'd had nothing to do with that death other than housing the deceased and finding him when I was on a walk. I could have fought Norm right there and then, but I wanted to protect my sister and get the body out of my basement more than I wanted to be right. That could be revisited later.

"My sister found him. We believe he might have been electrocuted. He was here doing work on the inn due to some issues we've been having lately with the underlying structure, and he's right near an outlet." I gestured to the wall to keep him in line with what I was saying and on topic and not think anything other than accident.

"Which sister?" he asked, narrowing his already squinty eyes.

"Does it matter?" Seriously!

"Yes."

"Mena."

And I watched as his whole body relaxed, and a genuine smile popped out on his face. "I'm absolutely certain then that it was indeed an accident. I'll need to speak with her, though, to get the facts straight. Where is she?"

"Don't you want to look at the body?"

"Not just yet. I think it's important that I see Mena before I see the body." He smoothed down his hair and then straightened his gun belt again.

The way he said her name made me itchy. And I did not like being itchy. What the hell was he doing now? He'd smoothed his hand over his head again and then brought his palm down over his mouth and blew into it. Was he checking to make sure his breath was okay? For the love of all that was holy. I could not handle this.

One of his officers led the way as we trooped up the stairs in a line, with me bringing up the rear. And then there was Mena, coming out of the door to the kitchen with a mug of something in her hand and tears still glistening in her eyes. She'd done something to remove the tear tracks that had been on her cheeks, but her face still looked a little swollen. The urge to hug her and tell her it was going to be okay was overwhelming, but Norm beat me to it.

"Oh, Mena, I'm so sorry you had to go through that. It's terrible. Something no one should ever have to see. I promise that you won't have to revisit it again if I have anything to say about it, and I do have a lot to say about it."

What in the name of Medusa's awesome hair was this man doing? When I'd found a dead body, he had automatically thought I had been the one to kill him and had made absolutely sure that I was not going anywhere until he asked all his questions, standing right in front of the corpse. With Mena, he was like a fawning sycophant...

I stopped myself in my tracks. Of course, he was. Mena was the golden child of all things in our family. She had been the cute one, the adorable one, the fun one. Our older sister had been the studious one and the serious one. And then there was me. No one had been sure what to do with me or how to define me, so I'd defined myself. Simply as Roxy and others could love or leave it.

But Mena was a different creature and had often been able to be a chameleon, bringing to the front whatever part of her most matched whoever she was standing with or interacting with. It was its own form of magic. Where I tended to fade back into the wallpaper and do whatever needed to be done not to be seen, she could change into whatever would bring her attention, but only the good kind. I would say it was an even better talent than her pyromancy, but she didn't agree. According to her, she didn't even acknowledge it was a thing the one time I'd tried to talk to her about it, so I'd never brought it up again. She hadn't been mad or even irritated. In all honesty, she'd been baffled, so I'd left it there.

Some would call it manipulation, but I didn't think that's what she intended. She did it without even realizing it.

But it was on full display right now, and it was something to behold.

Smiling shyly at Norm, she tucked her blonde hair behind her ear before tucking her hand under her chin. "Hey, Norm. I'm sorry you had to be called out. How have you been? It's been a long time since I've seen you. The uniform looks good on you."

I kept the eyeroll to myself because the behavior was working. And honestly, if it kept her out of jail, then I was not going to interrupt that as long as it worked in our favor.

He did some preening, almost making me lose the battle of the eyeroll, but I kept my cool at the very last second.

"Are you okay? That must have been so scary to find someone like that. I'm so sorry."

She bit her lip and dipped her chin. "I'm okay. I'm just a little bit scared because I got a text from Tyler to go to the basement, but then when I got there, it looked like he'd been electrocuted. I didn't touch him. Promise. I wasn't sure what had happened." She shook her head, and her hair tumbled around her shoulders. "And then my sister came downstairs and found me. She was able to tell that he wasn't breathing anymore so she called and talked to someone at the police station and then now you're here. It's all a kind of whirlwind."

All true and all without flourish. And I could tell it was hitting Norm in all the feels, unlike when I had found someone dead, and he'd immediately said it was me and that I was going to go to jail.

With her, he took her hand and led her to one of the settees in the hallway, and gently guided her to take a seat, then handed her a tissue. Where did he get that?

She crumbled it in her hand and gave him a sad smile. "Thanks."

"Of course, and don't worry at all. I'm sure it was an accident. We'll be able to figure that out right away so you can settle your mind. Horrible things happen sometimes. I'm just sorry it happened to you."

What in the hell had happened to her? Come on now. Again, though, I kept the words to myself. But I won't lie, it was getting harder and harder to do.

There was a heavy tread on the stairs to the basement, and then Norm's second in command, Micah, waved Norm over as soon as he opened the door into the hallway.

"Hey, Roxy," he said as Norm hesitated to leave my sister. "How's it going?"

"Not as good as it could be." I shrugged, and he nodded.

"It might be getting worse, sorry. I don't think this was an accident. I'm pretty sure somebody killed the guy downstairs. I'm going to have Norm come down and check it out, but you might want to have a list of who has access to the basement and who's here in case we need it like last time."

Oh, I didn't like that at all, and I definitely hadn't liked it last time, either.

Chapter 4

Norm's face took on the cast of a thunderstorm, ready to rumble as his brow furrowed and he cleared his throat. "Micah, we can handle that later. There's no need to distress Mena right now. Can't you see she's already upset?"

"Um, yes?" Micah shrugged. "I just thought that you might want to know what we found so we could begin questioning people, namely the person who found Ty dead. We have to collect evidence and information if we're going to catch the killer. We can't rule out anyone, especially whoever found him like that or whoever made him look like that. I'm just saying."

If possible, Norm's face went from thunderstorm to downright category-five hurricane. The two had clashed almost literally last time as Micah had had a part in Norm taking a header down the main staircase and landing at my feet. Norm had not been happy, and Micah had been horrified. He'd also been very new to the job. Six months in, though, it looked like that dynamic might have shifted. Part of me was interested in watching Norm rein himself in, and the other part wished Micah would shut the hell up.

"We'll talk back at the station," Norm ground out through clenched teeth. "For now, you can contact next of kin."

"Sir." And I was impressed he'd used the word when you could very clearly see that he probably wanted to use a different word that started with the letter S. "Sir, I'm going to have to insist that you come with me downstairs and check over the scene before we make any speculation on the cause of death."

This was the little boy who I used to watch in the afternoons while his mom worked at the local diner. The little boy who almost always had a sunny smile on his face and a real knack for being curious about everything. He wasn't curious now, though. He was very clearly irate. And if I had to guess, he was going to make a case that would stick with or without Norm.

Norm, who grunted, then turned to Mena. "I'm sorry. I'll go down and get this sorted out. Some people want everything to be a murder so that they can look like a hero."

That was a very unfair assessment, but I watched as Micah held his tongue and then the door for Norm to precede him down the stairs to the basement. I would bet almost anything he wanted to plant one of his police-issued boots square on his rear and shove him down the stairs intentionally this time.

As soon as they were gone, Mena popped up from the chaise lounge and started pacing. "Oh man, you don't think they're going to think I did it, do you? I didn't do anything. I went down there because I got a text. I don't hate the basement like you do. But I wouldn't have gone down there without a reason."

I leaned against the wall with my ankles crossed as she grew more agitated. "And what if they think your reason was to take out an old lover who was maybe trying to make demands on you that you weren't willing to fulfill? Maybe he knew something from back in the day that could ruin your new life, and he was demanding you take him back or else?"

She whipped around from the bottom of the staircase and glared at me. "You have got to be kidding me. You must be kidding me. Why on earth would I do that? I didn't even know he was around. I thought he had gone off traveling like he said he was going to. I was out in the backyard picking some flowers for my room when he said my name from the gazebo. First, I was shocked and then giddy for a moment. We started talking, and I remembered all the things I liked about him, but also some of the reasons I had been thankful that Mom and Dad asked me why someone so much older would be interested in someone so much younger. Mentally, our ages have seemed to reverse with aging, but I still was fond of him. We had talked about a book I was writing while I was in the gazebo with him. So, when he asked me to meet him in the basement, I thought that it was fine to just skip down there and say hi, then skip back up the stairs to continue preparing my room." She sat back down and cradled her forehead in her hands.

It all sounded legitimate and could have made a lot of sense. But if the police felt there was foul play here, then she might have to be a little more forthcoming with what she had been doing down there and what state exactly she found him in compared to how she had left him.

I loved my sister. I really did. And there was no way I thought she had actually done this horrible thing if it wasn't an accident. I would defend her to my very last breath, but something felt off here. I was going to have to do a little more digging. I needed another valid suspect to give the cops. Preferably one who had actually done it if, in fact, something untoward had been done.

Norm appeared at the top of the basement stairs again. "There's something wrong about the body. We'll be taking it to the medical examiner to confirm the cause of death. Don't go anywhere and be available for questioning. I'll contact the next of kin."

Mena gasped, but at this specific time, Norm appeared to only have eyes for me. Admittedly, they were filled with fire and daggers, but why me? I had only found the one who had found the body.

Although, I, at least, knew there was no way in any version of events where I was the murderer. I would gladly take the brunt of that look and the anger. If it would shield my sister, knowing there was no way he could accuse me of being the killer and making it stick, I was here for the duration.

Suddenly, I wished that I was an accountant or any other profession at the inn because I was vacationing with my handsome boyfriend, ready to take in all the sights and sounds, or just relaxing in the huge library with a good book and a delicious cup of hot chocolate.

But that was not what my purpose was. And I knew that until we figured out what had actually happened and who, if anyone, had done it, we were not going to be safe here. There would be lots of questions, possibly lots of accusations, and very likely lies and secrets exposed.

I was exhausted already.

But I also wasn't going to back down.

"We can answer any questions you might have. We have nothing to hide." Except for our talents, and I wasn't even going to go there until Norm and his team left. As soon as they did, though, I was going to invade the library like I had never done before. We needed answers, and I only hoped that the books would not let me down as they had lately.

"You know you will." His sneer remained solely for me, and I returned it with a short but terse nod.

"Fine."

"We'll look into this more to see if there are variables we haven't considered. For now, we're going to do more investigating in the basement, but I'll let you know if and when we're ready to leave."

It wasn't like they could sleep down there, and the lunch hour was just now coming upon us. I had every hope that they'd be out of here before our family dinner. Because after we sent Dean and his family on their way with their bellies full, I wanted to be able to talk candidly, and we couldn't do that with non-mancers in the vicinity.

I had a lot of questions and very few answers. However, I also had quite a few people around me that might be able to change that.

But first, I had to get rid of Norm and his crew.

They worked down in the basement for the next hour while I had my scheduled lunch with the employees who were on site. They all enjoyed the meal Glennis had made, and she preened under their compliments as I had hoped she would. It would butter her up for what I would be expecting of her over the next few days.

I tried to keep an ear out for anything happening in the basement, but I couldn't hear much of the conversation without going down there. There were hints of voices through the floorboards, and that was it. No one sounded angry, so that could be a good thing. I wished I knew what was happening in the basement, though. Ty's hair had been standing straight up from his head when normally it was laid down and was very styled. Had the ends been singed? Was he close enough to the wall outlet for it to be the reason? A wire in the wall?

I tried to map the wine room mentally and exactly where he had been. But I couldn't pull it up and still be present for everyone talking about the excitement of the 4th coming up and how they looked forward to some of our usuals coming in.

Besides that, I wasn't kidding when I said that I didn't go down there very much if I didn't have to. In fact, I hadn't made myself descend the steps in a month or two. Not since an anniversary weekend with a couple who had been together for fifty years and had rented the entire inn for a family party that had the wine flowing almost endlessly until they left. They were nice and calm drunks, and I had appreciated that more than I could say.

That was not germane to my situation now, though, so I let the thought go and focused more on what was going on right at this moment in the inn. And what was going on right at this moment in the inn was the sound of feet on the stairs as everyone went back to their jobs after finishing lunch. I had been sitting closest to the dining room entrance, where I could hear if the basement door opened, hoping to maybe hear something specific through the wooden panel. But I'd been unable to get any clarity about what they were focusing on.

Once they were all gone, I'd moved to stand right outside the door. A much better vantage spot, even if I still couldn't hear anything through the door.

I didn't want to ask Norm any questions when he came up, but maybe I wouldn't have to. I had talked with Micah last time, and we had been in and out of each other's lives for years without any angst. Hopefully, we could continue that, and he'd be willing to share some information in a way that Norm would not. Mainly nice versus nemesis. I was willing to try, at least.

Norm came out of the door first, and I was never happier than when I had decided to move away and appear to be fluffing some of the fake roses we kept at the front door. I'd taken a glue gun and had made them appear to have small drops of dew on them. I was actually very proud of them, so it wasn't hard to act like I was far more interested in what they looked like instead of caring at all what Norm had found. Though, of course, that was completely untrue.

I waited for the rest of the crew to come through the door, carrying their black bags, which I assumed held all the equipment they might need to take stock of the scene and determine if it was a crime or not. I really hoped it wasn't.

And then came the body on a stretcher. I closed my eyes and dropped my chin, taking a moment to wish Ty a safe journey into the afterlife. I didn't know what kind of person he had been in his last few years here on earth, but I hoped it was good. Even though his life was cut short, I also hoped it had been a life that he'd experienced the very best.

And if he hadn't, and that was what had gotten him killed, I really hoped I would be able to ferret out that information and hand it over to Norm, anything to keep his eyes off Mena. Once the last person came through the door, Norm closed it and then turned to me. I'd sent Mena off to the kitchen again to keep her out of his sight and way.

Obviously, he had some affinity for her. I would just hope for the possibility that his affinity would keep him from thinking she was capable of murder the way he'd thought I was. The problem with that, though, was he could be volatile, and I wasn't willing to risk having Mena out here where he could drag her off in handcuffs if she breathed wrong or maybe didn't react to him the way he would hope she would. I wanted to believe better in one of our top cops in our small and normally sleepy town, but I couldn't take any chances.

Once the door was closed, he stuck his hands on his hips and looked at me, staring really, without blinking. There was something in his gaze that made me absolutely itching to have a book in my hand, and a question to ask that would make things snap into a pattern I could understand. Since I was nowhere near that at the moment, I simply waited with my hands folded at my waist the way my Aunt Hellen waited for someone to stop being an ass and tell her what she wanted to know before she even had to ask.

I kept eye contact with him, not willing to be the first to look away just in case he took that as some kind of admission of guilt.

"So..." He dragged the word out, and I waited. I would not be goaded into adding anything he didn't already know. And I certainly wasn't going to tell him what to think because he'd probably do everything in his power to prove me wrong.

I'd thought at one time that we should probably have a conversation about whatever he thought I had done to him in ninth grade that was so horrible he was still swimming in it almost twenty years later, but when I'd asked a book if that would bring resolution it had almost shouted the word no at me, so I hadn't tried again, and I wasn't going to try now.

But as soon as he left, I was so going into the library like a forager looking for that magical orchid or the future king willing to do anything to pull that sword from the stone. And I was going to get some freaking answers, even if I had to ask every single book in the two-story space.

They would answer me. It was my talent, and I was going to make it work for me for once. I decreed it!

He blew out an exasperated breath like I hadn't followed the script he'd put together in his head. "There are some issues, and it is possible this was a murder. I don't want it to be, but since when has that mattered?"

I didn't think he actually wanted me to answer that last question.

"We'll be around. We're done here for the time being, but I'll be back with some questions, or people can come to the police station and answer them there."

"I think it would be easier if you did the questioning here. If you need a room for privacy, I have several."

He grunted and then turned away from me.

Of course, once I finally escorted Norm out of the house and shut and locked the door behind him, I leaned back against the oak monstrosity with the doorknob digging into my back and released a big, huge sigh.

And with the release of breath, my will skittered away with it. Who did I think I was? Yes, I had gotten some bigger answers last time with the sparkly letters and the actual phrases that had risen from the book, but I hadn't been able to do that since.

Heading toward the library anyway, I wondered why I thought this would work for me in a way that would help me and be informative when it usually was a crapshoot as to whether I could even get it to do the minimum of what others before me had managed with the same tool. Then again, most of them had had far more formal training, which I had not had due to some family issues.

Speaking of family issues and my not getting the full education I should have been able to expect, Aunt Hellen came waltzing into the library just as I found the first book that had a small sparkle.

And I wasn't kidding when I said she was waltzing. She, for real, was in the classic Sleeping Beauty in the Woods stance, arm up and curved to a beautiful angle, her feet moving in the three-step pattern as she swept across the floor. The vision was a little limited in that she had on a pair of black slacks and was wearing a red t-shirt with a cartoon of birds singing or squawking. But she still brought her magic to the moves as she wove her way through the conversational clusters of chairs and couches and counted from one to three to herself and anyone else who might be in the vicinity, like me, for example.

I stopped what I was doing and just watched her. For years, she had seemed a little subdued. She always did the right thing, and she was incredibly helpful with anything I had ever asked of her. A rock in a world that often seemed absolutely set on being a landslide of mud and sludge. And I appreciated that more than I could say. But over the last few months, she had started to... well, bloom was the only word I could think of to describe the way she now presented herself to the world. And it was truly lovely, even if I didn't understand what had brought out the change. Whatever it was, I was here for it.

I waited for her to finish the dance to the music only she could hear in her head.

She stopped at the chair next to me and then dropped into the fluffy velvet, perching on the end with her legs crossed, her elbow anchored on her knee, and her chin cupped in her upturned palm.

"My darling, my love, what are you doing in here, and why do you look like you should be armed for battle in a breastplate and with a sword at the ready?"

"You sound like Uncle Vince." He often started most of our conversations with a string of names for me that were neither my name nor anything I'd ever been called by anyone but him.

She blushed, and it set me back in my chair. What was going on there? They'd avoided each other for years. Even though they were often in the same house or inn, in this case, as each other, they often were almost never found in the same room. They had always gone out of their way to not be in each other's sphere. I'd asked my mom about it since Aunt Hellen was related to her and Uncle Vince was a relation of my dad, but my mom had told me I shouldn't ask and just let the two of them exist in whatever way they were comfortable. I'd followed that rule until I found out about six months ago that it had kept them from teaching me correctly because they were supposed to do it together, but that hadn't happened.

Each had said that they'd watched me and guided me from the sidelines, but that wasn't quite the same as getting formal training. Honestly, it had felt like I was way behind when I'd finally seen what my talent could do. During the time I was looking into the last murder, so much had occurred to expand my talent in that small time frame. I'd tried to replicate it, but never got close to that kind of magic again. But that didn't mean I stopped trying. Especially now that we had another dead body to look into.

"Oh, I am so here to do battle. Things are about to get a little dicey, and I have to know what's going on. If I have this dubious talent, it's going to freaking work for me, or I'm going to have a monumental fit like the Universe has never seen before."

She had the gall to laugh, but then I ran back over what I'd said and realized it absolutely required a laugh of epic proportions. What was I thinking? Norm could be a real pain in my backside, but he would do the right thing, especially if that meant keeping Mena out of the running as a real suspect.

I blew out a breath. "I'm not good at this."

"Of course, you are. In fact, you're better at it than pretty much anyone in our line, so you need to give yourself a break and maybe some credit."

"Ha! Credit for what? Always messing things up? Being able to get only glittery letters when it has to do with death?" I'd spit the words out, but it sparked something in my head and made me reconsider what exactly I was doing and the intention behind it.

I ran my hand over the back of the tome in my hands. A knock-off story of the gods and the way they messed with each other back in the day. It was a title that had come out in the seventies. One I'd never read all the way through, but it seemed to call me when I'd first entered the library like that warrior Aunt Hellen had asked about.

I turned the book over and over in my hands and concentrated on it, wondering how I was supposed to ask the question. Heck, I also wondered what the question itself should be.

But I didn't want to get too off track with this new line of reasoning. It could work. I closed my eyes again like I had when they'd brought Ty's body out past me in the hallway. I dipped my head, and said a short prayer and request for some help, anything that might get this rolling in the right direction.

When I opened my eyes, the book itself was glowing with an intensity that was almost blinding. The pages sparkled like a fairy was sitting in the middle of the book, just waiting to be released so she could sprinkle her wisdom all over the place.

"Something's going on there," Hellen said, leaning in over the book so far that our foreheads were almost touching.

"Yes, I see it too. Do I open the book and just let it do its thing? I don't want to dim the magic at all, but I also don't want whatever is there to go jaunting off once I release it."

"This is not really one of the things I can teach you, necessarily, but you're going to have to learn to lean into your talent and trust it. I get that the timing is later than for most people, but I also know you might just not have been exactly ready for it before."

That was up for debate, considering that no one had tried to help me in the here and now back then, and that wasn't my fault. But with the sparkle drawing me in more and more, I wasn't willing to fight that out at the moment. There would be time later if I still felt like it needed to be addressed.

"Okay, so then what do I do, oh, ballroom dancer of the library?"

She blushed again, and I wondered why. I hadn't said anything that should embarrass her.

But she dove right in and chased the question out of my head. "You can ask the question out loud if you want to. I could also ask you the question. But I think you should work on this completely by yourself right now to see what you're capable of without any interference, direct or indirect."

"Okay, so I just ask the question?" I had done this a hundred times and knew what usually happened. However, this time, it was strange to feel my nerves tingling in my back and then spreading up and down to race all over my entire body, from the tips of my toes to the tips of my hair.

"Yep, let's see what happens."

"Was Tyler killed?" The book started vibrating in my hands, and little poofs of fairy dust shot out from the pages' edges. It was like a boiling pot with the lid rattling. And then I opened it, and the whole world turned into a shower of gold sparkles.

Chapter 5

I was very happy that I was already sitting down because I was pretty sure I would have been knocked back on my butt if I had been standing. What on the good green earth was happening?

The sparkles danced and played in the sunlight that cascaded through the windows at the top of the library. This used to be a conservatory way back in the day. But then Poobah made the move to introduce custom-made bookshelves and books in every genre and time period through all the years he owned the place. Some had said it was because it would help me one day, but I believed it was because he liked books, and I was just a convenient excuse.

Regardless, the sparkles seemed to want to touch every available surface in the huge room as they showered over the chairs, couches, and books and then onto the lampshades, the table, and the end tables.

And yet, there were no words. Last time, there had been words and some vague images in the sparkles, but this time, it was nothing but burst after burst of gold.

What was I supposed to do with that? It told me nothing and did absolutely zip, zero, and zilch to help me figure anything out.

I looked over at Aunt Hellen, and she seemed extremely fascinated with one particular corner of the room that had a fountain of sparkles exploding over and over again.

"Look, Universe. I'm not going to say I don't love the show, but I need a little help here, and you're just making things more confusing. I'm not on board. Bring it down and help me the heck out instead of making me feel like I might go into a seizure."

Immediately, the sparkles waned and fell to the ground. Aunt Hellen made a sad sound, and I would have to admit I was a little sad it had gone away now that it was no longer blowing sparkles all willy-nilly. But at least I could see what was happening and didn't feel quite like I was in the middle of a fireworks show I had no control over.

"Well, that's sad." Aunt Hellen rearranged herself in her chair and frowned at me.

"I know, but it was too much. I can't have one thing happen for all of my almost thirty years, and then all of a sudden be expected to deal with a massive explosion of sparkles. It's too much."

"Or it could have been just enough. Maybe it was a celebration that you're vibrating at the right frequency. Maybe it was just wanting to throw you a little party, and instead, you made the theater turn the lights on and shut off the projector right before the climax of the film."

Was there anything like being shamed for not being thankful for what had felt like chaos, but really could have just been a celebration? Let me answer that for you––no, there wasn't anything like it.

And now I felt like an ungrateful wretch.

Excellent.

"I'm sorry. I didn't mean to take away your party. You can come back if you want to, but maybe turn it down just a notch or two?"

There was a hesitation in the air that I could feel cascade through my body and the whole house, not just the room. I wondered if others felt it, too, and were baffled as to what had just happened. As long as they stayed out of the library, they could feel whatever they wanted. We could talk about it at dinner.

And speaking of dinner...

"This is very exciting and a step in the right direction. We should have our own celebration tonight! Will we be able to speak freely when everyone is together for dinner?" Aunt Hellen asked.

I groaned because the answer was both yes and no. I had invited Dean and his family to eat with us, so that meant we'd have non-mancers in the room at the beginning, and we couldn't talk freely with them there. I couldn't uninvite them. That would be worse than asking the Universe to tone it down.

And speaking of that...a sparkle started dancing in the air right in front of me, about five feet away. It was even with the writing desk that Poobah had retrieved from the attic.

Months ago, we'd come into possession of a book that was related to the unfortunate death of one of our guests. A book that people had wondered about for years because it was surrounded by mystery and a hidden treasure. It referenced a second book that supposedly had a map in it to the treasure, which people thought was buried on an island out in the Susquehanna River. At the time, I had no idea that it was an ancestor of ours who had written the diaries or had hidden the treasure.

That is until Poobah found the second book in our dumbwaiter and handed it over. I'd combed through it, and while there wasn't a map, there had been a list of the things she'd supposedly buried. Once I'd shown the list to Uncle Vince, he and Poobah had gone on their own hunt without any kind of map because Poobah had recognized some of the pieces listed.

One of them was the writing desk. A beautiful, handmade oak writing desk with a front face that folded down and rested on a brass arm engraved with leaves that looked like they were blowing in the wind. It had been in the attic for years, according to Poobah. He had wondered aloud if that meant all the pieces were in the house since he also had a cane that was referenced in the list with its ebony base and mother-of-pearl handle set up as the butt of a sword hidden in the cane itself.

And so, we all began hunting down pieces at the inn, looking in nooks and crannies for everything on that list. And each piece of the treasure, the treasure everyone had thought was lost in the river, buried where no one could find it, turned out to be in the house. To think I hadn't even known it was part of our family legacy and had been hidden away in the attic and various other rooms, like the basement, was amazing.

My coffee table in my room was one of the pieces, too. There was also a letter opener that had sat at the front desk for several years and had been used numerous times with no one aware it was actually part of a treasure an ancestor of ours had hidden years ago.

She'd been on her way down the river to her betrothed, the diary told us. Before she got there, though, she decided to turn in here, to this little hamlet that sat on the banks of the river, and make a home here instead of following through on the promise of marriage to someone who would have expected her to completely put aside all her talents and instead exist only in the world you could see. She was the beginning of our legacy of being here and owning this inn.

The only things we hadn't found yet were an array of jewels and jewelry. I hadn't given up hope of finding them, though.

"We might have to wait," I said, finally answering Aunt Hellen's question about speaking freely at dinner.

Right as I said the words, the little cloud of sparkles grew and started swirling in a pattern, breaking and reforming as if trying to make up its mind as to what it wanted to be.

I waited a few more seconds, holding my breath because I didn't want to mess with whatever pattern it was trying to make happen. But then I got impatient because that seemed to be the base of my every personality trait when it came to this kind of thing.

"What do we need to know about Tyler's death?" I asked. Since my first question had created such an explosion, I was trying to go at it from a different direction.

The sparkles coalesced and made a phrase I probably could have done without.

Get your Watson. We're going murderer-hunting.

"You have got to be kidding me. Do you see this?" I asked Aunt Hellen. She started poking at the letters, and they hiccupped. I couldn't think of a different word to describe how they stopped and jumped and then reformed. For me, they had made a hole and then came back together after I'd moved my finger away. But for her, they seemed to hiccup and then jump away from her finger only to regroup right above where she had her hand. Very interesting that they reacted differently to different people. I'd have to see if they did something else with Mena.

Mena. My brain made a dozen connections all at once. "Do you think the books are doing this again because it has to do with murder or because it has to do with our bloodline?" That frightened me a little to think that those two might be related in a way I most definitely did not want them to be.

I took a deep breath because it would do me no good at all to start hyperventilating before I even knew what was going on.

What had happened to my staid and predictable life? I used to get up in the morning, wonder what shenanigans guests might get into that day, make some coffee, wander around, and put out any tiny flames that never had a chance to be a fire. And now I seemed to, yet again, be dealing with a huge conflagration of infernos.

"Darling, don't get yourself worked up." Aunt Hellen put her hand on my shoulder and leaned into my personal space.

I hadn't realized how much I needed someone to stop my spiral into the abyss of oh no until she did that. It gave me a chance to regroup and resituate myself. "Okay, no, okay, I've got this. It doesn't mean that Mena is the killer. I can't believe that." Even though I had found her standing over the dead body and not doing anything, she hadn't even checked for his pulse, just in case he was still alive. Because she had known he wasn't? No, I couldn't think that way.

"Whatever is going through that beautiful head of yours, I want you to stop it for a minute and just take some easy breaths. You have a very vivid imagination. I've never seen anyone make Mount Everest out of a chipmunk hole in my life like you can." Aunt Hellen gave my shoulder a squeeze.

Obviously, I was not pulling off my calm the way I thought I was. I leaned into her hand on my shoulder, and she kissed the top of my head. And there it was, the ability to channel that peace and bring it right into my whole body.

I blew out a breath slowly, kind of like the air leaking from a balloon without popping.

"What do you know about the sparkling letters?" I asked. Because I hadn't been able to really recreate it again after the last murder investigation, we hadn't talked much about it. It had frustrated me to no end that I couldn't make it recur, so I'd avoided it. Maybe now was the time to ask all the questions that felt backed up in my head like a log jam.

"Well, I did some research, and to be honest, I've only ever been able to find people who saw a few sparks flash to lead them to a correct book. I haven't been able to find any practitioners who have actually had the galaxy coalesce around them."

"That's both unhelpful and a little staggering. I thought I had the lamest talent in the world and that I wasn't even kind of up to par with anyone who came before me. And now you're telling me I can make things happen that have never happened to this level before?"

"Don't let it give you a big head." She laughed and pulled me in for a hug.

The door to the library swung open and smacked into the wall next to it. And there was Uncle Vince in his full gaudy get-up of a Hawaiian shirt with a pair of shorts that looked like they'd been patchworked together from every t-shirt that should have been left in the rag bin.

"What are you doing in here? It's like the whole house is shaking. I haven't seen anyone who isn't a mancer actually respond. But those of us with the talent are about to lose our ever-loving minds. What is happening?"

Aunt Hellen and I looked at each other, and I couldn't miss the way that blush from earlier was crowning her cheeks again. Had something happened between them that I wasn't aware of? I didn't see them together much, but they had never been near each other before if they could avoid it, at least, that I knew of. There was less tension in the air when they were in the same room together, and that made me happy, but if we were going from can't stand each other to being all romantic and blushy and stuff, I wasn't sure I was ready for that either.

"I asked about the dead guy in the basement."

"Wait, what? What dead guy in the basement? I didn't see anything about that in my scrying bowl this morning, and it's usually pretty good about giving me any and all beets I need."

"Beets? Do you mean deets?" Holy heck, dealing with these two could sometimes make me feel like my head was spinning. "Beyond that, what are you talking about? Do you ask every day if there's going to be a dead person?"

He scoffed at me even though I felt that was a very valid question when it came to what he had just said.

"Not precisely about a dead person. I'm not getting paid to write obituaries. I will just see if there's anything I need to know about the day that might be outside of the norm."

That was not at all what he had said, but I didn't have time to argue with him because the sparkles had dispersed and were reforming. A new word? A new phrase? Something else that I couldn't or didn't want to handle?

You've got this! It said and even put an exclamation point on the end of it.

Uncle Vince laughed his big belly laugh, and Aunt Hellen giggled. Their gazes met, causing her to blush and him to clear his throat. For the love of...I needed not to get involved here. We had too many other things going on that needed far more intervention and all of my concentration. Especially since we still had the dinner tonight, and then I'd have to make sure we could have a family talk after we walked Dean and his family out of the room.

And I had more questions than ever.

I asked a few of them now, but I wasn't getting anything of real value. I decided to abandon it and the two people who were acting much differently than I had expected so I could find my sister and ensure dinner was coming along to the finish line for all of us.

I'd put in an order for family-style spaghetti with sides of shrimp scampi, mozzarella-covered chicken, and a bowl of Glennis's special meatballs. We didn't often eat like this because there was so much food, but I felt like tonight was a night for something more since we would all be at the table at the same time.

While we might not be able to talk about the magical side of what was happening, we could still talk about the murder and everything else that seemed to be going on around here lately, like the structural problems involving the electricity and the plumbing and who we might have to hire now that we were out a contractor.

It felt weird to worry about that when someone was dead, but it was a definite game-changer in several ways, and I had to think about it. Which then made me pause because I'd never checked on Rand. Oh, my word! I hadn't even thought of him in the middle of all this, and that was horrible.

Grabbing my cell phone, I trooped up the stairs to the second floor. Had he left? I hadn't seen him walk out the door, but I also hadn't been on the first floor in the hallway the whole time. He could have left after Norm had gone. Maybe he'd left as soon as he'd seen the cops come in.

But he hadn't left at all. I found him in Room 13, and yes, we did have a Room 13. I knew that some hotels still refused to have that number anywhere, either as a room or a floor, but I wasn't afraid of a little superstition.

He was humming to himself and fixing a socket in the wall. For just a second, I was terrified that he, too, would manage to electrocute himself, which I still believed was what had happened to Ty, regardless of what Micah thought with his *something was wrong here* comments. He hadn't said what exactly was wrong or different. I knew for a fact that Ty's hair had not naturally looked like he had stuck his finger into an electrical charge, but maybe there had been something else.

I, however, was fully aware that I was trying to distract myself from bothering Rand. The terror that no one had gotten a hold of him filled my brain. What if he didn't know his son had been carried out of the basement just a few hours ago in a body bag? More than anything, I did *not* want to be the one who told him. But I also didn't want to call the station and have to talk to Shirleen, Micah, or Norm to verify what I figured had to be true.

Damn.

I knocked on the door frame, hoping he'd look up. With his earbuds in, I was pretty confident he would have at least seen a call coming through. Maybe he'd chosen to ignore it.

He never even looked up. It wasn't until I moved into the room and tried to stay to the side without taking him by surprise that he finally glanced up and smiled. I had been standing in his peripheral vision, and when he finally took his earbuds out, I realized they were attached to a cassette player my dad had called them Walkmans. I wasn't sure if that was the actual name, but I did know for sure that they did not come with a phone app. Uh oh.

"What can I do for you?" he asked, that smile still in place.

Oh man, I was going to ruin his day and his life with one sentence, and it was killing me inside. But he had to know. He should have already known. Norm should not have stopped looking for him or trying to contact him until the poor man was given the horrible news that his only child was no longer walking among us.

"Can you join me over here, please?" I gestured for him to follow me to the door. It was away from tools and away from electric sockets, but it was close enough to the wall and even the bed if he fell backward.

"Sure. Did Ty do something wrong? I'm so sorry. I keep telling him he has to do the best job possible if he wants to build this into a real livelihood. The kid had some hiccups when he was growing up, but I really thought we had grown out of that, and he was moving in the right direction. I can fix anything that wasn't done right. I hope no one got hurt due to an error."

I laid my hand on his arm to get him to stop talking. I couldn't let him keep coming up with new things that Ty might have done wrong when he might have done his last thing wrong on this green earth right under his father's feet.

"Rand, please hold on a moment. In fact, why don't you sit down?" Any other time, I might have asked him to follow me downstairs so we could talk in the sitting room. Maybe I would have texted Glennis to bring us a beer, or a hot chocolate, or a coffee, or something. But I wasn't willing to drag this out any further.

"There has been an accident, actually," I started.

He jumped up from the edge of the bed and headed for the doorway. "You tell me where it is, and I'll make it right. I'm so sorry. I told him he had to be more careful."

"Rand, please, wait." I was faster and closer, so I blocked the exit from the room. He stopped three feet away from me. I drew in a deep breath. "I'm so sorry that there is not an easier way to tell you this, and I'm so sorry for your loss. But your son is gone, Rand. The cops have probably been trying to get in touch with you to let you know he was electrocuted in the basement. They had to carry him away. They couldn't bring him back."

His whole body froze in place like he'd been stuffed in our walk-in freezer and locked in for too long. I reached out to put a hand on his shoulder, and he turned away, avoiding my fingers and my gaze. I could understand the need to absorb the news without being touched or seen, so I took an additional step back and waited.

This had to be horrible for him. I was going to fry Norm like an overdone omelet when I saw him next. And I knew I'd see him because something told me that no matter how much I wanted to believe this had been an accident, I was starting to have a feeling in my gut that could be just wishful thinking.

The book had told me as much when it had said I needed to go find my Watson so we could go murderer-hunting.

Watson was Dean, and maybe always would be as long as I could figure out how to make a life with someone I couldn't share my entire self with.

I avoided that line of thought because it did not help the situation I was currently in with a man who was grieving for his only child, his only son.

Finally, his shoulders started shaking, and I considered leaving the room. If he needed to have a good cry, I did not want to stop him from feeling free enough to let all the emotions overtake him. The inn wasn't filled just yet, and we had about an hour before anyone would start pulling up in the driveway to check-in.

If Rand needed a ride home, he could leave his work truck in the side parking lot, and I'd get someone to take him home. Poobah had said he'd be here in about an hour to start getting ready for dinner. Because we were a bed and breakfast, we weren't serving any of the guests. Most would either order delivery to their rooms from the many restaurants around the town, or maybe they would have brought something in with them. Some usually unpacked and then went out to look around the town, which was absolutely lined with vintage streetlights and adorable little cafes and sub shops.

I didn't hear any sobs coming from the man standing with his hands braced on the window frame. He had his arms spread wide and his feet planted about the same distance apart. He looked like he was using the old woodwork to keep himself in place, and I could understand that, too.

What I didn't understand was when he turned around, and the shaking was not from crying but from laughing, a little like a loon.

"Those motherf—" He gulped and glanced my way like I would be offended that the death of his son was causing him to swear. If it were me, I'd have turned the air blue above my head. "Mother truckers finally did it, and I am not going to stop until I see every single one of those goons in jail. Every. Single. One. All of them rotting in jail. Bastards."

Chapter 6

Okay then. I did not know how to interpret or even figure out that outburst, but I had a feeling that the laugh was not because anything was funny. I was convinced it was more because he was baffled and about to cause some mayhem to whoever he was talking about and calling bastards. My gut told me so, and I trusted it.

He balled his fists at his side and stalked toward the door I was still blocking.

"Now, Rand, I know this is devastating, but don't leave just yet. There's nothing you can do right now other than talk to the police." Though, I hated to send him to Norm in this current state. I was afraid he might punch Norm right in the nose if he asked one of his many inane questions or didn't take Rand seriously. Then again, maybe a bop in the nose wouldn't be so bad if it was Norm's nose.

"Move, Roxy."

"Rand, I can't do that. You are way too agitated to go anywhere, and wherever you do go, I'm afraid you're going to get yourself into trouble. You haven't thought your way through this entirely."

"You either move, or I move you." He growled the words, and I hesitated.

Was it worth it to have him manhandle me out of the way at my own inn when I had no real control over whatever he wanted to do to whoever he wanted to do it to?

On the other hand, I did not like being talked to as if this wasn't my house and, therefore, my rules. I also did not want him to get into a car crash or something else completely avoidable if he'd take a minute to calm down.

"Roxy, I'm not playing with you. Move, or I'll move you, and I doubt it will be pretty."

I felt a presence tingle at my back a second before Dean spoke.

"And I assure you that if you touch her, you will have me to deal with, and I have no doubt at all that it will not be pretty, so choose your next words wisely."

In a flash, the fight went out of Rand. He sank back onto the bed with his hands braced on his knees and his head dipped, staring at the floor. Actually, I couldn't tell if his eyes were open, so maybe he wasn't staring at the floor. For my part, I was staring at Dean.

"Thank you," I mouthed, and he kissed me on the nose and then gently moved me out into the hallway.

I was willing to go that far, but if he shut the door in my face, we were going to have words, and that I could certify would not only not be pretty, it would be catastrophically ugly.

He didn't close the door, though. Linking his fingers with mine, he bridged the doorframe with his arm behind him.

"Rand, I can't say I understand what you're feeling right now since I don't have any kids of my own, but you must be devastated and completely at a loss for what comes next." Dean kept his position in the doorway, but reached out his other hand to the poor man sitting on the bed.

Rand's head whipped up so quick, he should have had whiplash. In fact, if he had been talented with magic, I had a feeling he would have shot fire out of his eyes. As it was, he looked ready to deal a death blow to someone, maybe anyone. "I know exactly what comes next. I go find that horrible Jeff and I tear him from limb to limb."

"Wait, who's Jeff?" I could think of several men in town whose name was Jeff, but none of them struck me as someone who would have come into the inn, cornered a man in my wine cellar, and then killed him with electricity. One of them wouldn't even have attempted the stairs to reach the wrap-around porch on the front of the inn due to his ailments, much less than walking down the steep and narrow steps to the basement.

"He wouldn't be anyone you knew. He's someone who threatened me. And he might not be the actual person who killed my son, but he's the one who could have put the hit out and paid someone else to actually do the dirty deed."

Holy heck, were we talking about murder for hire or like a gangster-type setup where this Jeff person had a goon squad who'd take care of his "problems"? Either one I did not like, but the second seemed to carry things with it that I was not willing to contemplate.

"Are you talking about Jeff Ducy?" Dean asked.

Rand narrowed his eyes while giving a brief nod of his head. "How do you know him? Are you the one who's doing his business for him?" Each word came out sharper and harsher. I was very much afraid he was going to bum-rush my boyfriend, and there was nothing I could do about it, especially if it propelled us out the door and then knocked us down the stairs.

How had my life come to this?

"I know him because he threatened my brother once over some not-really-on-the-up-and-up escapades."

"And what did you do?"

"I punched him in the face and then waited for him to get up before doing it again." Dean stuck his hands in his jeans pockets.

Rand slapped a hand to his forehead, then dragged it down to pinch the bridge of his nose before dragging it the rest of the way down to yank on his own beard. "So, you know him. You want to come with me while I beat the daylights out of him?"

"No, I'm sorry, I can't do that, but I could find out if he actually had any kind of hit out on your son. What I'd need you to tell me is why he'd do that or how you managed to get mixed up with someone like that."

And that was when Rand finally started to cry. He lurched over to the wing-backed chair in the corner and tilted his head to the ceiling. The tortured groan that came out of his mouth and the tears sliding endlessly down his cheeks and into his beard tore my heart up in my chest.

But from what he'd just said, this guy was a menace, and it sounded like Rand had done a thing or two to cause his ire.

I took a step toward him, trying to get back through the door until Dean turned pleading eyes on me. "You don't want to get into the middle of this," he said. "Please trust me. It is not some random jerk who has nothing better to do. If it really was one of Jeff's people, then this thing just got a whole lot bigger than a dead electrician in your basement who got electrocuted by accident."

Well, I didn't like hearing that, but my Watson was not dumb, and I did trust him. Once I nodded, he let go of my hand to kneel in front of Rand.

"You're going to have to tell me what you owe them and what it's for if you want me to help. I won't say anything to the cops until we know for certain that he's the right guy, but I really need you to be honest with me right now."

Wow, this sounded like the script of one of those fast-action, absolutely whirlwind movies that people were loving these days––intrigue, secrets, bad behavior, and now a gangster thrown in for good measure. Yikes.

"I can't do it. I can't go into the details, and I can't be the one who says a word about anything, especially since they already took away my kid. What if my wife is next, or me?"

Who was this Jeff guy, and why would Rand be so afraid of him and also so certain that he had been the one to ensure Ty died? Although a part of me was itching to grab a book, I stayed right where I was to see if Rand would give up any of the details.

"I'm not saying you shouldn't be afraid, but if we can get him on this, then he might be taken out altogether. I have people I can talk to about these kinds of things." Dean stayed where he was, kneeling on the floor, and reached out a hand to place it on Rand's knee.

The other man jumped up, nearly knocking Dean over and surprising me so much that he barreled right past me into the hallway. I got knocked sideways into the wall and then had to watch helplessly as he rushed down the stairs two at a time. When he reached the front door, he whipped it open, then slammed it closed behind him. Immediately, I hustled over to the window to watch him pull away in his work truck and disappear around the corner, heading away from town.

I had bypassed Dean, but he had already been righting himself, so he didn't need me at that moment. I still walked back to him and gave him a boost by his elbow to get him to lumber all the way to his feet.

"Are you okay?"

He dusted off the knees of his work pants and shook his head. "Yeah, I'm fine. Just give me a moment." He walked to the window and stared out onto the street below, then turned back around. He nudged Rand's toolbox with the toe of his shoe. "I think we should probably put this somewhere safe until he decides to come back for it."

Because he seemed to be talking to himself, I didn't say anything.

Grabbing the back of his neck, he shook his head and sighed. "I'm going to have to talk to Caper, so we might not make it to dinner tonight. Would it be okay if the kids still came even though they won't have an adult with them?"

"You're not going to go start any trouble, are you?"

"No, I promise I won't start any trouble. And I won't respond to any, either. But if this Jeff is in town, then Caper might be able to ask around about him in a way I never could. I'm just going to have to convince him he wants to do that when he's been making real and good progress toward extracting himself from his previous world."

"If it is a murder, and if this Jeff guy was the one who made sure the trigger was pulled or whatever happened to kill Ty. Then I really don't want you or your brother involved in it. We could share it as a lead that should be followed up by...Norm." I swallowed hard on that last word because he was the very last person I'd want to talk to about any of this. But if it saved Dean and his brother, then I'd do it.

Dean kissed me full on the mouth this time and nearly took my breath away. "Nope. Normally, I would not fight with you, and I hate going against what you want, but this time, I'm going to have to ask you to really trust me. I don't want that guy anywhere near here. If it gets out that the tip came from you or anyone on this property, then we could be signing up for a world of hurt over something that had nothing to do with us."

"But he had someone killed on my property. You don't think that's something I should be concerned about?"

"Be as concerned as you want, but we can't be seen as the ones who called in the threat. You have way too many vulnerable people here. I will not let them be in jeopardy when this is someone we can access in different ways."

There was a large part of me that wanted to fight him and fight him hard on this, but my better sense won out. I didn't like it, but I guess I didn't have to. On the other hand, I wasn't all the way for it, so I would reserve the right to revisit this if nothing good came of it.

"I'll tell you what, let's make a deal," I finally said after running the possible scenarios through my head.

He narrowed his eyes and cocked his head at me. It wasn't a no.

I continued. "You and Caper do whatever you have to do to get some information, but I'm going to insist we also look into this from other angles and see if there are any other people who could be viable suspects."

He opened his mouth, probably to tell me no, but I was not having that. I'd compromise, and he'd better be happy with it.

"Doing it that way has two prongs to it that can help us," I jumped in again before he could say anything. "For one, it will look like I know nothing about this Jeff guy, so he's not even on my radar. Plus, there is every possibility, with the way Rand fled, that he is in way deeper than he's letting on. Your offer could have been cherry-picked for him, so why did he decide to bolt instead of taking you up on what could have really helped him? There must have been a threat there of some kind, or those people would have never crossed his mind. If it looks like I'm not doing anything, even though my sister could very well be a suspect, I don't think anyone would actually believe that after the way we went all-in on the last investigation, and you know it. Now, if we have a game plan and a way to execute it without showing all our cards, we might be in a far better place than ever before."

He opened his mouth again, and this time, I held up a hand to stop him.

"You're not going to be able to talk me out of it. I am all in on making sure the killer is caught. I'm also afraid that if we don't at least appear to be doing something, it will boomerang back on us. Not to mention that if this person is as horrible as you say he is, and no one brings him to task, then we have a bigger problem than just one dead person at the inn. We have a civic responsibility, Dean!" As I finished with a flourishing hand gesture to the heavens and my voice at full volume, Dean took my hand and kissed my knuckles.

"I agree."

"You really need to listen to...what?"

"I agree. And if you'd let me get a word in edgewise, I would have told you that from pretty close to the beginning. I'm not going to lie, I want you safe and everyone else here safe, too. I have a lot at stake, just as much as you do, and I want to make sure his man is caught and punished. His cronies, too, if he wasn't the one who actually did the deed. You're right. We do have to be smart. And I think it's a good idea to look like we are at least fumbling around in things so that he doesn't wonder. I'm not sure he knows anything about you, or who you are, or what you do, but that doesn't mean he couldn't figure it out pretty quickly. And that is the last thing we want. So yes, we should look into things. Yes, we should definitely put out feelers for information that doesn't appear to point to him. But I also think we need to get Caper to ask some of the questions we can't. And to get that ball rolling, I need to talk to him. I think it would be better to do so before dinner and get that moving. But if you're totally set on this dinner, and it being a family-type affair due to your sister being here, then I am totally willing to compromise there. In fact, that might actually be the better idea since you already set it up. It might cause more questions if suddenly my brother isn't here and neither am I. Good call."

Deflate my argument with a whole speech without actually saying there was an argument to deflate. Nicely done. But I wasn't going to tell him that. Because he already knew.

That cheeky smile and the way he kissed my knuckles and held my hand mere inches from his mouth, knowing I could feel the caress of his every breath, was something I hadn't yet figured out how to ignore. Honestly, I was pretty sure I never wanted to be able to ignore it, at least in my mind.

"If that's what you think, then that's what we'll go with," I said with my own cheeky smile.

He laughed, then kissed me, and made my whole body melt.

"We should agree more often," I said against his lips.

"Let's do that now, then." And he kissed me again. He backed away before I was ready, but just in time, as my sister came around the corner with her phone in front of her face and no actual awareness of the space around her.

"You might want to avoid that wall, Mena. I don't think it's going to embrace you."

Her gaze popped up from the screen in front of her, and she caught herself a foot from taking that wall on full body. "Oh!"

"Yeah. Oh. What are you looking at so very intently?"

Her lips went from tipped up to tipped down, and her brow crinkled in concentration. "I keep wondering about this text that Ty sent me right before I went down to the basement. The three before it all have full sentences and good punctuation. But the last is a bunch of abbreviations and shortcuts instead of the real words." She turned the phone to me, and Dean crowded right behind me, pushing his chest against my back to get a better look. I wasn't going to complain about that. Nope, not at all.

Ahem, back to the matter at hand.

"So great to see you again and get back in touch," I read out loud. "I really look forward to seeing you more while you're here. Maybe even after you leave, we can maintain whatever we manage to create over the next little while. Thanks for coming into the gazebo. Maybe this is the place we'll remember when…"

The first text was well thought out and entirely flushed out. He'd even spelled all the words right and seemed not to have been in a rush to get the words off to her. "It's very nice and hopeful without being pushy."

"Right," she said, scrolling down on her phone and then turning it back to us. "Now read this one."

"U n Me basement gotta go cu soon." That one literally made my skin crawl with its lack of grammar and proper capitalization, not to mention it had very little in the way of any real information.

"I guess he could have been in a hurry and wanted to just get the message off as quickly as he could. Maybe he knew something and was trying to warn you?" Dean held out his hand, and Mena gladly put the device onto his palm. "I mean, there's no way to tell if this is how he usually texts and the first one was drawn out and more formal because he was thinking hard about how to impress you?"

Good question. And it triggered me to remember that Dean's phone had me listed as Hottie even before we had started officially dating. How had Ty listed Mena in his phone? I had no way of finding out. I wouldn't be contacting Norm unless I absolutely had to, and this was not a "had to."

Mena wrapped her arms around her waist. "I got six total texts, and the other four were just like the first one. This last one was the only one that looked out of place."

"Do you think someone killed him and then scrolled through his phone to see who he or she could call down to find the body? Maybe the person didn't take into account the way Ty actually texted because the person was in a hurry to get out of the crime scene?" Dean asked.

"Good questions." I tapped my lip with my finger. "How would we be able to figure that out?"

"Well, for one thing, I know Ty had his phone locked. He told me that he never leaves it unlocked. Ever," Mena said. "If someone else did write the text, then they would have had to get Ty to open the phone, which means they'd have to get him to type in the code before he was dead, or it would have remained locked."

"Unless they took the phone from him while he was still alive. Maybe he was listening to music while he was working, and the person snuck up on him, grabbed the phone, and killed him at the same time."

It was, of course, all speculation. We had no way of knowing what had truly happened. Even if we found the killer, we couldn't be sure he would tell the whole story and the truth about what happened.

But we needed to start there. I put forth something I didn't want to believe, but thought it at least had to be said.

"Do we at all think his father might have killed him?" I asked, squinting as I said it because it felt nasty. "I came across him in room 13, and he'd had no idea that his son was gone, supposedly. When I told him, he did look distressed at first, but then he laughed and blamed it on some mob-type guy and laughed that the man had finally gotten to him. But when we asked what he meant and why this guy would be after Rand and his family, he took off running, then hopped in his car and drove away."

I hadn't told Mena the whole story about who Dean and his family were. That was on a need-to-know basis, and she did not need to know that Caper had previously been a thief and swindler. Nor did she need to know that he had tried many times to drag Dean into the life with him.

Instead, Dean had chosen to restart here with a new last name. Technically, his original name was Alberdean Winchester, but he'd always gone by Dean. The last name, though, was new. Seriously, I might have changed it just because I didn't want to constantly be asked if that was my real name or if I was trying to pretend like I was some super-hot demon hunter on the television.

But he'd chosen the new last name to move on from the life of crime and had offered to take Caper's children with him. Caper had kept the kids with him because he had been getting his life back on the right track. Unfortunately, six months ago, he'd fallen off the rails. He'd dropped the tween and teenager off to Dean and then finished out what he'd needed to do to keep them safe.

And then he'd remade the promise to do the right thing again, and I'd given him the time and the place to do it. Maybe he had some drain and wire skills that he could use to help me fix things here instead of having to hire a new contractor. I knew that was totally off track from where we were at the moment, but it was still valid, and it gave me a second to step out of this new drama. I'd think about it more later.

For right now, we had a murder to solve.

"I would think it would take a special kind of awful person to kill your own son to get bad people off your back, but that doesn't mean someone couldn't have done it," Mena said. "There was this murder in the south of France when I was there. It was similar in motive, but the guy was a billionaire. Would Rand's son's life really be worth whatever money he might owe someone? Ty said they're struggling to get back on track financially, so I can't imagine it was that much money."

She had a point, but I also wanted to start making a list. Norm might not want to charge Mena with murder, and he might actually do everything in his power to make sure no signs point to her, but not everyone in the department might feel that way. I wasn't willing to wait for them to arrest her to start looking into things.

"Let's have dinner, talk about what's going on, see if anyone knows anything, and then we'll reconvene to discuss more specifics between the three of us."

The book had only said I needed my Watson, but I was not throwing away the gift of Mena's gab and grab. It could come in handy if we couldn't find the right person and needed more information to move on down the line.

Plus, it might make her feel better about the whole situation if she was part of catching the person who had killed someone she could have come to care for a lot if things had stayed the same and Ty hadn't been taken too soon.

"Okay, so we're going to ask around and then report back. Since the kids will be at dinner, maybe we shouldn't go too far into what might have happened and how."

Dean sighed, then chuckled. "Those kids have seen more than any of us probably, and they're all in recently on the murder mystery thing. They probably have their own theories and notebooks of clues."

Which reminded me...Amelia had said that she had often been the secretary for her father when he was doing bad things. She wasn't allowed to talk to certain people because of how bad they were, but maybe she knew who Jeff was and how to get in touch with him. I'd be more circumspect about asking and make sure that I wasn't putting her in danger, of course. But if she had info that might help, I wasn't against at least asking and then telling her that Dean and I would handle it from there on out.

First, I needed to check on my crew and make sure they were okay and aware of what had happened before the investigation started, and we possibly got off the rails as my family was wont to do.

Chapter 7

As I pushed open the door to the kitchen, I found Glennis and Clara bickering over how to prepare the chicken parm that I'd asked for and whether they had enough mozzarella sticks. Ah, to only have to worry about that kind of stuff. And as much as I could have left it alone, just let them continue down their line of ridiculousness (since there was only one way to correctly prepare chicken parm–– crispy breading and lots of mozzarella cheese, and there was never a number that was enough mozzarella sticks) I did want them getting along. Currently, Taylor, my still-skittish kitchen helper, was cowering in the corner with words and attitude flying through the air. For her to do her job, I needed to stop the bickering. Namely, shred all the lettuce for the massive Caesar salad that was also on the menu. The five heads of romaine sat on the counter with a knife next to them that I hoped neither Clara nor Glennis would grab in their bid to end the cheese wars.

"Ladies, we do not have time for this today." I looked up at the TV monitor that hung in the kitchen. Primarily, it was used to show what was happening in the dining room in case someone had to rush out and help anyone out there. But then I realized that the picture was grainy because I had never flipped the switch in the fuse box back to on. The whole place was dark, with the chandelier and sconces still without power. Gah, that meant I'd have to head back down into the basement, and I very much did not want to do that. However, I also needed to grab the wine, and the place was no longer a crime scene. So I would be safe enough, as long as no one's ghost tried to accost me.

And I'd just made it worse for myself. Great job there, Roxy!

I took a deep breath because they hadn't stopped bickering at each other about whether they should use the pre-prepped and store-bought mozz sticks or if Clara could finally trot out her new recipe.

"I have everything on hand. I really want to try these. You've said a number of times that I could do it, Glennis, but that it was not the right time. I'm telling you now that I'm making it the right time, right now, at this time." She slammed her closed fist on the metal table, causing the lettuce to jump and the knife to skitter toward her.

Before anyone got any stupid ideas, I grabbed up the lettuce, placed most of them on the counter behind me out of everyone's reach, and then stuck my hands on my hips, the left one holding the very sharp and effective knife out to the side.

"We do not have time for this." I turned to Glennis. "What is the issue with the mozzarella sticks?"

"Nothing, that's why I want to use our usual. Family has even more expectations than the regular patrons who don't eat here all the time. If everyone is expecting mozzarella sticks, then they are expecting our normal ones. I'm not going to change that just because Miss Clara here thinks she knows how to spruce up something that is already amazing. I chose them myself years ago, and they've never failed me. We're not taking chances on that kind of thing."

"Clara, how are your sticks different?"

She pulled a card from the back pocket of her black Dickies. "I printed this off the internet. It's still the same mozzarella, but you crush those spicy, fiery Doritos and use them as the crust instead of the regular batter. They're amazing and unexpected."

I did not like the unexpected, and I was pretty sure that using a chip from the grocery store as an outer coating and trying to dip it into grease would not make for an awesome dish. But I also didn't want Glennis to always have the final say in what came out of the kitchen.

Decisions, decisions. Dang it! Why now when I had so many other things going on?

"Okay, here's what we're going to do. We're going to make two batches of the regular and one batch of these new ones."

Glennis groaned. I sent her a look that made her stop in her tracks.

"Clara, if they turn out wonderfully, then we'll consider mixing them in every once in a while."

"*If* being the operative word," Glennis said, tucking her arms around her middle over her apron. Obviously, she was irritated, but she was going to have to manage it.

"I do think, though, that most people have a specific kind of cheese stick they prefer, so I want to make sure those are always available, too. We can all get what we want as long as we make sure we also stick with the traditional. Now, is there anything else going on, or are we running on time to serve dinner?"

"Other than those atrocities, yes, we are very much on time to make dinner for when you requested it. Even if some of us seem to duck out when the real work happens."

Was there something I didn't know about? I looked back at the three women in the kitchen. "Is Nell still here?"

"That one," Glennis said in the voice she used when she was disgusted, much like with the mozz stick debate. Clara scoffed, and even Taylor didn't hold back from rolling her eyes and grunting. "She left to take care of a bloody nose. It didn't look bloody to me, just swollen, but what do I know? She said she'll be right back, but I guess we'll just have to wait and see, won't we?"

Okay, what the heck was going on? I thought everyone loved her, but maybe I had just assumed, not actually asked.

"What's going on? You all know you can always talk to me about what happens here. If there is something to fix, then I do that."

"Huh." Glennis shrugged and kept her head down, even when Clara nudged her.

"Come on, Glennis, you've seen more than we have, and if we have a chance to say something, we shouldn't miss out on the opportunity. Tell her what you saw the other day."

"Yes, Glennis, what did you see the other day?" I would hold off on asking her why she hadn't told me before now. Heck, I could probably just ask her if she had ever planned to tell me. Of course, that would be after I found out what was apparently going on under my nose that I was unaware of.

Running an inn could be a real pain in the keister, in case you hadn't noticed.

"It wasn't anything completely awful," Glennis started, and then she just stopped and fiddled with a washcloth at the sink.

I waited a beat, but it didn't look like she was planning on continuing. "I need more than that, Glennis. If something is going on at the inn, I need to know, or I can't make good decisions. And if I can't make good decisions or change things to run at our optimum level, then what are we doing here in the first place?"

She sighed, and it sounded so put upon that I wanted desperately to roll my eyes. However, that would help no one, and it would probably just piss her off. In fact, it would probably make her not talk about anything anymore, anyway.

See? Pain in the keister. If I thought I could exist without her, sometimes I thought a lot about just having her retire already.

But I knew that would be bad for me and the business, and probably bad for her too, so I held my tongue and hoped that she'd pull it together enough to actually and finally tell me what I needed to know.

"Well, the other day..."

And she trailed off again. Ugh!

"Look, if you think you're going to get in trouble or something, or you're afraid I'm going to fire her, and you don't want to be the cause of that, I do understand. But the inn is more important to me than a lot of things. The thing more important is the employees and making sure things are running as well as possible. I count on you, all of you actually, to help me make sure I'm running as tight a ship as possible. Please just tell me what you saw the other day."

Another sigh, but at least this time, she started talking as soon as she had let all the wind out of her windbag. That was mean, but I hadn't said it out loud, and I wouldn't, so I wasn't going to apologize.

"The other day, I saw her crawling around the floor with Ty up in the hallway. He was trying to fix something that she had said was broken, but he couldn't see exactly what was broken about it and told her as much. She got down on the floor and kept crowding him out with her posterior in the air, but he still couldn't see what the issue was. She pointed him in the direction by taking his hand, which she 'accidentally' brushed against her chest, then feigned surprise and apologized. He backed away quickly, saying he was sorry over and over again. But she said it was okay, she'd liked it, and she liked seeing him every day. And it was weird how all these things kept failing that would bring him around on the daily. He said he only came when called, and she laughed that sultry laugh like he was being naughty when I could tell he wasn't." She scoffed. "He wasn't, I tell you. He's like my nephew Norm, a little misunderstood, a little naïve, but he doesn't know how to play with the big girls when it comes to that kind of stuff, and I think that's better for all of us in the long run."

Did not need the proselytizing from the maven of the kitchen, but as long as she didn't keep going, I could let that pass.

She huffed out a breath. "Anyway, she finally got him to get back down on the floor, and I would have sworn that she'd pulled something out of the socket while she was down there. Suddenly, the things that were working before no longer worked, and he was able to fix it. Which got me to thinking. We haven't had this many malfunctions and failures in years. I'm not saying you missed anything or that it's your fault. I know you're new and this place is old. But maybe you don't exactly pay attention to things exactly as your grandfather did. We can't all be him or expect to be as wonderful as he was. But now I've told you, and now I can wash my hands of it."

She turned away, and I was left standing there stunned to be honest. Was she just trying to warn me about bad employee behavior, or did she really think that Nell had possibly been sabotaging the inn so that she could get Ty here?

"Did she have a crush on him in particular, or was she also trying to cozy up to other men?" I had to know.

"She has some trick for every guy she seems to walk near. She tried it with your man, but he was very quick to remove himself from the way she'd tried to cage him in against a wall. He was smooth about it, too, but I saw it happen in the dining room on the television. When she came into the kitchen and glanced up at the TV, she snickered and then winked at me and went about her business."

Well, I did not like that. I had hired Nell because she had come highly recommended by the family who ran the feed store.

However, now that I think about it, why didn't they hire her since she was family?

I did not need another thing to worry about, but I left it on the list for the minute because I also couldn't afford not to think about it. I'd keep an eye on her though just in case.

"I do appreciate the information, Glennis. If you or anyone else sees anything else that appears to be out of line or outside our normal operating procedures, please let me know. Finding out at the beginning can make a big difference." Why did I have to keep telling them this? We were supposed to be a team here. They had to know that if they saw something going wrong or questioned something about how we did things around here, that I was totally open to concerns and compliments both. I guess I would just have to keep saying it until they believed me. I also made a mental note to ask Poobah if he'd had the same issues or if it was just me or just the staff. Ugh.

"Okay, thank you. I really appreciate that. Thanks for staying on top of things."

"We always do, even as you're running around playing detective." Glennis had mumbled the words under her breath, but I still heard them. I was going to have to corner Poobah later and find out what she had on him and why he never shut her down. I couldn't continue working like this with her cutting me off at the knees every chance she got.

After a small shake of my head, I ignored her. The fact was, I didn't want to call her out in front of the others. I mentally added talking with her to my list, and I'd leave it there until later. Right now, I had to go down into the basement. I'd avoided it long enough, and the dining room lights had to be back on if I thought I was going to have dinner in there with a bunch of people.

"Okay. I'm going to head down to the fuse box and try to remember to do the things I meant to do earlier when I was down there."

"Hopefully, you don't find any more bodies," Clara chimed in not so helpfully.

I flipped a wave to her and kept the groan in instead of letting it out.

Opening the door to the basement, I took a second to catch my breath and prepare myself for whatever was going to be down there. It was safe to assume there would be some dust and maybe debris from the investigation. I could do this, though, and I didn't have to clean anything up yet. As I said before, I couldn't expect anyone to come down here if I wasn't willing to come down here myself.

I crept down the stairs instead of striding down them like I should have. But it was one thing to be brave and strong in front of the staff and another thing if I wanted to be a little smaller and more careful when I was all by myself.

There were eighteen steps to the bottom of the staircase. I counted each one as I took measured and quiet steps one at a time. Did I think that if I crept, I wouldn't scare anyone who happened to be down there? Hopefully there was no one to scare. Why would anyone be down there? I was freaking myself out for no reason.

Nothing would be down there, and nothing would hurt me down there. I could do this. Dammit!

This was ridiculous.

Irritated with myself, I stomped down the last three stairs and was finally in the hallway. All I had to do was go back the hall and then turn the corner, and I'd be in the wine room again. A place I hadn't been to since finding Mena standing over a dead Ty.

Once I hit the concrete floor, I hustled right along. I was going to just go straight to the fuse box, flip the switch that was on the wrong side, and then race back up the stairs. I didn't care who heard the noise I made on my ascent.

It was easy enough to go straight to the fuse box. I cranked open the door, found the right switch and flipped it to the on position. Done and very proud of myself, I turned around and found a book on the floor at my feet. That had not been there when I'd walked over here. If it had, I would have had to either step over it or kick the book out of the way by accident. There was no way I wouldn't have noticed if I had kicked a book that was in my way. I wouldn't have kicked it either way. I would have just picked up the book. But it hadn't been there.

I knew that in my soul.

But it was there now, and that meant I'd have to pick it up. Part of me was shaking inside. The other part of me scoffed at myself and bent over at the waist to then wrap my fingers around the binding. Books had always been my friends. I was not going to forget that.

"Is there something you need to tell me?" I asked the question and flipped open the book at the same time.

Now, normally, I would find a passage on that page and read it. Even if it didn't originally make sense when I first read it, I would reread it, and it would make some more sense. Sometimes it was a steamy exchange between two lovers, and the answer would be a yes, or a no, or maybe do the thing and find out what comes next. However, I usually had more pointed questions than the one I had just asked.

And yet, as soon as I opened the book, sparkling letters floated up off the page. They mingled around each other, coming up in different sequences, and with different phrases. It was going too fast for me to catch what they were saying. I had a feeling I wasn't supposed to be able to see them all. The last time this had happened, I had been able to have Aunt Hellen tell me the different phrases so I could write them down to deal with later, after the chaos was over.

This time, it was me, all by myself, and I had no way to write anything down. Also, there appeared to be no real pattern because the same word length did not come up in any kind of formation. This was not going well.

"Stop it," I said far more forcefully than I normally would. Admittedly, I was frustrated, and the letters were not helping.

And yet, this time, it worked. The letters settled down, moving in a circle like a carousel.

"'Take caution and know who you're near," I read out loud to no one but myself.

"Find a place to rest and know that it is one that will help."

"Come to the light and make things right."

And it kept going. It was too many phrases for me to keep straight in my head. I took a seat on a wine barrel and fumbled my phone out of my pocket. I had never tried to take pictures of the letters, but I was going to make an effort.

"Can you go again?" I scooted a few bottles of wine over and set the book in the space I had created. But as soon as my hand came off the book, the letters did that weird thing where they turned black and crumbled away like ash falling from the sky.

"Damn!"

I picked the book back up, and it was like someone had thrown a movie into reverse. The black ash rose from the shelf, still black, but slowly starting to sparkle back to its original gold, then began the slow-moving carousel. That was more like it.

I hadn't asked it to do anything. It was just doing it without me saying anything, so I stuck with that for the moment. It wasn't easy to keep my phone in one hand and the book in the other, but after a few fumbles and some stray ash and reverse action, I was finally able to make it work.

I would look at the pictures later, but for now I had read the three sentences so many times that they felt burned into my mind. But what did they mean?

It could be that knowing who I was near meant the killer was close? Or that someone who knew something about the killer was close?

Did the one about the light mean I had to bring the killer to the light and, therefore, justice?

I had no idea about the place of rest except that I owned an inn, and lots of people came here to rest. That seemed to point to the inn, and I had a little niggle at the back of my mind that my sister was at the inn, and all this had started when she arrived, which was literally a handful of hours ago. How on earth was that possible?

My cell rang in my hand and made me jump, dropping the book. All the letters scattered, but not into ash and dust this time. They just went away, and when I picked the book back up, nothing new happened.

Session over? Possibly.

Since I had already flipped the switch on the fuse box and the lights should be up and running, I walked away with the book in hand as I made my way back to the stairs. Cell reception was abysmal down here, and I didn't want to drop the call from whoever had themselves listed as an unknown number. Usually, I wouldn't answer the call. If your phone number wasn't in my phone, and we'd never talked before, then there was every possibility you did not need to get a hold of me, but this felt different. Call it trusting my gut.

I mounted the stairs and brushed through a section of frigid air. Was there a leak in the air conditioning? I couldn't even fathom that at this point, so I ignored it as I made my way to the top stair just as the phone hit the fifth ring when it would go to voicemail.

"Hello?"

"Keep your freaking nose out of my stuff, you hear me? I have no time for games. I did nothing. I had nothing done. I'm not your guy. Tell Dean to tell that to Norm, or it's not going to go well for any of you, including your dear grandpa. Poobah, right? That name I won't soon forget."

And then the call disconnected, and I put my shaking hand on the doorframe leading out of the basement. I stood there until I could get my legs, arms, and brain to stop shaking.

Chapter 8

The table was packed with all of those I loved, as well as some I was growing to love because I was around them more. Even Dean's brother Caper, who could be feisty, but also incredibly helpful, was quickly becoming a favorite.

The table was also packed with food, almost groaning under the weight of the chicken parmesan, spaghetti, and mozz sticks. Or that sound could have been the response to Uncle Vince telling yet one more dad joke, even though he'd never had any kids.

No one had actually sampled one of Clara's mozz stick concoctions yet. I had a feeling I was probably going to have to take one for the team on that, though I wasn't against trying to dare Dean into being the guinea pig or even his nephew Isaac, who sat next to him at our table for nine.

We'd stayed quiet while all the food was being delivered, and everyone had thanked Glennis, Clara, and Nell for doing the serving. I didn't get a chance to ask Nell about the bloody nose, but it had looked okay when she passed by me, so I left it there. Taylor had headed home shortly after I'd left the kitchen because her shift was over. The rest of them had readily agreed to pay extra for staying on when we technically did not serve full-on big dinners unless it was for a conference.

Despite everything that was going wrong around here, it was wonderful to have so many people at the table, all talking amongst themselves as they passed dishes and encouraged each other to try this thing or that. Aunt Hellen had situated herself between Amelia and Caper. She helped the younger girl cut up her chicken and put the right amount of sauce on the plate. Of course, she was also working with her to use a fork and spoon to correctly get her noodles in her mouth without flipping sauce over the white tablecloth for a second time. For a twelve-year-old, she was still a little feral, probably from how she'd been raised. Even if she hadn't been, Aunt Hellen couldn't help herself when it came to instructing people on proper table etiquette, even if you were in your twenties. I did see her give Caper the side-eye at least once that he caught, but he only shrugged and gave her a smile and a wink.

Even though I should have, I hadn't yet told anyone about the phone call I'd gotten. I was still trying to work out what it meant and who it might have been. I'd also kept the book information to myself for the moment, knowing I couldn't talk about it in front of Dean, Caper, Amelia, and Isaac.

"So now that everyone is here, I wanted to make sure we were all aware of what happened today and that there might be questions for us," I said, and everyone quieted down. "You don't have to answer them all if you don't know what to say." That was easy and generic enough not to scare the kids.

"Really, Hottie Roxy?" Amelia said, turning her fork around and around in her spaghetti with the spoon guiding the noodles. Aunt Hellen smiled at her and patted her on the hand. I could remember with utter clarity the way Aunt Hellen used to do the same to me and the glow it created in my chest. The way Amelia looked up at her from under lowered lashes was the exact same way I had reacted. There was a bond forming there, and I had a feeling that if Caper ever did anything wrong again, he'd have

Aunt Hellen to contend with. Without a doubt, he would never win that one.

Fair enough. I'd have to find a time to let Dean know so he could warn Caper. Maybe that was precisely what he needed to stay on the straight and narrow, like super narrow.

For now, though, we had a dinner to enjoy after I went through the information I could share and left out the parts that I couldn't.

I waited for the blush to subside on my face and then cleared my throat. "Okay, you want it simple and to the point?" Or as to the point as I could get.

"I think that might be best," Isaac said. He spoke so little that his deep voice, coming out of a fifteen-year-old boy, sometimes took me off guard.

"Fine then. Someone was most likely murdered in the basement. Mena found him after receiving a text asking her to meet him down there. We don't know if the text was sent before or after he was killed, but the police have the body now. Most likely, they will have some questions for everyone who is on the property or who was on the property at the time. I'm going to encourage you to answer any questions you definitely know the answers to, but don't give any info you don't actually know firsthand. They might ask things that could lead to other things, and you could be in trouble before you even know it just for trying to be helpful."

Glennis had come in halfway through my speech, and she glared at me until I looked at her head-on. She dropped her eyes, but did not unclench her hand from around the bread basket. Yes, Norm was her nephew, and I knew she was protective of him and the work he did, but I wasn't going to lie about how the force had fumbled the last murder. I hadn't named him specifically, so if she thought that was who I was talking about, that was on her. Since I hadn't said that part out loud, I was not going to feel bad about it.

"Basically, I just want everyone to be careful for the next little while. If you see or hear anything that seems out of the ordinary, please bring it to me."

"Or me," Dean said, taking the basket of rolls from Glennis and smiling at her. She smiled back, her whole demeanor softening. Until she looked at me again, since I was sitting right next to him, and her eyes went hard.

Why me? Why was it always me that got the nasty response? First Norm and then his aunt. You'd think I'd done something horrid to both of them. I couldn't remember anything. So that meant the one person was almost twenty years ago, and the other I employed for a lot of money and gave a lot of leeway. I should have been the good guy!

I let that go right now because it served no purpose.

"So, has anyone seen anyone who shouldn't have been here? Overheard anything that seemed out of character?"

I got several shrugs and not much else. People were digging into their salads or passing around the chicken or the huge steaming bowl of spaghetti. Dean had gotten the rolls from Glennis, but had passed them to his right instead of to me on his left. Which meant I had to wait for them to go all the way around the table before I'd get my greedy hands on some of the best carbohydrates to ever be baked.

Except he took one of the three rolls he'd placed on his plate and put it on mine. "To hold you over until the basket comes back this way."

I was mid-laugh when I saw something flicker in my peripheral vision. Who was here? And why were they hiding around the pocket doors into the dining room? Aunt Hellen sat up straighter in her chair, focusing on the same place I was, but no one else was looking. She glanced my way and seemed to be trying to signal something to me, but I wasn't getting the message.

The flicker happened again, and I whipped my gaze back to the doorway. Who was here? Why were they here? This was a private dinner, and everyone who had been invited was already seated at the table. Everyone else, namely guests, had been given their room keys and directions to cafes and restaurants in town where they could get dinner. Every one of them had taken one look at the short distance, dropped their stuff in their rooms, and then trooped out the door. Several of them stopped at the front desk to thank me for the wonderful directions I'd provided them. I appreciated that even if it shouldn't have been needed, they just looked at the website.

But I thanked them and sent them on their way before entering the dining room to find everyone already seated and just waiting for me and the food.

Now, there was someone new lurking around, and I didn't like it. I rose from my seat, but Aunt Hellen waved me back down. I plopped my butt back in my chair because, honestly, I did not think I could deal with anything new right now.

Aunt Hellen sailed out of the room with Uncle Vince right behind her. They'd been sitting across from each other at the table, and I hadn't seen him get up, but he could be quick sometimes when he wanted to be.

"What's going on?" Amelia asked.

"I'm not sure. It's possible a guest has a question and is at the front desk. With no one there, they peeked their head in to grab Hellen's attention without interrupting our dinner. Go ahead and eat. I'm sure they'll be right back."

Dean started a story about the people who had tried to bring an RV onto the ferry this morning and how furious they were when he'd had to turn them away. He added wild hand gestures and changed his voice when it came time for the woman's words versus the man's words. Everyone at the table was laughing when Aunt Hellen and Vince came walking back into the room and resumed their seats.

I tried to make eye contact with her since Vince was on my side of the table, and I'd never be able to make that happen without making a spectacle out of myself. But she was studiously avoiding my gaze. Was that an uh-oh or a dammit?

I went to grab my roll to stab it with a knife and then hopefully forcefully butter it when it was taken out of my hand and launched across the table at Hellen.

What in the hell was that? Who had taken my roll? After a quick glance around, I realized there was no one who would have. Definitely an uh-oh look from Aunt Hellen. Not good. Not good at all.

Dean looked at me, and I pretended to laugh like I had thrown my roll. I grabbed his next just in case *anything* happened to want to launch that also. Instead, my roll came sailing back through the air. Dean caught it before it beaned me in the nose. I shot my gaze to Aunt Hellen, and she too had that fake oopsy smile on her face, but she'd gone a little pale and uncomfortable.

"Are we having a food fight?" Amelia giggled and grabbed her own roll.

Isaac didn't look as sure, but he took up the roll, like if he didn't, something bad would happen—poor kid. But I was right there with him because I didn't know what the heck was going on either.

Rolls launched, and laughter ensued. Caper started stockpiling them like we were having a snowball fight. Isaac laughed uproariously as Amelia distracted their father, and Isaac scooped all of his rolls into a cradle made by holding out his t-shirt at the bottom. He scampered back to his seat with a huge, impish smile on his face. I had never seen him so childlike before, and I wanted more of that for him, even if it came at the cost of bread sailing across the table.

The laughter was loud and boisterous and seemed to shake the very room. The chandelier above us started swaying. At first, I thought it really was the commotion from the table, but then the lights flickered, and my heart dropped into my stomach. Aunt Hellen's eyes cut to mine, and she shook her head slightly. I had no idea what that meant and no chance to ask her because a phone rang. An old-sounding phone, the jingling sounding both near and…closeted was the only word I could think of at the moment to describe it.

This time, Aunt Hellen looked at Poobah, and they both got up out of their chairs.

What in the heck was going on? I ignored her when she shook her head at me again. The first time was fine. A ringing phone that didn't sound like any ringtone I had ever heard was something entirely different. They had to be out of their minds if they thought I was going to sit here and wait for something else to start flying across the table. However, I didn't want to ruin anyone's fun just in case it wasn't something that really needed my attention. Decisions, decisions.

But this didn't feel like something that didn't need my attention, and so there I was, getting out of my seat while resting a hand on Dean's shoulder as he also tried to get up.

"Your family is having so much fun. Let them keep going. I'm sure it's nothing, and if it is something, I promise I'll talk to you about it later."

He took my hand briefly and kissed the back of my knuckles. "Just be careful, whatever it is."

"Will do." I kissed him on the cheek and then ran into the hall as the phone jangled again.

Poobah and Aunt Hellen were arguing in fierce whispers that if they'd been at full volume, they would have probably brought the whole house down around us.

"What on earth is going on? And both of you better think long and hard before you try to slough me off with some weak excuse that has no basis in reality."

Poobah looked at the wall under the stairs and then leaned against it like he was just taking a little rest like a cool guy. "Nothing to see here."

"Need I remind you that this is now my inn? And if there is something going on here that I absolutely need to know about it? *And* if I don't know about it, and something happens to you, and I have no idea what is happening, then I am going to be totally at a loss. No doubt making me make mistakes I could have avoided if you had trusted me to actually run this place instead of just being a stand-in while you do the behind-the-scenes work."

"Wow, low blow, Roxy," Aunt Hellen said.

"But valid, my dear." Poobah took me in from head to toe and then back up to my head. He nodded, and I waited. I wasn't saying anything. I was not going to let him get out of things without answering any and all questions.

"That's the Earl," he said.

"Is he stuck in a wall? Did he get blocked in there like the *Cask of Amontillado*?" Now might not be time for jokes, but I needed something to hold on to.

"I don't think anyone walled him into anything. Do you know, Hellen?" Poobah had not yet moved from his fake casual stance against the wall, which told me all I needed to know about where the ringing was coming from.

"No, he wasn't walled in. My understanding, I think, is that he died here of natural causes."

"Wait, as in we have an actual earl who died in this inn, and he is haunting us?" Color me shocked.

"Well, we're not sure if that's his name or his station. I don't think anyone has ever asked. He doesn't tend to talk to anyone. Did he talk to you?" We were whispering back and forth, and I was getting tired of trying to use my secret voice.

"What is behind the wall?" I asked, stalking over to my grandfather and daring him to keep me away from what I wanted to see.

"Now, dear, it's nothing to worry about. It was walled up long ago because there was no need to keep it out in the open when no one used it anymore. It's perfectly safe, though, and it won't disturb you."

"Are you using what instead of he, or instead of a thing, like a radio?"

"It's nothing."

The phone rang again, and not only jangled, but also jingled, and there was no cutoff for at least ten seconds. If we didn't get this handled soon, others would come out, if for no other reason than they wanted to know what was taking us so long. I only hoped that no phantom hand was throwing the spaghetti.

"Move," I said.

"No."

"Move, or I move you," I said, feeling a little like Rand when he had wanted to go after Jeff for probably killing his son. This wasn't the same situation at all, but it was important.

"You wouldn't do that to your dear old, feeble Poobah, would you?" He put a hand on his chest and gave me the sad eyes.

Not surprisingly, I found myself not caring at all, which worked for me. I put my hand out to brush him away from the wall, and his face took on a shock I had not seen before. I guess that was what happened when you didn't listen. I could be the white sheep in my family of odd, black sheep. I could do all the right things all the time. But every once in a while, that veneer fell off outside my suite of rooms, and I could get what I wanted, when I wanted, without giving a freaking care as to what it cost, as long as I got it.

Poobah knew that. We'd only gone toe to toe on one other issue in my whole existence. I didn't want this to be our second, but I also wasn't backing down.

He must have seen all those thoughts in my stormy eyes because he unfolded his arms, sighed deeply, and then clasped his hands behind his back. I'd give him one more second to make the right decision on his own, and then I was going to make it for him.

He broke as I took one more step toward him.

"Hit the step, Hellen. She's not going to be satisfied until she sees what she wants to see, even if I wanted to protect her from it."

Usually, this was where I would back down, not wanting to disrupt things and trusting him to make good decisions for the family. I would have rethought my position, not wanting to be wrong, if I forced the issue when I should have just trusted him to know what was best when I didn't have all the needed information.

This was not that time.

Hellen hit the step. Actually, I watched like a hawk as she ran her hand along the middle of the fourth step, right above the one that squeaked, and then pushed gently right at the edge of the runner. Was that the reason the stair below it squeaked? Because something popped up that looked like a lever with a knob on it. As soon as it was flush with the floor, the panel on the wall right where Poobah had been standing swung open toward me. Which meant that my vision was blocked by the white wall with the blue wainscoting. I crept forward an inch at a time, carefully bracing myself for what I was about to see.

Would it be an old man? A dead man who had been gone for centuries? Is a skeleton literally hanging in the closet?

But no, it was a telephone booth built into the wall. A beautiful wooden bench stretched from wall to wall, a place where someone could sit while talking on an old-style receiver hanging from a silvered box with the numbers to dial, and a small slot where you would insert your coins before placing your call.

And as soon as I saw it, I wanted to go in and make a call to someone, anyone, really. How cool was this, and why on earth had we walled it up instead of using it as a vintage kind of furniture, like everything else in this darn inn? I would have to wait to get an answer to that at a later time because instead of me making a call, something made a call to me. It rang again and again. Poobah moved his hand like a prize girl on the Price Is Right, waving me into the booth that hadn't seen the light of day in all my years and probably long before that, too.

"You want me to answer it?" Now I was nervous. Who or what would be on the other end of the line?

"You wanted in, I've let you in, now do whatever you think you should do. It's your inn, after all, as you just made sure to tell me."

Oh, I knew he was going to hit with that, and now I had to take the challenge or back down and apologize for claiming that it was actually mine.

I stepped into the booth, praying to anyone and everyone who might be listening to please protect me from anything and everything. Yes, it was a broad plea, and no, I was not at all embarrassed that I had sent it out far and wide.

I lifted the receiver to my ear. "Hello?" I squeaked.

"Girl, you'd better have more chutzpah than that if you want to talk on this phone," a strong male voice said.

"You're the one who called me during a dinner party with family and friends who can't know about you. So, I think we're at an impasse on that. Tell me what you need, and stop throwing food, and we'll be much better off so I can go back and eat my chicken parm in peace."

"That's what I'm talking about," he said with pride evident in his voice. "Now, I set that book down in front of you because there are things you need to know and things you need to do. I can't cross too many boundaries, or others will be able to counter-cross. You'd better get your study hat on because you're about to get schooled. I can wait, though. Go to the gazebo at the witching hour, and we'll talk. Make sure you have a notepad and a pen. Whatever that flashy thing you were using earlier to try to see those letters is not going to work with me. It gives me a headache, and I haven't had one of those in almost two hundred years. Talk soon, and maybe think about how much fun everyone had at that table with the roll throwing. Plus, it could have been worse if I'd decided to wing the chickens around instead."

And he hung up, whoever he was. Earl. Right. His name was Earl, but we didn't know if he was an earl or if that was his first name. But I did know he'd been dead for somewhere around at least two hundred years. I also knew he could physically move objects. And that somehow, he was able to make calls through a phone that was no longer hooked up under our main staircase that people used day in and day out. And I might never fix the third step.

I hung up the phone carefully, making sure to put the receiver on the cradle very gently. I held onto it to keep it in place for just a moment as I took in a deep breath and prepared to turn and address the two people who I had trusted more than anyone else in my life for my whole life.

"Who wants to go first? You both have a lot of explaining to do. And just for fun, it sounds as if I only have until the witching hour to be completely caught up about anything and everything that might have to do with three phrases I got from a book that a ghost threw at my feet in the wine cellar where someone was killed. So, who's going first?"

Chapter 9

Poobah and Aunt Hellen looked at each other. Something passed between them that I would probably never fully understand. I didn't know if I needed to, and definitely not right at this moment. I did need to get back to dinner, though, before people started drifting out of the dining room to see what was going on and what I was doing while they threw food at each other.

"Now, dear," Poobah started, and I slit my eyes at him.

He cleared his throat and tried again. Good idea.

"Roxy, there are bound to be secrets that everyone holds within them. No one in this world knows everything about another person. You must see that with what you have going with Dean."

"Low blow," Aunt Hellen said and put her arm around my shoulders. I shrugged her off.

"You don't get a pass just yet and have many questions to answer from your own knowledge." I turned back to the old man who I loved more than almost anyone on this whole planet. "I do understand that and have never expected you to divulge your every secret to me." Though, I might have found a way to press him about what Glennis had on him that had made her so confident that she had total control over certain aspects of the inn. Control he had let her have that I was now fighting to get back. But that was for another time.

"You're right."

"Of course I'm right, and don't try to shift this away from me. What is this, and who was that, and why don't I know anything about it?" Step one, I would restate my goal and then stare at him until he gave in to my demands. At this point, I was going to force myself not to even blink because I was afraid he'd take that fraction of a second to disappear, leaving me without answers or any clarity.

He blew out a sigh, and I felt it in my soul, but I wasn't letting him off the hook.

He finally seemed to resign himself to the fact that I wasn't leaving until he told me at least some of what had been hidden for so long. "The phone was put in around 1930. It was for any patron who needed to make a phone call. It was one of three numbers connected to the house, but they shared the same line. Something called a party line."

Surprisingly enough, I knew what that was due to a history class I'd taken in high school. There was one line for a whole house, sometimes a whole neighborhood, and it could be used with different numbers.

"We had a phone at the front desk to take reservations and help with any kind of thing the outside world needed. We also had a number to your suite and another to what is now the library. We did not have in-suite phones, since those were incredibly expensive, and people could just come down for whatever they needed."

"Yep, got it. I know what a party line phone is. I also know how it works now with a number in each room and at the front desk. I remember when you decided to not only rely on cellular service. There are many places in the house that have notoriously bad reception, like the basement, where I found a book. Which I then put aside to have dinner with my family, and people who are like family even if they don't know the whole me. And I did that right up until a ghost started a food fight and then called me to tell me it was my fault. Let's get back to the phone booth."

He spread his hands in front of him. "What do you want to know?"

"Does it make real calls?"

"No. Not anymore."

"Why did we block it off when it could have been a wonderful antique like the rest of the decor in the house?"

Aunt Hellen stepped forward. As Poobah shook his head, she made a cutting motion with her hand. "She needs to know." She took my hand in hers and squeezed. "Because spirits can make contact through it. We tried, but couldn't keep people from trying it out and getting the shock of their lives. You can put up all the signs you want for people to please not touch something, yet there's always going to be someone who tries regardless of the warning. We almost lost a child to a random spirit who was not nice like Earl. We couldn't risk that, so we decided to close off the booth, but not destroy it, just in case..."

"Just in case something like this ever happened?" I asked, eyeing them both.

"Yes, just in case of that," Poobah said, massaging his bushy eyebrows with his left hand. "Look, to be honest, I had forgotten about the thing until it started ringing and sent me right back to when we closed it down. The sound alone was enough to make what little hair I had left stand on end. I didn't think it would ever come into our lives again. We've been so concentrated on transferring ownership and getting things working, then had the murder occur six months ago, and it just never occurred to me to talk about it."

"It seems like it would be pretty important if I were here all by myself and a phone started ringing, but I had no idea where it was coming from or how to answer it."

"You're right, and we're sorry," Aunt Hellen said, hooking her arm through Poobah's. They were presenting a united front, but not against me, thankfully. It did make sense with everything that had needed to happen to get things moved over to my name and phasing him out. Then, I had to take into account how busy we had been over the last year and a half. It would make sense that it was something he might not have thought of. But now I was certain I would probably think of it every single freaking time that step squeaked.

"Why now?" I asked. "Why is he calling now when he hasn't in a very long time, I'm assuming?"

"Honestly, I don't think he's ever called before," Aunt Hellen said. "But I recognized him earlier in the hallway during dinner from when I used to sneak into the basement to spend time with one of my boyfriends and maybe figure out how to pour out a glass of wine and replace the liquid with water, thinking no one would ever notice the difference."

"That was you?" Poobah moved away from her, unhooking their arms and standing with his fists on his hips.

Oops.

"We don't have time for that right now. People are going to start coming out to see where we are and what we're doing, and I don't want that." But I really wanted to hear more about the sneaking later.

"I put a brief spell over everyone, actually, so that they don't even notice we're not there. Vince might have been able to shield himself from it, but that's okay because he would keep anyone who tried to wander off in the room."

"Well, Aunt Hellen, it seems you think of everything." Points for not-so-subtle sarcasm.

"Please don't be mad at me, Roxy. I honestly don't think I can handle that right now with everything else happening in the world. I said I was sorry, and I will try to answer anything I can after dinner is over and before the witching hour, okay?"

It wasn't like I could say no to that. I nodded to her and then to Poobah before turning on my heel and heading back into a room where no one had missed me because they hadn't even known I was gone.

It did give me a second, though, to really take in who my people were. There was Dean, who I had never thought would be anything more than a best friend. And my sister, who I hadn't seen for a long time and hadn't really had a good talk with in a lot longer than we should have let pass. Caper and his two kids were a joy, even if they did worry me with what they might do and how they might do it. Then there was Uncle Vince, who appeared not to be under the spell Aunt Hellen had put on the room. He waved me over as soon as he saw me and hugged me.

"Was it Earl?" he asked.

He knew, too?

"Don't be mad. It's something I haven't thought of in years, not since Hellen and I were almost caught down there trying to see if we could replace some of the wine with water so we could drink without anyone knowing."

Oh my, that meant the boyfriend Aunt Hellen was talking about sneaking away to have time and wine with was...Uncle Vince. Now, wasn't that interesting?

"Yes, it was Earl. What did you know about him? Is he dangerous?" I would leave the speculation about Hellen and Vince for another time, but I wasn't going to let it out of my sight.

"He's not dangerous, per se, as in he wouldn't do something to hurt anyone, but he's been here for a long time while making almost no contact with the outside world. We might want to try to figure out why now."

"I'll just add it to my list of things I don't know and have no clue on how to have a better understanding of. You know, right under figuring out who killed Ty."

"That is priority one, I think, right now."

"You'd be right."

The room brightened suddenly with a flash of the chandelier above our heads, and the shift made it so that everyone else could see me now. I made a point to take my seat as if I'd just run to the ladies' room or something. Caper shot a look at Isaac, who grinned, putting all the rolls back into the basket and lobbing one underhand to his dad. Caper caught it without missing a beat and then cut it open to put butter on it.

So, we ate dinner, laughed, and talked. There was a brief pause in the frivolity when Amelia asked if the cops were going to be coming back.

"I'm sure they mean well, but that Norm guy scares me a little with how intense he is, and I've met some intense guys before." She glanced over at her dad and then went back to buttering her fourth roll. Aunt Hellen had also returned and whispered in Amelia's ear. The girl smiled devilishly and then took a big chunk out of the roll. I had no idea what she'd heard, but I knew my Aunt Hellen. And it was probably something about women being far better at handling the struggles of life than men and that she was right there if Amelia needed anything. I'd heard it a hundred times and often had the same smile on my own face.

We were bringing this band of four, not always on the up-and-up people, into our family, and I loved that, but I also feared it might not last if this weird stuff kept happening. I found Poobah across the table and down three spots. He raised his glass of wine to me and then took a swig. I didn't know what that meant, but I did know that we had some more talking to do.

"I am going to ask everyone again to please let me know if you see anything strange around here. Any person who shouldn't be on the property, any packages that we aren't expecting, anything that stands out as different."

"Did any of you know Ty that well?" Caper asked as the kitchen door swung open, and Nell and Clara came out to clear dishes before dessert. I happened to be looking at my new hire to see if she had her earbuds in, so I caught the way she bit her lip hard and blinked rapidly.

I snagged her as she moved past me. "Are you okay?"

"I just, well, maybe, not really? It's just so sad."

"I understand, and I'm sorry this is part of your first few weeks with us. It's not how we normally operate."

"I get it, and I wouldn't have hired on if I thought this was some kind of death trap, but Ty was a really good guy, and it's horrible that he's gone." Tears glistened and threatened to spill over.

"Did you know Ty?" I hadn't thought about that when all the commotion was going on earlier.

"We, um..." She blew her bangs out of her eyes and lowered her head. "We had started talking about dating and maybe seeing where it took us. We had talked about it years ago, but it just hadn't worked out at the time." Her eyes shifted away from me as she drew in a deep breath. "I guess that dream is dead, too." She sucked in a sob, and I was out of my chair and leading her back to the kitchen as quickly as I could without causing yet another commotion.

Glennis stood at the sink and didn't turn as the kitchen door swung outward to let us into the bright and warm room. I had always loved the kitchen, even though I typically could not be trusted to make anything in the least bit edible in here. If you wanted hot tea, I was your girl, but that was pretty much where my talents ended.

Once the door swung shut behind us, Nell crumbled into a seat on the island and wept. I placed a hand on her back and made eye contact with Glennis. I mouthed, "What should I do?" and she shrugged, then turned back to her whipped cream application to a berry and strawberry cobbler that was making my mouth water just by looking at it.

But I had other things to focus on first. Dessert could wait even if I never thought I'd actually think and mean those words.

"I'm so sorry, Nell. I had no idea you were dating."

"We weren't, not yet, not really, but the possibility was there, and now it's gone. We'd had some great conversations and really had started to reform our connection when he was doing all the work here. I loved to see him. I don't have any family around anymore since my dad moved to Europe. At first, it was nice just having someone to do things with. I had hoped it could become more, but that hope is dead now, along with Tyler." She gulped a sob back.

Since Nell's head was still bowed, I caught Glennis looking at me, and she tipped her knife toward the girl at the breakfast bar. Her thoughts on Nell doing some shady stuff came roaring back into my head. Obviously, this was not the time to ask about it, but it would make more sense if Nell had been pulling a cord here or blocking a toilet there, knowing that it would keep Ty around for one more set of jobs. I would deal with that thought and possible repercussions later.

"If you need to go home, you can. I think we've got the rest of this handled." And I really didn't want to talk about her when she was still in the building, but I knew I might have at least a few things to say to Glennis involving her role here and in the overall picture.

"Do you mind?" she asked, raising her head and giving me the saddest smile ever to cross someone's face. "If you don't mind, I'd really appreciate it. I've been trying to hold myself together all day since I saw them bring Ty out of the wine room, and I just think I'd like to go into my cocoon and maybe take a bath and read a funny book or something."

"Absolutely." I didn't even look at Glennis. If she had a problem with this, then I could fill in and do whatever Nell would have normally done. I knew my way around clean-up.

"Okay, thanks." She rose from the counter and took off her apron. After stashing it in a cubby near the door, she took out her bag and her keys. Her cell phone tipped out of the bag, and she caught it mid-air. The screen lit up with its saver, and it was a big red heart with something scrawled on the front.

There was a series of moving bars at the bottom, and it looked like something was playing on it.

"You might have activated something when you dropped the phone."

She looked down and laughed softly. "Oh, that's just a podcast thing. But thanks, my battery's been low the last couple of days, so I need to shut everything down. I might not be available if you need me, so I can just sink into relaxing and figuring out what comes next."

"You weren't on the schedule for tomorrow, anyway, so that's not an issue. Let me know how you're doing, though, if you don't mind. That way, we can keep up with you. Let us know if you need anything, too."

"You could have Mena bring it over!" she said brightly. "I might need my old friend back just to be able to find some small joy with Ty gone." Ty, who had texted Mena to say that he wanted to see if they might be good together this time, unlike the last time. Yikes.

"I'll see what I can do, but her family comes in tomorrow, and then she's not going to be able to skip away when she's supposed to be watching the little one they're bringing with them."

"Right, duty first," she said and then gave a sighing laugh. "I'm going to go. Please tell everyone I'm sorry, and I'll see them again soon."

"Drive carefully."

"I do everything carefully," she said and then walked out the back door onto the patio, took a left, and was gone.

I leaned against the counter, knowing I should go back out into the dining room. Maybe explain that Nell was having a rough time and she'd be in another day. However, no one in there really needed that info other than Mena, and Nell could text her herself. I was not the secretary.

Clara came back through the kitchen door with a smile on her face that dropped when she saw us.

"What's wrong?" I asked.

"Where did Nell go? Am I going to have to do the dishes all by myself tonight? I do not get paid enough for that. Why can't she ever do her job?"

"Why do you say that?" I asked, glancing back and forth between the two women.

"She's a good worker," Glennis said from her post at the sink without turning back toward me.

"I know, it's why I hired her. But you seemed to think she was doing shady things this morning when we talked about her, and now you're defending her. What changed?"

"I ended up talking with her, and she was a little upset that I misunderstood what she had done and why she was doing it. She was trying to help because Ty asked her to help. He wasn't quite as knowledgeable about the job you hired him for as he led you to believe. She does know how to fix everything since her dad was a handyman, and she used to ride along with him to learn all the tricks of the trade. She wanted him to be able to shine here so that maybe other people would also hire him. She planned to help him do his job the right way and hope he'd learn, like an apprentice."

"Wow. What about the brush against the body comment?"

"I misheard her. She swears she said it was okay, to not worry if he needed to rest, not that she liked how he touched her chest."

Those two phrases didn't sound exactly alike, but Glennis had been known to embellish things to get what she wanted or sway your opinion to her side of things. I should have remembered that when she was telling me the story earlier.

So, between Rand and Nell, they had been trying to help Ty get back on his feet. What had knocked him down? Was he trying to escape it, but it found him in our basement and took him out once and for all?

But then there was still this Jeff guy, and also, we didn't know what had killed Ty in the first place. I still had hope, as weird as it sounded, that he'd been electrocuted because he had not been safeguarding himself when he ripped into an outlet.

And if that wasn't a weird thought in a day absolutely chock full of weird thoughts and happenings, I didn't know what was.

"Well, we'll keep an eye on things around here, and if you end up needing help, just let me know. I have a few people I could call in to see if they are a good fit for the interim."

"Most things are already chopped and prepped and portioned out. All I have to do is cook them. Clara and Taylor can do the running around. We'll be fine, just like I told you we would before you hired Nell."

This was a conversation we had had before, and I was not having it at the moment when there was so much more right outside this door. Glennis thought I was trying to replace her, or I didn't trust her in her advancing age. That couldn't be further from the truth. What I was really trying to do was give her a break from doing all the things all the time so that she'd want to stay here longer. But nothing I said or did ever seemed to get through the resistance in her brain that was the size of the Hoover Dam. Damn.

I left without saying anything else because it wasn't worth diving into this again when we would not come to a compromise.

When I re-entered the dining room, it was to find everyone crowded around Mena as she showed them videos she'd captured on her many travels. She'd been all over Europe, sailed through the oceans, took vacations that doubled as work on far-flung islands and in small and large towns across the world. I had never left the States, but I loved seeing what she had done and how much fun she'd had doing it.

But I didn't join the crowd because I had yet to do anything more than put food on my plate. My plate was gone. Earl again?

Nope, it was Dean who must have gone into the kitchen right after I came out. He was carrying a steaming plate and put it down in front of me. The smell alone was enough to make me almost giddy, and I wasn't talking about the chicken parm with all its herbs and spices.

I tipped my head up to thank him and got a lovely kiss that made my toes curl in my very sensible shoes. I could get used to this. I really could. And that both made me incredibly happy and extremely nervous. I'd never had a real relationship that lasted for any significant length of time, and never one that I could see lasting for years and years to come. And yet, with this man, who I had talked myself into only being my best friend, I could see all the way out to the horizon of time.

"Thanks," I said when he stepped back.

"Of course, you remind me of my mom sometimes. Always the last one to eat, making sure everyone else has what they need before you allow yourself to sit down and enjoy your own dinner. I admire you for it, but sometimes you really do need to do what you want and need to do instead of always trying to anticipate what everyone else might want or would like to have happen."

He wasn't wrong. However, I wasn't going to admit that.

"Did you get a chance to eat?" I asked, cutting up my crispy and cheesy chicken.

"Plate's clean, so I'd say yes. I had to stop myself from licking the last of the sauce off of the dish because the food was so incredibly good. And speaking of sauce, you have a little bit..." And he kissed me again, swiping the tip of his tongue along the seam of my lips and making me shiver as I had downstairs, but for a completely different reason.

Fortunately, Glennis saved me from snatching him up and seeing what kind of trouble we could get into under the table without anyone noticing. That was so unlike me, but I wasn't against the mental fantasy even one bit.

After everyone was sated and the last berry crumble had been fought over and finally divided into nearly (per Mena) equal portions, Dean and Caper took the kids to the cottage at the back of the property. They were out of school for the summer, but Caper still tried to keep them on a pretty even schedule. They'd lived for years erratically, and he seemed to really be trying to take this third chance and do something with it.

I was totally on board with them leaving, too, because it meant we were getting closer to the time when I'd be able to actually talk to just family, just mancers. Maybe we could get some things taken care of and answered so we could move on to bigger questions, like who had killed Ty and how we corner the killer into a confession. I had a couple of suspects, but maybe someone else at the table had more.

I said goodnight to Glennis and escorted her out of the kitchen after we checked that all the burners were off, set the coffeemaker for the next morning, and then made sure the muffins, granola, and yogurt were ready for the next morning. I couldn't get her to leave. And the longer she dragged her feet, the more I wanted to catapult her out the door and to her house. She stayed here sometimes if we had a big crowd, like with the writers' convention from six months ago. But since we only had three rooms filled, I didn't need her until the day after tomorrow when we'd be at full capacity.

I really wished we could answer all my questions now and put Norm on the path to getting things sorted out and finished up before the influx of vacationers for the Fourth of July weekend. But unless I came up with something very quickly with no facts then we were going to be stuck doing this for the foreseeable future.

Except that my brain finally started working right, and I remembered that Earl had asked me to meet with him at the witching hour. Was that midnight or three in the morning? I'd heard both and didn't want to sit and wait for three hours just in case I got it wrong.

I had a whole slew of people to ask, though, and they were right in the next room.

When I came back into the dining room, the atmosphere was a little more subdued than it had been before, with the laughing children and stories being thrown around like confetti. But that made sense because while I enjoyed the joy, I also knew we were in no way out of the woods when it came to finding the murderer and keeping the house safe from whatever was happening in the basement.

I plopped down into my chair and swirled my leftover crumble. I was not always a huge fan of crust, so I would often move things away from the breadiness below and eat just the filling.

That left me with something to smash over and over again with the tines of my fork. I made little crisscrosses that could have held an epic game of Tic Tac Toe or grids for a crossword puzzle like no one had ever seen before. It was also a great distraction when I didn't know what to say or even where to start.

"So...Earl." Poobah sat with his arms crossed and that pipe he never actually smoked hanging out of the left side of his mouth.

"Right, Earl." Taking a few minutes, I explained to Mena what had happened in the hallway. I honestly didn't know what to make of him. I did not have the power of talking to ghosts like Aunt Hellen through her seances. How did I think I was even going to be able to speak to him? Would he call me on the phone at the witching hour? Whenever that was.

"Has anyone else ever talked to Earl?" I asked, not sure which answer I was hoping for.

"Not since my generation, not to our knowledge." That was Poobah again.

"He's never even called you on the phone?"

"No. He's very secretive and isolated. I was told he prefers that. I'm not sure why he's reaching out now, but it must be important. At least to him for him to break his silence. What was he saying?"

"In all honestly, nothing much. I got more out of the book, but I don't know what that means either." I pulled my phone out of my pocket and put it on the table. I opened it and then scrolled through my pictures, and all of them were void of any kind of sparkle. Damn. "Well, I guess that didn't work."

"What?" Uncle Vince rose from his chair and came around to sit next to me where Dean had been just a little while ago.

"I tried to take pictures of the book in my hand with the sparkly letters, but it didn't work. They were going around in a carousel-type thing, and I knew I wouldn't remember everything, so I made a point to take a picture to capture it."

"Spirits and magic don't like pictures," Uncle Vince said.

"Yeah, I get that now."

"But it was worth a try, Roxy, and I'm glad you managed it." Aunt Hellen sat next to me on the other side, and the three of us put our heads together over my phone.

There was a long sigh from someone, and then the table was set on fire.

Chapter 10

The dining room table set aflame had not been on my bingo card for what might happen at a family dinner, but then neither had a food fight. Maybe I should the card away and go with the flow.

It took me two seconds to see that the fire was not real and that it was actually coming from Mena.

"Stop that," I said, and she grinned.

"I just wanted to get things back on track for what we're actually doing here. We need to figure out what comes next. You all staring at blank pictures where there should be these sparkly letters you keep talking about is not moving us forward."

"And what do you suggest instead?"

"I suggest we have a seance with the brilliant Aunt Hell leading us in song and dance, and then we ask Ty what he knows and who he knows that did it. I highly doubt someone snuck up on him down there. Once the text was sent, it is very possible he was either already dead or close to it. I hadn't seen him in years, but I never knew him to be stupid. So I'm thinking someone else sent that text, wanting me to come down there and find him so that I could be framed. Now, tell me more about this Earl."

I spread my arms wide. "Today is the first time I've ever heard of him, and I've never had interactions with ghosts before. They're not my forte. At all."

"Well, yes, you have," Aunt Hellen chimed in, and every gaze rotated to her.

"Explain, please." And do it fast, I thought, because there was no way I was letting her slip out of this one to move on to another topic.

"You don't remember falling into the river when you were a little girl? You were so focused on reading your book and loving getting answers to whether or not you could talk your mom into letting you have a second serving of ice cream that you walked right off the end of the pier?"

"I have never walked off the end of a pier in my whole life."

"Right, because the ghost of Mary Margaret turned you around at the last second and sent you back the way you'd come. If not for her, then you and your precious book would have been in the drink with no one around to grab you. Your mom wasn't sure where you were when I asked because she was in the middle of one of her projects. You and I were supposed to go to lunch. When I went out to your favorite place at the ferry launch, I was too far away to save you, but close enough to see you angle out over the water with the edges of your sneakers on the very last inch of the pier and then you were turned around, still talking to yourself and poking at the words on the page."

I was frozen in time, that memory shrieking back into my mind in full color with a distortion I had never seen before. A ghost flickering in my peripheral that didn't register as anything but a stray cloud.

"And how about that time you were so into your book you nearly fell down the stairs? Someone opened the secret back staircase painting at the top and kept you from falling by holding you back by your ponytail. You laughed that the door was open and then ran down the stairs to see where it led, and you found it was an entrance to the kitchen. Your giggles were contagious, and the ghost of Wallace Seagrave joined you. But you thought it was birdsong out the window and tried to catch a glimpse of what bird made that pretty noise. You asked for days."

I had asked ad nauseum, that I remembered.

"I never said anything or answered your question with anything but vague statements because I didn't know what you knew. Beyond that, I wasn't sure if it would be something you could use or only something that would be used when needed, not on call. And, you were young and not yet fully in your own talent. I wasn't going to burden you with something more when you were still struggling with something you had convinced yourself was going to be a fun but ultimately dumb talent. I wasn't introducing a new one you would think was cooler and therefore ignore the one that was your core strength."

There was so much information and many truths and yet lies. What was I supposed to do with all this? And how did it factor into my life in general and then more specifically? If I acknowledged this new ability while I still didn't have a good handle on my core talent, would I get distracted? Be overwhelmed?

What on earth was happening to my world? And then there was Dean. If random ghosts were going to turn me around on piers or open doors and expect me to interact with them, how was I going to explain that to someone who knew nothing about the supernatural at all?

Why was life so freaking complicated? All I wanted to do was run a successful inn and make sure our sheets were up to the highest standards. I wanted the food rolling out of the kitchen to be top-notch. I did not want to be all these other things. I had been fine at this point on just answering random questions with my minor talent and doing it for a lark whenever I felt like it. Living more in the real world than the other where fantastic and magical things happened had served me well up until now. I should have thought about that and appreciated where I was then instead of always wishing for more.

Now that I had more, it might put everything I wanted in jeopardy.

Part of me wanted to shake a fist at the sky, and the other part wanted to just sit down in a chair and have a good cry. Neither of those parts of me were going to get what they wanted any time soon, so I bucked up and faced everyone in the room.

"Okay, so I've had interactions with ghosts before, and now I'll have one tonight. Who knows when the witching hour is? I've heard midnight and three in the morning." My tone obviously did not invite any more memories or information than what I was specifically asking for.

"Three," Aunt Hellen said.

While at the same time, I heard "Midnight definitely" from Mena.

Aunt Hellen looked over at her, and Mena shrugged.

"Most European witches think of it as midnight. I wasn't only out there traveling and blogging. I also stopped in and met with many different family groups throughout my time in Europe and all those little islands I'd been on. I didn't miss a chance to find out who was where and what they believed. And statistically, they believed that midnight was the correct time."

"What else did you find out?" I asked.

"You'll have to go check out my blog for that, maybe after we get the info we need and see where it leads us. I have a feeling, though, that if Earl sees you out at the gazebo at midnight, he'll show up even if he originally meant three in the morning and down in the basement. I wouldn't go down there again if you don't have to. At least not until we get some stuff sorted out."

"One of the things I'd like to start with then, dear sister, is why you were talking with Ty so much?" I clasped my hands in front of me on the table that was no longer awash with flames. "Didn't the two of you part ways a long time ago and not under the best of circumstances?"

She sighed. "So, you were there that day."

Uh oh. I had not meant to reveal that or even talk about it. I just wanted information from the present, not the past. But I couldn't lie to her, so I nodded.

"He offered to wait until I turned eighteen so that Mom and Dad wouldn't be mad. The idea was that we could stay friends for the next three years, and then, when we were old enough, we'd try to have a real relationship. I didn't want to do that to him or to myself. He was nice enough, and I did really like him, but my friends had started getting boyfriends, and I was missing out on going to the movies with people my own age. I had other boys I was in school with who would have made more sense anyway, and there was a part of me that was a little wary of why a guy so much older would want to be with someone so much younger."

"So, you had heard your parents' warnings, but you just didn't want to acknowledge that they might know what they were talking about." Poobah leaned forward with his pipe in his hand, and his left eyebrow almost arched to his receding hairline.

She looked down at the table and pulled a couple of shreds off her paper napkin. "Yes, I had heard them, but I was very sad and angry. I did like him. Once I yelled at them, I didn't know how to go back without having to admit I was wrong. And to be fair, I was fifteen."

"To be fair, you are absolutely correct, and they probably could have handled it better." My heart had broken for her, but I had been older and had seen both sides of the issue from the older set and the younger. First, love sucked when it was put on ice, no matter how you looked at it.

"Right, so he left, and then he did some things that got him into trouble. I don't know to what level. When we saw each other yesterday, I didn't want to start with what bad things had happened. I only asked about the good things, and there were a few of them. He said he was getting his life back together, and he'd love to be friends again, with possibly more on the horizon if and when that ever happened. And that's when I gave him my phone number. We talked a little bit more. I left, he texted, and then texted a few more times. Then came the one about meeting him in the basement that was spelled weird and fractured sounding. When I went down the stairs, I turned the corner and found him on the ground, and then that's when you came in, Roxy. You know the rest."

I did know the rest, but I wasn't sure how it all worked together. Was it really the bad guy putting out a hit on Ty in my place of business and my home? Or was it something else from his not-so-good past? What about something from his just-now-budding present? Still so many questions, but at least now I had a little more of a basis to build from.

"Aunt Hellen, I know you don't like to do impromptu seances, but do you think we'd be able to talk to Ty?" It was not my favorite thing to do, either. And honestly, it might even be worse now that I knew the ghosts had interacted with me before without my realizing it. How weird would it be if I was waiting for one of them to touch my shoulder or say something only Aunt Hellen and I could hear?

Too weird to think about, honestly.

"I don't think that's going to work this time, and since Earl already called you, I think we might want to work with that first. I can certainly start gathering the things I need to try to speak with Ty. But because he's a murder victim, there might be things

I can't access due to the brain shielding him from things that would hurt worse in death than in life."

"Let's not do that." I tapped my fingers on the table. "Let's try the Earl way, and then we can make decisions from there. I'll meet him out in the gazebo by myself at midnight."

Several people started talking at once, and I cut them all off. "I know you want to protect me, but with the messages I received from the book and then the information I got from Earl over the phone, I'm going to put my foot down on this one. It has to be by myself. My personal space. We'll talk tomorrow about how it went, okay?"

There were some grumblings, but they subsided when everyone could see they weren't going to be able to move me from what I wanted and how I was going to do it. Fair enough, and it worked for me.

We moved all the dishes into the kitchen, and I started the dishwasher for Glennis. She might not like the way I had stacked it since we were diametrically opposed on how these things were supposed to work. But I did it anyway so that she wouldn't have to fuss with dirty dishes from the night before. Plus, I could check on it on my way out to the gazebo if I remembered and probably empty it into the cupboards if I was feeling particularly ambitious.

The next four hours passed in chunks. I'd look at the clock, and it seemed to have moved backward. Well, not really, because it had only clocked the longest two minutes of my life. That alternated with me glancing up from reading about some of the people in my family who had dealt exclusively with ghosts.

I found an entry for a sciomancer, someone who communicated with the spirits and the dead, which was slightly different from a necromancer, who could summon them. I did not want summoning powers, so I stayed with the first term until I was told differently.

That put a new wrinkle in things, though, since I knew nothing about either one of those terms. I'd only ever really studied bibliomancy because that was what I was told I could do. I'd always thought it was kind of a weird and silly talent compared to things like being able to predict the future through a bowl of water like Uncle Vince, reading tea leaves like Aunt Hellen, or raising fire like Mena could do.

I had always had one of the lower talents. And while I had hoped for something big and different and amazing, I was finding myself wishing I'd never wished for anything more than I had.

And then, finally, it was two minutes to midnight. I knew I'd better get out there now. I didn't want to miss Earl and whatever he had to share with me.

I put on a light jacket, but stayed in my sleep shorts and T-shirt. I did have a bra and underwear on under them, so I was counting that as good enough.

The gentle breeze carried the scent of the many flowers we had growing around the perimeter of the house, and it gently played with my short hair. I'd put flip-flops on to come out and also brought a blanket with me to cover my lap if I got cold, not just from the weather, but also from remembering that I had walked through that cold spot earlier, and it could have been Earl. If it was, and he was going to be that close to me, I didn't want to be shivering and miss what he said because I couldn't hear it over the chattering of my teeth.

I quietly closed the French door behind me as I left through the dining room. It was the easiest path there, and we'd recently redone the stone pathway, so it was sturdy and no longer had weeds growing up through the pavers.

I had the book I'd found in the basement tucked under my arm and had snagged a soda from the kitchen before heading out. I was certain I would need the caffeine and also something to keep myself from blurting out whatever words were running through my head. It was a habit of mine to think after I spoke without giving myself a second to consider how I wanted to position myself.

As I got closer to the gazebo, my heart sped up. Was I really going to do this? Sit out here and converse with a ghost during the witching hour in a gazebo? There could be spiders crawling all over the place or other creepy crawly things that I did not want to know if they were from this world or another.

Stepping up to the gazebo, I said a brief prayer, much like the one I'd made before--that anyone listening could please be alert and save me from anything bad happening. But I did remind myself that Earl had been around for a lot of years, and he'd never caused any trouble that I knew about, so I was *probably* safe.

It was that *probably* that concerned me.

And the fact that as I went into the gazebo itself, I had a feeling Earl was not just his first name.

His way of speaking might have been a little rough over the phone, and I had not detected an accent. But he was dressed to the nines like he was attending a soiree at the royal court in the sixteen hundreds. From the cravat to the short tight pants that I assumed would have been velvet, even if they were faded in his ghost form, to the big wig he had perched on his head, there was a lot to take in.

I waited on the last step for him to turn and acknowledge me. What would happen if you scared a ghost?

I didn't want to find out. I'd watched all the movies, and there were scenes that I never wanted to take part in when they were created in CGI. I certainly didn't want to participate if they were here, in real life, in my freaking backyard.

Finally, he turned fully toward me.

"I guess I should have been more specific about the time," he said, bowing at the waist and catching his wig in his hand as it shifted and appeared to be heading for the wooden slats that made up the floor of the gazebo.

"Yeah, I don't know if you were listening in to the dinner conversation, but we weren't sure if it was midnight or three in the morning, so I thought I'd go for the earlier one and wait as long as I had to in order to follow your request." I was rambling, so I shut my mouth. I could have said demand in place of request since that was really what it was, but I didn't want to start on the wrong foot.

"This time is acceptable. It's not like I have anything else going on, really, and I do have all the time in the world to do all of that nothing."

"Do you ever want to move on?"

His face contorted into a frown, which was better than becoming some shrieking banshee, which my mind had just conjured up out of nowhere. Gah!

"I'm sorry if that was too personal. This is my first time talking to something other than a human. If I do it wrong, it's only because there's no information on how this is supposed to work."

"Looked, did you?"

He sounded like Yoda, but I kept that to myself at the last minute. I'd already stepped too close to the line with that frown. Telling him he looked like a puppet from a franchise would most likely not work in my favor.

"I did. I went through all the books I have about powers and the ancestors and couldn't find much."

"Hmmm, that's because you don't have the right book. We'll talk about that at a later time, though."

Oh, great, so this wasn't going to be a one-off. Darn it.

"So why am I here?"

"We'll get to that in a moment, also. I haven't had a conversation with anyone but myself in many decades, and I'm finding it enlightening to listen to you and watch your body language."

I sat down on the bench and put the blanket over my lap to give him less body to look at. Giving away my nervousness and the fear I felt wouldn't help. Not toward him necessarily, but to what he might say. I had the utmost belief that it wasn't my sister who had killed Ty, but there was still a niggling doubt back there. What could she do with the fire? Could she burn someone from the inside out and make it look like he'd been electrocuted? Would she have been angry if Ty had pressed her on issues she had thought were over long ago? Issues he hadn't let go in all these years where she was floating around and doing all the fun things she'd wanted without giving him a second thought? The murder podcasts were flooded with untimely deaths involving that very motive.

I loved my sister, but she had a tendency sometimes to think more about her needs and wants than anyone else's. While that was probably a good thing when you were traveling alone and needed to be your own best advocate. That didn't take away from the sting if you were the one who was thinking about someone else when you didn't even cross their mind.

"Okay, so, time to get down to business. What did you need to tell me that you couldn't tell me in the phone booth, so you made me come out here instead? Is there a reason this had to be done in person?" I realized my gaff after I said the words, but since he didn't do anything more than raise his eyebrow at me, I didn't think it was worth taking it back and trying to explain myself. He knew what I meant, and I was sticking to that.

"I'm glad to see that you brought the book with you. I need to show you some things. Beyond that, the Universe is interested in being able to communicate with you better, more consistently, instead of the willy-nilly way you seem to take any and all instructions."

"Now, hold on a minute. I do the best I can every time I open a book with a question. I'm not playing around." But that was a lie, and I knew it as soon as the words came out of my mouth. I always played with it. I had only ever really taken it seriously when we were looking for answers six months ago. Because of the murder, I only tried to figure out what it was saying without giving a flippant answer when the letters started rising off the page in all their sparkly gold beauty.

But I wasn't going to tell him that. From the look on his face, though, I didn't need to tell him because he already knew. He nodded at me and began pacing. I could see every slat of the woodwork behind him as he crossed back and forth in front of the lattice lining the gazebo. He was in full color, but like a transparency or one of those stained-glass windows, my mother had loved collecting.

Thinking all these things weren't getting me anywhere, especially when he was talking and I wasn't paying attention.

"I said, please open the book. I swear, it's like you just zone out. I don't understand how that Dean of yours doesn't lose his mind sometimes."

"You know about Dean?"

"I know about everyone. So, let's try this again. Please open the book, put your palm a few inches above it, spread your fingers wide, and concentrate all your thoughts and effort on bringing the letters to life. If you like the sparkle, then they'll give you the sparkle. There are few limitations on the way this can work because it is only curbed by your imagination."

How did you focus everything on your hand? I didn't want to ask, so I did what I thought he was talking about and watched as the letters rose in a stuttered way, rising and then dropping back a little, then rising again. They faded and then shone so bright that the whole inside of the gazebo was lit as if I had a chandelier out there. They faded again, and the letters weren't making any particular words at this time, just floating. I hadn't asked a question, though, and Earl hadn't told me to just yet. For now, I went from gold to an array of colors, stopping to admire the way the purple letters seemed to be more melty-looking than the original sparkle. Eventually, I went back to gold because it gave off a soft and beautiful glow that spoke to my soul.

"Okay, so now that you're prepared, let's ask a question."

I heard a noise behind me that could have been a gasp, and then words shot out of the air, not in sparkle form but from a human.

"What is that, and how can I get one of my own?" Amelia exclaimed.

Uh oh, to the nth power!

Chapter 11

I was stuck, and I didn't know what to do. I flipped the book closed as quickly as I could and cut off the sparkle, but I had no way of making Earl go away. Amelia shouldn't be able to see anything, anyway, since she wasn't a mancer.

What on earth was going on?

"Your blanket is the cutest thing ever. Would you mind, like really mind, if I stole it from you? I could ask my dad to do it, but he's trying to be better. Oh, maybe I should, too, then. Let me try again. Could I please know where you got the blanket, and is it expensive? Or do you think I could find someone who'd want to let me give them the five dollars I have on me to be able to have it?"

The blanket. She was talking about the blanket. Holy wow, that was close and made my heart almost stop. Finally, it started beating again, allowing me to breathe.

"You can have the blanket. I have a few others in the house I can use instead. I don't want you to pay me for it, though. It'll just be a gift."

"You have a lot of gifts, don't you?" she asked, glancing over to where Earl had been standing. And now it was just the latticework. What did that mean? And what should I say? She was very adept at playing situations to the best of her ability. After going through her first twelve years with someone who was always on the take, it would not be unheard of for her to be able to talk around things or pivot faster than most people her age.

But I also didn't want to assume anything because she didn't have the blood. I would have recognized her if she'd been a mancer. I was positive about that. And Dean and Caper weren't either. I'd never felt anything off Isaac either, but to be fair here, I didn't have much interaction with him since he'd moved in at the cottage at the bottom of the property. The cottage where this young girl should be, not out in a gazebo in the dead of night. Gah!

"Does your dad know where you are?" I worked very hard to keep my eyes from looking back over to where Earl had been standing. Where had he gone? Was he still hanging around, but we just couldn't see him?

I still flicked my eyes toward the house, and in that second, she stole the book out of my lap and flipped it open. My hand whipped out without thinking, but I stopped myself a second later. Pretending like I was merely patting her on the shoulder might not work usually, but it was all I had. No sparkling letters. Phew. Now, as long as I didn't ask any questions or demand any answers, we should be fine. Or at least I hoped so.

"We should go back in," I told her. "I'll walk you to your house. It's usually pretty safe around here, but I don't think your dad would want you out this late at night, especially not by yourself."

When she leaned into me, I felt terrible for not being truthful with her. Even though she hadn't asked me anything and I hadn't told her any untruths, it still felt like lying. I did not like that in the least, in particular with her, since she had told me more than once she had no women in her life and loved the thought of being with us. Over the last six months, she had really taken to Aunt Hellen, and I wanted her to take to me too, but I couldn't tell her about the glowing letters or the ghost.

Unless she was one of us, and I didn't see how that was possible. But that didn't mean I wasn't going to research the hell out of it and probably have to ask Dean some questions that I wouldn't be able to back up why I was asking.

Talk about complicated.

I rose from my seat in the gazebo and waited for Amelia to do the same. Her face was sad for a moment, and my heart broke. But then I draped the blanket she'd wanted to steal over her shoulders, and she looked at me with a bashful smile. She leaned into my body, and I put an arm around her, like a half hug but with my whole being.

She was adorable and deserved the best possible life that anyone could offer.

"Let's get you back to the cottage." I tucked the book into my pocket and hoped with all I was that it wouldn't start glowing. It was funny to go from desperately wishing it would glow to hoping against hope that it wouldn't. Such was my life lately.

"I'm not tired." Amelia swung her hands far as she walked, like a trooper out on a parade march.

"I get it, but it's after midnight, and if your dad were to wake up and not find you at least in your room, if not your bed, then he's going to be worried."

She scoffed at that. I wasn't sure if she was just putting on a show or really did believe her dad wouldn't care if he found her missing.

"He's probably out doing that thing, that thing he said he wouldn't so I'm not too worried about him not finding me since he's not here to look."

Oh, well, I did not want to touch that one with a ten-foot ferry-guiding pole.

Instead, I put my arm around her shoulders again and made sure the blanket wasn't dragging on the ground behind her.

We approached the little, sunny, yellow cottage at the back of the property where she and her family had been staying for the last six months. I had always loved this place and had considered installing myself here when I first took over the inn. I would have been in close proximity and readily available, but not in the thick of things. However, I much preferred being within the inn, just in case. Well, I appreciated it most days, anyway.

"Do you have a key?" I asked, knowing that I had all the keys at my waist if she didn't and had accidentally locked herself out.

She shook her head. "I didn't lock the door behind me."

Part of me was very tempted to ask if she had come out after seeing me in the gazebo or if she'd already been out. But I was getting very tired, and that was a conversation we could have at another time.

I reached for the shiny black knob on the white front door when it was whipped out of my hand.

Caper stood in the doorway in a pair of boxers and not much else. He did have one sock on, so I could give him credit for that.

His hair was a wild shock sticking up from his scalp as if it were trying to run off, and his eyes weren't much calmer.

He grabbed Amelia into a hug that had her squeaking, but I noticed she didn't try to get away. She sank her head onto his shoulder, and her shoulders shook.

When Caper looked up at me, I smiled at him. I would admit that I had wondered if he really was out at this time of night. And even if he had been, I was pretty sure he would have called Dean over to help with the kids. Especially since he was looking into some things for us regarding the murderer, not getting back into his own unique means of trouble. Although, I couldn't guarantee that last part.

"Thank you," he mouthed.

I nodded at him and then stepped forward to kiss Amelia's crown and stroke a hand down her back. "The blanket is hers. A gift for coming out to check and see if I was okay so late at night, sitting in the gazebo by myself."

He nodded back at me before releasing Amelia only long enough to grab her hand and lead her into the house. There was a glow in the back of the structure where the kitchen was. Had he been restless and gone into the kitchen for a snack and then realized his youngest was not in the house? I didn't know, and right now, it wasn't any of my business.

I pulled the door closed behind them, figuring tomorrow was soon enough to check in on her and make sure she had what she needed. I believed Caper gave her everything he thought she needed, but maybe there was something more she hadn't asked for, but would love to have. Like more women to talk to. Maybe some friends. My cousin had a kid near her age. Maybe I could get them to meet up at the fireworks this weekend.

It was worth considering, but it was also way past my bedtime, and after a good rest would be soon enough.

On top of that, I also had to think about how I was going to approach what she may or may not have seen in the gazebo.

I would readily admit that I didn't want to. In fact, I would have rather just swept it all under the rug and completely forgotten about it, kind of like the door under the stairs to the phone booth.

But that wasn't how I was built, and if, for some reason, Amelia did have even a little power, I would not leave her floating out there all by herself with no real knowledge. Of course, I'd have to figure out how to tell her father first because I was not going to go behind his back.

Which led me to actually confront the real part of this that was speaking to me. And that was that if Amelia was one of us, then that meant I could tell Dean and see if that was the end of us or a whole new beginning.

I shook my head at myself as I opened the French door to the dining room and then pulled it closed behind me. I glanced out at the cottage and saw that there was still a light on, casting a soft glow on the small, wooded area in the back.

Were they up talking? Was she telling her dad that she saw a ghost and I played with ghosts?

I won't lie, that made me feel a little sick to my stomach. Yes, some people thought that magic or supernatural abilities were cool. And others called us demons and had once tried to burn us at the stake. It could go either way or neither.

As I was passing by the staircase, the phone rang, and I didn't mean the one in my pocket.

Gah! How had Aunt Hellen opened the door under the stairs? I knew it was the fourth step right above the squeaky third, but had she pushed something? Turned something? Put in a code?

The grandfather clock in the foyer chimed one, and the phone kept ringing.

"Earl, if that is you, give me a second. I don't know how to get into the phone booth, but I am trying."

The ringing ceased immediately, and I was tempted to sneak away just because I was that tired and wanted to do nothing else tonight except lie down and hope tomorrow was a better day.

But even after knowing Earl for a short time, I was fully aware that was not going to work for him. Besides, who knew how he could escalate things if I ignored him?

All right, to the stairs.

It couldn't be something difficult because Aunt Hellen had opened the door pretty easily and within a fraction of time. I hadn't seen her take anything out of her pocket, like a key or a card or anything to open the door, so it probably was just a type of latching mechanism. I could do this. I'd watched enough DIY videos that one of them had to deal with something like this.

I reached through the spindles on the staircase as I remembered Aunt Hellen doing and felt around under the edge of the carpet for anything that didn't feel like well-worn wooden treads on a step.

There was a short ring in the booth, and it cut off before it was done. I scowled at where I figured Earl was calling me from, namely the basement, and kept checking.

And then I found a small button, almost like an imperfection on the wood, a slight dip, that when I pushed on it triggered a clicking sound, and then the door on the other side of the banister swung open.

He'd better not start calling again.

And he didn't. I sat there for five full minutes, waiting for it to ring. I'd picked it up off the cradle as soon as I'd gotten in the door, but there was nothing on the other end. So maybe he did actually have to call me instead of me just picking up the phone and being able to talk to him?

I sure wished I knew the rules of this kind of thing.

Picking up the receiver again, I decided to give it one more try. It was a rotating dial, and the zero was at the very bottom. So I stuck my finger in the circular dial and dragged the wheel around, then let it slide back with a clicking sound from old movies when someone was dialing.

As soon as it hit the end of the dial, the phone gave one short ring in my ear, and then there was Earl.

"Why did you bring her with you?"

"Well, hello to you, too. And I didn't bring her with me. She didn't come with me at all. She showed up from her house. Could she see you?"

He harrumphed. "Not that I could tell, but she felt something beyond what a non-mancer would feel, and that could be concerning, or it's just her youth. Children are far more open to the possibilities than adults."

I wanted to blow out a sigh of relief, but I couldn't yet.

"I'm sorry our conversation was interrupted. Is there more you can tell me? Were you in the room when Tyler was killed? Do you know who killed him? Is it someone you could identify if shown a picture?"

"No, I cannot." His voice sounded almost the same as it had out in the gazebo. Briefly, I wondered if he was actually talking over the phone or just pretending to, but that seemed weird even to me. "I wasn't in the room and only heard a brief scuffle and then a thud, which I assume was the body dropping to the floor."

"What can you tell me?" At this point, I'd take pretty much anything if it would help me.

"I believe you still have the book? You did get it back from the little girl, didn't you?"

"Yes, I did get it back from Amelia."

"I do not need to know her name, only the role she plays in this, which is none now since you have the book. I'm hoping this is the very last time I have to talk to you or anyone."

Rude much? But I didn't say anything because it wouldn't change the tone of this conversation, and I really wanted whatever he had to share. He had said in the gazebo that we'd have future conversations, but maybe Amelia had scared him off from that.

"Begin again by hovering your palm above the pages. I'll wait, but not too long."

Jeez, talk about pressure. I cocked my head to the side to clamp the phone between my ear and my shoulder. It was so uncomfortable, but I was afraid he'd leave if I broke the phone connection. Honestly, I was also hoping he had other wisdom to impart if I could get him to keep talking.

"Okay, hovering is happening."

"And are you concentrating your all into your hand?"

"I'm certainly trying." The letters stuttered and rose and fell again as they had out in the gazebo. What was I doing wrong?

I bore down hard, thinking my whole self was in my hand.

"You're trying too hard."

I let out the breath I'd apparently been holding and kept back the tears I could feel brimming in my eyes and the back of my throat.

"Please do not cry. There is no crying in bibliomancy."

"What do you want me to do? I've been at this for years and never knew much about what I was doing, so I always just played with it. They forgot to teach me how. Instead, they just boosted whatever I managed to learn on my own. I'm operating on very low info here, and you're being mean."

His sigh probably would have ruffled my hair if he'd been standing next to me, even if he was dead. "I am not being mean. I am trying to help you, but your admission does answer a few of my questions that I had not thought to pose." He paused, and I wasn't sure if I was supposed to fill the silence.

"Let's attempt this a different way. There is no information you absolutely need tonight, and since I cannot identify the person who committed this evil deed, perhaps we can get some answers from someone else. Ask your aunt and uncle to scry together during a seance. You will need to be there to hold the room, but I believe you are up to that. Contact me after you've done this, and we will see what happens next."

And then, of course, the line went dead––pun totally intended.

I rested my head back against the hardwood interior wall of the phone booth. It was a beautiful oak stained to a warm golden perfection. I wanted to explore this little nook more, but honestly, I was beat after everything that had happened today, and I desperately needed sleep, like ASAP.

After closing the door under the stairs and making sure it wasn't going to randomly pop open, I shuffled myself off to bed. Once there, I waited for the nightmares or dreams or whatever to come to show me what I'd done wrong today and how I might never have a chance to redeem it.

Instead, I got sunny visions of standing on the ferry with Dean as it crossed the river. We leaned on the railing overlooking the current moving slowly through the river. Our shoulders touched, and I had my head cocked to rest against his. I had no idea what we were talking about, but we laughed uproariously at something. And then darkness shrouded everything, and I sat up soaking wet with sweat.

What the heck was that?

Pounding on my door kept me from contemplating the dream too much. The last time I had to open the door to someone making that much noise, Aunt Hellen had been in trouble. After rolling out of bed, literally, since I landed on all fours and then stuck a hand on the bed to bring myself to my feet, I headed through my sitting room at a clipped pace. What new horror was being rained down upon us at--I glanced at my watch--six in the freaking morning?

I'd texted Aunt Hellen asking her to take the morning, knowing no one should be checking in until four this afternoon. Plus, since we currently only have three sets of guests, I figured they wouldn't need much.

That was a lot to think about in the ten seconds it took me to whip open the door and come face to face with a smiling Mena, her arm locked through Nell's.

"You really need to think about getting a haircut that flatters you at any time of the day, Roxy. This one is not doing it for you."

She and Nell giggled, and I nearly slammed the door in their faces. I handled very few things well before my first cup of coffee, but could usually muster at least some civility if it involved the inn and something that needed to be handled.

I wouldn't deny that Mena might need to be handled, but that was not my job.

"Unless you are bleeding or there is a terrible fire somewhere, I am sleeping." I had barely slept last night with all the dreams. This was not how I wanted to start off my day.

"I just wanted to let you know that I'm going to be helping Nell around the house so we can hang out and we don't take her off the schedule. You don't mind if I help, do you? I've worked around here before."

Nell was scheduled to work this morning to prepare for that family coming in and others. We were going to be fuller this afternoon, so I really needed her. And Mena had worked here every summer during school. I wasn't sure why she felt she had to ask to help around here, but if I had an extra pair of hands, I wasn't against that at all. As long as they actually worked...

"Can I talk to you for a minute since you're here?" I asked Mena.

"Of course. Nell, I'll meet you in the hallway in a few minutes, okay?"

Nell's gaze dropped to the floor, then came right back up along with her smile. "Sure. See you in a few. Thanks, Roxy."

I smiled at her, and as soon as she walked away, I closed the door behind her. Gesturing for Mena to move into my bedroom, which was the furthest from anyone being able to eavesdrop on us, I went first. I wasn't worried about Nell, of course, but more about anyone else who might come through the hall or possibly that little girl who might have seen more than she should.

"I have issues." Wasn't that the understatement of the year?

Chapter 12

"There's no need to state the obvious." Mena turned her back to my bed, then launched herself to flop on top of my covers and pretended to make snow angels. She was ridiculous, but this was almost better than coffee. I'd still need it, of course, because my body couldn't exist without caffeine. But her humor and joy in so much of life was a kick toward feeling human far earlier than I usually did. She was good for my soul and also for my need to connect with more people closer to my age. I loved my older folks intensely, but I often felt like I had a bunch of mentors and mothers and fathers around instead of peers.

That hadn't actually occurred to me until she'd walked in the door yesterday morning. Something from one of my dreams had triggered it, and now I was thinking about it a lot.

"Can we be serious for a minute?"

She sat up on the bed and immediately fell into the role I needed from her. It was uncanny how she could switch like that, but very much appreciated.

"What's up? I know I make fun of you for being anal-retentive. But you seem closer to the ceiling of being overloaded on stress than normal."

"Where to start?"

"Like Grand Duchess always said, at the beginning."

I smiled at the reference to our grandmother, Poobah's wife, who passed away a little over five years ago. She'd been someone you could climb into a chair with or snuggle up against on the couch. You didn't have to say anything, and neither did she, and suddenly, you just felt better. That kid who had made fun of you on the playground only had power if you gave it to him. You and your mom would get along again one day after you both survived teenagerhood. You could do better with the grades if you really applied yourself.

I needed that right now more than I had realized.

"I'm scared."

She patted the bed next to her and grabbed my favorite blanket, the one right behind the one I had gifted to Amelia. Moose, short for Mustafa, my errant black cat, entered the room as he owned it. He took one look at the pair of us sitting on the bed with a blanket on our laps and apparently discerned that this was his new throne.

Taking a leap, he then settled right where our legs were against each other. After doing a few turns and meowing at us every time he came back around, he finally decided to curl up in my lap with his head on Mena's lap.

"It's good to see him again. I've missed him." She stroked her hand over his head and tipped his chin up so she could kiss his nose.

"I've missed you." I stared down at Moose as my eyes burned a little.

"I've missed you, too. Now let's talk about what's going on."

So, I ran her through all the stuff about how the murder six months ago had really put all of us through the wringer. How Glennis might have Poobah secrets that had made them equals, but now I was the boss. How I had never thought Dean would be anything more than a friend, but now he was. And I was concerned that I wouldn't be able to hold on to him because I was never going to be able to be fully myself with him. I told her about the ghost, the phone booth, and how Aunt Hellen and Uncle Vince were probably once an item. How they had avoided each other after something happened years ago, and so I never got correctly trained. About how that led to my excitement, but also concern over the way my gift worked now. And the ghost thing.

"Wow, I mean, wow, you're going to have to give me a minute to digest all of this. You have tea?"

I sure did, and normally, I would be having my coffee right now, but I decided to join her for tea instead.

She took my electric kettle, got water from the fridge, topped it off, and set it on the stand. Next, she grabbed two cups from the pegs under a bookshelf and held up my favorite to me. I nodded, and she went about putting in tea bags and sugar.

"Now," she said with her back still turned to me. "I know all of that feels super important to you, and it is super important, in general, but especially to you. However..." She turned to me sideways so I could see her profile. "There's a lot in there that is completely out of your control."

I sputtered, and she put her hand up.

"I'm not saying you should ignore it, or go with the flow, or pivot, or yell plot twist, and then run in the other direction. I'm simply saying Uncle Vince and Aunt Hellen are not your issues other than they had better be teaching you things now, or I will have a word with them."

"They are, and I think they might be seeing each other on the sly."

She whistled. "Ohh, on the sly? Do you think we could catch them in a compromising position and then blackmail them for things like that earring set I've always wanted her to give me?"

That made me laugh, and I appreciated it.

"And we could make Uncle Vince pick up the extra donuts off the special menu that only those in the know would know about." The kettle clicked off, and she went back to work, creating a cup of tea that was probably going to be the best I had in a long time simply because of the company.

I hadn't thought of that menu in forever. I wanted a sprinkled Boston cream with chocolate pudding right now.

"I get why you want to look into the murder and interact with the ghost, as needed, especially since Ty's death happened here. And we can definitely talk about what you have and what you might need in the way of evidence for Norm, who I am not a fan of, but I can fake it if needed."

"I just don't want him to pull you in on this. I'm afraid he's going to feel pressured to arrest you, no matter what he says now."

"We'll handle that when it comes knocking on the door." She took the creamer out of the small fridge and topped off both of our cups with heavenly creaminess.

I did appreciate that she didn't try to hit me with the Irish cream that was also in the fridge.

"I know what you're thinking, and it's way too early, and we have way too much to do to indulge in tipsy times this early in the morning. Maybe at the end of the day, when everything is settled. Unless you spend that time with Dean?" She shot me a sly smile. "Which leads me to the one thing I think you absolutely can control."

"I wouldn't say I can control Dean." Since he was the only one left out of all the things I'd told her, she must have meant him.

"Dean," she sighed his name and clasped her hands in front of her heart. "Have I told you how incredibly adorable I think he is? I promise not to try anything out on him, but my goodness, sister, you sure do pick them well when you finally decide to pick them."

A blush heated my cheeks. "I don't know that I picked him. It's like we picked each other, even though I had a crush on him and wasn't going to tell him. But then I found out he has me listed in his phone as Hottie, and I thought maybe it wasn't as out of the picture as I originally thought it was."

"Oh, my word, are you kidding? He has you in his phone as Hottie? See? Freaking adorable. Abso-freaking-lutely adorable." She sighed again as she brought our cups to the antique coffee table I'd inherited from our grandmother. Well, it had come from further back than that in time since it was linked to that shipment that had never made it down the river. Everyone had thought our ancestor had buried treasure. But really, she had hidden it in the house and had just let people believe it was on an island, waiting to be dug up so no one would look too closely at what was already there. Though, I had heard, and then read, from the book that Poobah had handed me that there was more somewhere in the house––like a stash of jewels that no one had seen in over a century. But that was a mystery for another time.

Taking a seat on the couch in the next room, she beckoned me in. I simply picked up Moose and moved him with me. And found that she had given me new coasters to go under our mugs. She'd done that for all her travels. In fact, a lot of my family often gave me coasters. I had a whole cabinet of them. These coasters were a beautiful ceramic, painted with big sunflowers. When you set your mug down, it was perfectly centered with the petals wreathed around the base.

"I hope you like them," she said. "I was going to try to get you something different this time, but I love bringing the coasters. I hope that's all right."

"Absolutely. They're lovely, and I appreciate you thinking of me while you're out taking over the world." I settled us into the couch right next to Mena. The cat resumed his position of body on me and head on her, stretched, and then promptly closed his eyes.

"I'm afraid you're going to be a little bit later than Nell had expected if we're having tea and talking about all this." I was no longer really worried about anyone trying to listen in on us. We weren't talking specifically about talents, but more about boy stuff. I hadn't had boy stuff to talk about for years, and now that I did, I really valued having my sister here to talk it through with.

"I'm assuming you're concerned about the *rules*," she said, then took a sip of her tea, keeping her eyes on me over the rim.

"Of course, I am. We're not allowed to talk to anyone outside the mancer community about our talents. I'd have to give it or him up, and I don't want to do either. But I'm not sure how I can keep both."

"I have thoughts on that. We could go to the council." She held up her hand as I gasped. "Hear me out. It's been a very long time since that rule was made. It was mainly to protect us from a world that hated us and wanted us dead, even if all we did was make the harvest more plentiful so no one died in the winter. It's time to shake things up a little bit. You would be the perfect test case."

"I don't know if I have it in me to be a test of anything."

"Oh, you do. I know you do, but we can table that for the moment. I do want you to think about it, though. And enjoy your time with the hunky Dean. There's so much going on out in the world. We absolutely must take our joy where we can find it."

I turned my cup around and around in my hands. "I get that, and I want to believe it, but I'm also nervous about getting too close or breaking his and my heart at the same time. But I'm not willing to give him up."

She gripped my hand. "I don't know that he'd even give you the choice to try that. We'll figure something out."

"Later."

She quirked an eyebrow at me as she sipped from her cup again. "Later, but not never."

"I can live with that."

"Are you still scared?"

Surprisingly enough, I really wasn't. Of course, there was still a lot to take in and a lot to take care of, and I was here for all of it. But I felt like I had at least floated down from the ceiling enough not to crack my nose on the plaster every time any little thing happened. To be fair to myself, a lot of what was going on was not little, but there were some things I could only do my best with. The rest would have to be up to the Universe.

She must have read my face because she said, "Good, my work here is done," and then got off the couch and drained the last of her tea.

"Are you heading out to find Nell?"

"Yep." She stared at the bottom of her cup. "I wish I had tea leaves so I could go bother Aunt Hellen."

"She would take you in any way possible, with or without tea leaves."

"I'm sure she would," she said cheekily. "But if I do find her in that compromising position, that could benefit both of us. And if I also had a cup with tea leaves, I could use it as a prop to tell her I've been trying to learn tasseomancy. And this couple in the bottom of my cup that I'd never seen before led me to her, and I was wondering why."

"Dubious." I laughed.

"Delightful," she said and then bent down to hug me and kiss Moose on the head.

"Nell should be in the dining room making certain we have enough utensils for tomorrow morning's breakfast. Glennis is doing it big since a lot of people are coming in tonight, including your employers. I can't wait to meet them. I'm so glad you found some good people to work with."

"And an adorable baby that I don't have to take home at night."

"And that." I smiled and blew her a kiss since Moose was not moving. "Can you let Hellen know I will be down in a little bit? I know she gets up at dawn on every given day and seats herself at the counter, but I usually stop at about eight. I think I might take a power nap so that I'm ready for everything today. I feel better knowing you're going to be in and around here so I can sleep."

"Don't put too much faith in me. I might ruin everything." Something about the way she said that gave me pause, but then she was out the door. Moose ran right out with her. I wasn't worried about him patrolling the hallways. He did that often and usually would end up in the library looking for a sunbeam to bathe in.

So, I took my time getting ready after I took a quick snooze in the middle of the blanket angel Mena had made. I stood in the shower a little longer than I usually did. I set my hair in some small curlers to give it a little extra bounce. I applied eyeliner and mascara just to spruce things up a bit. And the whole time, I had the book from Earl at my elbow.

It hadn't said anything since I'd talked to him last night. I'd tried hovering my hand over the words, but maybe I was on the wrong page or focusing incorrectly. There had to be an easier way to do this. I needed to call on the talent and then expect it to be there to help me in any way it could. That was the basic principle of bibliomancy. I knew that, but I had not expected the golden sparkly letters rising above the page and spelling things out. Before, I had always just read a passage, got some idea of the answer from whatever I had read, and then passed it along.

These were actual answers, and I couldn't say I was mad about that, even though they were more often metaphors, wordy phrases instead of direct answers, and something I still had to figure out, like those three from yesterday.

I knew who was in the house. Although, did I really? It could be referencing ghosts in the house, too. I had never encountered one of those before. Well, not that I remembered. I couldn't say I was happy I'd encountered one now.

Although...I hadn't heard from him since late last night. We still had a lot to talk about, but I was going to have to see if he'd let me down in his basement to talk or maybe allow him to come into my rooms. I couldn't take a chance of Amelia finding us again. And me, yet again, being unable to explain what was going on without lying to her.

I'd figure it out. I always did. But first, I needed to get myself into gear now that I was feeling super cute and maybe even a little bit sassy in my skirt with its 1920s vibe and a lapel pin my aunt had purchased in Italy on one of her many trips.

Taking a deep breath, I asked whoever might be listening from on high to please help me get some more information. I needed to make sure everyone in the inn was safe. Along with that, I needed confirmation that if what happened to Ty was not an accident, at least it was the end of whatever was going on, instead of a start, as I had feared last time.

The book sat there, not vibrating, not making any noise, and not throwing off any sparks. I needed it to do something if I was going to move forward on this investigation. I probably shouldn't be involved in an investigation, no matter how you looked at it. But I couldn't help myself. Call me nosy. Call me wanting to protect my sister. Call me wanting to solve this last murder so we could move into the holiday weekend with pure joy and nothing more to worry about than something low-level, like breakfast being too hot, or not having enough coffee on hand. Those I wouldn't love, but at least I could deal with them. This murder stuff was not in my lane. In fact, I wanted it off my road altogether.

Okay, I'd procrastinated enough. I needed to see what, if anything, I could find out from the book. I could do this. I took another breath, opened the book on my lap, and hovered my hand over the text. A small spark of golden dust shot out of the book and hit my palm. It didn't hurt, and it wasn't hot, but I had to force myself to stay still instead of flinching like I wanted to do.

"Do you need a question?" I asked.

Several puffs of spark went up, circling my hand to form above it into a very clear Y. I was going to take that as a yes.

"Okay, here's a question for you. Do you know who the killer is?"

The Y turned black and then fell like ash back onto the page. I was going to take that as a no.

"Is Dean my Watson, and will he help me figure out who the killer is?"

The sparks rose again and formed a little cloud of fireflies that tumbled over and over themselves like a flock of birds in the sky. It turned into a little tornado, but I didn't feel any wind moving, and the pages below stayed flat. It was fascinating, to be honest, and I could probably sit there and watch it all day long, just spinning and spinning, in all its glory, no matter how small it was.

You'll need to move more into the process and less on the prohibition.

"What the heck does that mean?" I didn't mean to yell it, and I certainly was happy that no one else was currently in the room with me.

The book was not happy, though, or at least the sparkles weren't, because they turned to black again and sank back to the page in ash.

I tried a few more questions, but that yelling had put it out with me. It apparently was no longer in the mood to talk. Maybe I'd try again later. Or maybe I could do this without the book.

The sparks flew off the page, this time in reverse lightning strike patterns and coalesced very quickly into a stark answer that I could not misinterpret even if I tried really hard.

NO.

Okay then.

I grabbed the book I'd received from Earl and tucked it into a small crossbody bag that I planned on taking with me wherever I had to go today. It wasn't exactly fashionable, and it did take away a little from my bouncy hair, lined eyes, and sparkly lips. But ultimately, I was practical, and this was practical.

As I emerged from the hallway into the foyer, there was the man I'd been thinking about—more than I should.

"Loving the bag there, Roxy, very cosmopolitan."

Dean Manchester, or Winchester, depending on if he was using his real name or the one he'd given himself when he tried to distance himself from the crimes some of his family members had committed. I'd met him eighteen months ago when he'd moved to town and had fixed a few things at the inn. He worked at the ferry launch and around town under the supervision of the town council. He had wanted to make a new life for himself, but I hadn't known why until we'd found a dead body together on the beached ferry.

And my whole life had changed.

We'd been friends before that. Admittedly, I had had a crush on him. But I'd told myself it was impossible, and there was no way a relationship would ever happen. I had made peace with that reality and just enjoyed him as a good friend.

But once things had gotten dicey around here and the book had told me that he was my Watson, I'd started rethinking those limits I had put on myself and what could be.

And now we were an item, and I loved it so much that it scared me sometimes, as I'd told Mena.

"What are you up to today?" I asked, leaving my fear in the dust, but keeping the book close at my side. I knew that he couldn't see the sparkles as I feared Amelia might have last night. But sometimes, if a book was being persistent, he could hear a loud humming that made him look around and wonder where it was coming from.

"Stopping by to see how things are going. Did you find anything new?"

"Not really. I was hoping that maybe Caper had been able to come up with some information about the Jeff guy. I'm still concerned that Rand took off so quickly without helping me out, too. Do you think he could have done it for another reason and is just trying to get us off track by throwing this Jeff out there for us to look into?"

He rubbed his chin and then blew out a sigh. "I talked with Caper. He said no one is willing to say anything about Jeff. Now, he couldn't tell if it was because there was nothing to say or if they were too afraid to talk. But right now, that looks like a dead end until we can get anyone to help us out there."

"Dang it!"

"Such harsh language," he said, then pulled me into a hug that I did not resist at all. "We'll have more today, hopefully. Caper is asking around about Rand and Ty, in general, this time instead of going directly for the crime aspect. It's weird, though.

I'd talked to Ty a couple of times. He seemed like a good guy, so I don't think he was mixed up in anything. Unless it really was a threat against his dad and his debt that they just followed through on. Either way, it's sad."

"It is." And that reminded me I hadn't really asked Mena how she felt about all of this. She and Ty might not have talked in a lot of years, and she'd said she had understood why they wouldn't have worked, but she had still found someone dead who she had cared about at one point.

She was off working currently, so I'd see if I could snatch some time with her before her family came in this afternoon.

In the meantime, I had things to do and a man in front of me who could help me do them if he wasn't busy at the moment.

"Do you have a sec?"

"I have a full minute if you need it."

I bumped him with my shoulder and smiled up at him. "I do. Can you go down to the basement with me? I really don't want to go down there by myself right now, but I need a few wines. I want to check on the fuse box again to make sure everything is where it's supposed to be before people start checking in."

"Are you afraid there might be a ghost down there or something?" He brushed my bangs out of my eyes and smiled at me.

Oh, if only he knew.

Chapter 13

I let Dean go down the stairs first. To be fair, he offered. It wasn't as if I had hidden behind him and forced him to open the door and then started my own descent. I'd contemplated that very scenario, but he'd taken the lead. I didn't even have to ask.

"Did the cops do any damage down here when they were checking things out?" he asked as we neared the bottom of the staircase.

I wanted to shut my eyes so I wouldn't accidentally see Earl and gasp, but I also didn't want to miss the last step and fall into Dean's back. It was all about choices.

Fortunately, there was nothing unusual in the hallway, around the corner, or in the wine room. The cops had left everything pretty close to pristine, which I appreciated very much. There was still a me-made hole in the rack from when I'd tried to use the book, but I fixed it before Dean noticed anything. He had gone directly to the fuse box and was fiddling with the switches, making sure each was in the correct position.

I shuffled the bottles, making sure not to clank them together, and then joined him at the box.

"I sure hope nothing else happens this week." Had I just jinxed myself? Could I jinx more than I already had? I hoped not.

"I hope not, too. You deserve a break, and honestly, I think things are going to go well. There is still a chance Micah was feeling a little like he needed to prove all the things now that he got moved up a rank without Norm's blessing. It's possible there might be a little opposition or in-fighting. But no matter what they think or are spouting, they'd still have to prove it."

"True." I saw a streak of black on the floor and wondered if they'd been dusting for prints and left some behind just after I'd said they'd left it pristine.

"Did you find something?"

Now that I was down at the level of the black, it looked more like ink than it did any kind of powder. "Do you have your phone? Can I use the flashlight?"

"Sure."

And then there was light. The light was shining right on the back of my head and creating quite a shadow on the floor in front of me. I reached back for the phone, and he handed it over without a word.

"I'm not sure what this is." I was a little afraid it was blood at first, but it was too gelatinous for that. Wouldn't Norm and his crew have been able to find it and take a sample or at least clean it up? I highly doubted they would have left it there.

There was a sharp burst of light from above, and then everything but the flashlight went dark. A second later, there was a face in the light, and it wasn't Dean's. I drew in a gasp and then tried to hold it. Could Dean see Earl with his face up close to mine? Did he hear a humming like he had when the books were active? How on earth was I going to explain this?

"Wow, it is dark down here," Dean said, sounding like he was out of place. "Let me see if the switch flipped. I don't want to take the phone from you, but I might have to. Sorry. I can't see anything over here." He dropped a gentle hand on my shoulder, and I passed the flashlight up to him.

I thought once it was no longer on Earl that he would be lost in the darkness, but I was very wrong. Very, very wrong, in fact.

He glowed. Not quite like he had out in the gazebo where I had been able to see through him with his clothes in full color. Down here, he was all black and white, like the television my great-uncle still refused to change out for anything. It wasn't his main television since he was a huge sound system and action movie fan. But he kept it in the spare bedroom in case he ever got to feeling nostalgic for a bygone era.

And now the picture before me mimicked that coloring. Earl didn't look angry or upset. He looked resigned. He pointed at the sludge on the floor and then to his nose.

I had no idea what he was getting at. And it wasn't as if I could ask any questions. I jerked my head to the left, trying to signal that I wanted him to move along and that we'd talk later.

He repeated the same gesture with the sludge and nose. Was he saying it was leaking out of his nose? Was it not just some mud or something else innocuous?

I knew for sure that I did not want to touch it, but Earl kept pointing to it and his nose.

And then the lights blazed overhead, and Earl and the sludge were gone.

What in the heck was going on? I had to hide my shock and uncertainty when I faced Dean again. He tapped me on the shoulder and held a hand out under my nose to help me stand.

"What was that all about? You sounded like you gasped after the lights went out."

"I just was taken off guard." I really didn't want to lie to him. I *had* been taken off guard. If he assumed it was because we'd been plunged into darkness, then that was going to have to be okay with me. I couldn't exactly tell him it was because a ghost was trying to tell me something about his nose and a gob of goo that was now gone.

Why did my life always seem to be full of questions but few, if any, answers?

"I think everything is in the right place, but I really think you might need to see if there's someone else who can come in and help with the electricity. It keeps going out, and I don't want anything to go up in flames. I know a guy, if you want me to call him and see if he can at least take a look at things."

I gulped because I'd already paid Rand for the work he and Ty were going to do, but hadn't yet done. I highly doubted Rand would give me anything back, and I knew Ty wouldn't be finishing up any work unless he was down here with Earl and could move things.

That stopped me in my tracks. Did the goo have something to do with Ty's murder? But then why would Earl have been pointing at his nose? I'd have to call him later on our secret phone. I felt like it was the Bat phone in the commissioner's office. The problem was I didn't have his number. Darn it!

"If you don't want me to call him, I won't."

I latched onto Dean's hand and let him pull me to my feet. I didn't drop his hand when I was at my full just-over-five-feet in height. "Actually, I would love that. Do you think he might give me an estimate, and then I can decide from there? I have to make sure I can afford him."

He cocked his head to the side. "Did you prepay with Rand and Ty?"

Another gulp. I didn't want to sound stupid. This was the first major fix I had ever done to a building, heck to any building. And I was afraid I had made a very bad decision. Instead of answering, I dipped my head and nodded.

Using just one finger, he tipped my chin up. "Normally, with anyone else, that should have been perfectly okay. Most people at least ask for a deposit because they don't want to get the whole job done and then have the check supposedly be in the mail."

"Right."

"Very right. I'll see if I can find Rand tomorrow and go from there. I'll also call Oscar. He owes me a favor, anyway. I'm sure he'd be happy to pay off that debt with an inspection and a reduced price."

"I don't want to..." But I didn't get to finish my sentence because Dean held up a hand, stopping me in my tracks.

"Please, let me do this for you. You've done so much for my family, people you didn't even know. And they're thriving here, even if Amelia is growing a little strange with all this exposure to the women of your family and Poobah, oh, and Vince. Did you know the other day, she came up to me to discuss the various forms of donut-making? Apparently, Vince was convinced that if Glennis would let him in the kitchen, he could make a donut that was just short of magical. She laughed and laughed and said she and Glennis had a bet on how long it would take him to actually talk to her about it. So far, Amelia is winning the bet since Vince hasn't shown his face in the kitchen for almost three days now."

I could feel moisture welling in my eyes. I adored that girl. Someone had better stop cutting onions down here.

"Okay, if Oscar can do the walkthrough and let me know what needs to be done, where, and how long it will take him, I will happily pay in installments with whatever discount he thinks is appropriate, but doesn't take him out of higher-paying jobs."

"Working on this inn would be a serious boom to his business. He's doing accounting as a full-time job right now, but old houses and renovations are his passion. If he could say he worked here, that would be an automatic boost to his credentials."

"I'm game then. As long as he can get here before four or after eight."

"I'll call him as soon as we get upstairs. The cell service down here is horrible." He looked at the screen of his phone and then turned it to me. "Barely half a bar. At least we didn't need that for the flashlight, right?"

"Right."

I let him take the lead up the stairs again, hoping that nothing would shove me in the back as I left what was a little like a first or second ring of hell. Maybe that's a little harsh.

We parted ways when we got to the foyer. He had work to do on the ferry, and I had an inn that I could only hope would work well while all the rooms were filled.

I found Nell and Mena in the dining room, folding napkins and talking about all manner of things. I stood in the doorway for a moment and just watched the animation on Mena's face as she regaled homebody Nell with all her adventures. When it seemed she might never take a breath where I could jump in, she finally stopped and gestured to Nell. "What have you been up to?"

Nell laughed, but it sounded mocking, like she was not at all going to be able to compete. So why try? "There's nothing quite like never leaving your small little town. Everyone knows me, and I know everyone, and we're all good with that." Nell had been here her whole life, and it sounded like she loved it. Maybe that would convince Mena to seriously consider staying. I liked having her here more than I thought I would when I first saw her yesterday in the kitchen.

"I've loved traveling, but I think I missed out on some good things by leaving and not coming back until now."

"Well, if you have any questions, I'm sure I know all the gossip, where everyone is, and what they're doing. It's like a superpower. Everyone likes to tell me their business."

That could come in handy. I put that thought in the back of my head and stepped into the room. "I love the little swans you're making with the napkins. I don't think we've had those for a very long time."

Mena showed off her creations, and then so did Nell. The lines were crisper on Mena's, but there was no need to point that out. Everyone would love them tomorrow morning, and with both of them working, things would get done in half the usual time.

But I had to break that chain just for a moment to check in with Mena. "Hey, sister of mine, can I borrow you for a second? I wanted to ask about some plants."

She gave me a funny look since we both knew I killed any and every plant I touched. I even had fake little trees and pots of flowers with rocks instead of dirt in the rooms because I'd once gone as low as to annihilate a plastic plant. Nothing was safe with me.

But she followed along out into the hallway and then into the kitchen. This way, I could keep an eye on things, but have privacy. Glennis had the rest of the day off since she'd be working a lot tomorrow. Clara and Taylor had also taken the day off because they were going to be working some twelve-hour shifts coming up. I'd only asked Nell to work today when she'd said she didn't have any other plans and could really use the money.

"What's up? You look like you saw a ghost, or should I say another ghost?" Mena chuckled and grabbed an apple out of the bowl on the island.

"The same one, but he kept pointing at some stuff on the floor, and the lights went out, and I had no idea what he wanted.

Then, when the lights came back on, he and the goop were gone. But that's not why I asked you to come in here."

"Right, supposedly you were in desperate need of plant advice, which I would not give to you and would not know what to tell you even if you didn't kill everything in sight. So again, what's up?"

Now that my time was here to ask how she was feeling, I almost chickened out. What if it just brought things back up that she didn't want to think about? What if she was grieving, and she was at the anger point and would lash out because I was making her face things again?

However, I had to ask. I mustered my courage and dove in with both feet. I glanced up at the television in the corner, watching Nell folding napkins and fiddling with her phone for a few seconds before I turned back to Mena. "I hadn't asked you how you were doing after the death of Ty. I'm sorry for not thinking about how much it might have affected you. I was so focused on keeping you out of trouble that I never gave your feelings any thought. And I am sorry about that."

She draped an arm around my shoulders. "I appreciate that. It was more the memories I was thinking of when I first saw him, but the more we talked, the more I wondered if it would be worth pursuing. I'm sure he was a great guy, but I have changed a lot since I was fifteen. And he hadn't seemed to have done the same kind of growing. I don't think we would have ended up being anything. Not that I want him to not be in this world, but I don't think it would have gone much past where it already was. I'm heartbroken for those who loved him, but not heartbroken for myself."

I cupped her hand in mine. "You know that if for some reason that changes, and you get blindsided by a different kind of grief, that I'm here, right?"

"You've always been here, Roxy, and I cannot tell you how much I've relied on that throughout the years." She cleared her throat, stood up straight, and snapped her hand out, palm up. A tiny flame began dancing on her lifelines etched into her flesh. The fire never burned her, and the way it flickered was mesmerizing.

She'd been able to do this since she was little. At first, she was incredibly erratic and would chuck real fire at anything and everything she was irritated with. She'd tried burning a blanket she'd accidentally tripped over when she was ten. Then she'd fricasseed a peanut butter and jelly when she realized Glennis had given her strawberry jam instead of the blackberry she had asked for. Precocious was one word that had been used for her, but also stubborn, ornery, and sassy. They all fit depending on which day of the week it was and where her current mood fell on the stormy to sunny scale. My mom had threatened to make her wear a mood ring just so we could keep on our toes while she was being trained.

However, right now, there was no denying her absolute control of the flame that was building in her hand. She blew a soft breath, and the flame danced like the hula girl Poobah used to keep on the dash of his '69 Dodge Dart.

I couldn't take my eyes off it, but that didn't mean I wasn't aware of her in my peripheral vision. The flame was mirrored in her eyes as she devoted her absolute concentration to what she was doing. As she rolled her hand over for her palm to face the ground, the fire worked to keep pointing up. It was like it was taking a walk along her hand. From this position, she made the fire dance and then flipped her hand back over and cupped a smaller flame in her hand.

"What do you want to know?" she asked in a voice that was incredibly monotone and different from her normal speaking voice.

"I would take any answer that you might want to give me." It wasn't a question, but I didn't know exactly how things worked for her with her power. She'd mastered it at a young age and had been the envy of others trying to test their limits. I knew she was powerful, yet I still didn't want to do anything that could hurt her by accident. Because, let's be honest, if something bad was going to happen, it would most likely originate with me.

"I see a crowd standing behind a man with steel in his chest and promise, but no one standing next to him. They all are reaching out toward him, but none of them can touch him. Interesting."

She snapped her fingers, and the flame was gone. Her skin didn't even look slightly pink from the fire.

"Did I say anything interesting?" she asked, her voice going up a register and bubbling out of her like I was used to.

"Wait, why are you asking me that?"

"Oh, because I don't always remember what I say when the fire is lit. It's like something moves through me to make the magic, and I get…" She cocked her head to the side. "It's like I get shuffled aside when I go that deep." She shrugged and smiled. "I'm very careful to only use it to that extent when I'm with someone I trust, so it's been a few years, but hopefully, it gave you something that will help."

My first thought was that she should never again use the power to that level if it made her unaware of what was happening at the moment she was being "shuffled aside." My next thought was that we needed some answers if she was going to do that again. "That can't be right. We should talk to Aunt Hellen. I can't imagine that you're supposed to be blind and deaf to what is going on while your power is at full capacity. That goes against everything we were ever taught."

She shrugged again. "It's like I said, I don't do it unless I am very clear on where I am and who I'm with before trying.

I just thought it could help you with this. You didn't answer my question. Did it help?"

"I'll have to think about that. You said something about a guy with steel in his chest and a bunch of people behind him, but no one could touch him."

"Hmmm, do you think that's the killer? I mean, Ty was a big guy, so I can't imagine anyone who wasn't at least as big as him being able to get close enough to do any damage. I suppose the steel could have been like a lightning rod, though, and that's how he got electrocuted. And the vision was just working with what it knew? You are not alone in wishing it could just answer straight out instead of always trying to give us these metaphor things or analogies. Surely, we've evolved enough as a race to be trusted with just the full-on, straight-out info. Am I right?"

"I would love that, to be honest."

"Well, since we're being honest, I'll confess to wishing I had your talent instead of mine. You can sneak around and do all the reading you want to get answers to anything you want. Me? I have to go hide and hope there are no cameras to catch me looking like I lit my hand on fire, and I'm just too dumb to put out the flames."

"I..." Didn't know what to say in the least. She was jealous of my talent? She thought the ability to literally harness fire on her hand was subpar to flipping open a book when someone asked about the weather, reading a death scene with knives and bullets in a thriller, and betting on it meaning that the weather was going to be nasty was better than what she did?

Holy wow.

"My word, it's like I can actually see the gears turning in your brain and the smoke pouring out of your ears. Don't get too big of a head. I still like that I can pretend to set things on fire if I'm irritated. And there's nothing quite like being able to set my very own marshmallows on literal fire without having to wait for anyone to get it started. But there are drawbacks." She put her hand on her hip. "And one of those is that I guess I wasn't much help."

"No worries. We have avenues, and I appreciate you trying. It's entirely possible you totally just solved the mystery, and we simply have to figure out what it means and get the puzzle together enough to come back for the steel in his chest."

"I should get back to work before Nell thinks I abandoned her."

"Are you enjoying yourself, at least?" I asked.

"Actually, yes, I am. I always thought I would never want to work here and that you were chaining yourself to something you'd never be able to escape. But the more I'm here, surrounded by family and all the objects that have been passed down through the years, there's a certain vibe that's resonating with me."

"You're always welcome here."

"We'll see how you feel after this weekend." She chuckled as she left the kitchen. Once the door swung shut behind her, there was a commotion and a yell. I tried to open the door, but something was blocking it.

Chapter 14

I put my back into it, my butt into it, my shoulder into it, and still the door wasn't budging. The scream at least had been short-lived, but I still wanted through the door. For all I knew, it could be quiet because someone had killed someone again, and that someone might be my sister.

Taking a deep breath, I tried one more time with my butt, back, and shoulder. And managed to crash the door open with no resistance. Which, of course, meant I stumbled out and onto the floor. Fortunately, I stumbled toward the staircase, so I landed on the carpet instead of nailing my head on the old oak floorboard, but wow. I saw sparkles that had nothing to do with my books or my talent.

Suddenly, I felt like I was being crowded in on all sides. People were bent over at the waist, peering down at me. A few were even talking, but my ears were ringing, and I couldn't say for sure if the noise was from someone else or only in my head.

Oh man, this was going to hurt as soon as I could feel anything but claustrophobia.

"Back up and let her get some air," a male voice said. I had not heard it before, and I couldn't see him since it seemed everyone who was bending over me was female, even the small child with a big smile on her face.

"Boo," she said and then giggled.

I cracked a smile, though a painful one, and everyone backed up, then stood up. A strong, large hand reached down to help me up, and I clasped his wrist, allowing him to help me sit. But he had other ideas and propelled me all the way to my feet in one smooth motion as if I weighed absolutely nothing.

He was dressed in a suit that had to be tailored and custom-made. He had a lovely silk tie in bright blue that sat against the snowy white of his blindingly white dress shirt. Or maybe that was just the sparkles that seemed to be stuck in my vision.

"You look a little worse for wear. I'm so sorry we startled you." His accent was different, but I couldn't exactly place it, even though I was usually pretty good about stuff like that. Irish? Scottish? No matter where he was from, I would probably have gladly listened to him recite his grocery list.

And next to him, smiling with her pearly whites showing, was a stunning woman with red hair swept up into an elegant twist. She was also in a suit. This one was also tailored and custom-made. She radiated beauty and calm in a way I was pretty sure I'd never seen before.

And between them was the little girl who had said boo. She was a perfect melding of the two perfect people. I had no idea why they were here or what they were doing here, but something about them just radiated calm.

Until Mena picked up the toddler and rubbed noses with her. "That's Roxy. She trips over stuff and is usually much better about catching herself, but not this time. While we're here, we'll see if we can get her to do some other fun stuff like she used to when I was little. She makes a good elephant if you can get her to wear pants to protect her knees."

The little girl screamed in joy, and it was the same tone and enthusiasm as the one that sent me through the door. Was this Mena's family finally coming in to stay for the five days? They were stunning, though I thought I might have already said that once or twice.

"Roxy, this is Sean and Nora Tullaine. And this little nugget of adorableness is Hannah Bear." She rubbed noses with her again, and the little girl slapped both her hands to Mena's cheeks and gave her a big wet kiss on her chin.

Adorable, yes. Messy and loud, also yes. I'd reserve judgment on if that was going to be a problem if it happened at three in the morning.

"Nice to meet you," Nora said, wrapping her arm around her husband's elbow. "I'm sorry our entrance was a little rambunctious. Hannah tends to be super excited when she sees Mena. She'll settle down now that we're here." The curve of her perfectly shaped red lips made my own lips curve in a smile. There was some power there, but I didn't think it was the mancer kind, just an overload of personality shared by all three of these people.

I put my inn-owner hat on a second later and welcomed them to the hotel.

"We're happy to have you and hope your stay is everything you want it to be. Mena might have oversold the place, though. We're just a small town, and while we do the fireworks big on the holiday, we're pretty low-key around here."

Sean laughed with a shade of bass, and I gulped. "Anything and everything the inn provides will be perfect and just right. We wanted a place to get away, and this is beautiful. The floors are original?" he asked, looking down with his hands flapping the side of his jacket out and showing off how well-fitted that shirt was. Phew!

He'd asked a question before I'd let myself ogle him. What on earth was it? Oh, right. Floors.

"Yes, the inn has stood for almost two centuries, and the floors are the original. I've been told that my great-great-great-grandfather put them down to last forever."

He stood back up from his inspection and smiled. "They're amazing. I have a feeling I'm going to be looking into all the nooks and crannies of the house if you don't mind."

His wife laughed and leaned her head onto his shoulder. "He just loves architecture. I'll try to keep him out of any private areas."

Man, oh man, I'd have to make sure certain things were locked up, like my rooms. But I smiled back. "There are only a few places that are off-limits."

"I'm going to hold you to that," Sean said.

Aunt Hellen came bustling in, all smiles and trailing our two valets, who I contracted to work on and off over the summer. Harvey Betts and Malcolm Freeman were in their sixties and had worked here almost as long as Glennis. They'd started about fifty years ago as workers over the summer and had come back year after year, even when they had regular full-time jobs.

Now they were both retired and still here with smiles and the outfits they had asked to have made for them last year. It was a simple get-up, just a pair of tan pants, a short-sleeved dress shirt, and a vest that had books on endless shelves. They'd asked, and I'd been happy to answer. And Bea, a seamstress in town, had been thrilled to be asked to make them. I'd heard a few other employees ask about them, but no one had said they wanted to wear it all the time, so I'd wait and see what they thought of the idea after the season.

"Looking smart," I said quietly out of the side of my mouth.

They both smiled and tucked their fingertips into the little pockets Bea had made at their stomachs. Malcolm even had a pocket watch chain hanging from his, and it was attached to his belt loop.

"Nice touch."

He smiled bigger and elbowed Harvey. "Told you that you should have taken me up on my offer to lend you my other one. You, too, could have gotten the second compliment. Just saying."

Harvey groaned under his breath. "I'm never going to live that down, Roxy. Thanks so much."

"My pleasure," I said as I straightened his matching bowtie. It was a clip-on, which he had not been happy about. Apparently, those were only for small children and old men. But I'd insisted, just in case something happened and he needed to pop it off. I'd had nightmares about bow ties a few months ago. This was my compromise, and I appreciated that he'd met me halfway.

"Malcolm and Harvey are here to take your bags to your room while Hellen gets you checked in."

"And you have a room for Mena?" Nora asked.

"Oh, yeah," Mena answered. "I've already got my stuff all setup and unpacked. Roxy even let me have my favorite sheets from when we used to stay here for vacations."

"I thought you lived in town while you were growing up," Sean said as he signed some paperwork Hellen had slid in front of him. Usually, she would have explained that they were waivers, but he'd smiled at her and just shook his head, saying no need, then started signing.

"We did, but my grandparents ran the inn. We would go on mock vacation. We always thought it was for us to get out of the house and explore, but I have been thinking that it was probably so our parents could have a break from us."

"Wild, were you?" Sean said, giving a half smile that had probably melted quite a few hearts right on the spot.

"Abso-freaking-lutely, as Roxy likes to say."

I hadn't said that in quite some time, but I let it go since both Nora and Sean chuckled. But when Hannah yelled "freaking," I rethought that decision.

"I'm so sorry," I said, even though I had not been the one to actually say it.

"No need to worry. We've been using words like that to teach Hannah what is and is not allowed to be said. It's much better than trying to teach her when she starts dropping the four-letter versions of things."

They seemed so laid-back, just as Mena had said. But I had expected two people in super-casual clothes, with maybe some sandals and cargo shorts and the mom's hair up in a messy bun.

What I'd gotten instead was the ultimate power couple. However, this power couple came with much softer edges than I would have thought if I had happened to see them on the street and judged the books solely on the covers.

I waved to Hannah as she leaned sideways over Mena's shoulder and tried to touch every single spindle on the staircase. She was a handful. I could tell already. Mena would probably earn every penny, but that meant I got to have my sister here. It also meant I could hopefully get Nell back to working at her top speed instead of lagging along while she and Mena had caught up on everything that had happened while they'd been apart. My thought that two sets of hands would be faster had not proven to work out.

Speaking of Nell, I checked in on her back in the dining room. She was still sitting there doing what they'd been doing earlier.

"Mena's family got here, so she had to go."

"I kind of gathered that from the screaming and talking. I'm almost done here, and then I'll check on any last-minute things. We're all set, though, for whatever happens next."

I sure did hope so.

***

An hour later, I knew I was most definitely not all set up for what happened next. Aunt Hellen had called me to the front desk, then had called me as I was walking down the back steps to go to the library. I tried for the library again, and I was halfway there when she called a third time to tell me to meet "them" out in the gazebo. Whoever "them" was.

"Them" turned out to be Micah, escorted by Aunt Hellen. The first thing I noticed was that he wasn't dressed in his uniform. I had about forty-five seconds to hope maybe he was here for a summer job to supplement his cop salary before I sat down on the same wooden slats I'd sat on last night, and he opened his mouth.

"Look, I do not want to be the one to do this, okay? Let's start there."

Dread filled my stomach. "I don't want to be the one hearing this. I'd rather start there."

He pinched the bridge of his nose and heaved out a sigh. "Fine, neither of us want, to do this, but I think it has to be done, so here I am because Norm isn't willing to do it. Actually, he refuses to do it."

It was strange to think that I agreed with Norm for once. I let that go, though, and settled myself more firmly on the bench, gripping the edges with my fingers until they ached. "Just tell me, and we'll go from there. My brain can come up with some awful things, and I'd rather know what you think than let my imagination run wild."

He fixed his gaze on me, and I couldn't look away. "Something is not right with this whole investigation. The body appears to have been electrocuted, but there's more. I'm not really supposed to be telling anyone this, and if it was anyone but you, I wouldn't. However, I have to ask some questions, and I'd rather have the real answers instead of burying my head in the river and hoping for different results."

That was convoluted, but I followed, so I just nodded my head for him to continue.

"So, yes, his hair is singed, and his body definitely took a jolt from what the medical examiner is saying. But I knew it had to be something else. There was a small spot of dark red on his shirt in the back, so I asked the medical examiner to check it, just in case. After further investigation, the medical examiner found there was also a rod, extremely thin and something that was almost missed, in his chest. It goes right through his heart. He bled internally, and that was the only reason the doctor found it because an electric shock shouldn't have made that happen."

"A rod?" I gulped, but hoped it didn't show.

"Steel. He has a steel rod embedded in his heart. We have to find out where it came from and who would have done that to him. We're thinking the killer just hoped no one would see it because they'd assume he had zapped himself to death on your faulty wiring."

"I don't know that I have faulty wiring. It was just a few fuses that kept blowing, not the whole system."

"See, and that's another thing. Why just sudden bursts of outages? There are too many questions and not enough answers, Roxy. I know you don't want it to be your sister, and from the information I gathered from your staff, the outages started before she got here. I have many doubts that she was the one who planned them all along. She didn't have access while she was in Greece. And I can't imagine she'd set up the scenario where he'd get electrocuted, and it wouldn't be looked at too closely when he did get a shock. But I can't let the rod go, and I can't tell anyone else about it."

That sinking stomach went all the way to my knees. Mena had seen a piece of steel in a man's chest in her flames. She said she didn't remember what she said when she went into a trance like that, but was that true, or just her trying to throw me off? I could not for the life of me honestly believe she had killed anyone, much less Ty, even if he had been pressing for them to resume a relationship that had never really been.

But still...

"I'll keep the information to myself, but I can tell you that as far as I know, we have nothing here that would be a thin piece of steel that anyone would have been able to stick in poor Ty's chest."

"I'd like to look in the basement again if that's okay. I just need to be able to say I covered every angle. Norm is looking for anyone else at all that it could be, but he's got pretty much nothing. He's ready to ignore the medical examiner and go with the electrocution angle, and I just can't do that."

"Why would he want to have the report be wrong? I mean, I get that he might think my sister didn't do it. He said as much. But last time, he was all gung-ho to make sure he got the right person. And this time, he seems to be protecting the person it could potentially be. No matter who that is." That stomach dropped to my toes.

"I asked Norm," Micah said. "And it turns out that right after Mena told Ty to go away, right before he left town, Norm found her in the park, sitting on the ground crying. They talked, and he walked her back to the inn. He thought maybe she would like him if he showed her how a real man should treat her. And he's never totally given up on it, even though she told him you absolutely forbade her from dating him."

Oh my. Well, that would explain a lot then, wouldn't it?

"I'll talk to her while you check out the basement. I appreciate you coming over in plain clothes because we have a lot of people checking in right now. I'd rather not have to explain why you're here and what you're doing. If anyone asks, just say you're looking into the wine cellar. I have someone hopefully coming tomorrow to look at the wiring in the house, and if I hear anything about the state of things or how the electrocution could have happened, I promise to call you right away."

"I'd appreciate it, Roxy. If you know anything at all, please tell me. Yes, we need to solve this, but I want it done right."

"So do I, Micah. So do I."

I sat outside for a little bit longer once he went back into the house. He knew where the wine cellar was, and he could let himself in. I needed a moment to collect myself and think about what to do going forward. At this point, I had two possibilities and not much else. Maybe I should give both of them to Micah and let him sort things out. Except, I was afraid he wouldn't be able to make the connections I could and would scare people away from actually talking to Caper if they knew the police were involved, instead of just a brother thief who was looking out for his own interests and where he was staying.

I was going to have to call Dean again and see if he had heard anything. What I really wanted to do was call him and see if he had time to snuggle on the couch and watch a movie with me, but with ferry season right on top of us and the inn full, there was no time for that.

A murder investigation it was then. It was time to call in my Watson and see what I could explain without giving away my secrets, along with Mena's and Micah's. Man, the list was getting long.

But I made the call, and within ten minutes, Dean was in the library in one of his favorite chairs. There were many small conversation and study areas throughout the enormous room. Poobah had taken the original conservatory and put bookshelves on three of the four walls, leaving the last for windows so that the sun could stream in. I'd always loved the rolling ladder I'd put in when I'd first taken ownership of the place. It had been a dream of mine to be like Belle from *Beauty and the Beast*. We did not, however, talk about how horrible things had gone that one time I'd tried to push off from one side and very much did not make it to the other side.

I had found Dean in the heart-backed chair he said was the most comfortable out of the fifteen chairs and couches spread out in the space. It was one of the places where we'd sat before and where I'd finally admitted that maybe there really was something more to us if I'd let myself unbend enough to find out.

Now, seeing him sitting in that chair filled my heart with all kinds of emotions, some absolutely pure, like love, and others confusing and messy, like how could I not tell him all of who I was and still think we could really be together?

That was way too deep for this moment, and we had many more things to do before I even tried to figure that one out.

As I passed the side of his chair, he snagged my arm and pulled me down across his lap. I squeaked in surprise because who wouldn't? But then I sighed when he held me close and kissed me.

This I could get used to.

"My word, it's like every time I see the two of you together, there's some kind of lip lock going on. Isn't that against the house rules? I remember very clearly being told I was not allowed to kiss anyone when I came here two summers ago, and Poobah still owned the place, but you were running it. You nearly ran me off the porch just for saying good night to someone I had liked back in high school."

Mena. Of course, it was Mena.

Dean smiled against my lips and then rotated my legs out to the front and helped me set my feet on the floor. I wasn't yet quite steady enough to get up and be sure I wouldn't fall back because of the quivers he gave me just by holding me. Taking my time, I moved to sit on the arm of the chair to take a moment to get up, walk the two steps, and seat myself without collapsing. Sometimes, you went with the deal you knew you could do. There's no shame in that.

"What are you doing here, sister dear? I thought you had your small charge now and had to switch jobs to nanny extraordinaire. She's adorable, by the way, but also very loud. Kid's got a set of lungs."

She decided to take the chair I usually sat in and draped her legs over the arm as I had. She sank further down since she didn't have a boyfriend to cradle her, but her legs stuck out further due to her being a lot taller than me. She swung her leg up and nudged me with the toe of her shoe. "You should hear her mother sing. It's amazing what that woman can do without a microphone. Anyway, they're going out to dinner at the Wooden Nickel and don't need me for that since I can have dinner here. I showed them where to go, and they were happy to see it was right around the corner. They've been on the road most of the day, so they just wanted to grab something that wasn't fast food, but wasn't slow service. Marcy will take care of them over there."

"She will. How do you know she's still over there?"

"I saw her when I came in yesterday. I can't believe it's only been twenty-four hours that I've been here because it feels like a week, seriously."

Seriously. I couldn't have agreed more. But I didn't say that out loud.

"What is it that you need now?"

"Well, first, I wanted to know what was for dinner, but second, I saw Micah coming out of the cellar. Didn't you say that he's with the police now? What was he doing here? Did they find anything?"

"Not that I know of." I hoped desperately she wouldn't say anything about her vision in the flames. There was no way I'd be able to tell Dean about Micah finding steel and explain how Mena would have known that without talking about her vision or having Dean think she might have actually been the one who had killed Ty.

"Well, what are we doing to solve this thing? If any of the information I saw is true, then we have problems."

Why, oh why, had she said that?

"What information did you see?" Dean asked, resting an elbow on my leg.

"I meant heard, sorry. I heard that there were some bad people after Ty, or maybe Rand, or maybe both?"

Nice save, or at least I hoped it was a nice save. At this point, there were so many versions of stories flying around that I couldn't remember who knew what, and I did not like that. Not one single bit.

"Mena, if you have time now, why don't you go talk to Glennis and see if she can make those burgers you love so much? It's just us tonight." I shot her a look, hoping she would understand that I needed her to leave so we didn't accidentally say anything in front of Dean that couldn't be saved in quite the same way.

"Oh, that's a great idea. Dean, are you in for dinner?"

"Not tonight. Caper and I have a few things we have to do, and the kids are going with us. We'll just pick something up while we're out."

Where was he going, and what were they doing with the kids? I'd gladly have them here if it meant they wouldn't be in harm's way while their errant dad and reforming uncle asked around and interacted with some of the more nefarious people in town.

"Where are you going?" I asked. Hopefully, it sounded casual, not like an interrogation.

He smiled at me and cupped my knee. "It's a surprise that Amelia wants to do for you, so don't ask anything else, or I'll have to decide between lying to you or keeping my mouth shut. I'd rather not do either."

A surprise? For me? I generally detested surprises, but I could put that aside this one time. I covered his hand with mine and squeezed. "Well, have fun doing whatever it is that you're doing." I shot Mena another look, and she finally got a clue.

"Well, I'm off to talk very nice to Glennis so that she will not only make me the burgers I love, but also some fries with brown gravy. I haven't had the good kind in forever." She waved on her way out, and then Dean scooted me back into his lap.

"Now, where were we before I have to go get everyone at the cottage?" He took my face in his hands, and I tipped slightly to the left as he went right.

And then someone cleared their throat behind us.

"Sorry to interrupt," Poobah said. "But we have a situation, and I don't know what you want to do about it."

Chapter 15

I rested my forehead against Dean's. When I said I didn't usually like surprises, I liked anything Poobah would call a situation less.

"Nothing bad?" Dean asked, helping me off his lap again. This time, I just stood up instead of taking the arm of the chair. He needed to do his thing, and I apparently had a thing to do now, too. Or at least I would, as soon as Poobah told me what was going on, and it looked like he was not going to divulge anything until Dean was gone.

"No, nothing bad, just inn business." Poobah had his customary pipe sticking out of the left side of his mouth. He hadn't smoked it in decades, but apparently still felt the need to hang on to it like a habit. It was the same with the cane he'd gotten back six months ago. He didn't need it, but he liked to carry it. He'd said he felt regal, but I thought it was more that he felt lethal because there was an actual sword inside the cane itself.

Dean slid a hand down my cheek as he left, saying goodbye to both of us with a quick wave as he let himself out of the library and closed the door behind him.

"Things getting serious?" Poobah asked, taking the chair next to where Dean had been sitting and gesturing with his pipe for me to take the other chair.

I shook my head. "I don't know. I'm aware of the rules regarding the mancer community, but I can't imagine giving up Dean or my talent. Why do I have to choose?"

"There are a lot of reasons for that, but none you should have to worry about just now. Give it some time."

"Why does it sound like you know something I don't? You know how I hate secrets and surprises."

"This is not a secret or a surprise. It's just a gut feeling. I saw a vision in my scrying this morning that told me there's something we're missing. I don't know what it pertains to, but I'm putting all big decisions on hold for the time being until we know what it's in reference to. You should think about doing the same."

"I don't have much choice at this point. I have nothing to make any big decisions on, and everything else I'm refusing to even look at until I am forced to."

He stroked my hand. "Everything will work out. I promise. We'll make time for the séance and scrying Earl requested if we must, once the house goes to sleep."

"Well, then maybe we could get started finding out who or what killed Ty because the police were by a little bit ago, and they think it's murder, not accidental electrocution."

"Hmmm." He tapped his pipe in his leg.

I waited to see if he'd follow that up with anything helpful. When he didn't, I groaned. "What is that supposed to mean? There's every possibility that Norm isn't going to want to pursue Mena as a suspect because, apparently, he likes her. There are others at the department that might like her, but they also want the right person taken into custody, and one of them could very well think it's her."

"Do they have a theory as to why it would be her?"

"You're awfully nonchalant about this whole thing. It's not Mena, no matter what they say, but it's not always innocent until proven guilty around here. I'd rather not have her get arrested in the middle of her job because of false, or limited, information."

"Then I guess you'd better put that deerstalker hat back on your head, grab your Watson, and start figuring out who it was instead." With that, he rose from the chair and kissed me on the head. "I'd recommend getting down to business with your books. You've learned a lot. You're learning more. But you have to trust your gut and get those babies to answer you."

"What do you know about Earl?" I asked, and that stopped him in his tracks. "He's a ghost in the wine room who keeps trying to talk to me, but I'm not able to always understand him. Isn't that a whole different kind of talent from bibliomancy? Why do I have two abilities when I barely thought I had even one good one, and I'm not sure I want the other one?"

At that point, he turned back around and sat in the chair. "What has happened since we showed you the phone booth under the stairs? What has he said?"

I ran down the facts for him as I knew them. He either shook his head or nodded every other sentence.

"Why are you acting like a bobblehead?"

"It's just a lot to take in. And what did you say about Amelia? You had a blanket she wanted or said she wanted, but you're concerned she either saw the glowing letters or the ghost? Is she of the blood?"

What an odd way to frame the question. "I have no idea. I put Mena on looking into things like their family tree, but I'm not sure how that's going or if it even is going. Dean and Caper are pretty quiet about family. Heck, I didn't even know Dean had anyone but himself until six months ago, so it's not like they're rolling out the genealogy for me. And I don't know how to ask since the reason I need the information is not something I'm allowed to tell him about until I know for sure."

"That does present some issues. Okay, we'll think about how to get things rolling in the right direction."

"I also am scared about the Mena connection."

That had his gaze whipping up to mine and locking in. "Why do you say that?"

"Look, I love my sister, but the last time the letters glowed like that, it was because the mystery had to do with someone who was related to us. My question then is, since there are no new diaries, what is the other connection?"

"Well, it has to be something other than that. Okay, tonight I'm coming back, and we're going to put together a game plan. We have several levels here, and if we can close one down, then maybe we can make room for the next to be closed down, and then the next and the next."

"I would give almost anything for that."

"Don't make that offer too soon, my darling. You never know what the Universe is going to want from you in situations like these. Making that promise too early might have you giving up something you'd never dreamed possible."

This time, he really did get up and leave. I didn't try to stop him. There were so many avenues here and so much going on that shuffling it all around felt like trying to bail water from the backyard when it was still raining.

I used a couple of books to see if they had anything new to tell me, but no matter what genre I was in, the only thing that kept coming off the page was *LOOK DEEPER*.

Into what? Or who?

I had no way of knowing and no direction of where that deeper might be. I left the library feeling like either it had failed me or I had failed it, and I couldn't have either, especially if that failure meant that my sister was going to be called in as the culprit.

Despite the fact that I would have much rather been almost anywhere but back in the wine cellar, I decided to head down and see if I could get a word in with Earl. I had considered using the hidden telephone booth, but I had hours before I could do that without at least some assurance I wouldn't be seen. And with the inn filling up, it could be possible that I would have no chance of doing that stealthily.

I heard voices as I descended the staircase. Who was it? Were they talking with Earl? I didn't hear an accent, but that could mean anything. And who was down here without my knowing?

I slipped along the wall, keeping close to the plaster, just in case. As I made my way down the hallway, I realized that whoever it was, they were in the wine room. No one should have been down here that I knew of.

I peeked around the corner and saw two guys I'd never met before moving bottles back and forth and talking about the value of what we had on the shelf. First off, how had they slipped past the front desk, and second, how did they even know where to look?

Third, should I get someone to help me? I wasn't one of those women in horror films who would run into the attic and hide under a cover, hoping the monster wouldn't find me. But I also wasn't a modern-day version of Xena Warrior Princess. I had some choices. If I went back upstairs, they'd have to come out past me to be able to leave unless they were planning on staying down here all night.

Maybe they, too, were going to meet someone, and then they'd be dead.

Oh, that was not a good thought to have. It made me shudder, knocking against the shelf at my elbow.

"Who's there?" a man yelled, and I heard footsteps on the concrete. No matter how fast I went, I was not going to be able to hide from them. And I was the freaking owner of the inn, dammit. If I wanted to be down here in *my* basement, looking for *my* wine or whatever else I wanted, then I was not going to be scared to do whatever had to be done.

I walked out from my hiding place like I owned the place because I did.

"What are you doing in here? This is a restricted area. Kindly leave."

"I told you we should have stopped in at the front desk instead of just following Dean's instructions." An older man with a head full of salt and pepper hair rubbed his hand down his face while another one shook his blond head.

"Dean sent you here?" Why hadn't he texted me? Or had he? I hadn't taken my phone or the book out of my little crossbody bag since I'd first put it on in my room. What felt like days ago was really only a few hours.

"Yeah, he said he'd call ahead. He got stuck down at the ferry because they thought they had some leakage. He was going to walk us up, but he didn't want this to wait too long, so he told us to let someone named Hellen know we were there. But there was no one at the front desk, and the whole place seemed quiet. We didn't want to stand around doing nothing, so we texted Dean, and he told us which door and to go ahead and get started."

I had taken my phone out of the bag by now, making sure not to let the book slide out, too. I thumbed the phone on and then saw all the messages Dean had sent. He'd even called twice within the span of ten minutes. The ten minutes I was in the library with Poobah, before I snuck down my own stairs and tried to hide from people I thought might be killers. Maybe I was that too-stupid-to-live heroine after all, and the Universe just thought it had too much left for me to do to let me be killed, something to contemplate later.

"You're here to check over the electricity then." Dean had laid out the whole plan, including names and license numbers, previous clients I could call if I needed to hear live reviews, and that their rates were nothing because they were paying off a debt to him.

"Which is Oscar, and which is Paul?" I asked.

"Oscar." Salt and Pepper hooked a thumb at his chest. "Paul." He gestured to the other guy.

"And did you find anything?"

"So that's where things are a little bit strange."

"Things are often strange here," I said as I saw Earl pop his head out of a wine bottle at Oscar's hip.

"Well, by strange, I actually mean normal." Oscar pointed to the electrical outlet on the wall with his screwdriver. "I don't see anything new down here, and everything you have might be about fifteen years old. But it's all in good working condition. Paul looked around in the fuse box, and it was the same thing. Nothing is wrong, nothing is broken, and there is no real reason why your electricity is turning off. I checked each of the breakers myself."

"He never believes me," Paul finally joined the conversation and shot a look at Oscar. "I'm always right, but for some reason, he has to prove it to himself first."

"Wow, that must be annoying." I was getting a very good vibe from both of these men, and that made me feel better. I would still be cautious, though. They could have made the whole thing up and were about to swarm me and kidnap me, but I had a pretty good feeling that was just my stupid imagination running away with me.

"So, you're not finding anything wrong?"

"Nope, in fact, I'd say whoever did this work years ago knew a thing or two and loaded you not only for bear, but for the grizzlies and for the next fifty years."

"Since you're already here, would you mind going through the rest of the main inn and just checking the other sockets? All of my rooms will be full soon, so I will get a list of the rooms that are empty. I don't want to invade my guests' space, but anything in common areas and empty rooms would be great. I'll pay you for your time at whatever your rate is."

"No, you won't. This one is on Dean, and he'd take us to church if we took anything from you. We're happy to do it. He saved us from some nasty work and business. If Dean asks, we show up."

It was on the tip of my tongue to ask for more details, but I didn't want to intrude on their lives. I was thankful I had people who seemed to know what they were doing and how to do it.

"I'll leave you alone then. If you need anything at all, like water or snacks, or anything, just stop by the kitchen and ask for Glennis. I'll let her know you're here and might be in need of sustenance. She loves feeding people. Oh, and Aunt Hellen should be back up front when you come up. Thanks for doing this. I really appreciate it."

"We appreciate the time and trust. Thank you."

Oh, right! They were starting their new business. They needed some wins to put on their resume so people would know that they could trust them.

"Are you just electricians?" I asked.

They looked at each other. "We're kind of jacks of all trades, masters of many." Oscar chuckled. "We also have some shady things in our past, but we're clean now and happy to do the real work."

Paul rolled his eyes. "We're not making the best impression here, my friend. First, we're in the basement without announcing ourselves, talking about how much the wine is worth, and then you tell her we have a shady past. Pretty sure that might not have been how to go straight out of the gate."

I smiled at them both because, really, this was just my life now. I was surprised at how much I didn't mind the messiness when I had always been so focused on control and making sure everything was done right and on the up and up.

"As long as you don't steal anything from the house, I'm fine. I've heard there are ghosts here, and anything you take could have a spirit attached to the spirit if you get my meaning."

That stopped both of them in their tracks, and they looked around wildly. Earl leaned on the rack between them, shooting me a very mischievous smile.

"I'll leave you to it. But remember to get snacks and some juice, or water, or soda from Glennis. Have the front desk let me know when you're leaving. That way, I can make sure I write down how long you were here and present it to Dean so he knows the debt is paid."

With that, I also left the basement like I owned it because I did.

But the whole way up the stairs, I kept coming back to what they had said about nothing being new and nothing being wrong with the old. Lights had gone out throughout the house over and over again, small things that sprung up every couple of days and caused a commotion. Maybe it really had been Earl. I'd have to talk to him later on the ghost phone under the stairs and ask him to please stop if he was playing tricks.

And how weird was my life that thinking that not only made sense, but also made me feel better?

The rest of the afternoon went by pretty quickly. We did have burgers and fries with gravy from Glennis, who seemed far happier than usual. I'd take it.

Mena heaped praise on her so extensive that it rivaled the sheer amount of gravy she used on said fries.

"You want some fries with that gravy?" Uncle Vince had asked at one point. Mena dipped her spoon in the gravy and made it look like she was going to flick it across the table. She put it down before I had to yell that we were not having another food fight and I'd make all of them go to bed early if they didn't quit messing around.

I didn't see Dean come back from his surprise errands with Caper and the kids, but I was at the front desk when Oscar and Paul came down the stairs lugging all their tools and attitudes. I thanked them for their time and got the lowdown that, again, they had found nothing wrong with the wiring in the house. There was nothing to indicate that these outages should have been happening at all, much less on the daily. This perplexed me, but not enough to keep me up at night. No, what kept me up at night was seeing if I'd be able to sneak downstairs at midnight again. I desperately wanted to give Earl a call to check in with him and let him know that something was wrong with the way he thought I could read the books, which wasn't working for me.

My time finally came at half past midnight. Fortunately, I was already downstairs, so I didn't have to creep along the stairs, hoping that I wouldn't fall. Instead, I used the dimmed hallway lights and muted desk lamp to lead myself over to the staircase.

Where the door to the secret phone booth was already open.

Uh oh.

Chapter 16

What to do? What to do? Part of me wanted to scurry away. I could just decide not to deal with anything at this very moment. But the other part of me was still wearing that like-a-boss mode from earlier. And I was tired of running away when things got dicey. I was the one with the knife.

Well, not really, but I did grab an umbrella from the stand next to the front desk before approaching the open doorway to the booth.

I did not know who I had expected to find in there, but it most definitely was not Amelia.

How do I approach the young girl who was sitting in there with the phone up to her ear and a drawing pad in her hands? Was she talking to a ghost, or was she just pretending because, yet again, she was bored in the middle of the night? Was Caper letting her drink caffeine after eight? I'd have to check. But first, I had to assess what was going on and how she'd gotten into the booth in the first place.

I lightly rapped my knuckles on the exterior panel. It covered the whole thing and looked as smooth as the rest of the wall under the staircase. Per Poobah, though, it had been added years after the phone booth was no longer needed.

She looked up and smiled. "Hi!"

There was no embarrassment for being where she wasn't supposed to be, and she didn't look scared as if she had heard or met someone or something she hadn't intended to meet. That was something, at least.

"What are you doing down here?" I could have said in here, as in within the inn, since she had a house at the edge of the property she should have been at instead of here, but I let that go. It was more important to know how she'd found something in two days that I hadn't known about for my whole life.

"No one is awake at my house, and I snuck an espresso earlier when Glennis wasn't looking, so I'm wired."

This child. Ack!

"Maybe let's not do that anymore. Soon, you'll be doing school stuff again, and you don't want to get your days and nights mixed up."

"We've always homeschooled. I can do my work whenever I want to as long as I get it all done in the right week." She swung her legs back and forth as she sat on the wooden bench. Leaning forward, she hung up the phone and then clasped her notebook in her lap as if I might take it away.

I had thoughts on the schooling thing. But now was not the time to share them. "What if your dad wakes up and finds you gone?"

"You said that last time, and he was fine after I told him I was with you, so I think I'm pretty safe being with you again. Plus, I left him a note about where I'd be. I saw this door close earlier, and then it seemed to like sink into the wall. You couldn't even tell where the door seam was. But I felt around, and there's this little groove on the outside. It was the latch, but it was hard to get it to release. I thought since I hadn't seen anyone else use it before, maybe I shouldn't be messing with it while everyone was awake. But then Glennis made one of the guests an espresso, and there was some left, so I took it, and then I was awake, so I thought, why not now?"

Why not now, indeed.

"Are you usually up and about at this time of night?" I moved into the booth, scooting her over so we could both sit on the bench. She wiggled over enough for me to fit then wiggled back to be able to sit right up against me. This child.

"Well, there was really no normal before this, if you know what I mean. Sometimes we had an apartment, and sometimes we slept in the car, and sometimes we stayed at other people's houses." She drew in a breath and gripped the notebook to her chest. "It was always safe. We were always safe, but sometimes I stayed up to take a turn at the watch."

"You had a watch, like a schedule of who stayed awake so everyone would be safe?" This child?

"Well, not in a way that there was an actual schedule of anything, but I could tell when my dad was really tired, so sometimes I'd just stay up to make sure he was okay while he slept. He thought I was sleeping. He'd always come over and tuck the blanket around me and kiss my forehead, and I'd pretend I was asleep. But then, as soon as he laid down, I would open my eyes and then pinch myself if I started to fall asleep. I got pretty good at it."

This child. I put my arm around her as if there just wasn't enough room for me to have both my arms at my side, and she scooted in a little closer. "I'm sure your dad appreciated your vigilance."

"I don't think he ever really knew, but I did, and that was enough. Sometimes, Isaac would stay up with me, too, but he's a growing boy, from what I learned, and that means he probably needed more sleep."

"And did you go walking around the neighborhoods and sneak into places to check things out while everyone else was asleep?" It was a valid question for a child who had been raised in a strange environment. I had no doubt that Dean's brother Caper had often done his best with what little he had to work with, but the more I learned, the more my heart ached for this child and her brother. Even for Caper, sometimes.

"Oh, my goodness, no, that would have been a horrible idea. But now that we're here and we're very safe, I can wander around the property without having to worry about anything. Well, except for this murder thing. I think I probably should be more careful about the murder thing. But last night, when I saw you sitting in the gazebo, I knew it was okay to come out. And tonight, I saw your sister out in the gazebo, too. I went to talk to her, but by the time I got there, she was gone. You both have this glow-in-the-dark thing. It's very cool. Hers is more red, and yours is gold, but it's there." She sighed and rested her head on my chest right above my heart. "Anyway, she was gone by the time I got there. And then, since I was already out, and I know where the spare key is because I saw Taylor use it one day, I decided to come in and see if I could get the door to open, so I did."

Wow. I had no idea where to start. I had a feeling I would need to talk to Dean and then have him speak to Caper or maybe have a talk with Dean and Caper at the same time. I didn't want her to get into trouble, though, and it wasn't as if she'd done anything wrong, and she was safe, but still. This child.

"The glow you see, is it real or is it like an..." I almost said aura, but if she didn't know what that was, or if she did and I opened a Pandora's box I was not supposed to open, I was afraid of the consequences.

"Yours was on your lap. You had a book open, and the glow was from that. It shone on your face, kind of like you can do with buttercups in the summer to see if someone likes butter?"

I hadn't done that in years, but I knew exactly what she was talking about. I also knew that it could mean some other things that might make my conversation with Dean and Caper that much more important.

"And what about Mena?"

"Well, hers was from flames dancing on her hand, but then I wiped my eyes because that couldn't be real, and it wasn't."

I barely stopped myself from jumping off the bench. I could not let her know that what she had seen was real. But, oh man, this threw a serious wrench into all kinds of things, and I had no idea how to handle it. I needed to talk to Poobah, Aunt Hellen, and Uncle Vince. But it was after midnight, and now was not the time. Plus, I had some thinking to do and questions to ask before I went anywhere with this. Yikes.

"Do all books glow when they're in your lap?" she asked, gripping that notebook until her knuckles turned white in the dim glow from the reception area.

I did not want to lie to her, but I did not want her to put that book in my lap either. "I'm not sure, but I am very tired, and I think you are, too."

She yawned and tried to hide it.

"See? We'll talk more tomorrow. Let me walk you home again and make sure you're tucked in tight, and then tomorrow is fireworks, so you want to make sure that you're all ready for a fun evening, right?"

She looked at me for a few seconds longer than I was comfortable with, but I didn't look away. I couldn't. This child.

"Okay. But I can get back by myself. If you're tired, you don't have to walk me."

"Oh, but I do. It's what people do for other people they care about. Make sure they're safe."

"But then, who's going to make sure you get back to the house safe? Why isn't Uncle Dean here? I bet if you asked him, he'd come over from his little apartment and walk you back to the inn."

I kissed her on the head without thinking about it, and she clung to me in the most intense hug I had ever received in my life. She buried her head in my chest, and I could feel the edges of her notebook gouging into my stomach, but I didn't care.

I let her hold on for as long as she needed to.

And then she bounced up from the bench, notebook in hand, and that blanket I'd given her under her other arm. Where had that come from?

"Okay, Dad will come looking for me in about ten minutes, so I should definitely get back there. I watched him have a fit one time because he didn't realize I was actually on the floor in a nest of blankets. It wasn't this bed. This bed is awesome, but it was a bed that just didn't feel right, so I slept on the floor. He tore the covers off and started crying, so I made sure to always know when he was going to wake up because that way, nothing like that would ever happen again."

More to take in, more to process. Did she have some kind of clairvoyance? Did I need to see if Aunt Hellen was ready to take on another pupil? Did her dad know what she could do? Did it come from his side of the family?

Too many questions, especially when I was still trying to look into who had killed Ty, and I had a nearly full inn. She was not quite at the age when studying would begin, so we might have some time, at least enough, to shut down this investigation before we started something completely new. But wow.

Just wow.

She took my hand in hers as soon as we stepped out through the French doors, and then she dropped it to run back and tuck the key back into its hiding place outside the kitchen door.

As she skipped back to me, her smile could have lit up a whole city. It absolutely lit up my heart.

I got her into the house and tucked her in, then kissed her forehead as I made sure she had her blankets and her book with her. I quietly let myself out of the house, and then shut the door and leaned back against it. What was I going to do with that girl?

"Amelia out and about again?" Dean said from the far side of the porch. He sat in a rocking chair with his feet up on the railing like a gunslinger from the Old West. If he lit a cheroot, I was leaving.

"I..." I had no idea what to say or how to say it.

"Caper knows when she's gone and has always followed her to make sure she is never in trouble, but he lets her have some leeway around here since it's much safer than anywhere they've been before." He stood and walked toward me. When he reached me, he picked up my hand and kissed my knuckles, then led me off the porch and down into the yard. We stopped at the gazebo, and he turned me so that my back was against the raised lattice work on the far side of the house and the cottage. No one could see us back here, and I took the opportunity to use that for all I was worth.

His kiss did things to me that I had never dreamed possible. I'd had boyfriends, some casual, some that I had thought things might go somewhere maybe, but no one had ever made me feel like Dean did. And the thought of having to let that go because I couldn't be all of me with him had shattered me more times than I would have wanted to remember. But if Amelia was a mancer of some sort, then he would be let into the circle of knowledge by association.

The real question then would be, did he want that, or would he think being with a real-life witch was just one step too far?

I broke the kiss and rested my head on his chest. "Is he mad that I don't just send her right back to bed?"

"No, he appreciates that you think she's worth spending time with."

"How could anyone not think she's worth that?"

He blew out a breath. "That's a subject for another time. Right now, I have some new information regarding the murder, and I think we might want to sit down because it's going to require paper and pencils and being able to string things together."

I knew I had to get up early tomorrow morning, and I would probably regret this as soon as my alarm went off. However, I wasn't going to stop myself from asking him to my rooms, where I had a table, plenty of notebooks, and pencils galore.

I shushed him as we entered through the French doors and then took a right to my rooms. With the way my life had been going lately, I almost expected a welcoming committee outside my door. But everything was quiet except the swish of our feet against the carpet lining the hallway.

I opened my door, backing in while pulling him along behind me, and then flipped the lights on. If there was someone on my couch waiting for me, I would kick them right out into the hall and slam the door in their face, especially if it was a ghost.

But there was no one. It was just me, Dean, and Moose, who came strolling out of my bedroom. That made me sigh in relief.

"Tea?" I asked.

"It's almost one in the morning. I'm thinking probably not on the tea."

"Makes sense." I still grabbed a small bag of cheesy popcorn from my snack basket and sat myself down on the couch next to him. He pulled a sheaf of papers out of his pocket and smoothed them out on the coffee table my grandmother had made sure I received before she passed.

"So, I have a bunch of info, but I need your eagle eye to help me wade through it all. I know the players, but you seem to think more like the criminals."

"Ha. Ha. Ha."

"Must be all those books you read."

"Must be." I tucked myself in next to him and waited for him to start.

He picked the pages up off the table and arranged them in some order that made sense to him.

Then he tapped them on the table and cleared his throat.

"What's going on?"

"I'm preparing myself. Last time, I felt like I barely did anything, even though you called me your Watson. So, this time, I wanted to live up to the name. Give me some grace here, okay?"

He gave me that lopsided grin, and all the grace was his.

"Begin when you're ready. I am here to learn from the master."

He tugged at the neckline of his t-shirt. "So much pressure!"

"You're fine. Just get on with it then."

"So, I was finally able to talk to some people about Jeff. Caper also confirmed that the guy hasn't been in the area in about two years. We looked into why, and it turns out he fled to somewhere in Europe to escape doing time. He's got what he called a 'lieutenant' running things for him here. But the word on the street is that the guy is just using all of Jeff's money to take care of the wife Jeff left behind, and he's spending the rest with wild abandon until the money runs out. If Jeff steps foot back in the country, he'll be taken right away."

"And you're sure that he didn't send anyone in his team to take care of business?"

"See, look at you thinking like the criminal. Yes, actually, he did send out an order, but the hired man and this new highest-up person talked, and he was paid off without having to do the dirty deed. Apparently, the hired man likes this guy way better because he's getting them actual jobs with for-real pay. They even have insurance. At this point, everyone is just desperately hoping Jeff never actually comes back. In fact, one guy told me they have people throughout several countries making sure Jeff is continuously on the run so that he's never going to come back here. Others already know what to do if he does land on US soil. It's actually pretty brilliant."

"It sounds that way. Who knew?"

"Unfortunately, though, that means it's probably not Jeff or anyone working for Jeff, especially since Rand only owes thirteen grand, and that's not enough to kill for, usually."

"I'm not sure I needed to know that."

"I didn't want to know it, either, but since I had to, you have to." He laughed. "Moving on. I did find out that Rand has been messing with some projects recently and cutting corners. Didn't you say that Glennis thought they were bad people?"

"I think she said that was because Norm's mom had some work done to her house, but then didn't pay for it. She pretended like it was bad work so she could tell him she didn't owe him anything."

"Okay." He very carefully crossed out something on his page.

"I wanted to thank you for sending over Oscar and Paul. They were very nice and seemed to know what they were doing."

"Strangely enough, they were two of the guys from that crew that was run by Jeff. They're really hoping not to have to go back, so any little jobs you have for them, make sure you send their way, and if you could talk them up around town, that would really help."

"Of course."

"What else can we look into?" he asked, tapping his papers together again. "I feel like we must know something we just aren't putting together. It's driving me batty."

"Maybe we're just not making the right connections." I glanced at the clock. "Eek, it's two in the morning. You'd better go. You have to work in the morning?"

"I do, and so do you. I'll lock the door behind me. Sleep tight."

We hugged at the doorway, and then I watched him walk down the hall and then take the turn to the French doors through the dining room. Those things had been used more today than probably ever in the last year. With his family living in the cottage at the back of the yard and me going in and out, along with Amelia, it was a good thing the hinges had been replaced last year so they weren't constantly squeaking.

Now that I was by myself in my room and had a moment, I removed the book Earl had given me and tried the hand thing again. I hovered over the paper, hoping and praying that something would come to me. Maybe I just hadn't asked the right questions. Maybe I wasn't phrasing them right. Maybe I just needed to go to bed and let my brain rest.

Funny enough, that was exactly when the words started glowing and circling in the air above the page.

Keeping one hand on the book, I used my toes to stretch out and bring my notebook to me. Fortunately, the pencil I'd been using had a grippy on it, so it came right along instead of rolling off onto the floor.

Beware the wayward.

What the heck was that supposed to mean?

From light, there is dark.

Okay, then.

Take caution when making a bed.

Um...

Now, I would admit that I had hoped the books would talk to me, but this was strange. I checked the pages and flipped a few to see if I could get anything more concrete. But it never happened, and then I woke up to my alarm with my face planted on the open book and the pencil on the floor.

I had no more answers at this point and a deep frustration that nothing seemed to be working the way I had hoped. And I had a full house and a breakfast to oversee since we were serving this morning. I warned myself that Glennis might be in a mood and that Taylor might drop a plate. Clara might give me the cold shoulder for some reason unknown to me. And Nell would probably find some new issue with the house that had to be taken care of right now, all while she listened to whatever podcast through her earbuds.

Hopefully, Oscar and Paul would already be here to handle whatever that issue might be. Clara could handle herself. Glennis could get over herself. And Taylor, well, Taylor was just going to have to buck up and handle whatever was thrown at her today.

We had things to do and not a ton of time to do them in, so it was all hands on deck.

Malcolm and Harvey would not be in until much later to help anyone who might need directions around town or a ride. I knew I could trust them to do what was needed when it was needed, so I marked them off my list of people and things to worry about. It only took the list from one hundred to ninety-eight, but I was taking any bonuses I could get. Now, if the lights could stay on and everyone go about their merry business, I would be a very happy girl.

Breakfast went off without a hitch. Glennis was a star in the kitchen, and I appreciated everything she did, even if it sometimes came with a double side of crispy attitude. We were going to have that talk soon. I had meant to corner Poobah to get him to tell me what Glennis had on him, but I had no time. Things were going relatively smoothly, so the talk could wait until all these wonderful people went home.

I walked through the dining room, making sure the muffins were light, the coffee was hot, and the quiche was to die for. I might have wanted to choose a different phrase, what with the murder still hanging over our heads, but so far, no one had asked about it, and I wasn't going to be the one to bring it up.

Mena went with her wonderful family to provide nanny services as they took a ride on the ferry across the river. Finally, after everyone was gone, I was able to take a quick run down to the wine room. I didn't hate it as much anymore, though it was still not my favorite place to be. But I had business down there and was aiming to kill two birds with one stone.

The Tullaines, Mena's family, had requested a bottle of wine to celebrate a real estate deal that had come through this morning over in Ireland. I heard them ask Mena if she might want to be a more permanent fixture in their household now that they had the property Sean had dreamed of since he was a small toddler. I walked away before I could hear the answer because I didn't think I could face that right now on top of everything else. There would be time to congratulate her on her own dream come true later.

Right now, I was walking down the steep stairs to the basement and hoping that Earl would design to visit me while I was there. I had questions, and I was pretty confident he had answers.

All was quiet down here, as it was supposed to be. Oscar and Paul had shown up about ten minutes ago and were continuing to work through the list of rooms Aunt Hellen had handed them to check over. I was still having trouble understanding how the electricity kept flickering when both men had not found a single thing wrong with the system.

So maybe that was three birds with one stone by coming down here because I had other questions for Earl, too, involving if he was playing with me and the electricity.

I rounded the corner into the wine room just in time to see Earl moving an entire wine rack out of the way and opening a secret door.

Chapter 17

I had a decision to make here. Should I scare the ghost and just announce myself by asking Earl what in the world he was doing? Or did I take a page out of Amelia's book and wait until he left, then try to open the door myself later?

The first problem I saw though was that he could be anywhere, anytime, and I wouldn't be able to see him if he didn't want me to. So, I couldn't exactly sneak around him unless I sent him on some kind of errand and waited until he was embroiled in said errand to come back down here. The problem with that was that he would most likely either balk at any errand I gave him, or he'd just say he was going somewhere and then come right back to see why I wanted him out of his normal domain.

Scare it was.

But that was taken off the table when he turned around and looked right at me. "You might as well come in. I had hoped to do this before you came down, but I had a feeling you would not do as I wished, since you never seem to at any other time."

Hey now! "That's not fair. We literally just met like twenty-four hours ago, and I've done everything you've asked when you asked. I might have messed up a little on when the witching hour was, but I didn't ghost you." That pun I hadn't intended, but I wasn't going to flinch. I would own my pun. I was not a coward, especially because I was in the right here.

He shot a glance over his shoulder and then turned to face me fully. I took in the tight knee-length pants, the cravat, the flowing shirt sleeves, and the heeled, pointy shoes. He was in full color, and I would have bet that he was a ladies' man when he was alive. Heck, maybe he still was one in the afterlife. However, he said he hadn't interacted with anyone in a long time. So, why me?

I felt like I asked that question a lot, but it was a valid one.

"So, I'm here, and you're apparently opening a door to a place that, again, I had no idea existed, even though I own this monstrosity. What were you going to do? Was there something you needed to tell me? And while we're at it, what on earth was with the phantom sludge on the floor and you pointing at your nose?"

"All in due time." He walked away from me into the hidden room and then looked back. To see if I was following? I didn't know if I wanted to do that.

But curiosity probably should have been my middle name.

I hesitated for about three more seconds and then just couldn't hold myself back. What was in there? Did Poobah know about it? Did Aunt Hellen? I had come across many things over the last six months that people apparently didn't think I needed to know. Was this just one more, or was I the first living person to enter this secret place in centuries?

All questions that were going to have to wait because, *Holy Wow*, it was like entering into Aladdin's treasure cave.

There were leather chests and racks of deteriorating clothing, shelves of frames and barrels galore. All the barrels were sealed shut, so I had no idea what was in them, but I wasn't going to try to pry the top off of one of them. I didn't need any more surprises than what I was dealing with at the moment.

The space wasn't enormous, but it went back a ways to the point where the far wall was shrouded in shadows. My mind was trying to place where under the first floor this was located. The kitchen? No, too far away. The stairs? Very possible. And in fact, I saw an electrical line that ran up the wall and then through the floor. Was this where the phone was hooked up and why it could transmit with no working power or a real phone line attached?

While I had been looking around like a gawking toddler in my first toy store, Earl had silently watched me from over to my left. I'd get to him just as soon as I came to terms with the fact that there was an entire glass case of china that I had never seen. And I knew exactly where I would put something like that, right in the dining room, next to the sideboard.

I spotted a sewing machine with a black metal foot rocker and an exquisitely detailed hand wheel. It was black with a spray of vibrantly painted colors. What was all this doing down here?

Finally, I came to Earl, who was leaning very nonchalantly against a bookcase crammed with all shapes and sizes of books. I'd been so studiously avoiding him that I had almost missed the best treasure trove down here. But when I went to move around him to get my hands on all those lovely pages, he straightened up from his lean and stood between me and what I wanted to touch more than anything.

How did ghosts react if you just went right through them? Did they slime you like in *Ghostbusters*? Did it hurt them? Did they disperse and then reform away from you like the word sparkles above my books sometimes did when I poked my finger into them?

"There are rules," he said, stopping me in my tracks.

Well, now, I didn't like rules in my own house that I did not make.

"These rules are non-negotiable. I found that out the hard way. Please listen to what I have to say before you touch anything in here." His tone was so serious that I clasped my hands behind my back and waited for what came next.

He paced back and forth in front of the bookshelves. They were lovely, a patinaed mahogany that shone in the bare overhead bulb dangling from the ceiling. There were any number of spines presenting themselves in a full-color display from black to purple and deepest red to a shell pink that my grandmother would have loved. What were they? Were there any first editions of things that people sought after, like a vintage music collector on a mission for an original recording of The Beatles?

To say I was giddy was probably a gross understatement, but I was also cautious. I did not want to find out what the consequences of breaking the rules were, even if I didn't like the unknown rules simply on principle.

"A long time ago…"

"In a galaxy far, far away?" I asked.

He whipped around and shot his left eyebrow up as far as I've ever seen one go.

"Sorry."

"Do you take anything seriously, Roxanne?" The pacing had stopped, and now he had his hands on his hips. He tapped one of his pointy-toed shoes on the stone floor, but it made no sound.

"Actually, yes, I do. I take the running of this inn very seriously. I take the commitment I made to my employees very seriously. I take my connections and love for my family very seriously, too. But few people have ever taken *me* seriously, so I'm good at hiding that behind the jokes."

He studied me for a moment, this ghost who supposedly hadn't spoken to anyone in years and kept guard over a portion of the cellar that I didn't think anyone had entered in decades, maybe even a century.

He could have simply closed the door behind him and not let me in. He could have never called me on the phone or given me the book that made the sparkles with will instead of willy-nilly.

"Why me?" I asked. "Poobah and Aunt Hellen are almost certain that you've had nothing to do with anyone for probably close to two hundred years, and yet you show yourself to me. You call me on the phone. You ask me to meet you in the gazebo at the witching hour. Why me?"

"That's a question I've been asking myself for the last twenty-four hours."

"No answers yet, huh?"

"No, I'm pretty sure I know why. I'm just trying to make peace with it."

What did that mean?

But he jumped back into the rules. "Things can leave this room, but they cannot leave the premises of the house. I was once a highway robber and had heard that this place existed and had jewels and hand-carved fine items from far-flung destinations. Did you know Fionella's father had been a traveler?"

"To be honest, I didn't know about Fionella at all until six months ago when I was told she was the woman who started our family here and wrote the diaries about the treasure and not being able to let her magic go, so she ducked out of a betrothal that she hadn't wanted in the first place."

"And do you know who she was betrothed to?" Our stances mirrored each other as he stood in front of the bookshelf with his hands clasped behind his back, too.

"No." But I had a sneaking suspicion.

"I had no idea she had any kind of magic. I had been presented with a portrait of her and thought her worthy of gracing my arm and my home, bearing my children, and taking on polite society. So, I offered for her, without having met her. She came from a good family name and had quite the dowry that would have helped my family immensely after some debt we had gotten ourselves into."

Yeah, I hadn't been wrong about who he was. "But I thought you never found her? I thought you went on to live your life, and she was lost to you."

"That doesn't mean I didn't come looking for her." His brow lowered, and his lips dipped down into a frown that bordered on hate.

"I take it you found her?"

"I did, but she was unaware of my presence. I stopped in as a weary traveler, asking for hospitality, and she graced me with that and so much more. The house was warm, it was lovely, it was everything I would never have thought to offer her. She deserved to be here with her light and her graciousness, but at that time, I was unable to separate my desires from what was right."

Uh oh, it didn't sound like this story was going to end well. "And?"

"And, well, I tried to take her with me in the dead of night. I'd pulled the carriage around myself and loaded it with any number of items that I was sure would have fetched good prices. I had every intention of leaving it there, but she came down those stairs from the upper floor with a candle illuminating her face and throwing her body into shadowed relief through her night dress." He closed his eyes, and I wasn't sure if he was wracked with guilt or reliving the memory of seeing her silhouetted on the staircase.

"What did you do?" I couldn't hide the horror in my voice.

He lasered his gaze on me. "I ran." He sighed. "I tried to run. But when I was staring at Fionella, her husband came up behind me and slammed something into my head. She was the last thing I saw as my soul left my body. They buried me in the backyard, under the gazebo that was under construction at the time."

I gasped, feeling sick to my stomach. Murder? My great times, whatever grandparents had murdered a man and then hid his body away from the world as if nothing had happened?

He held up a hand. "Before you begin condemning your family as murderers, they had every right to protect what was theirs, and I didn't run from the house right away. It's time for honesty. I ran up the stairs first, and I grabbed Fionella. I had every intention of taking her and the bounty of her dowry with me. She belonged to me, not to him. She was promised to me, and back in the day, I was horrible enough to think that what was mine was mine whether she wanted to be or not. I had no thought to what she had built here or that she deserved better than some indebted shyster who had no intention of allowing her to be anything but what I wanted."

Stunned was not a strong enough word, so I settled on aghast. I was totally and completely aghast. At Earl's behavior, at his audacity, at his callousness. But more than that, at the way that he admitted all of this to a descendant of that couple without any expectation of sympathy.

"I'm not sure what to say." And if that wasn't the truth, I didn't know what was.

"I am stuck here because of the choices I made that night. At first, I was angry and would try to break things and make their lives miserable. But I could do nothing but watch them grow old together, have children, laugh, and build a life I could never have given her. One I would have never even considered because it was not in line with what I wanted. They had no idea my spirit haunted their home, and that, more than anything, might have been the catalyst for my transformation."

"How so?"

"Have you ever been in a position where no one sees you? No one hears you? You are left to view life through a lens that is clear to you, but no one else understands?"

"I can't really say that I have. I might be the white sheep in my black sheep family, but I am heard, and I matter. I know that, even without being told."

"That's because you come from a family who values you for exactly who you are. Every woman who has ever graced this inn with her beauty and her forbearance has led to you."

I scoffed. "Hardly. And I'm one of three, the most boring one out of all of us."

Surprisingly, he smiled at that. "If you say so."

"I do." I didn't go as far as to stamp my foot, but it was a close thing.

"I wouldn't expect anything different from you, and I've known you since you were tiny. I had no idea you were the one I was waiting for, though, until the diary was brought back into the house by that writer. As soon as it crossed the threshold, it sparked something in my soul. I began paying attention for the first time in decades, and what I saw was fortitude, thoughtfulness, and a lack of understanding of how very powerful you actually are."

I could feel the blush creep up my cheeks even as my mind rejected the praise. I cleared my throat. "This is all great and stuff, but it doesn't explain the rules and why I can't touch the books." Way to go, me! Deflection back to what I actually wanted to discuss.

"Perhaps in time you'll come to see yourself as others do." He straightened his sleeves and ran a hand over his hair. "Very well then, let's move on to what the rules are. Nothing can be removed from the house that is in this room. You may use it to decorate and study or even to showcase some of the wonderful antiquities that have resided here for years, but nothing can go outside this property."

"Got it."

"This is serious," he said.

"And I'm being serious. I heard you the first time and the fourth time, maybe not the second time, since I wasn't paying attention too much. I can't fully speak to time three, either. But that last time, I absolutely got what you were laying down."

He shook his head as many people were wont to do when dealing with me. "The last book I gave you came from these shelves."

I patted the crossbody bag where it rested and then realized that I could have really hurt myself without even knowing if I'd walked off with it, not knowing the dangers. "You should have warned a girl way before now, then. Holy cow. I've been wearing the thing at my waist all morning."

"Interesting. May I see it?"

I pulled it out, and it glowed until I set it in his hands. There, it took on the shadows of the back corners of this hidden basement room.

"Ah, my theory is proved wrong then. The rules only apply to me. I suppose that makes sense." He sighed, and I felt it in the depths of my own soul. "I've been here a long time. I'd never thought I'd move on, so I'd made peace with it. I had hope that maybe if I could make things right with you, that I could move on, but the books are never wrong."

"Hold on a second. Are you saying that you think you've been here this whole time waiting for me or someone else so that you could redeem yourself?"

"Is that so strange?" He took up his leaning position against the bookshelf again. I desperately wanted to get my hands on the tomes, but this felt much more important.

I never thought I'd say that when books were my life.

"Not strange, but who told you that?"

"I don't know that anyone ever told me anything, to be honest. But it made sense. When you showed up, something changed, and I had hope for the first time in a very long time.

I put it aside, believing there was no way it could be true, and perhaps I was right in the first." He shrugged. "It certainly wouldn't be the first time I was wrong, and I highly doubt it would be the last."

"I was told you didn't want to leave."

"It's a story I scrawled on a wall to your grandfather many years ago. Your grandmother––you called her Grand Duchess, if I remember correctly, a nice compliment to the name Poobah––saw it first and brought Benson down to view it. They couldn't see me, but they stayed away after that, and I could wallow in my own self-disgust, so it worked for everyone, really."

"You're not wallowing anymore, are you?" This had to be the strangest conversation I had ever had, and for an innkeeper, that said a lot, just in case you were wondering.

"I may or may not take it back up." He tapped his chin. "At this point, who knows what comes next? I do know that you need one last book and a tool to define your talents. You have some resentment toward Hellen and Vince for not teaching you properly. They have their own issues, but this is not one of them. They were thwarted without them knowing because your talent apex can only be achieved with something I've hoarded down here for years, long before you were even born."

I waited several seconds for him to either produce the tool or tell me where it was, but he left it there and shrugged again. "Seriously? Do you want me to beg for it? Would it make you move faster if I cried? Do you need the theatrics?"

"Not at all, but the sass was a nice touch. Well, done." He reached behind him and produced a leather-bound book that was very much like the first and second diaries of Fionella. On top of it sat a magnifying glass with a handle that was sculpted and carved just like the head of Poobah's cane. "Be careful. It's set up just like its counterpart."

"Do you mean to tell me there's a knife in the handle?"

"I told you that you were a smart one." He handed the book and glass to me, and as soon as it touched my palms, he vanished.

By design? Willingly? Or had he been taken to wherever he was destined for now that his task was complete?

I spent a few seconds looking around the room to see if he would reappear, but then I couldn't stand holding the book and not cracking it open anymore. I wasn't going to do it down here, though. Secret rooms were cool, but I was a little concerned that something would close that hidden door, and I'd never get out.

As soon as I cleared the doorway, the door slammed behind me, rattling the whole rack of high-priced spirits. I raised an eyebrow and stuck my tongue out just in case Earl was watching, and then ran up the stairs with the new book and the magnifying glass tucked into my crossbody bag.

Surprisingly enough, I made it to my rooms without being stopped. It was far from my usual, but I preferred it, so I didn't question it. Once I was locked in my sitting room, I took the book and laid my hand on the cover like I had done hundreds of times. I opened the book and waited for anything to happen, but nothing did, no sparkles, no words, no hints.

Then I shook my head at myself. I needed a question, but it felt like the question had to be super good, like really spot on.

"Do you want to talk to me?" I asked, and yes, that was the best I could come up with. The whole page glowed, and that light seemed to seep into my every pore. Part of me thought I should be scared as hell, and the other part told that first part to calm the heck down.

Just to make the experience a full-on, what the hell did I think I was doing without any instructions? I also lifted the magnifying glass to peer at the page, and the explosion of pure color nearly blinded me.

No longer was it just words. It was a scene playing out like a movie viewed through the magnifying lens as if it were a television or something. Scene after scene whisked by so fast that I couldn't catch on to what was actually happening in any one of them.

"Please stop." It had worked before with the sparkly letters when they were moving too fast, and it worked this time, too. The scene was frozen on a red splatter on a concrete floor. Right on the edge, I could see the signature build of a wine rack, which meant this was the basement. But I didn't remember ever seeing blood on the floor, even when I first found Mena standing over Ty.

And then it hit me…it was in the same place where Earl had pointed at the sludge in the dark, then pointed at his nose.

Is that what he had been trying to tell me? To check the place where the blood was? To let me know there had been blood and I should use my clue sniffer to figure it out? I needed him here now, and I had no idea how to get him back.

This called for another trip to the basement. And this time, I was going to get all the answers I wanted, or I was going to start kicking some ass and taking some names.

Chapter 18

I came running out of my rooms in my little kitten heels. My curly hair bounced along the way with me, and my sleuther's heart was about to combust. I was going to figure this out, hell or hiding ghosts aside!

In my flurry of speed, I almost tripped over Oscar and Paul, who were sitting on the floor on opposite sides of the hallway, using their tools to check the electric sockets. Slamming on the brake kept me from actually colliding with them, but it was close.

"You're in a hurry," Paul said. "Sorry to be blocking your path."

"No problem. Sorry for coming in hot like a rocket."

"Meh," Oscar said. "If you need to be somewhere, then you need to be somewhere. We get it."

They both scooched closer to the wall and gave me ample room to get around them, but I stopped for just a moment more. "Are you finding anything?"

"No, it's kind of bizarre. Your wiring isn't new, but it is the best shape of anything we've seen in all our jobs together. Even the ones we used to do for the boss, and he only had the very best of everything. You're top of the line here."

"That's good."

"It is, but then it makes me wonder how things kept going wrong. There is no indication anywhere that any shorts have been happening." Paul replaced the wall plate with his socket and pushed himself to his feet.

Oscar did the same. "I feel bad using this as a repayment to Dean. It seems like stealing. We've literally done nothing but get to be inside a beautiful establishment and talk to very nice people. And that Glennis, man, can she make a mean potato salad. Then she wouldn't let us leave without some shoofly pie she's testing out. I'd weigh far more than I do right now if I worked here on the daily." He snickered.

"It's an issue, seriously." Smiling at them came naturally, and they smiled back, but then Paul gripped his toolbox tighter and took a step back with a frown on his face.

"Everything okay?" I asked him. Had he seen Earl and was afraid of ghosts? I turned around and found no one but Mena and her family leaving through the front door, being waved out by Nell.

"Yeah, yeah. We are so thankful for this second chance. Well, really, it's a first chance at this kind of thing. I know we didn't really do anything, but if you wouldn't mind putting in a good word for us with your friends and colleagues, we'd really appreciate it." Paul glanced down the hallway again and ducked his head. "We should get going. Do you mind if we go through the kitchen? Maybe Glennis has a little something we can grab for a snack on the way home."

"No, that's fine, and tell her to make you a plate of leftovers if you like spaghetti and chicken parm."

Oscar nodded and then pushed Paul along in front of him. "Everyone deserves a second chance, dude. Just as much as us."

What did that mean? I watched them walk away and wondered if I could get them to tell me what they meant. Maybe I could talk Dean into talking with them since he knew them far better than I did. At least enough for them to owe him something.

I didn't think it was Mena. Neither of them probably knew her unless they were talking about thinking she was the murderer, and this would be her second chance. Or was there something about the couple she was nannying for that she and I both didn't know? Did they know those two lovely people who had seemed to be maybe a little too perfect and had a lot of money? Where did it come from? What did they do for a living?

So many questions swirled in my head, and I almost followed them to the kitchen to ask, to heck with waiting for Dean to be my intermediary. But then I was taken in yet another direction when Earl popped out of the phone booth wall, looking far worse for wear. Half his color was gone, leaving him black and white from the toes of his pointy shoes to his waist, and the color from his waist to his hair was muted like he'd been sent through a dryer when he'd clearly been labeled dry clean only.

What the heck was going on around here?

"Downstairs. Now. Please."

No one else seemed to see anything out of the ordinary, so despite the urgency in his tone, I did a stroll instead of a run. I waved to Aunt Hellena at the front desk and let her know that I'd be right back to take over if she needed a quick break. She waved me off and welcomed the next set of guests arriving. As far as I knew, we were only one more set of people from being full to the gills at The Charmed Inn, and that was both awesome and yet also daunting because I still had a killer to find and now ghosts to deal with and unrest of the previously wicked, but hopefully now redeemed.

Just a day in the life of me, I suppose.

Entering the basement staircase, I brace myself against the wall as I crept down the stairs. After seeing Earl in such a rough state, I was afraid of what had happened, but also keen to find out what it was. He was growing on me, and I'd been sad when I thought he'd left without saying goodbye, but this version of him was hard to look at. What had happened?

I made it to the bottom of the stairs without any obstacles and was about to round the corner when I was stopped in my tracks because somehow, I was hearing my sister down in the basement with me, even though I had just watched her walk out the door with her family.

"Yeah, there's a lot to do around here," she said, clear as day, like she was standing next to me. "We're a small town, but everyone here watches out for each other. And so many wonderful things are well within driving distance," she said.

"Oh, we have no plans to really get back in the car until we leave. It's so pretty around here. We'll just take some walks, maybe hit some of the closer restaurants. We'd love to be able to go on a date with just the two of us also if you wouldn't mind keeping Hannah Bear by yourself for a bit one night?" That was the father, Sean.

I knew that there was no way they were in my basement. Especially when I heard the ferry horn blast at the riverfront. Was Earl projecting something? Was he watching on some portal I knew nothing about? The magnifying glass had played many scenes. Did he have something else that could also pick up the audio?

For some reason, I kept silent as I crept around the corner, doing my best to keep my heels from clicking on the concrete. I wouldn't have been able to tell you exactly why, but once I rounded the corner and found myself face-to-face with the very last person I would have expected, I was glad I did.

Because there was Nell with another bloody nose. How could I tell when her back was to me? Because she had a bloody tissue in her hand and kept bringing it up to her face. And because her back was to me, I could see what she was watching on her phone, which was propped up on a wine rack. She'd moved several bottles out of the way to make room for it.

No earbuds this time, and I was both thankful and scared by that. Should I creep away and use my own cell phone to call the police? I'd even take Norm storming in here and doing some serious damage to anything in his way if it meant that the killer would be caught.

It had to be her. Everything lined up. From the messages in the books about knowing who was in the house to beds being made and beyond. From Glennis not being sure that she was doing a good job. And if she had some kind of mirroring malware on Mena's phone, then she would have known exactly where she was and what she was talking about with Tyler, as well as how to get her down into the basement.

The big question was, why?

Unfortunately, I said that last word out loud when I very much didn't mean to, which had Nell whipping around, the tissue stuffed up her right nostril, and a bottle of wine in her hand. A very old bottle. One that cost about three grand on today's market. I was not going to be injured by overpriced wine, even if it was from the old country.

"Why, you ask?" she said, waving the bottle at me.

I stumbled back without thinking about it and knocked my head on the wall behind me. My vision went blurry, and my ankle twisted. I barely saved myself from falling to the ground. But within those few seconds, she had positioned herself at the entrance of the wine cellar, and there was no way I was going to get past her without running her over.

I was stuck, and Earl was nowhere in sight.

Aunt Hellen knew I was down here, but she'd waved me off while looking at her computer and helping a family check-in, so there was every possibility that she did not actually hear what I had said.

This was very bad.

"Victim number two." She sneered at me. "You know there was never even supposed to be a victim number one, if I were being honest, which I think I can be now that it's just you and me, and soon it will be just me and your corpse. I'm getting better at staging things, so maybe we'll make it look like you fell down the stairs in those stupid shoes. It could happen."

How dare she make fun of my adorable shoes? I'd paid good money for these things, and I knew that they made my short legs look longer, and my wider feet appear narrow.

"Or maybe you were checking out the same electric socket as Tyler had been, and oops, it turns out it really is faulty, and you too suffered a shock of your life. Or would that be death?" She appeared to be talking to herself and laughed at what she apparently considered a good joke.

She was wrong, but I wasn't going to be the one to tell her. I kept my mouth shut. If this was going to be the monologue of the villain, then I was here for it. I had reached into my pocket earlier and turned my phone onto record. So even if she did manage to end my life, there would still be proof. Of course, that was assuming if she knew how to use malware, she wouldn't know how to erase a video. Great.

"We don't have to do this," I said, finally, lifting my hands in the air. "The police think it was an accident. We can leave it at that. I won't press for anything, and I'll make sure that they keep it that way. I'll have Mena talk to Norm and ask him very nicely to make sure Ty's death is listed as an accident."

"Mena!" She nearly yelled the word, then must have realized that it was possible people upstairs might be able to hear her. "Mena." She practically growled the word this time. "The bane of my very existence."

"What? How is that even possible? You were besties. Are going back to besties."

"I can think of a different word that starts with b that I think fits her much better than that one."

"Now, hold on." I put my hands on my waist and stared her down.

In turn, she raised the wine bottle at me again, and I responded by putting my hands back in the air. Volatile did not even begin to characterize this situation. What had happened and when?

"Did she do something to you that I don't know about? I know she can be a little forgetful sometimes, but she doesn't ever do it to be mean. She's just built that way." And didn't I know that better than anyone?

"Forgetful? Again, I can think of another word that starts with f that isn't quite as long as forgetful, but definitely fits her better."

Wow. Okay. Time to start digging. If I was here, then I figured I might as well give her a chance to unload while I considered how to get around her, even though I was about half her size and not nearly as agitated.

I would not die in my own freaking cellar and then have to spend eternity with Earl. I wouldn't!

"But you were so excited to see her that you both screamed and nearly had me falling down the stairs. She said you were her best friend in high school. She was looking forward to staying here and being able to get that back."

"The screaming was real, and I was happy to see her. But I also know her and know that she would probably ruin everything, and I was right. Not even a few hours here, and she was already trying to take my man."

"So, you killed him?" That seemed like an odd thing to do unless you went with the "if she couldn't have him, then no one could" thing. "Mena didn't even want him after talking to him for a few minutes and exchanging texts. She didn't think they were a good match when they first were circling each other, and this time, it was even faster than last time before she realized they didn't go well together."

"And there's that b-word again, just floating around in my head." She stabbed the wine bottle at me, and I put myself flush against the wall behind me.

Maybe if I could move my head fast enough when she took a swing, then the bottle would break on the stone. Of course, that would then leave her with a very sharp weapon of broken glass to stab me with.

"He texted me and told me that he was so excited to see her, that it was just like old times, and that he was so happy he had gotten out of the trouble he'd been in so that he could be with her as a good guy." She scoffed. "A good guy. Please."

"But you still wanted him?"

"He was already good way before he got in or out of that trouble, and she never saw it."

"To be fair, she was fifteen to his twenty. Our parents forbade her from seeing him because she was underage."

"Yeah, I remember that. And I remember him crying because she'd turned him away even though he'd offered to be her friend and wait until she was the right age. He loved her like I loved him, and she threw him away like garbage."

It was on the tip of my tongue to ask her why she would want Mena's garbage, but I stopped myself at the last second. "So, you killed him because he showed an interest in someone who was not interested in him? That seems like shooting yourself in the foot."

Maybe if I could keep her talking, an idea would occur to me on how to get out of this, or maybe Earl would come along. Or maybe someone would notice that I was missing and come to find me. I was open to anything at this point.

"Ha!" she burst out, but it didn't sound like she thought it was funny.

"Am I wrong?"

She shook her head, and I almost bolted past her. Unfortunately, she looked up with what could only be considered cold, dead eyes before I'd even moved one foot.

"You're not wrong. But it was different than that. We were working together on a few projects for my father before he left for Europe. But then things went awry, and he got cold feet. I tried to get him to warm them up again, but he'd made his decision. So, I made mine. I was going to follow him wherever he went."

I gulped. "Your father is in Europe?" Like the Jeff guy who might have put a hit out on Tyler because of Rand's debts? But that seemed a little far-fetched. Plenty of people went to Europe, and I'd bet that some of them were also named Jeff.

"Yeah, I heard you talking with Dean about that. Jeff is my dad, and yes, he did put a hit out on Rand, but would have also taken Ty. He'd assigned the job, but then the jerk turned him down. I agreed to take it as my first real step into the family business. But I was going to double-cross my dad and save Ty by using all my experience to move us away from all of this."

"But then Mena showed up."

"Are you telling the story, or am I?"

Honestly, at this point, I wasn't sure, but it all made sense now. She could have sent that text to Mena, hoping to frame her and have her put in jail. If she knew that Tyler wasn't going to leave with her, then she could still make points with her dad. Wow, maybe Dean wasn't wrong when I really could think like the criminals with little to no effort once it was out there in front of me.

"You are, of course. Sorry."

She huffed out a breath. "Okay then. So, my dad wanted him gone, but no one was listening to him anymore. I was going to totally jump ship with Ty, and we could have made a good life together somewhere else, but he dropped me as soon as the b-girl showed up. At that point, it made more sense to just take him away permanently. He was never going to give up on wishing for Mena, and I was not going to be a second choice."

"Why make it look like an accident then?" I grabbed the crossbody bag at my chest and wished that I had more time to come up with a plan. The zipper dug into my hand, as well as the decorated end of the magnifying glass.

"Because at first, I was not going to make her the scapegoat. I was just going to take him away from her. But once he started talking about how excited he was that she was back in town and how much he realized he'd never gotten over her or given up on her, I knew there was no chance for us. But there was a chance for me to get her down here and take the fall. And even if it looked like an accident, I knew that the medical examiner would find the piece of steel in his heart eventually, and even Norm couldn't deny that was what killed him and not the electricity."

"So, you really had it all planned out." I very slowly worked the zipper down just enough to get two fingers inside the bag. I covered one hand with the other like Aunt Hellen liked to do when she was about to make a statement that everyone should listen to.

"More like it all fell right into place once I decided to do the right thing. Funny how that can work. And so that's the end of our story." She paused and raised the bottle above her head. "And the end of you. You've been an okay boss. Maybe Mena will take over the inn and use her charm to make it truly The Charmed Inn. You won't be here to see it, but maybe you can watch it from heaven. You're an innocent bystander, but unfortunately, you still have to go."

"See now, I have a problem with that," Norm said from behind me, and for the first time in our entire acquaintance, I was happy to hear his voice.

***

Glennis scoffed at my idea for all of us to head down to the waterfront for the fireworks display scheduled in an hour. I'd told her we could get something from the food trucks. And you'd think I had told her that I'd rather eat a pizza out of the frozen section of the grocery store than let Pete down at The Pie Shop spin me a dough I couldn't resist.

It had been two hours since Nell had been escorted out of the house in handcuffs. She'd yelled a few choice things as Norm had manhandled her up the steep stairs and out to his waiting patrol car. Some of them started with the letters b and f, in case you were wondering. I'd promised to send him the recording from my phone, even though he probably couldn't use it in court, and then closed the door and the case.

There was plenty of other evidence, though, once we knew who the killer was. Micah had come in and done a swab on the exact place where Earl had shown me the sludge in the dark. Earl had apparently fought his way back from the afterlife in order to help point me in the right direction and save me by popping out of the wall. And it had worked in his favor because where he had originally gone was no picnic, and he should have stocked up on ice cubes. But now he was back in the cellar and had made me promise that we'd talk on the phone tonight as he brought his space back to rights after Mena had gone down and used her fire to clear all the horribleness out of the basement.

I hadn't told anyone about the secret room yet. I wanted to wait until I got a second look inside before telling a secret that currently was just between me and Earl, my new ghosty friend and savior. I was hoping he wouldn't hold that over my head, but I had a feeling that he was just happy to be back among the living, even if he was dead.

And speaking of the living and happiness, I gratefully took Dean's hand as we walked down to the waterfront twenty minutes before the fireworks were going to go off from a small island in the middle of the Susquehanna. Everyone from the inn was with us, and we all decided that funnel cake was in order as soon as we weren't so stuffed from all the leftovers Glennis had put out in a buffet-style dinner that wasn't usually a part of our stay package.

She'd even smiled at me and thanked me for helping Norm on this case, so maybe that talk I kept thinking we'd have to have could wait just a little bit longer.

I leaned into Dean as he matched my step on our way to the festivities. I loved being with him and treasured it even more tonight when it could have been touch and go there between me and a wine bottle of death.

I was feeling as dreamy as the sunset, so I wasn't entirely surprised when I jumped a little when Amelia grabbed my hand and leaned into me as I leaned into Dean. We must have looked like a bunch of weirdos, but I was finding myself to be very much okay with that.

Standing straight again, she began skipping along beside us, still holding my hand. "So glad I could find you," she said softly so only I could hear her. "I knew if I focused everything I had on you, the clouds and stars would tell me where we should look for you. They're never wrong you know, but I can't always get them to answer me. I don't know why, but I so appreciate that they decided to help me tonight. I'd be lost without you, and so would Dean and Dad and even Isaac, but I don't think he'd actually tell you that without having to be bribed. It's a thing with him. You understand."

I looked at her, and she smiled a cherubic smile that melted my heart. Yes, I understood. I understood that she was talking about having access to a power called aeromancy, the ability to use atmospheric elements to channel into magic.

And that changed my whole world. I was here for it, just not tonight. Tonight, I'd enjoy a normal white sheep of the family outing with my white sheep boyfriend, and we'd go from there.

It was the least the Universe could do for me after all it had put me through in the last few days. It owed me, and I was collecting.

CHECK OUT THE WHOLE SERIES!

CHECK OUT THESE OTHER GREAT READS FROM ROWAN PROSE:

Misty Simon, who also writes as Gabby Allan, always wanted to be a storyteller. Today, she has more than 30 titles to date in the romance and mystery genres. She lives with her husband in Central Pennsylvania where she is hard at work on her next novel or three.
www.mistysimon.wordpress.com

www.ingramcontent.com/pod-product-compliance
Lightning Source LLC
LaVergne TN
LVHW040725180825
818903LV00006B/153